Images of the Anthropocene in Speculative Fiction

Images of the Anthropocene in Speculative Fiction

Narrating the Future

Edited by
Tereza Dědinová, Weronika Łaszkiewicz
and Sylwia Borowska-Szerszun

LEXINGTON BOOKS
Lanham • Boulder • New York • London

Published by Lexington Books
An imprint of The Rowman & Littlefield Publishing Group, Inc.
4501 Forbes Boulevard, Suite 200, Lanham, Maryland 20706
www.rowman.com

6 Tinworth Street, London SE11 5AL, United Kingdom

Copyright © 2021 The Rowman & Littlefield Publishing Group, Inc.

All rights reserved. No part of this book may be reproduced in any form or by any electronic or mechanical means, including information storage and retrieval systems, without written permission from the publisher, except by a reviewer who may quote passages in a review.

British Library Cataloguing in Publication Information Available

Library of Congress Cataloging-in-Publication Data

Library of Congress Control Number: 2020052399
ISBN 9781793636638 (cloth) | ISBN 9781793636652 (pbk)

Contents

The Anthropocene and Speculative Fiction: Introduction   1
Tereza Dědinová, Weronika Łaszkiewicz, Sylwia Borowska-Szerszun

PART I: NATURE AND CULTURE IN THE ANTHROPOCENE   25

1. "The Being that Can be Told": *The Telling* by Ursula K. Le Guin as a Remedy for the Anthropocene   27
   Tereza Dědinová

2. Young Adult Fantasy to Save the World? Retelling the Quest in Maggie Stiefvater's Raven Cycle   45
   Carrie Spencer

3. The Forest as a Voice for Nature: Ecocriticism in Fantasy Literature   67
   Britta Maria Colligs

4. The Fantasy of Wilderness: Reconfiguring Heroism in the Anthropocene, Facing the Age of Ecocentrism   87
   Lykke Guanio-Uluru

PART II: (POST)APOCALYPTIC WORLD AND THE ANTHROPOCENE   103

5. Anthropocene vs. Plague: Disastrous Diseases and Their Impact on Society as Seen in Literature from Thucydides to Modern Speculative Fiction   105
   Jiří Jelínek

6   Fantasy, Myth, and the End of Humanity in M. R. Carey's
    The Girl with All the Gifts   121
    Maria Quigley

7   Beyond the Anthropocene: Human Enhancement, Mythology,
    and Utopia in James Patterson's *Maximum Ride* Cycle   135
    Anna Bugajska

8   At the Crossroads of Ideas: The Russian View on the
    Anthropocene in *Metro* Series by Dmitry Glukhovsky   157
    Joanna Krystyna Radosz

**PART III: SOCIETY AND POLITICS IN THE
ANTHROPOCENE**   **175**

9   Apocalyptic Visions: N. K. Jemisin's *The Stone Sky* and the
    Sociocultural Origins of the Anthropocene   177
    Keygan Sands

10 The Politics of Language and Culture in China Miéville's
    Novel *Embassytown*   191
    Aleksandr Kolesnikov

11 Mythological Aspect of Immigration in Fantasy:
    Case Study of *Mercy Thompson* and *Alpha and Omega*
    Series by Patricia Briggs   213
    Dariya Khokhel

12 The Development of Realist Speculative Narratives to
    Represent and Confront the Anthropocene   235
    Dwight Tanner

Index   257

About the Authors   267

The Anthropocene and Speculative Fiction

Introduction

Tereza Dědinová, Weronika Łaszkiewicz, Sylwia Borowska-Szerszun

Finland, once called "the land of a thousand lakes," sometime in the future. Water is the essence of life. It unceasingly transcends boundaries, connecting individuals, times, and places. It represents continuity, constantly renewing itself and everything it circulates through. It does not differentiate between human and non-human organisms, equally sustaining all. It can be tamed and controlled, but never permanently and fully. Although it is the essence of life, water is scarce.

In *Memory of Water*, the debut novel by Emmi Itäranta (published in Finnish in 2013 and English in 2014), the map of the world is completely different from the one we know. Due to global warming, waters rose much faster than people had imagined and many lands were lost to oceans. Countless homes in the middle of continents were destroyed by raging storms. Large areas of former Sweden and Norway became uninhabitable due to the contamination of freshwater reserves. The so-called eternal ice that used to cover both poles is now just a name. Oil ran dry during the Twilight Century, economic and political centers of power shifted, and most past-world technologies were forgotten. The best places to learn about the past are the so-called "plastic graves," that is, vast dumping grounds bearing witness to the unimaginable wealth, prodigality, and irresponsibility of the people long gone.

The problem of climate change, which underlies Itäranta's novel and which has been gaining attention in global media due to the increase in the number of extreme weather events occurring in recent years, is only one of the manifestations and consequences of the Anthropocene—the recently identified geological age of severe human impact on the planet. There are many more. People are effectively altering the world through massive urbanization and development of infrastructure, constant mining for resources, extensive deforestation, large-scale food production, and other activities which have led to the loss of pristine lands, numerous species (the so-called Sixth Extinction), and biodiversity in general. As a result, many thinkers now claim there is no nature left, only the environment.[1]

While the age of the Anthropocene has not yet been officially recognized by The International Commission on Stratigraphy and there is no agreement about its beginning,[2] the global community has adopted the label readily. The concept of the Anthropocene was popularized in 2000 by the geobiologist Eugene Stoermer, who coined the term in the 1980s, and the Nobel-winning chemist Paul J. Crutzen. Ever since, the name "Anthropocene" has spread far beyond the scientific debate and entered the world of media, art, and academia. The many disputes about the origins, nature, and consequences of the Anthropocene have brought these issues to the attention of various communities across the globe. That these issues are also repeatedly approached through stories indicates the major and universal role of storytelling across various communities. The power of stories is emphasized also by *Memory of Water*. The novel's protagonist, the seventeen-year-old Noria Kaito, who trespassed the harsh laws of her society and now awaits death in her empty house, is writing down the story of her short life, of secrete and dangerous knowledge, of loss and hope. She devotes her last moments to sharing her story because she believes that words, same as water, can transcend boundaries and bring renewal and hope. Noria's story is like the journey of a hidden spring, originating in the darkness inside/underground, then gaining strength, and spurting out at last:

> The words were slow to come at first, faint and wan in the darkness where they'd been stowed away for a long time. But as I reached for them, they began to flicker and flash and float towards me, and their shapes grew clearer. When they finally burst to the surface, bright and bold, I caught what I could and let them pour out of me. [. . .] The sentences on the paper broke the circle of place and time. (Itäranta 187)

Memory of Water is a novel depicting broken continuities and damaged relationships between individual people, people and the environment, and the hidden past and the dystopian present in which people lack the power and knowledge to build a better future. However, humanity cannot exist without hope, and it is hope that drives Noria to delve into history as "somewhere under the sky, there must be a reason to believe that the world was not dry and scorched and dying beyond all repair" (104). That hope, faint and fragile, is represented in the novel by water, always flowing and changing, never static, trapped, or dead. Likening words and stories to water emphasizes their nature and power. While Noria's story is intended, in the limits of the fictional world, for her contemporaries or future generations, Itäranta's *Memory of Water* aims at today's readers who, with their every decision, create the future not only for themselves, but also for all not yet born—the future that might, but does not need to be, similar to the fictional world of Itäranta's novel.

The novel is filled with powerful images that encourage the readers to reflect on their habits and choices. For instance, Noria's exploration of the local plastic grave is driven by a desire to learn about the people of the past, whereas her best friend, Sanja, disapproves of her actions: "It's not worth thinking about them, Noria. They didn't think about us, either" (24). However, Noria cannot resist thinking about the people long gone, since the world she lives in is a result of their choices:

> I have tried not to think about them, but their past-world bleeds into our present-world, into its sky, into its dust. Did the present-world, the world that is, ever bleed into theirs, the world that was? I imagine one of them standing by the river that is now a dry scar in our landscape, a woman who is not young or old, or perhaps a man, it doesn't matter. Her hair is pale brown and she is looking into the water that rushes by, muddy perhaps, perhaps clear, and something that has not yet been is bleeding into her thoughts.
>
> I would like to think she turns around and goes home and does one thing differently that day because of what she has imagined, and again the day after, and the day after that. (Itäranta 24)

Noria and Sanja's exchange can easily make the readers feel more than a little pang of guilt for how they treat the world around them and for the legacy they will leave for future generations. The novel's faint images of people from the past pertain to us—readers of the novel—and the dystopian imagery of the narrative might help us overcome the short-sighted day-to-day thinking so that, rather than ignore the troubling reality, we learn to accept the responsibility for our deeds.

THE QUESTION OF SCALE

It is now beyond dispute that humankind bears responsibility for changes so vast and extensive that it can be identified as a global geophysical force that has profoundly transformed the face of the planet. William Steffen—a climate scientist and the author of *The Critical Decade: Climate Science, Risks and Responses* (2011)—and his coauthors point to this issue already in the title of their article: "The Anthropocene: Are Humans Now Overwhelming the Great Forces of Nature?" (2007) However, to accept that to "a large extent the future of the only place where life is known to exist is being determined by the actions of humans" (Lewis and Maslin 178) seems to be too demanding for the vast majority,[3] especially when considering what the German sociologist Ulrich Beck called the "age of unintended consequences" (119). The variation of the butterfly effect demonstrates how small everyday decisions (e.g., deciding whether to drive a car or ride a bike to work) gain large-scale and highly politicized consequences. Thus, it becomes necessary to assess individual decisions on a scale of time and space so vast that it borders with the unimaginable and then to initiate fundamental lifestyle changes on both a personal and global level. Fortunately, Steffen's words in "The Anthropocene: From Global Change to Planetary Stewardship" (2011) convey not only a warning but also hope: "We are the first generation with the knowledge of how our activities influence the Earth System, and thus the first generation with the power and the responsibility to change our relationship with the planet" (749).[4]

The issue of scale refers also to the need to embrace the non-human agenda and recognize the planetary context. In 1990, Michel Serres called for a "natural contract" (*Le Contract Naturel*, 1990; *The Natural Contract*, 1995) to complement an interhuman social contract—an approach that would "acknowledge and address the violence humanity has waged against the Earth itself" (Clark, *Ecocriticism* 4). The concept of the natural contract can be one of the possible instruments for grasping hyperobjects[5]—which the Anthropocene or global warming undoubtedly are—that is, "entities of such vast temporal and spatial dimensions that they defeat traditional ideas about what a thing is in the first place" ("Hyperobjects"). As Timothy Clark observes, the Anthropocene confuses the essential categories that people use to reach the meaning of things. The crucial feature of the Anthropocene is its overwhelming incomprehensibility and ensuing confusion: there is "no simple or unitary object directly to confront, or delimit, let alone to 'fix' or to 'tackle.' There is no 'it,' only a kind of dissolution into innumerable issues" (Clark, *Ecocriticism* 10).

And this is where literature enters to play its fundamental role. Literature can grasp the unimaginable, furnish solid contours to the yet only foreseen consequences, turn dry statistics into an embodied story, and transform the readers' understanding of the subject with the use of metaphors and powerful images. Paolo Bacigalupi's short story "The People of Sand and Slag" (2004), which was nominated for the Hugo and Nebula Awards, is a fine example. The story offers its readers a glimpse into the possible future in which the relationship between people and the world was disrupted even more than in Itäranta's *Memory of Water*. Paradoxically, though the environment is destroyed (e.g., oceans glisten with spilled petroleum and sandy beaches are full of acid puddles) and all non-human life is almost extinct, humanity, or at least what remains of it, is thriving. People have mastered advanced bioengineering, yet instead of saving even a fragment of the natural world, they adapted to the new circumstances and became almost immortal (they heal with enormous speed and gain nutrients from any source, sand and slag included). In the story, three guards in a mining conglomerate find a rarity: a real unmodified dog. Yet even though the narrator starts to feel something unusual and surprising toward the helpless animal, in the end the group decides to kill the dog since to take care of it in the new world is too demanding and expensive. Thus, they roast the animal on a spit and share its flesh—an appalling crime by the standards of Philip K. Dick's *Do Androids Dream of Electric Sheep?* (1968), a seminal science fiction story of the ruined Earth, in which living animals are the most desirable possession.

The people in Bacigalupi's story have traded their humanness for indestructibility; they are a parody of perfect adaptation, more than fit to live and prosper on the wreckage of the murdered Earth. They feel like gods—invincible and powerful—yet they lack the essential human competence of feeling fellowship and love to anything besides themselves. Their society has not changed at all: it is still driven by greed, consumption, and unwillingness to sacrifice one's own pleasures. Disposing of the dog frees the characters from unwanted responsibility: "Without the dog, we could really enjoy the beach. We didn't have to worry about whether it was going to step in acid, or tangle in barbwire half-buried in the sand, or eat something that would keep it up vomiting half the night" (Bacigalupi 63). And even though the narrator experiences some unnamed loss, the sensation is too fleeting and insignificant to change anything: "Still, I remember when the dog licked my face and hauled its shaggy bulk onto my bed, and I remember its warm breathing beside me, and sometimes, I miss it" (63). There is hardly any hope in Bacigalupi's story, both for humanity and nature.

Yet such bleak narratives also encourage readers to acknowledge the reality of the Anthropocene and contextualize its challenges. On May 18, 2011, *Nature* published an editorial entitled "The Human Epoch" that claims: "Official recognition for the Anthropocene would focus minds on the challenges to come" (254). The authors of the editorial consider the act of naming the recent epoch beneficial even if "[s]o far, it is more a prediction than a fact of Earth's history because many of its defining features are only starting to register in the rock record" (254). While the geological record will give its full evidence only in the future, to name the epoch now helps to grasp the pressing reality and provides a framework for proper consideration of the occurring transformation and, most importantly, for taking necessary action. It motivates people to realize that "we are in the driver's seat" ("The Human Epoch" 254). Manuel Arias-Maldonado also emphasizes the usefulness of the label "Anthropocene," because this term allows for "a wider perspective on a number of socionatural processes and events that used to be contemplated separately" (80). In fact, the Anthropocene challenges people to cross various boundaries:

> Previously accepted demarcations between the natural sciences, the social sciences and the humanities are not just coming under pressure but are effectively being transgressed and disregarded in many environmental issues and controversies. A question such as how much CO_2 an industry should be allowed to emit is at once a matter of politics, economics, climate studies, chemistry, social welfare, intergenerational ethics and even animal rights. (Clark, *Cambridge Introduction* 8)

Even the decision concerning the actual starting point of the Anthropocene has far-reaching implications. In *Defining the Anthropocene* (2015), Simon Lewis and Mark Andrew Maslin conclude that either the so-called Orbit spike in 1610 or the Bomb spike in 1964 is the most promising candidate. They argue,[6] and rightly so, that "[t]he event or date chosen as the inception of the Anthropocene will affect the stories people construct about the ongoing development of human societies" (Lewis and Maslin 178).

Since times immemorial, people have created stories in order to preserve their knowledge, confirm their identities, roles, and relations, and—most importantly—describe and, in that way, control their surroundings. "You can't understand the world without telling a story [. . .]. There isn't any center to the world but story," declares the Native American scholar Gerald Vizenor (qtd. in Coltelli 156). By this statement Vizenor indicates that the act of narration is a primary skill in our cognitive repertoire and a link between our subjective perception and the objective reality. A story is a powerful entity that transcends time and place, facilitating both a return to the past and speculation about the future. Within the frame of a single narrative, we can reflect on our heritage, assess our present condition, and ponder the possible consequences of our actions. Taking this into consideration, it seems vital to regard the discourse on the Anthropocene as an enlightening narrative which depicts humankind's transformation into a geological agent that exerts a lasting impact on the world. Moreover, if we create other narratives of the Anthropocene, that is, if we tell more stories about the present challenges and their future consequences, we might reach a better understanding of what needs to be done to ensure not only humanity's survival but also the restoration of the natural world and its non-human inhabitants.

Scholars of the Anthropocene have already recognized the potential hidden in narratives—or art in general—and their significance for the problems of the contemporary world. For instance, in *Minimal Ethics for the Anthropocene* (2014), Joanna Zylinska observes that "stories have a performative nature: they can enact and not just describe things—even if there are of course limits to what they are capable of enacting" (11). Thus, while Zylinska is aware of the constraints of storytelling, since stories alone will not solve the complex problems of our world, she highlights the influence which narratives can exercise over our mindsets, in that way initiating critical thinking which leads to change. In *Ecocriticism on the Edge* (2015), Timothy Clark argues, "The work of the environmental critic then becomes to consider and appreciate work in literature, criticism and the arts that helps articulate this shift towards a new kind of eco-cosmopolitanism capable of uniting people across the world without erasing important cultural and political differences" (17). Clark firmly asserts that stories can contribute to the creation of meaningful bonds between separate groups, which is necessary for forming a global network of relationships required to tackle the many problems at hand. Finally, Gina Comos and Caroline Rosenthal declare, in *Anglophone Literature and Culture in the Anthropocene* (2019), that "literature and art play a vital role in making tangible in various ways the abstract horrors of climate change and the destruction of planet earth" (xxi). Comos and Rosenthal rightly indicate that narratives of the Anthropocene provide some embodiment to the complex relations and hyperobjects which might otherwise escape our notice. By and large, narratives of the Anthropocene function as a platform for experimenting with ideas concerning the (de) evolution of humanity in respect to the planet.[7] They can actively shape our understanding of the present crisis, allow us to recognize our collective responsibility for the state of the planet, and encourage us to change our ways. Lewis and Maslin claim optimistically that

> the power that humans wield is unlike any other force of nature, because it is reflexive and therefore can be used, withdrawn or modified. More widespread recognition that human actions are driving far-reaching changes to the life-supporting infrastructure of Earth may well have increasing philosophical, social, economic and political implications over the coming decades. (178)

However, not all thinkers are equally optimistic in their assessment of humankind's ability to reflect on their position and actions. Richard Grusin, for instance, argues that the epoch of the Anthropocene means realizing humans are "climatological or geological planetary forces that operate just as nonhumans would, independent of human will, belief, or desires" (ix). For John Michael Greer the name "Anthropocene" is a plain manifestation of human arrogance and an embodiment of "the delusion that what our civilization is doing just now is going to keep on long enough to fill a geological epoch" (Greer).[8]

WHOSE ANTHROPOCENE?

While both *Memory of Water* and "The People of Sand and Slag" are set in the far future from the perspective of today's readers and show outcomes of a profoundly changed world, in *The Bone Clocks* (2014) David Mitchell describes a painful process of the "end of the good old days"—our days to be precise. The novel consists of six sections (the first starts in 1984 and the last in 2043), and the final episode describes a near-future only five years after the so-called Endarkment. The scarcity of resources caused by climate change coerced people into leading much simpler and dangerous lives. The world, which used to be interconnected by numerous links and in which every place was within reach, shrunk into isolated communities haunted by ghosts of the past. The remains of a once all-pervading Net are increasingly unreliable and most of the memories (pictures, videos, and texts) were lost when the Net first collapsed—almost nobody kept printed copies before the Endarkment. The elders, children, and the weak are at the mercy of violent groups exploiting the absence of authorities. Bandits are not motivated solely by practical reasons; they are driven by anger. It is, at least partially, rightful anger against the older generations who let the world fall apart.

> "The good old days are good and gone, old lady. Winter's coming."
> "You call yourself 'Hood,'" Mo tells him, "but it's 'Robbing Hood,' not Robin Hood, from where I'm standing. Would you treat your elderly relatives like this?"
> "Number one is to survive," answers Hood, watching the men on the roof. "They're all dead, like my parents. They had a better life than I did, mind. So did you. Your power stations, your cars, your creature comforts. Well, you lived too long. The bill's due. Today," up on the roof the bolt is cut on the first panel, "you start to pay. Think of us as the bailiffs."
> "But it wasn't us, personally, who trashed the world," says Mo. "It was the system. We couldn't change it."
> "Then it's not us, personally, taking your panels," says Hood. "It's the system. We can't change it." (Mitchell 571)

The above dialogue hints at an issue of major importance: the recognition of the Anthropocene as a narrative invokes questions about the identity of the narrator and the protagonist and, consequently, about responsibility and guilt. On the most general level, the Anthropocene is yet another chapter—hopefully, not the final one—in the grand story of humanity's existence on Earth. However, in terms of questions about the "narrators" and "protagonists" of the Anthropocene, this answer is far from being satisfactory for several reasons.

In his seminal book, *The Postmodern Condition: A Report on Knowledge* (1979), Jean-François Lyotard heralds the fall of grand (meta) narratives, warns against a belief in the inevitability of progress, and questions both the reign of reason and existence of objective truth. Shaped by the horrors of World War II and responding to the injustice of imperialistic colonialism, postmodernism discards the illusion of a universal discourse and knowledge of objective reality, and instead tries to accommodate the plethora of voices, identities, and experiences coming not only from the dominant majority but also from those historically and culturally oppressed by the majority. In fact, it is the voices of indigenous people that the contemporary world might now need the most. As it has been succinctly argued,

> If our species does not survive the ecological crisis, it will probably be due to our failure to imagine and work out new ways to live with the earth [. . .]. We struggle to adjust because we're still largely trapped inside the enlightenment tale of progress as human control over a passive and "dead" nature that justifies both colonial conquests and commodity economies. The real threat is not so much global warming itself, [. . .] as our own inability to see past the post-enlightenment energy, control and consumption extravaganza we so naively identify with the good, civilised life to a sustainable form of human culture. [. . .] We will go onwards in a different mode of humanity, or not at all. (Plumwood)

The notion that the Anthropocene is a universal narrative of humankind has been questioned by many scholars who demand diversity in the place of artificial uniformity (see Comos and Rosenthal). Of course, the challenges posed by the Anthropocene do pertain to all people, since the planet is our shared home. Inarguably, the problems of climate change, exploitation of natural resources, and ubiquitous pollution transgress nation-based geography and thus invoke Manfred B. Steger's concept of the global imaginary, that is, "a shared sense of a thickening world community, bound together by processes of globalization that are daily shrinking our planet" ("Rise"). However, while Steger is right to emphasize the global scale of certain challenges, we cannot neglect the fact that the shaping of and responses to the Anthropocene differ across communities. As Ursula K. Heise rightly observes, on the one hand, "the Anthropocene has turned humankind at large into the protagonist of a new deep-time narrative," yet, on the other, it has "generated heated debates over the merits of such a species narrative as opposed to an emphasis on economic and geopolitical inequality" (1).

Moreover, the label "Anthropocene" has been rejected by some scholars who suggest alternative names emphasizing what they regard as central features of the era. Jason Moore (2017), for instance, proposes the widely adopted Capitalocene as a term highlighting the crucial role of capitalism in organizing the culture–nature relations with all its tragic consequences. The terms Occidentalocene, coined by historian Christophe Bonneuil (2015), or Eurocene and Technocene (Sloterdijk 2015) accentuate the responsibility of highly industrialized Western nations. Plantationocene is also self-explanatory (see Haraway 162). Nicholas Mirzoeff follows up with an even more direct label: his chapter in *After Extinction* (2018) is revealingly entitled "It's Not the Anthropocene, It's the White Supremacy Scene; or, The Geological Color Line." Bruno Latour takes a contradicting approach when recommending to focus less on the contemporary political labeling of responsibility for changes and more on the geological and biological scales (54). Following up, Heather Davis and Etienne Turpin wonder in the introduction to *Art in the Anthropocene* (2015): "do we really want the epoch to be named as such for the next 10,000 years?" (9) Donna Haraway suggests Chthulucene as a description of the future in which both human and non-human survivors will come together into interspecies assemblages (4–10).

Inarguably, though it enables us to reflect on the human impact on the planet, the concept of the Anthropocene creates a problematic narrative. When humanity is compared to tectonic plates (Serres 160), to the super-subject (Ford), or a universal geological force, these comparisons overshadow the undeniable fact of the unequal influence of different societies and individuals. As the alternative names (e.g., Capitalocene) indicate, not all people take part in "the fossil fuel economy that is causing climate change" (Arias-Maldonado 89). Moreover, not only the distribution of responsibility but also the distribution of suffering is highly uneven. Many indigenous and less industrialized societies are more pressingly endangered by climate change than the generally affluent West. The Marshall Islands, for instance, which lie about 6 feet above sea level on average, contribute less than 0.00001 percent of global emissions, yet the rising sea level puts them at considerable risk and can render their home uninhabitable within decades (Larson). Likewise, many indigenous societies throughout the world must adapt to the changing environment at a substantial cost—economic, cultural, and political (Chief et al., 165–170).

Thus, Dipesh Chakrabarty is right when he claims in his influential essay "The Climate of History: Four Theses" (2009) that it is impossible to speak about humanity as a single collective entity, because the ways in which indigenous communities have experienced the Anthropocene differ significantly from the participation of highly industrialized Western countries. Chakrabarty's argument that the Anthropocene "calls for a global approach to politics without the myth of a global identity" (222) has been supported by numerous demands for more ethnic diversity and the recognition of indigenous narratives in the discourse on the Anthropocene (see Arias-Maldonado; Davis and Todd; Comos and Rosenthal; Zapf). Zoe Todd argues against the hegemonic tendencies of the Anthropocene narrative; instead of engaging with the Anthropocene as a teleological fact, she proposes "joyful and critical engagement through many forms of praxis" (252) and emphasizes the contribution of indigenous thought, praxis, and art. Similarly, Chief et al. indicate that many indigenous communities already readjusting to the global environmental changes have devised valuable adaptive strategies (169–170). As a means against the universalization of the Anthropocene, Arias-Maldonado recommends comprehending it as "emerging from different socio-cultural settings that have different context-specific implications and will therefore most likely generate different social responses" (89). As if in direct response to these dilemmas, Clark articulates a belief that "an emergent culture, coterminous with the species, will make up a collective force strong enough to help counter the day-to-day forces and decisions accelerating the extinction of terrestrial life" (*Ecocriticism* 17–18). It is only vital that people do not lose sight of diversity in this collective force. The Anthropocene can be conceptualized as a narrative, but it is not a universal narrative of humankind. It is a story woven from various voices and identities, with no omniscient narrator and no single protagonist—yet, hopefully, it is a story that will reach a happy ending.

Provided that humankind is, indeed, an agent that can intentionally and successfully affect the development of the Anthropocene, Clark indicates a paradox created by the comparison of humanity to a geological force: humanity becomes an impersonal agent beyond the ability to reflect and plan. Clark notes that while, on the one hand, this geological force is "a total effect of innumerable human decisions," on the other, "it can seem as imperturbably closed to human direction as is a hurricane or the tilt of the planet's orbit" (*Ecocriticism* 16). The optimistic stance suggests that the Anthropocene does require humanity to reflect globally and that individual actions must "be conceived at this higher, unprecedented level of self-reflection" (Clark, "Nature" 16). Art, paired with environmental criticism, may serve as a tool for reaching that level of reflection and articulating a "shift towards a new kind of eco-cosmopolitanism capable of uniting people across the world without erasing important cultural and political differences. It is hoped that an emergent culture, coterminous with the species, will make up a collective force strong enough to help counter the day-to-day" (Clark, *Ecocriticism* 17). The less optimistic approach, also expressed by Clark, warns against exaggerating the influence of imagination when considering the changes required in human–nature relations (*Ecocriticism* 19–21).

VOCALIZING THE ANTHROPOCENE VIA SPECULATIVE FICTION

Speculative fiction is one of the most potent media for analyzing the condition of contemporary world because it can explore the causes and consequences of the Anthropocene in ways inaccessible to other fields. Clark firmly declares that various forms of the fantastic can be a fine tool for understanding the Anthropocene:

> With its bizarre kinds of action at a distance, the collapse of safe distinctions between the trivial and the disastrous, and the proliferation of forces that cannot be directly perceived, the Anthropocene becomes deeply counterintuitive. It may find its analogue in modes of the fantastic, new forms of magic realism, or texts in which old distinctions between "character" and "environment" become fragile or break down. [. . .] Thus some forms of gothic, myth, or science fiction may well seem more interesting than a new novel displaying the latest subtleties of nuance in psychological or social observation, confining itself, that is, to the anthropocentric and arguably illusory world of conventional realism. (*Value* 99)

Writers of speculative fiction—be it fantasy, science, dystopian, climate, or post-apocalyptic fiction—invent (semi)fantastic realities which can freely dismantle existing power structures, undermine established laws, and provide provoking scenarios of alternative history by pursuing the simple question: "what if?" In that way, speculative fiction can alter the ways in which we perceive and interact with our surroundings. This is a major feat, given the ease with which we lose sight of the wonders of our world and treat familiar things as forever granted. Terry Pratchett aptly illustrates this ailment of the human mind in *A Hat Full of Sky* (2004), when one of his characters comments on the popular lullaby about a star:

> What power! What wondrous power! You can take a billion trillion tons of flaming matter, a furnace of unimaginable strength, and turn it into a little song for children! You build little worlds, little stories, little shells around your minds, and that keeps infinity at bay and allows you to wake up in the morning without screaming! (346)

Speculative fiction can open the readers' eyes so that they regain awareness of the world they take for granted. J. R. R. Tolkien, in the seminal essay "On Fairy-Stories" (1947), described this act as one of the four qualities of fantasy narratives, "Recovery" (53). Johanna Sinisalo, while discussing her own genre affiliation, provides an example which is a perfect illustration of Tolkien's concept:

Using non-realistic elements in my stories helps me to create a subtext and a fresh perspective on events. We might compare this to the ways in which we light a given object: if realism is when you light a statue from the front, I would move the light source so that the light hits the statue at a steep, diagonal angle. The object remains the same, but it looks different as new details are lit up while familiar details are hidden in shadow. ("Weird")

To defamiliarize the familiar is a key role of speculative fiction, and one thanks to which we can rediscover the world and its inhabitants.

This role is all the more important given the fact one of the major ailments of the Anthropocene is the distorted relationship between humankind and non-human species. The assumption that man is the pinnacle of divine creation, paired with the capitalist pursuit of profit, has led highly industrialized Western countries to exploit the natural environment and thereby damage their connection with the rest of the living world. Davis and Todd recognize this "severing of relations between humans and the soil, between plants and animals, between minerals and our bones" as the harmful "logic of the Anthropocene" (770), which needs to be exposed and challenged. Speculative fiction responds to the challenge by calling to life worlds in which humanity, just one among the many species, is forced to acknowledge the needs of non-human communities, cooperate with other sentient beings, and reevaluate its perception of the world. As Ursula K. Le Guin explains in relation to her own fiction: "Animals were once more to us than meat, pests, or pets: they were fellow-creatures, colleagues, dangerous equals. We might eat them; but then, they might eat us. That is at least part of the truth of my dragons. They remind us that the human is not the universal. What fantasy often does that the realistic novel generally cannot do is include the non-human as essential" (364). Le Guin then adds: "realistic fiction is drawn towards anthropocentrism, fantasy away from it. Although the green country of fantasy seems to be entirely the invention of human imaginations, it verges on and partakes of actual realms in which humanity is not lord and master, is not central, is not even important" (365). The idea about the insignificance of humanity might be a hard pill to swallow, yet such a shift of perspective is necessary to counter the detrimental effects of the Anthropocene. This necessity has been voiced, for instance, by Arias-Maldonado who argues, in *Environment and Society* (2015), that "we need to change our understanding of reality in a way that allows us to accommodate very long processes with formidable potential side-effects" (80).

THE ROLE OF THE APOCALYPSE

The most formidable "side-effect" of our attitude toward the natural environment might be the Apocalypse of the world as we know it—a scenario that is one of the most recurring themes of speculative fiction, or popular culture in general. The number of works which have gained popularity in recent years, for example, Suzanne Collins's *The Hunger Games* (2008–2010), James Dashner's *The Maze Runner* (2009–2016), Veronica Roth's *Divergent* (2011–2013), *Game of Thrones* TV series based on George R. R. Martin's multivolume *A Song of Ice and Fire* (2011–2019), and the Marvel movies (e.g., *Avengers: Endgame*, 2019)—which all, in one way or another, deal with the themes of extinction and survival—support Lawrence Buell's claim that "apocalypse is the single most powerful metaphor that the contemporary environmental imagination has at its disposal" (93). While Michael Harvey argues that in recent years dystopias have become more popular than utopias (7), overall it seems that our fear of the ultimate end has inspired numerous authors to create hopeful scenarios of survival (if not of prosperity) in the post-apocalyptic world. It is noteworthy that many of those works are aimed at young adult readers and feature similar protagonists as if preparing the younger audiences for the global challenges and, at the same time, assuring them that they will prevail and recover from their traumatizing experiences.

Such reassurance is much needed, given the fact that visions of the Apocalypse might have a twofold effect on people. On the one hand, some might respond with denial and refuse to take precautionary actions, insisting, for example, that climate change is a fiction they choose not to acknowledge. Such stubborn rejections have even gained a parodical diagnosis as the "Climate Change Denial Disorder" (2015). Such self-deception comes at a price both to the individual and the world since unattended problems are more likely to escalate than conveniently disappear. On the other hand, because visions of the Apocalypse are typically filled with horrors and suffering, it is easy to forget about the restorative aspect of this event: the rebirth that comes after the cleansing. In biblical tradition the Apocalypse precedes the rise of the Kingdom of God. As one is not possible without the other, humanity has to first experience the transformative power of destruction which will facilitate the arrival of a new order of things. Thus, paradoxically, the Apocalypse might be beneficial to the world and its inhabitants, but our fear of change obscures that opportunity. And of course, following the biblical context, first we need to pay for our sins—for the damage we have done to the world.

Thus, it seems that now, more than ever, we are in need of narratives which will tame our fear of destruction and transformation, and motivate us to search for solutions that will ensure not only the survival of humankind but the rebirth of a better world. Claire P. Curtis argues in *Postapocalyptic Fiction and the Social Contract* (2010) that "the catharsis of seeing total destruction either relieves that fear or awakens a need to act to prevent it" (5). The collapse of civilization is "a casual fait accompli" (Davis and Turpin 10), and to deny it is to reject the opportunity for reflection, change, and healing (assuming that the world and its inhabitants are not yet beyond the possibility of healing). That is why it is important that speculative fiction allows us to experience (post)apocalyptic scenarios before they become a reality; it is a safety mechanism that allows us to test certain solutions without the need to actually deal with their consequences. Moreover, as Curtis explains,

> Rather than simply dwelling on and inevitably glorying in the facts of destruction, these novels raise important questions about our expectations for a flourishing community—and thus, ultimately, about our own contributions to the violence that can bring about our destruction. So even when these novels fail spectacularly in their answers to how a community can flourish, that they even raise the question moves the conversation forward. (188)

In addition, "the blank slate" scenarios generated by post-apocalyptic narratives offer us a creative space for imagining a better future (Curtis 2–5). Jason Heller concludes:

> Post-apocalyptic books are thriving for a simple reason: The world feels more precariously perched on the lip of the abyss than ever, and facing those fears through fiction helps us deal with it. These stories are cathartic as well as cautionary. But they also reaffirm why we struggle to keep our world together in the first place. By imagining what it's like to lose everything, we can value what we have. ("Does Post-Apocalyptic")

Apart from learning to value what we have, we need to realize that every day we shape the future of our world with our decisions—that the distorted world of Itäranta's *Memory of Water* can be the fruit of our labor. Thus, we need to take responsibility for our actions and be prepared to deal with their consequences. Speculative fiction can aid us also in this process. As Robert Scholes explains, "As sublimation, fiction is a way of turning our concerns into satisfying shape, a way of relieving anxiety, of making life bearable. [. . .] As feedback, fiction is a means toward correcting our behavior in the world" (213–214). Scholes believes that "our experience with simulated situations" (214) can considerably affect our perception and actions. Following Scholes's reasoning, it can be argued that the simulated experiences offered by speculative fiction might help people dismantle the psychological barriers (e.g., limited awareness of the situation, certain ideological convictions, fear of the risks of change, etc.) which Robert Gifford blames for the still inadequate awareness about our daily contribution to sustainability. Given its wide readership among different age groups, speculative fiction is a medium that can engage audiences otherwise not academically or professionally interested in the debate on the Anthropocene. And by changing the ways in which we interact with the life around us, speculative fiction may ultimately contribute to the creation of the Anthropocene as "a new phase of history in which non-humans are no longer excluded or merely decorative features of [. . .] social, psychic, and philosophical space" (Morton 22).

STRUCTURE OF THE COLLECTION

This volume is divided into three interconnected thematic sections, reflecting the variety of angles and critical perspectives adopted by our contributors. The chapters testify to the potential of speculative fiction in its many guises to explore the problems we are facing in the Anthropocene epoch, offering insight into how various literary texts engage with the issues related to the threat of climatic Apocalypse, the destruction and protection of the natural environment, the relationships between human and non-human inhabitants of the planet, as well as the social and political dimensions of the Anthropocene, including the effects of global capitalism on the world we are living in. Transcending the boundaries between the genres and cultures, the chapters, when set dialogically against each other, provide a critical and multiperspective reflection on the complexity of the problems related to the Anthropocene, the advent of which "challenges some established boundaries between nature and culture, between climate and politics, between natural sciences and the social sciences and humanities" (Hamilton et al., 5).

The chapters in the first part, "Nature and Culture in the Anthropocene," all deal with destabilizing the long-held opposition between the self and the environment, humans and non-humans, nature and culture. In the opening chapter, Tereza Dědinová analyzes different levels of mimesis in Ursula K. Le Guin's *The Telling* (2000), a novel that takes place on an alien planet in a distant future and creates a sophisticated fantastic world. Drawing on the current findings of cognitive sciences, the chapter focuses on the function of mimesis as a means of crossing the boundary between the imagined and the perceived, and demonstrates how the embodied reading may facilitate the conveying of the story-driven experience into the reader's real world. Emphasizing the central concept of interconnectedness between the part and the whole through the complex metaphors of the human body as the body of the world, Dědinová reads Le Guin's novel as an exquisite attempt to show readers a possibility of harmonious participation in the ever-changing world, in which a human body operates in an intimate connection with both its physical and non-physical environments.

The other three chapters in this part are engaged in a discussion about the relationship between the natural environment and cultural heritage. Carrie Spencer examines Maggie Stiefvater's Raven Cycle (2012–2016), where the tensions in people's relationship with the environment are explored through multiple retellings of the legend of Owen Glendower (a descendant of King Arthur), problematizing traditional hero myths of conquest that conceptualize space and people in terms of the domination of the latter over the former. Adopting an eco-cosmopolitan approach, Spencer argues that the novels respond to the challenges of the Anthropocene by suggesting a possibility of the future in which both cultural and ecological difference and connectedness are understood. Retelling the legend from various points of view, including a non-human one, the cycle connects the past and present, humans and their environment, nature and myth, participating in the process of mythopoeisis— "the making of narratives that reshape the world" (Attebery 8) in response to irreversible planetary change. The non-anthropocentric concerns evident in numerous fantasy texts are further examined by Britta Maria Colligs in her ecocritical analysis of the depiction and purpose of literary forests in various narratives—from J. R. R. Tolkien's *The Lord of the Rings* (1954) through Ursula K. Le Guin's *The Word for World is Forest* (1976) to Ali Shaw's environmental apocalypse *The Trees* (2016). Observing that speculative genres often draw on the paradigm shift envisaged by ecocriticism and based on the key concepts of animism and interrelatedness, Colligs demonstrates that the fantastic forests can become independent characters with their own agency, functioning as representatives for their entire environment with their own specific voices capable of an environmental message. On the one hand, the forest and individual tree-characters act as memorials for nature and educators for the characters and ultimately for the reader as well. On the other hand, functioning as complex living ecosystems, they become active participants in their narratives and provide us with a powerful image of nature actively fighting against its enemies. Finally, Lykke Guanio-Uluru investigates Stephenie Meyer's *Twilight* series (2005–2008) and Scott Westfield's *Uglies* (2005) as narratives that offer insight into the opposition between civilization with its consumerist opulence and an alternative myth of the wilderness present in American literature since Thoreau's *Walden* (1854). The focus on the female protagonists of the novels allows for a discussion of the problematic aspects of transhumanism from an environmentalist angle and invites a re-consideration of the notion of heroism in the Anthropocene.

The second part, "(Post)Apocalyptic Worlds and the Anthropocene," contains the chapters on (post)apocalyptic narratives, whose growing popularity reflects cultural anxieties about the destruction of the world as a result of an imminent, natural, or human-induced catastrophe. The 9/11 terrorist attacks, natural disasters, pandemic outbreaks of SARS, Ebola, and COVID-19, have all contributed to the apocalyptic sense of doom that seems to have permeated the twenty-first-century popular imagination. As the fear of the apocalyptic event has always been present in our culture, this section of the volume opens with Jiří Jelínek's chapter, which analyzes the key aspects of the disastrous pandemics and their relation to the evolution of catastrophic thinking in a wide range of narratives, including both premodern and contemporary texts. Concerned in particular with comparing the images and functions of the catastrophic diseases, Jelínek also demonstrates the potential of the plague narratives to act as agents of social change. Some of these texts, he argues, can even be interpreted as a type of social experiment, with the plague becoming the main catalyst of the desirable cultural shift. Both Maria Quigley and Anna Bugajska further contribute to the discussion on (post)apocalyptic imagery and its relationship with the discourses of the Anthropocene. Quigley discusses the theme of hybridity in M. R. Carey's *The Girl with All the Gifts* (2014), a novel that seems to go against the major trend of post-apocalyptic fiction, which usually proposes that nothing can annihilate the human race entirely. In Carey's work, in contrast, a fungal infection has wiped out a massive amount of the population, by turning them into zombie-like creatures. Situating her chapter within a wider context of post-apocalyptic and zombie narratives, Quigley is particularly interested in how Carey's text diverts from established patterns by showing that humans are not the future of the Earth but an obsolete part of the past, and that the world can continue without them at its center. Bugajska critically examines James Patterson's *Maximum Ride* cycle (2005–2015), a narrative implying that while the pristine natural environment is perhaps beyond recall, humans can survive in another form, enhanced through the processes of chimerization and genetic modification. In her chapter she focuses on how Patterson's reworking of the mythical images of chimeras and other mythological creatures are combined with Christian eschatology and contemporary transhumanist utopianism within the framework of evantropia/dysantropia dichotomy. Noting that Patterson's novels, on the one hand, play on the fear of human–animal crossovers in mythology and folklore and, on the other hand, are influenced by the transhumanist hopes and contemporary superhero mythology, she reads them as texts that move beyond the anthropocentric apocalyptic imagery and make a case for an after-Anthropocene world, where the survival of humanity depends on relational, not oppositional, approach to the animal world. In the final chapter of this section, Joanna Krystyna Radosz examines the phenomenon of the Metro universe, which began with the release of Dmitry Glukhovsky's *Metro 2033* novel in 2005 and soon extended into an international project, comprising novels, novellas, and video games set in the same world. Her chapter adds yet another dimension to the discussion of the Anthropocene, as it approaches the subject from a non-Anglocentric perspective, offering fresh insight into the Russian tradition of portraying human-induced disasters in speculative fiction and examining the role of the underground in preserving humankind. Radosz's chapter focuses on the literary and cultural context of the particular geocultural region, which is less explored in English and American criticism, thus providing an opportunity for establishing new interpretative possibilities and comparative analyses.

In the opening chapter of the third part, "Society and Politics in the Anthropocene," Keygan Sands explores how N. K. Jemisin's Hugo Award-winning *The Stone Sky* (2017), the last installment of the *Broken Earth* trilogy (2015–2017), uses the strategies of fantasy to expose the roots of systems, particularly energy extraction and colonialism, that catalyze and propagate the Anthropocene epoch. Although colonial societies are ultimately ephemeral in the face of geologic processes, the novel reveals the origins of cataclysmic and recurrent events as consequences of actions undertaken by the resource-consuming, imperial-derived civilization. As Sands argues, Jemisin creates her own systems of oppression and colonialism that, because they are entirely removed from our world, clarify our understanding of real systems—a particular advantage of fantasy genre conventions. Through the lenses of multiple disciplines, Sands reads *The Stone Sky* as a powerful example of how we can reimagine ourselves as existing in geologic time and global space, demonstrating that fantasy literature can act as a vehicle of understanding and enacting social criticism. Criticism of colonial relations is also the theme of China Miéville's novel *Embassytown* (2011), examined in this volume by Aleksandr Kolesnikov, who focuses on the politics of language and culture. Drawing from L. Wittgenstein's works on language games as well as fundamental studies of the Other, this chapter analyzes the representation of the model of relations between the Own and the Other. Discussing the politics of language and culture as addressed in the novel, Koleshnikov argues that Miéville's handling of the problem is quite inadequate to the Chthulucene criticism and suggests that although *Embassytown* succeeds as a piece of postcolonial fiction, it fails as the narrative of the Anthropocene. Dariya Khokhel interrogates yet another aspect of the globalized world: the process of immigration as rendered in Patricia Briggs's *Mercy Thompson* (2006–2020) and *Alpha and Omega* (2008–2018) urban fantasy series. Demonstrating that urban fantasy is a genre suited for the discussion of the issues related to the Urban Anthropocene, with its emphasis on the social rather than geological dimensions, Khokhel analyzes the depiction of supernatural characters and their communities in order to explore the issues of immigration and the effects they have on both newcomers and indigenous creatures. This section concludes with Dwight Tanner's discussion of Ian McEwan's *Solar* (2010) and Barbara Kingsolver's *Flight Behavior* (2011) as narratives that develop new literary strategies and hermeneutics for representing and confronting climate change. Relying largely on formalism and narratology, Tanner demonstrates how these novels accomplish Amitav Ghosh's crucial call to demythologize the climate crisis by developing a realist speculative approach to representing climate change that would combine both the fantastic consequences of humanity's quotidian choices and the ways these fantastic, destructive consequences are becoming increasingly quotidian. Acknowledging that it might result in reifying anthropocentric thinking, the chapter proposes that speculative realism can still reveal and critique human-centricity, and challenge practices of understanding and approaching the natural world through human-centric metaphors.

In *Anthropocene: A Very Short Introduction* (2018), Erle C. Ellis asks, "Does an age of humans mean the end of nature? [...] And is the Anthropocene necessarily a catastrophe—a environmental disaster and the end of humanity—or could there be a 'good Anthropocene' in which both humans and nature might thrive together into the deep future?" (4) The chapters in this collection do not provide a straightforward answer to these questions. Yet they do suggest a shift in the collective imagination is needed if we are to handle the problems we are facing. Speculative fiction in its many guises can push its readers, by "help[ing] to liberate [them] from lazily relying on standard assumptions about culture and society" (Hume 162), to depart from the constraints of reality, not to escape it, but to question and challenge the *status quo*. Focusing on various genres, examined from a variety of theoretical vantage points, our contributors demonstrate that speculative fiction encourages a serious reflection about what the Anthropocene is, what it means to us, and what actions we might take. Through this, speculative fiction might play an important role in re-framing social and cultural narratives by challenging our sense of the self, transforming our relationship with the non-human other, and influencing our understanding of the future. While it does not necessarily offer immediate workable solutions, speculative fiction forces its readers to imagine both positive and negative outcomes, thus promoting a broader perspective on the ways we might take to arrive at the desired destination.

NOTES

1. As Timothy Clark claims: "In the limited sense of places unaffected by human activity there is no 'nature' as such left on the planet, but there are various 'environments,' some more pristine than others" (*Cambridge Introduction* 6).
2. President of the Commission, Stanley Finn, sees the Anthropocene as a valuable tool when it is understood as a historical and not geological epoch (Arias-Maldonado 79). For a detailed discussion concerning the start of the epoch, see Simon L. Lewis and Mark A. Maslin's article "Defining the Anthropocene" (*Nature News*, 2015).
3. As John Michael Greer dryly remarks: "the vast majority of people in the industrial world seem content to insist that they can have their planet and eat it too" ("Myth").
4. The recognition of the Anthropocene entails a change in our perception of human histories. Timothy Clark indicates the striking difference between the "understanding of recent centuries of human history as the advance of human freedoms through various peoples' struggle for rights" and "a boom in numbers, possibilities,

and in some cases at least, in liberties and security, through the discovery of vast resources of fossil fuels" (*Ecocriticism* 13).

5. Clark compares (*Ecocriticism* 6) hyperobjects to the Level III system as presented by Braden R. Allenby and Daniel Sarewitz in *The Techno-Human Condition* (2011).

6. "The choice of either 1610 or 1964 as the beginning of the Anthropocene would probably affect the perception of human actions on the environment. The Orbis spike implies that colonialism, global trade and coal brought about the Anthropocene. [...] Choosing the bomb spike tells a story of an elite-driven technological development that threatens planet-wide destruction. The long-term advancement of technology deployed to kill people, from spears to nuclear weapons, highlights the more general problem of 'progress traps'" (Lewis and Maslin 177).

7. Manuel Arias-Maldonado in the chapter "Moralizing the Anthropocene" (in *Environment and Society: Socionatural Relations in the Anthropocene*, 2015) gathered contributions contemplating the moral core of the Anthropocene debate, considering it a suggestion to rethink the culture–nature relationship (85–88).

8. Fortunately, there are more voices arguing that the Anthropocene, in spite of its dangers and deadly traps, can also introduce hope and direct our efforts toward the necessary transformation of humanity and its relationship to nature. For instance, the opening lines of "An Ecomodernist Manifesto" (2015) sound very encouraging: "We offer this statement in the belief that both human prosperity and an ecologically vibrant planet are not only possible, but also inseparable. By committing to the real processes, already underway, that have begun to decouple human well-being from environmental destruction, we believe that such a future might be achieved. As such, we embrace an optimistic view toward human capacities and the future" (Asafu-Adjaye et al.). Ecomodernists or ecopragmatists claim that a good Anthropocene can be achieved through technological innovations. They are very close to the group represented by Peter Kareiva, whose "new conservationism" shifts focus from nature preservation to strengthening of chosen natural systems most beneficial for people with particular attention paid to the poor. Serious criticism of these approaches aims at the centrality of humanity (nature should be preserved since people need nature) and lack of consideration for the non-human inhabitants of the planet.

Moreover, the "Seeds of Good Anthropocenes" project (available for exploration at https://goodanthropocenes.net/) aims at sharing optimistic and realistic visions of a desirable and sustainable future in an endeavor to empower and motivate beneficial changes. The founders of the project seek to create a counterweight to widespread dystopian images of the future, believing that hopeful images might reinforce positive actions and choices. Only where to look for reasons to hope without falling into the pitfall of wishful thinking? To inspire the global community, participants of the project identify and collect elements (Seeds) of the Good Anthropocene from diverse communities around the world to embrace as many of various regions, values, disciplines, and worldviews as possible. While the Anthropocene is a global issue, models of adaptation need to meet local circumstances. The good seeds are in the majority focused on connecting people to nature (Bennet et al., 443), and as such they should be beneficial for both human and non-human species.

WORKS CITED

Arias-Maldonado, Manuel. *Environment and Society: Socionatural Relations in the Anthropocene*. Springer, 2015.

Asafu-Adjaye, John, et al. "An Ecomodernist Manifesto." *Ecomodernism.org*, 2015, www.ecomodernism.org/. Accessed 20 February 2020.

Attebery, Brian. *Stories about Stories: Fantasy and the Remaking of Myth*. Oxford UP, 2014.

Bacigalupi, Paolo. *Pump Six and Other Stories*. Night Shade Books, 2008.

Beck, Ulrich. *World Risk Society*. Polity Press, 2009.

Bennett, Elena M., et al. "Bright Spots: Seeds of a Good Anthropocene." *Frontiers in Ecology and the Environment*, vol. 14, no. 8, 2016, pp. 441–448.

Bonneuil, Christophe. "The Geological Turn." In *The Anthropocene and the Global Environmental Crisis: Rethinking Modernity in a New Epoch*, edited by Clive Hamilton et al. Routledge, 2015, pp. 17–31.

Buell, Lawrence. *The Environmental Imagination: Thoreau, Nature Writing and the Formation of American Culture*. Princeton UP, 1995.

Chakrabarty, Dipesh. "The Climate of History: Four Theses." *Critical Inquiry*, vol. 35, no. 2, 2009, pp. 197–222.

Chief, Karletta, et al. "Indigenous Experiences in the U.S. with Climate Change and Environmental Stewardship in the Anthropocene." *USDA Forest Service, RMRS*, 2014, pp. 161–176. www.fs.fed.us/rm/pubs/rmrs_p071/rmrs_p071_161_176.pdf. Accessed 10 February 2020.

Clark, Timothy. *The Cambridge Introduction to Literature and the Environment*. Cambridge UP, 2011.

———. *Ecocriticism on the Edge: The Anthropocene as a Threshold Concept*. Bloomsbury, 2015.

———. "Nature, Post Nature." In *The Cambridge Companion to Literature and the Environment*, edited by Louise Westling. Cambridge UP, 2014, pp. 75–89.

———. *The Value of Ecocriticism*. Cambridge UP, 2019.

"Climate Change Denial Disorder." *Youtube*, uploaded by Funny or Die, 16 April 2015. www.youtube.com/watch?v=fZTTI_0mHN0. Accessed 9 March 2020.

Coltelli, Laura. *Winged Words: American Indian Writers Speak*. U of Nebraska P, 1990.

Comos, Gina, and Caroline Rosenthal. "Introduction." In *Anglophone Literature and Culture in the Anthropocene*, edited by Gina Comos and Caroline Rosenthal. Cambridge Scholars Publishing, 2019, pp. viii–xxii.

Curtis, Claire P. *Postapocalyptic Fiction and the Social Contract: "We'll Not Go Home Again."* Lexington, 2010.

Davis, Heather, and Zoe Todd. "On the Importance of a Date, or Decolonizing the Anthropocene." *ACME: An International Journal for Critical Geographies*, vol. 16, no. 4, 2017, pp. 761–780.

Davis, Heather, and Etienne Turpin. "Art & Death: Lives Between the Fifth Assessment & the Sixth Extinction." In *Art in the Anthropocene: Encounters Among Aesthetics, Politics, Environments and Epistemologies*, edited by Heather Davis and Etienne Turpin. Open Humanities Press, 2014, pp. 3–30.

Ellis, Erle C. *Anthropocene: A Very Short Introduction*. Oxford UP, 2018.
Ford, Thomas H. "Aura in the Anthropocene." *Symploke*, vol. 21, no. 1–2, 2013, pp. 65–82.
Gifford, Robert. "The Dragons of Inaction: Psychological Barriers That Limit Climate Change Mitigation and Adaptation." *American Psychologist*, vol. 66, no. 4, 2011, pp. 290–302.
Greer, John Michael. "The Myth of the Anthropocene." *Resilience.org*, 6 October 2016. www.resilience.org/stories/2016-10-06/the-myth-of-the-anthropocene/. Accessed 10 February 2020.
Grusin, Richard A. *Anthropocene Feminism*. U of Minnesota P, 2017.
Hamilton, Clive, et al. "Thinking the Anthropocene." In *The Anthropocene and the Global Environmental Crisis: Rethinking Modernity in a New Epoch*, edited by Clive Hamilton et al. Routledge, 2015, pp. 1–14.
Haraway, Donna. "Anthropocene, Capitalocene, Plantationocene, Chthulucene: Making Kin." *Environmental Humanities*, vol. 6, no. 1, 2015, pp. 159–165.
Harvey, Michael. *Utopia in the Anthropocene: A Change Plan for a Sustainable and Equitable World*. Routledge, 2019.
Heise, Ursula K. "Preface: The Anthropocene and the Challenge of Cultural Difference." In *German Ecocriticism in the Anthropocene*, edited by Caroline Schaumann and Heather I. Sullivan. Palgrave Macmillan, 2017, pp. 1–6.
Heller, Jason. "Does Post-Apocalyptic Literature Have a (Non-Dystopian) Future?" *NPR*, 2 May 2015. www.npr.org/2015/05/02/402852849/does-post-apocalyptic-literature-have-a-non-dystopian-future. Accessed 12 February 2015.
Hume, Kathryn. *Fantasy and Mimesis*. Methuen, 1984.
"Hyperobjects." *upress.umn.edu*. U of Minnesota P, 2013. www.upress.umn.edu/book-division/books/hyperobjects. Accessed 26 March 2020.
Itäranta, Emmi. *Memory of Water*. HarperCollins Publishers, 2014.
Kareiva, Peter. "New Conservation: Setting the Record Straight and Finding Common Ground." *Conservation Biology*, vol. 28, no. 3, 2014, pp. 634–636.
Larson, Nina. "Marshall Islanders 'Sitting Ducks' as Sea Level Rises, Says President." *phys.org*, 21 June 2019. www.phys.org/news/2019-06-marshall-islanders-ducks-sea.html. Accessed 11 March 2020.
Le Guin, Ursula K. "The Critics, the Monsters, and the Fantasists." In *The Secret History of Fantasy*, edited by Peter S. Beagle. Tachyon, 2010, pp. 355–366.
Lewis, Simon L., and Mark A. Maslin. "Defining the Anthropocene." *Nature News*. Nature Publishing Group, 11 March 2015. www.nature.com/articles/nature14258. Accessed 20 February 2020.
Lyotard, Jean-François. *The Postmodern Condition: A Report on Knowledge*. Translated by Geoff Bennington and Brian Massumi. *Theory and History of Literature*, vol. 10. U of Minnesota P, 1984.
Mirzoeff, Nicholas. "It's Not the Anthropocene, it's the White Supremacy Scene; or, the Geological Color Line." In *After Extinction*, edited by Richard Grusin. U of Minnesota P, 2018, pp. 123–149.
Mitchell, David. *The Bone Clocks*. Random House, 2014.

Moore, Jason W. "The Capitalocene, Part I: on the Nature and Origins of Our Ecological Crisis." *The Journal of Peasant Studies*, vol. 44, no. 3, 2017, pp. 594–630.

Morton, Timothy. *Hyperobjects: Philosophy and Ecology after the End of the World*. U of Minnesota P, 2013.

Plumwood, Val. "A Review of Deborah Bird Rose's 'Reports from a Wild Country: Ethics for Decolonisation'." *Australian Humanities Review*, no. 42, August 2007. australianhumanitiesreview.org/2007/08/01/a-review-of-deborah-bird-roses-reports-from-a-wild-country-ethics-for-decolonisation/. Accessed 9 February 2020.

Pratchett, Terry. *A Hat Full of Sky*. Doubleday, 2004.

Serres, Michel. *The Natural Contract*. U of Michigan P, 2011.

Scholes, Robert. *Structural Fabulation: An Essay on Fiction of the Future*. U of Notre Dame P, 1975.

Sinisalo, Johanna. "Weird and Proud of It." *Books from Finland, A Literary Journal*, 05 September 2011. www.booksfromfinland.fi/2011/09/weird-and-proud-of-it/. Accessed 9 February 2020.

Steffen, Will, and Lesley Hughes. *The Critical Decade 2013: Climate Change Science, Risks and Responses*. Canberra: A.C.T. Climate Commission Secretariat, 2013. researchers.mq.edu.au/en/publications/the-critical-decade-2013-climate-change-science-risks-and-respons. Accessed 25 February 2020.

Steffen, Will, et al. "The Anthropocene: Are Humans Now Overwhelming the Great Forces of Nature?" *Ambio*, vol. 36, no. 8, 2007, pp. 614–621.

———. "The Anthropocene: From Global Change to Planetary Stewardship." *Ambio*, vol. 40, no. 7, 2011, pp. 739–761.

Sloterdijk, Peter. "The Anthropocene: A Process-State at the Edge of Geohistory?" In *Art in the Anthropocene: Encounters Among Aesthetics, Politics, Environments and Epistemologies*, edited by Heather Davis and Etienne Turpin. Open Humanities Press, 2014, pp. 327–340.

Steger, Manfred B. "The Rise of the Global Imaginary and the Persistence of Ideology." *Global-E Journal*, vol. 3, no. 7, 30 July 2009. www.21global.ucsb.edu/global-e/july-2009/rise-global-imaginary-and-persistence-of%C2%A0ideology. Accessed 9 February 2020.

"The Human Epoch." *Nature*, vol. 473, no. 254, 18 May 2011. www.nature.com/articles/473254a. Accessed 25 February 2020.

Todd, Zoe. "Indigenizing the Anthropocene." In *Art in the Anthropocene: Encounters Among Aesthetics, Politics, Environments and Epistemologies*, edited by Heather Davis and Etienne Turpin. Open Humanities Press, 2014, pp. 241–254.

Tolkien, J. R. R. "On Fairy-Stories." In *Tree and Leaf*. Unwin Hyman, 1988.

Zapf, Hubert. "The Challenge of the Anthropocene and the Sustainability of Texts." In *Anglophone Literature and Culture in the Anthropocene*, edited by Gina Comos and Caroline Rosenthal. Cambridge Scholars Publishing, 2019, pp. 2–22.

Zylinska, Joanna. *Minimal Ethics for the Anthropocene*. Open Humanities Press, 2014.

Part I

NATURE AND CULTURE IN THE ANTHROPOCENE

Chapter 1

"The Being that Can be Told"
The Telling *by Ursula K. Le Guin as a Remedy for the Anthropocene*

Tereza Dědinová

OPENING

The term *Anthropocene* has many connotations, one of them being a culture–nature divide; humanity sees itself as separated from its environment, global society understands itself as superior and entitled to rule the world and to use and abuse it up to its liking. This short-sighted arrogance is possible only when we, the people, feel no responsibility to our future generations but also when we ignore the simple fact that we are not alone in this world. When exploiting, damaging, and perhaps even destroying our home, we thereby exploit, damage, and destroy the homes of countless beings, sentient and suffering due to our deeds. We chose to see our planet as a resource instead of as a complex system interwoven by myriads of connections. We chose to understand ourselves as detached from this web of life and as superordinate to it. The everyday reality of (and not only) climate change proves us horribly wrong, yet we continue *en masse* further and further to cause irreversible changes.

The power of art lies in its potential to be eye-opening, to tell new stories, to offer new visions, and to help humanity to understand its place within the biosphere, within the web of life. *The Telling* (2000) by Ursula K. Le Guin does not offer a strongly actual story directly aiming at the consequences of the Anthropocene. Instead, it shows its readers what it could feel like to be an integral part of the ever-changing whole, to move, to dance in harmony in the flow of being which connects the human body with its both physical and non-physical environment. However, Le Guin is not describing utopia in her novel; the culture based on harmony and interconnectedness of being is broken in the time of the story, and its remains are hidden in secluded places and under constant threat of disappearance. It is not possible to undo the history of human deeds—not on Aka, nor on Terra in Le Guin's novel, nor on planet Earth—however, we can, and we must try and find a way to heal the broken integrity, to heal both the people and the planet.

In *The Telling*, Le Guin builds an elaborate metaphor connecting the human body with the entire world and storytelling as both a part of the world and a means of how to grasp this connection. She does not only describe it but, through mimesis, manages to transmit a vivid impression, a compelling and unsentimental story-driven experience. This chapter aims to analyze the relationship between fantastic and mimetic elements and to examine the importance of the (story)telling in the text, to illustrate the role of mimesis on the level of story and discourse, and with the support of cognitive science to point out how the experience of the fantastic fictional world enriches the understanding of the actual world. I argue that an enactive, embodied perception of the story and the fictional world of *The Telling*, invited by its discourse, enables the reader to grasp a meaning valuable and perhaps essential for the interaction between humanity and our environment in the Anthropocene.

The Telling belongs to the *Hainish* or *Ekumen Cycle*, a loosely interwoven series of novels and shorter texts set in a fictional world, in which a number of planets inhabited by intelligent beings, through technologies that allow faster-than-light communication and interstellar distance travel, are connected in Ekumen (from Greek *oikoumene*, meaning "the inhabited world"), a community based on the exchange and free sharing of information and technology. In the first stories from the *Hainish Cycle: Rocannon's World* (1966), *Planet Exile* (1966), and *City of Illusions* (1967), a League of All Worlds is introduced, which may be a predecessor of Ekumen (see *Left Hand of Darkness*). However, Le Guin rejected the idea of the *Hainish Cycle* as a consistent saga with a fixed history.[1]

To the *Hainish Cycle* belong some of her award-winning novels: *The Left Hand of Darkness* (1969) and *Outcast* (1974), the novella *The Word for World Is Forest* (1972), and the short story "The Day Before the Revolution" (1974). Although Le Guin wrote and published more minor texts from the *Hainish Cycle* during the following years, *The Telling* is the first and, unfortunately, the last novel set in Ekumen for over a quarter of a century. The very loose connection within the cycle and the number of clues provided in the opening passages allow the reader to place the described events into a broader context—however partial—even without knowledge of the *Hainish Cycle*.

As is usual for Le Guin's work, while it is not an extensive text, it is rich in meaning and offers vast possibilities for interpretation. Raffaella Baccolini (2003) focuses on history, memory, and options of reconciliation, whereas

Susan M. Bernardo and Graham J. Murphy (2006) analyze the development of both the main characters Sutty and Yara, and they identify a Taoist search for balance as a central theme of the book, while also offering a reading of the novel as a critical dystopia. Sandra J. Lindow, in her comprehensive study *Dancing the Tao* (2012), reveals a strong connection between moral development and self-awareness not only in the case of characters of Le Guin's work but with significance to its readers as well.

Owing much to these insightful studies, in this chapter I focus on the function of mimesis as a means of crossing the divide between the imagined and the perceived, in other words, on the analysis of how overlapping levels of mimesis and an embodied reading empower the conveying of the story-driven experience into the reader's real world. Considering the length of this chapter, I will not focus on the development of Sutty and leave aside her relationship with Yara (already analyzed in detail by Lindow, Bernardo, and Murphy). Also, I will not pay much attention to the cause of recent changes of the Akan society, the need for Aka to realize non-uniformity and imperfection of Ekumen, nor the emerging solution to the conflict, and how it is introduced at the end of the novel (for a detailed study see Bernardo and Murphy).

INTRODUCTION TO THE STORY

As a representative of the galactic union Ekumen, the central character and narrator of the story, Sutty, accepts the location on the newly discovered planet Aka and sets out for a world with a rich cultural, philosophical, and literary tradition, fascinating and tempting her for its open society, not subjected to dogmatism, religious fanaticism, or homophobia. Aka seems to promise a new beginning in a happier and wiser world for Sutty, who is deeply traumatized by her life on Terra, where under the rule of theocratic fundamentalists, her family was forced to leave their home in India and move to the free zone in Canada. Years later, her beloved girlfriend is killed during the Holy Wars. However, before Sutty even set foot on the planet, everything changed. During the seven-decade-long interstellar travel (which, due to the time dilatation, takes only months for Sutty), Aka changes beyond recognition.

As a result of encountering the technically highly advanced Ekumen and meeting with the fundamentalists ruling Terra, Aka rejects its history and culture, everything old and traditional is outlawed, including the whole system of spiritual and physical well-being and the use of ideographic writing which has been replaced by a simpler alphabet free of symbolic meanings. Literary and philosophical works are burned under the supervision of the ironically named Ministry of Poetry,[2] *umyazu* (centers of learning) are destroyed, and *maz* (people of education, narrators, herbalists, and philosophers) are sent to re-education camps. If there are some old books still discovered, they are recycled and converted into thermal insulation; their owners receive cruel punishment and denunciators are publicly awarded. The entire planet is supposed to be almost cleansed of ancient—according to the current view of the world, barbaric—past, so that the new "producer-consumers" state governed by a capitalist corporation can march gloriously and effectively toward the stars.[3]

First, the new regime seems to have achieved absolute success, and Sutty fails to discover any trace of the old culture in the capital Dovza City. Only after leaving the metropolis, far in the country, in a secluded village below a mighty mountain, Sutty finds out that the old traditions are not lost entirely, and slowly learns about the elaborate system of a fulfilled life in both natural and cultural environment, in harmony with body, mind, and nature. The old tradition, so despised by the technocratic government, is created by an elaborate net of countless tellings both abstract and practical, of small and big subjects, concerning community living, love, and death or instructions for physical exercise, food preparation, and the use of herbs. All this allows for the preservation of harmony between people, between man and his surroundings, between the human body and the planet, civilization and nature, solitude and society, life and death. When studying the "old ways," Sutty gradually gains strength to overcome the shadows of her past and at the end of the book, her position as an observer for Ekumen and her close experience with the Akan culture allow her to take the first step toward healing the broken Akan society.

MIMESIS IN FANTASTIC LITERATURE

While fantastic literature hugely benefits from the transcending limits of the actual reality and offers countless non-realistic fictional worlds stimulating both aesthetically and cognitively,[4] mimesis remains a significant means of filling the gaps in the texture of the fictional world and thus contributing to readers' immersion into the story. As Brian Attebery observed, a "property of extension" is a great advantage of the reportorial mode of discourse (*Strategies* 131) and without the possibility to extend the fantastic world according to our shared knowledge of the reality "many fantasies suffer from certain thinness even while they seem to be overdetermined" (132). In the following passages, I will analyze the different levels of mimesis in the novel, starting from the most obvious ones and leading to the deepest levels of mimesis which are wholly dependent on the reader's embodied cognition.

LEVELS OF MIMESIS IN *THE TELLING*

In the fictional world of *The Telling*, planet Earth, called Terra, is explicitly remembered primarily due to the influence of troublesome historical incidents (which probably can be seen as an alternative future from the reader's perspective) on the narrator and the formation of her personality. Important events of the story itself are set on an alien planet. However, the awareness of the actual world, its culture, history, and present are essential to appreciate the novel. If we only read *The Telling* as a fascinating fantasy from another world that does not reflect our reality, we will deprive ourselves of the immense wealth of thought that the novel offers by overlapping the actual and the fictional worlds.

In *The Telling*, we can identify several levels of mimesis. On an explicit level, there are places from the actual world transferred to the fictional world: the protagonist Sutty was born on Earth, she has Indian and British roots, her entire family was forced to flee the clerofascist regime of the so-called Unists from India to Vancouver in Canada, where one of the free zones opened to those who did not follow the unified teachings of the government. Other places and nationalities transferred from the actual world are also mentioned in the text.

The first deeper level of mimesis involves implicit references to historical events and traumas of the actual world. Both Aka and Terra come under the domination of an aggressive regime that imposes its ideology on the whole society, and both are subjected to breaking away from their past and denying the idea of learning from it. As Sutty realizes during her stay on Aka, "the government of this world, to gain technological power and intellectual freedom, had outlawed the past" (Le Guin, *Telling* 33). Deleting history necessarily reminds her of the home planet: "we on Terra are living the future of a people who denied their past" (9).

We can easily find reflections of the actual world in the characteristic features of both regimes. The Corporation rejecting all cultural and religious traditions in the name of progress inevitably brings the Chinese Cultural Revolution to mind—the phrase "cultural revolution" appears twice in the text when the government that imposed fundamental transformation of the general worldview is described (9, 56)—and the Great Leap Forward by Mao Zedong.[5] Even more specifically, the history of Taoism during the rule of Mao was a direct inspiration for writing the novel, thus answering to the "silent enormity" (Lindow 158) with telling its story.[6]

Propaganda inscriptions, slogans, and songs glorifying the new regime are almost unavoidable in the Dovza City. They can allude to different totalitarian regimes and their persistent manipulation, with which the actual world has far too much experience. Propaganda disrupts the boundaries of intimate space, forcing itself into the ears and souls of its voluntary and involuntary listeners. As at the times of the Cultural Revolution in China or during the construction of socialism in Central and Eastern Europe (to name just a few of the many allusions),[7] Aka's regime considers silence and solitude as enemies, since they allow, even though within one's mind only, to break free from the unified crowd and engage in independent thinking, reflection, and self-reflection:

> FORWARD TO THE FUTURE. PRODUCER-CONSUMERS OF AKA MARCH TO THE STARS.
> Music hovered with them, highly rhythmic, multi-voiced, crowding the air. "Onward, onward to the stars!" an invisible choir shrilled to the stalled traffic at the intersection where Sutty's robo cab sat. She turned up the cab sound to drown the tune out. "Superstition is a rotting corpse," the sound system said [. . .]. "Superstitious practices defile youthful minds." (Le Guin, *Telling* 7)

The contrast between the recent past of Aka—highly spiritual, with a developed system of well-being in the world—and its present reality could hardly be any bigger. People are not considered people anymore; they are producers-consumers,[8] a crowd, marching, singing in forced unity, and destroying everything different, alternative, non-conformist. While there are direct allusions to the Cultural Revolution, we can generalize a universal implication of the situation in Dovza City, pointing to both physical and emotional unbalance as the desired state of people to be susceptible to manipulation.

The continuous noise imposing simplistic views indeed refers not only to the past, as the author itself confirmed in an interview with Mary Jo Schimelpfenig, published at the end of September 2017. In response to the question about the passage above, Le Guin recalls that social networks are powerful tools of propaganda and how difficult it is to avoid manipulation through them:

> TV and electronic media make propaganda incredibly easy to propagate and extremely hard to avoid. I don't want to say, "Well, if it's a noisy hole, why not climb up out of it?"—that's smug and simplistic. All the same, if the noise is coming from something I turned on, I could consider the option of turning it off. (Le Guin in Schimelpfenig)

The clerofascist regime on Terra, in turn, refers to past and present religious radicalism and to power systems in which religion becomes a platform for oppression and persecution of all those guilty of a different attitude to the world. References start at the level of language used by the Unists: "Fathers" as top state leaders, "God's army," "Time of cleansing" as a label for burning books, destroying cultural artifacts, and the bombing of the so-called Washington Library, which is the allusion to the library of Congress, the most extensive library in the actual world. The barbaric act of destroying the library, a symbol of wickedness for the Unists, is an embodiment of arrogance of the power exercising its right to stand above the cultural and historical heritage, to replace the polyphony of cultural diversity with the united roar of the only truth: "Only one Word, only one Book. All other words, all other books were darkness, error" (Le Guin, *Telling* 5).

The second level of mimesis is evoked by often implicit, yet obvious, inspiration by the philosophical and religious systems of the actual world. We can find many direct allusions bringing the relationship among Aka, Terra, and the actual world into focus. *The Telling* is introduced by a citation from the Mahabharata. The name Sutty refers to the goddess Sati or Shakti, the wife of Shiva—the dancer, who both destroys and at the same time creates, protects, and transforms the universe.[9] And *The Telling*—like other works by Le Guin—is strongly connected to the principles of Taoism and the Chinese thinking generally. Le Guin was captivated by Taoism since childhood when she watched her father lovingly browse through the yellowed leaves of the abundantly read copy translated by Paul Carus in 1898 (Le Guin, "Introduction" ix). As she later recalls in the foreword to her rewriting of the book, a meeting with the work of the sage Lao Tzu influenced her entire life: "I was lucky to discover him so young, so that I could live with his book my whole life long" (ix). The emphasis on the inseparability of the part from the whole and the whole from the part, the constant movement of the world, the non-existence of stability, and the interdependence of opposites belong to the frequently analyzed features of Le Guin's work (see Rochelle).

Both Taoism and Hinduism emphasize the necessity of balance and harmony linked to nature's constant flow and change. Sutty herself, at least at the beginning of the story, suffers tangibly by the lack of precisely these qualities. Traumatized by her life under the theocratic regime and thus primed to be extremely suspicious toward any religion, she struggles in Aka to remain objective, not to judge, to disengage from her personal experience, and not to interpret all religiosity as the oppressive force that stole her home and lover on Terra. When slowly discovering the hidden net of old ways of thinking on Aka, which she starts calling the Telling, she worries at first to find links to the religion as she knows and fears it. After immersing herself more into the elaborate net of the former Akan culture, she grows to realize that her concerns were unfounded.

Sutty's development in the story can be characterized as a seeking for balance, loss of which is personalized on more than one level by her dead partner, Pao. Sandra J. Lindow observes that in Chinese the name Pao reads the same as Tao, so with losing Pao, Sutty lost much more than a lover; she was deprived of her own "loving centre of life" (158). While getting into contact with the hidden remains of the ancient Akan culture, she slowly regains the center of herself, the sense of balance and harmony, and undergoes both a spiritual and physical awakening.

The character of Sutty invites empathic responses from readers for her many flaws, perpetual experiences of self-doubt, anxiety, unresolved grieving and anger over the death of Pao, and inability to refrain from subjective judgments conditioned by her past when dealing with situations on Aka. As Bernardo and Murphy observe: "Sutty's struggles are personal ones shared by all who have doubted their abilities, grieved over the loss of a loved one, or found themselves stymied by a dominant religious/political ideology" (83). The above-mentioned traumas, widely spread in the actual world, effectively open a means of connection between the story's character and its readers based on the shared experience; fictional facts thus relate to the reader's experiential background and contribute to the understanding of meanings offered by the novel.[10]

MIMESIS THROUGH THE LANGUAGE

The third level of mimesis can be approached through the language of *The Telling*. Le Guin was not only fascinated by the principles introduced by Lao Tzu, which have become well-known due to several translations of the text; she felt captivated by the language itself, its beauty and richness, which can be translated into another language only with difficulties. In her rewriting of the ancient text, she attempted to capture the substance of the original and to retell it using words and concepts inspiring contemporary readers. While the old translations of the book, according to Le Guin, were mainly focused on content, she intended to capture the poetry of its telling that often disappeared from previous translations. And along with it not only the beauty but a substantial part of the meaning of the text itself evaporated:

> The Tao Te Ching is partly in prose, partly in verse; but as we define poetry now, not by rhyme and meter but as a patterned intensity of language, the whole thing is poetry. I wanted to catch that poetry, its terse, strange beauty. Most translations have caught meanings in their net, but prosily, letting the beauty slip through. And in poetry, beauty is no ornament; it is the meaning. It is the truth. (Le Guin, "Introduction" ix)

The intense attention devoted to the language of her stories is characteristic of Le Guin's entire work: "the patterned intensity of language" reflects precisely her mode of writing. Her stories cannot be easily summarized; they resist easy translation and prevent the search for a message that can be extracted from the text without distortion. As Le Guin claims in essays dedicated to her writing, storytelling cannot be reduced to meaning, a message to the reader, it lies in the narrative itself, in its uniqueness, complexity, and interdependence.[11] As in Taoism, the whole and the part cannot be separated:

> I believe storytelling is one of the most useful tools we have for achieving meaning: it serves to keep our communities together by asking and saying who we are, and it's one of the best tools an individual has to find out who I am, what life may ask of me and how I can respond.
>
> But that's not the same as having a message. The complex meanings of a serious story or novel can be understood only by participation in the language of the story itself. To translate them into a message or reduce them to a sermon distorts, betrays, and destroys them.
>
> This is because a work of art is understood not by the mind only, but by the emotions and by the body itself. (Le Guin, "Message")

The last quoted sentence opens a path to the deepest level of mimesis in the novel, which is created by its readers, through their emotions, bodies, and minds. It lies in the multilayered network of meanings, stories, and evoked images, drawn from the fictional world of the novel and the fate of its characters through the reader's consciousness to the actual world.

Although every attempt to grasp the meaning of a story outside its natural environment within the text itself is condemned to be partial at best, let us try to approach the means Le Guin employs for conveying the strong relationship between being in the world and telling the world, in other words, the interconnection of the bodily experience with thoughts and language.

When considering this connection, we need to address the importance of physicality that is crucial in *The Telling* on two subsequent levels. First is the level of the story and the fictional facts, where an elaborate metaphor of the Telling as the world and as being in the world unfolds from the metaphor of the body as a tree. Second is the level of reflection of the text as its perception through the body, the so-called embodied cognition which claims that the (human) cognition (including language) is shaped by aspects of the entire body: "The core tenet of embodied cognitive science is that all psychological processes—including those that are traditionally seen as abstract and independent of bodily experience—reflect patterns derived from our physical engagement with the world" (Caracciolo, "Degrees" 14).

EMBODIMENT AS A KEY ASPECT OF THE TELLING

In *The Telling*, Le Guin employs an archetypal metaphor connecting the human body and the world. The primary metaphor lies in the likeness of a man to the tree—his skin to the bark (57), his blood to the sap (37), while the tree trunk forms the body of the man. At the same time, the body of the tree, thus the body of the man, creates the body of the world: "The body is the body of the world. The world's body is my body" (51). The connection between the body and the world is further enhanced by the allusion of the Akan Telling to the philosophical and religious systems of the actual world. Sandra J. Lindow notices that "[a]lthough there is no god, the sense of being right with god or Dharma comes from self-discipline in ways that support the health of the body and the world" (164). And the body is linked with the soul; in the ancient Akan culture, physical, spiritual, and emotional well-being is inseparable.[12] In the local language Rangma, one phrase means both "good digestion" and "peaceful heart" (Le Guin, *Telling* 54).

The world is inextricably linked with the telling, with "being that can be told" (54); individual tellings are like the leaves that disappear, but they reappear when told again (67). The being and telling are indivisible, since perception involves description (55). To tell means to comprehend, to participate, to appreciate: "By naming the names they rejoiced in the complexity and specificity, the wealth and beauty of the world, they participated in the fullness of being" (69).

The metaphors mentioned above link the physical space with the abstract system of the Telling (meaning the whole of the old Akan ways) and with the individual tellings, all of them living, changeable, breathing. Pictograms of recently forbidden writings seem to move and breathe like a man or an animal: "evenly, regularly, as if they are inflating and contracting again as if they were breathing" (31). Similarly, people are not separated from nature: group meditation exercises, also prohibited in the new Akan regime, evoke the impression of a harmonious shared breath, like that of a sea billowing, or "pulsing of jellyfish in a dim aquarium" (38). Rhythmically moving people remind of "rooted sea creatures, anemones, a kelp forest" (39). At the same time, Sutty perceives the movements as beautiful and full of meaning (40).

The movement and specifically the dance bear many allusions, further enhancing the relationship between the individual body and the body of the world. Sutty is connected to the dance by her name ("You are the dance" (115)), she first saw her beloved Pao leading a round dance (45), and when she starts to understand the Akan Telling, she compares the experience to the dance: "she was beginning to hear the music and to learn how to move to it" (52). Not only people but the entire world is capable of dance and Sutty learns how to join it, so people and the world can move in harmony.[13]

THE TELLING AS MEANING AND COHERENCE

The Telling as a whole, inherently incomprehensible, is in the novel referred to as the "path through the forest" or "the path to the mountain" (Le Guin, *Telling* 98); the compendium of some key tellings is called "Arbor" (58). Individual tellings are intertwined together, but the resultant whole cannot be approached otherwise than through its parts: Sutty cannot find the central telling that would give her the key to the old Akan philosophical system or the fundamental set of tellings since all tellings are equally important: "No bible. No koran. Dozens of upanishads, a million sutras" (58). She also fails to figure out the proper naming of the system that she slowly comprehends. It is neither religion nor philosophy. It does not count with the Creator, only with Creation. Eternity is not the end but the continuation. It is focused not on life after death but on life in the world; there is nothing "holier than the world," no power greater than nature is sought (70).

The Telling in the novel is a strand that extends into all aspects of life and being in the world, connecting the small with the great, the past with the present and the future, the real with the dream, and the concrete with the abstract. There is no set boundary between the profane and the sacred, for telling is a way of "holding and keeping things sacred" (102), and when appropriately perceived, with great attention, anything (all deeds and places) is potentially sacred (55). Sacredness is nothing outside the world: "The sacredness is there. In the truth, the pain, the beauty. So that the Telling of it is sacred" (102).

There are no irreconcilable opposites within the Telling, just two aspects of the one. In a harmonious whole, there is a place for antitheses, for it does not bear the one truth, it is simultaneously spiritual and down-to-earth, it does not contain rules and rewards for their observance, there is always room for alternatives. The single, unique is included in the whole, in the unity—"the One that is Two giving rise to the Three, to the Five, to the Myriad, and the Myriad again to the Five, the Three, the Two, the One" (67). The interdependence of unity and infinite variety creates the cornerstone of the Telling, "the mystery plain as day" (67). However, the Telling is still a mystery, not an explanation, and remains ungraspable by reason (72).

And above all, it is continually evolving, growing up as a tree-world body from its hidden roots and as long as it is told, the leaves on its branches renew. The leaves are not of the same color and shape, and there is no fixed meaning to any single story; they modify and change depending on the situation, narrator, audience, and so on. Thus, tellings function as myths in the actual world, shaped by their storytellers.[14] The relationship between the Telling and myth and the importance of storytelling create a strong connection between fictional and actual worlds: In both worlds, by storytelling, we relate to the world; the storytelling is anchoring the unstable and ever-changing into a net of space, time, and meaning. Through storytelling, we keep balance in the middle of unceasingly arising and vanishing moments.

The Telling in the novel is a means of connection between individuals, community, and their environment: "We are the world. We're its language. So we live and it lives. You see? If we don't say the words, what is there in our world?" (Le Guin, *Telling* 73). Without the Telling, people lose contact not only with their history and traditions but with their present community, with themselves, and with their environment as well. To be a part of the ever-variable unity, human beings lacking direct connection with nature need the Telling to remind them that they are an integral part of the whole. According to Lindow, the former Akan culture built a minimalist utopia that satisfied most needs of the people and offered "the sweetness of ordinary life lived mindfully" (Le Guin, *Telling* 84)[15] without leaving the heavy burden of ecological damage on the world. When the old ways were banned, people ceased to take care of their world; the rivers and the land were filled with poison, while both people and their environment were neglected and sick. The capitalist Corporation ruthlessly exploits nature for swift technological progress; the earth itself is perceived as a resource, not a living whole that embraces people too. For Sutty, this development is unpleasantly familiar since on Terra neglecting nature and its damage led to a series of plagues and famines that in turn gave rise to the aggressive theocracy and Holy Wars.

READING WITH THE BODY AND THE SOUL

In the already quoted essay *A Message About Messages*, Le Guin writes:

> Reading is a passionate act. If you read a story not just with your head, but also with your body and feelings and soul, the way you dance or listen to music, then it becomes your story. And it can mean infinitely more than any message. It can offer beauty. It can take you through pain. It can signify freedom. And it can mean something different every time you reread it. (Le Guin, "Message")

Claiming the act of reading as not a primarily intellectual but physical and emotional activity, Le Guin approaches the current knowledge of cognitive literary science that emphasizes the connection between the experience of the actual and fictional worlds as: "reading fiction makes the brain simulate cognitive and affective reactions to the actual world, and therefore [. . .] can improve our understanding of the real world" (Nikolajeva 8). The transfer of experience between the actual and fictional world is thus essential for the reflection of a literary work—no matter how fantastic the fictional world is.

Research on an emotional response to arts shows that emotions experienced when reading the text are "the result of the emotion-laden memories that have been triggered by literary events, characters, and so on, but are not self-consciously recalled" (Hogan, *Cognitive Science* 157). In other words, the reader reacts strongly to fictional events if they remind her of emotionally powerful real-life experiences (a feeling of falling in love, the death of a loved one, etc.). Therefore, during the reading, the emotion is transferred to the emotional reading experience, but it does not evoke the memory that is associated with that emotion—unless the memory is so strong that it penetrates from the subconscious into consciousness, thereby disturbing the perception of the text. Text-driven emotions are thus fundamentally dependent on the world outside the text and on the reader's experience of it.

If we imagine an object, our brain reacts just as if we saw it (Hogan, *Cognitive Science* 181) and when we read that the hero of the story smiled and raised his hand, the same (motor) centers are activated in our brain as if we smiled and raised our hand. We do not experience reading and knowledge primarily on the intellectual level, but through our own body,[16] experience, and memories. As Marco Caracciolo summarizes, "cognition is embodied and situated—in other words, inseparable from the subject's body and the context in which it is found" ("The Experientiality" 19).

In his recent study, Caracciolo develops three permeable degrees of the embodiment of literary reading introduced by linguist David Ritchie. Zero embodiment: language is processed in an "exclusively semantic way" ("Degrees" 18), all associations triggered by language are purely abstract and conceptual. As Caracciolo reminds, this degree is to be understood as a limit case, since "If cognitive scientists of the embodied stripe are right, embodiment shapes our mental—and linguistic—capacities through and through" (18). Second degree: only traces of the reader's past bodily experience are activated, while activation remains unconscious or produces phenomenologically weak imagery, which is likely to be soon forgotten by the reader. The third degree of embodiment leads to "detailed and fully conscious, imagery of verbally described action or scene" (18).

When contemplating literary texts as a form of simulation, Patrick Colm Hogan points out that the difference between factual and aesthetic knowledge—often emphasized as a core distinction between fiction and nonfiction—might be less crucial than the degree of simulation. Put differently, the essential quality concerning the impact of reading might be the degree of embodiment: "the most critical issue may be the degree to which a chosen narrative involves simulation that goes beyond experience and logical inference. In other words, the most important opposition may not be fiction/fact, but simulation/report" (*How* 5). Simulation in texts raises emotional engagement with the narrative and as Hogan observes, the emotional profiles produced by fiction "may have consequences for real-world behaviour" (*How* 5).

Le Guin allows readers of *The Telling* to experience the third degree of embodiment through sparse impressive descriptions that are likely to catch the readers' attention not only due to their relative rarity but also since they appeal to all the senses and often further strengthen the association between the body, the world, and the Telling. Also, as Caracciolo observes, alternation of high-embodiment and low-embodiment sections in literature brings the reader's attention to the former and prevents habituation and the loss of sensitivity ("Degrees" 25).

Apart from the already mentioned metaphors (directly connecting the body, tree, world, and telling), linking abstract and tangible, part and whole, sign and image evoked by the sign also manifest in *The Telling* in concise yet captivating descriptions, even more firmly relating human body, world, and telling. Bernardo and Murphy observe that "*The Telling* is almost poetic in its use of sparse descriptions and evocative language that capture the 'human' spirit of its characters" (75). I argue that the above mentioned poetic use of language is not aimed at characters of the book only, but it enables and strengthens the experiential quality of images mediating the blending of boundaries between the body and its environment within the narration. Le Guin masterfully managed to invoke a living image in a few words, associations drawing not only on the visual imagination of the reader but engaging her other senses alike. Sensory imagination supports immersion in the story and elicits the rise of emotion through which the connection of the fictional world of narration and the reader's experience of the actual world is reinforced.

Some descriptions not only evoke a picture made by few brush strokes but literally are compared to the actual drawing: "A stream ran through a concrete ditch between high dark walls to join the great river. Above it, a fisherman leaned on the rail of a humpback bridge: a silhouette, simple, immobile, timeless—the image of a drawing in one of the Akan books" (Le Guin, *Telling* 19). The landscape and the man as its part implicitly approximate the pictograms of the scriptures that are telling the world. Thus, the blended boundaries between part and the whole, concrete and abstract, man and world, world and the Telling are evoked in the novel not only on the level of the story and fictional facts but at the same time on the level of discourse. "The river, now clear as the wind, rushed by so silently that the boat seemed to float above it, between two airs. [. . .] Land, and sky, and the river crossing from one to the other" (22–23). The reader is encouraged to associate seemingly discontinuous facts, to grasp the intangible network of contexts wrapping up the narrated story, the fictional world, the way they are told, as well as the way how they can be read and transmitted through the reader's experience to her world.

CONCLUSION

In Le Guin's novel, mimesis substantially enhances reading on several subsequent levels: it supports interconnections between the narrative and readers' experience (both direct and mediated) of the actual world by providing many allusions to the past and the present of our reality and by overt inspiration by philosophical systems and religions—specifically Hinduism and Taoism—for creating the Akan Telling.

The central idea of the interconnectedness of the part and the whole, including human beings and their environment, is accented through the complex metaphors of the human body as the body of the world and through linking being in the world with telling the world. On the level of the reader's response to the story, embodied reading is invited through scarce yet highly immersive descriptions, further developing the central issue of blended boundaries.

The reflection through physicality is conveyed directly on two levels. First, linking the thought content, attributes, and experiences of the characters (Sutty experiences everything personally, and very strongly, she is by no means a non-participating observer) encourages the embodied reading, through the reader's own body and emotions. Second, relating body and narration, body and world on the level of the story evokes the connection on a deeper level, between the fictional body and the reader's body, and thus between the reader and his world.

The three key aspects of *The Telling* can be highlighted as follows.

Dynamics—beginning at the level of Sutty's name and reaching to the very deepest level of mimesis, to the need to keep balance in the constant changes, the flow of life when nothing is static, forever, everything must change, to evolve, to flow, and to dance in harmony.

Poetry—the patterned intensity of the language; vivid images help to immerse in the story and to convey its meaning.

Universality—*The Telling* is based on the principles of Taoism and Hinduism. The very familiarity of the central ideas of interconnection and mutual dependency of the part and the whole fortifies the effect of the novel. Similarly, as Le Guin's actualized Tao Te Ching for today's readers, *The Telling* echoes in her readers' bodies and minds with the power of already gained albeit possibly forgotten knowledge. The novel helps us see it with fresh eyes and recover a clear vision of not only the fictional but primarily actual reality.

Given the central theme of this book, we can conclude that Le Guin in *The Telling* suggests a remedy for Anthropocene, not a strikingly new one; on the contrary, through her writing she helps her readers to reconnect with ancient wisdom. It is not a practical solution; it cannot teach humanity how to harvest solar energy efficiently or how to stop overheating of the Earth, but it can offer a change of mind. Through the reading experience, it helps rewiring the readers' brains to see humanity as a part of the whole, and not something overborne, detached, excluding ourselves from the Telling of the planet Earth, from the story in which we participate. If we accept the story experience of *The Telling*, the need for harmony and balance in the ever-changing environment, if we experience ourselves in oneness with everything surrounding us—with the trees, mountains, cities, other people, and their stories—how could we possibly not care about the nature, the well-being of all other beings, the Earth? *The Telling* provides its readers with guidelines for a transition from the isolated humanity to humanity as a part of the whole, an inseparable component of the biosphere.

NOTES

1. As she wrote on her website: "The thing is, they aren't a cycle or a saga. They do not form a coherent history. There are some clear connections among them, yes, but also some extremely murky ones. And some great discontinuities" (Le Guin, "Frequently").

2. Sandra J. Lindow comments on the ministry name as echoing the doublethink familiar from famous dystopias as *1984* or *Fahrenheit 451* (160).

3. The irony of the new Akan regime is enhanced by possible inspiration of planet name Aka by Hindu term *akâs* referring to "the energy that flows through and unites creation" (Warner 196, qtd. in Lindow 162).

4. For the advantages of fantasy see, e.g., Marek Oziewicz's *Justice in Young Adult Speculative Fiction: A Cognitive Reading* (2015) or Maria Nikolajeva's *Reading for Learning: Cognitive Approaches to Children's Literature* (2014).

5. An ostensible purpose of the radical measures applied by the Great Leap Forward was to force the People's Republic of China among the supreme world economic powers. Instead, it resulted in an economic downturn followed by the greatest people-caused famine in known history.

6. As Le Guin commented in an interview: "Actually, it was not Tibetan Buddhism, but what happened to the practice and teaching of Taoism under Mao that was the initial impetus of the book. I was shocked to find that a 2500-year-old body of thought, belief, ritual, and art could be, had been, essentially destroyed within ten years, and shocked to find I hadn't known it, though it happened during my adult lifetime. The atrocity, and my long ignorance of it, haunted me. I had to write about it, in my own sidelong fashion" (Le Guin in Gevers).

7. Sandra J. Lindow reads the "Dovzan material culture as a critique of American capitalism, consumerism and planned obsolence" (161).

8. As Bernardo and Murphy observed in their analysis of *The Telling*: "Consumer economies don't have 'fellow' persons but only negotiating parties" (77).

9. Sandra J. Lindow offers quite a thorough analysis of the allusions to Hinduism in *The Telling*.

10. Bernardo and Murphy also comment on the connection between ideas and characters in Le Guin's work: "This has always been Le Guin's strength; her thought experiments are closely tied to the real-world experiences of her characters" (83).

11. Serious reservations toward the literal reading are stated explicitly also in *The Telling*: "Reducing thought to formula, replacing choice by obedience, these preachers turned the living word into dead law" (68).

12. As Lindow also observes when commenting on Corporation's fear of the old Akan culture: "People who are healthy, physically and emotionally, are free to devote their time to spiritual development" (163).

13. Bernardo and Murphy call the relationship of Sutty to the Telling as an evocation of the Taoist concept "wu wei" (literary meaning "without exertion") referring to the effortless accomplishment, action through inaction, based on "studying the nature and patterns of life" (85) and achieving "effect in the least disruptive manner" (85).

14. In *Stories about Stories: Fantasy and the Remaking of Myth*, Brian Attebery highlights the essential role of a storyteller on the evolving meaning of myth here and now (18).

15. See also Lindow 164.

16. "Experimental studies have focused on three areas, which relate to different aspects of linguistic comprehension: motor resonance in understanding action verbs, embodied metaphors, and situation models in reconstructing a linguistically described scene" (Caracciolo, "Degrees" 15).

WORKS CITED

Attebery, Brian. *Stories about Stories: Fantasy and the Remaking of Myth*. Oxford UP, 2013.

———. *Strategies of Fantasy*. Indiana UP, 1992.

Baccolini, Raffaela. "'A Useful Knowledge of the Present is Rooted in the Past': Memory and Historical Reconciliation in Ursula K. Le Guin's The Telling." In *Dark Horizons: Science Fiction and the Dystopian Imagination*, edited by Raffaella Baccolini and Tom Moylan. Routledge, 2003.

Bernardo, Susan M., and Graham J. Murphy. *Ursula K. Le Guin: A Critical Companion*. Greenwood Press, 2006.

Caracciolo, Marco. "Degrees of Embodiment in Literary Reading: Notes for a Theoretical Model, with *American Psycho* as a Case Study." In *Expressive Minds and Artistic Creations: Studies in Cognitive Poetics*, edited by Szilvia Csabi. Oxford UP, 2018, pp. 11–27.

———. *The Experientiality of Narrative: An Enactivist Approach*. De Gruyter, 2014.

Gevers, Nick. "Driven By A Different Chauffeur: An Interview With Ursula K. Le Guin." *www.sfsite.com*, 2001. www.sfsite.com/03a/ul123.htm. Accessed 6 March 2019.

Hogan, Patrick Colm. *Cognitive Science, Literature, and the Arts: A Guide for Humanists*. Routledge, 2003.

———. *How Authors' Minds Make Stories*. Cambridge UP, 2014.

Le Guin, Ursula K. "A Message About Messages." *ursulakleguin.com*, 2017. www.ursulakleguin.com/MessageAboutMessages.html. Accessed 6 March 2019.

———. "Frequently Asked Questions." *ursulakleguin.com*, 2014. www.ursulakleguin.com/FAQ_Questionnaire5_01.html. Accessed 7 April 2019.

———. "Introduction." In *Lao Tzu: Tao Te Ching: A Book About the Way and the Power of the Way*. Shambhala, 1998.

———. *The Telling*. Harcourt, Inc., 2000.

Lindow, Sandra J. *Dancing the Tao: Le Guin and Moral Development*. Cambridge Scholars Publishing, 2012.

Nikolajeva, Maria. *Reading for Learning: Cognitive Approaches to Children's Literature*. John Benjamins Publishing Company, 2014.

Oziewicz, Marek. *Justice in Young Adult Speculative Fiction: A Cognitive Reading*. Routledge, 2015.

Rochelle, Warren G. "Ursula K. Le Guin." In *A Companion to Science Fiction*, edited by David Seed. Blackwell Publishing, 2008, pp. 408–419.

Schimelpfenig, Mary Jo. "Powell's Interview: Ursula K. Le Guin, Author of 'The Hainish Novels and Stories'." *www.powells.com*, 2017. www.powells.com/post/interviews/powells-interview-ursula-k-le-guin-author-of-the-hainish-novels-and-stories. Accessed 7 March 2019.

Chapter 2

Young Adult Fantasy to Save the World?

Retelling the Quest in Maggie Stiefvater's Raven Cycle

Carrie Spencer

INTRODUCTION

An overwhelming global scientific consensus has confirmed that human activity has changed and continues to alter ecological systems on a planetary scale (e.g., see IPCC). Although the warming effect of greenhouse gases, including carbon dioxide, was identified in the nineteenth century, it was not until later in the twentieth century that climate change gained significant scientific and cultural attention (e.g., Heise, *Sense of Place* 206; Buell, "Global Warming" 264). As evidence for anthropogenic climate change grew, along with social activism and political commitments, the term *Anthropocene* was proposed by two scientists, Paul J. Crutzen and Eugene F. Stoermer, in 2000, to denote that the pace and scale at which human activity is changing planetary systems has defined a new geological epoch (e.g., Buell, "Global Warming" 272; De Cristofaro and Cordle 2). The Anthropocene does not only measure climate change in terms of fossil fuels burned or greenhouse gases accumulated, but encompasses the shifting processes of the planet through "a complex family of interconnected problems, all adding up to [. . .] a growing human footprint" (Chakrabarty, "Politics" 27). Human activity is an irrevocable part of these interconnected challenges that demand political, legal, economic, and social responses to the entwined complexities of greenhouse gas emissions, warming oceans, species extinction, ecosystem degradation, and deforestation. In this chapter, I use Anthropocene, rather than climate change, as a term that draws attention to the complex networks of relations between humans, non-humans, and non-biological physical processes.

Conceptualizing humans and non-humans within complex networks challenges dominant ontologies that position humans as superior to and separate from nature. In the 1990s, scholars from a number of fields (including anthropologists such as James Clifford; Marxists such as David Harvey; and geographers such as Doreen Massey) increasingly turned their attention to the phenomenon of globalization and theories of place and space. Humanist histories in which social "progress entails the conquest of space" (Harvey 205) were increasingly recognized as problematic due to ontologies that not only positioned humans over non-humans but European men over other people. Humanist narratives of progress and conquest relied upon colonizing constructions of "empty" space inhabited by first peoples, as well as non-humans, such that "the conquest of space" elided the conquest of peoples and cultures as well as physical environments (e.g., Harvey 203; Buell, *Future* 67). In humanist histories "the non-human world is there for the taking, to be transformed and molded into whatever humans see fit" (Williams 167). However, the Western concept of space as static and waiting for conquest underpins narratives of history which rely upon "the age-old humanist distinction between natural history and human history" (Chakrabarty, "The Climate of History" 201) that is no longer tenable in the Anthropocene. The notion of an environment under human control is exposed as folly by extreme and volatile weather events that demonstrate the agency of systems and processes that are far from "molded" to human desires. Furthermore, these unanticipated climatic shifts were unintentionally caused by humans, rupturing the illusion of mastery. Inattention to the life forms and systems that humans sought to master has exposed the dominant ontology that positions humans over nature as deeply flawed. The activities of humans that denied environmental embeddedness have produced global threats, not control.

In contrast to dominant ontologies, environmental and spatial approaches developed over the last few decades propose alternative theories of space and time that respond to the coexistence of all life forms and physical processes. These approaches de-center humans and reimagine complex interconnections across a variety of temporal and spatial scales conceptualizing living species and physical processes as variously "embedded" (Williams 171), interconnected in dynamic networks (Heise, "Science Fiction" 283) or "connected in a mesh" (Morton 169). The concept of space is no longer an abstract, empty backdrop to human endeavor; rather, "space is *relational*: made of the very relations among things" (Williams 162). This concept of relational space is fruitful for understanding complex networks between heterogeneous humans, non-humans, and physical processes that are continuously producing changing spaces from microscopic to planetary scales in the Anthropocene. The concept of relational space encompasses time: because space is produced through the interactions of multiple coexisting beings and things, it is always shifting (no longer mere backdrop). The simultaneous heterogeneity of life forms and physical processes produces a dynamic concept of relational space that cannot be neatly contained, as trajectories extend in all directions. Relational space is multiply scalar, produced through dynamic networks that are not enclosed in any dimension. Once humans and non-humans are conceptualized as co-producing space through these networks, human and natural histories are no longer "immiscible" (Chakrabarty, "The Climate of History" 206) but entwined. It is this concept of relational space that I apply to my reading of the Raven cycle (Stiefvater 2012–2016) in this chapter.

The increasing volume of climate fiction through the later part of the twentieth and into the twenty-first centuries followed a similar trajectory to the developing scientific, political, and cultural discourses on the Anthropocene. Although literature has, for millennia, engaged with ideas and ethics around human relations with nature and non-humans, Ursula K. Le Guin's novel *Lathe of Heaven* (1971) has been suggested as the first example in the now rapidly growing corpus of climate fiction (e.g., Goodbody and Johns-Putra 3; Trexler 8). In a number of studies literary critics are identifying emerging trends that suggest that climate fiction often remains human-centric, following "the same pattern, warning readers of impending disaster" (Trexler 25) due to unpredictable global ecological changes. The narrative focus on the threat of extreme weather to Western middle-class lifestyles has spawned numerous dystopian novels exploring a climate crisis within the text as justification for more oppressive government and social systems in narratives that explore human freedom and identity (e.g., Colebrook 272; Farzin 187). Even in climate fiction, frequently "the depiction of the human drama takes precedence over that of ecological process" (Goodbody and Johns-Putra 12) with the result that the environment "becomes a mere symbolic representation of a turning point in the protagonist's life" (12). Similarly, in children's and young adult (YA) literature, an "environmental(ist) agenda by no means automatically equates to counter-hegemonic position-taking" (Buell, "Environmental Writing" 418) as texts may adhere to well-established anthropocentric narrative patterns and tropes that restore mainstream social order. Although human–nature relationships can be explored with various degrees of ambivalence and subtlety, the underlying assumption that human culture is superior to a separate "nature" seems to be difficult for some (Western) twenty-first-century texts to reimagine.

Yet neither anthropocentrism nor dominant Western concepts of space-time are inevitable. The ontology that places humans over nature is a "particularly Euro-American idea" (Alaimo "Ecology"), traced to Ancient Greek philosophy and Judeo-Christian origin stories such as the expulsion of Adam and Eve from the Garden of Eden and Noah's Ark (Markley 18; Goga et al., 4). This ontology and its values regarding the role of humans in relation to nature has a long history of representation in children's literature (Jaques 113–114) and fantasy literature of the last century (Ekman 133). Although there is no need for fantasy novels to reproduce dominant ontologies or concepts, particularly as the secondary (supernatural) world in fantasy texts "can have quite different rules for how [...] time, space, and causality work" (Ekman 68), fantasies such as the Raven cycle also describe a recognizable primary (ordinary) world. The Raven cycle is a YA quest fantasy that, unlike traditional quests such as *The Lord of the Rings* (Tolkien 1954/1994), "merge[s] fantasy and realism" (Waller 1) as supernatural and magical events occur in a recognizable fictional world. However, such YA fantasies are typically conservative, asserting mainstream ideologies and ensuring the assimilation of even supernatural adolescent characters into acceptable social roles (Waller 89). As such, teenage characters with supernatural abilities and their human allies usually work to maintain the boundaries between the supernatural and human. However, the Anthropocene demands a reimagining of relations between humans and non-human animals, plants, and physical processes through which we are co-producing and changing space, such that it has been argued that "climate change necessarily transforms generic conventions" (Trexler 14). The Raven cycle is thus an unusual YA quest fantasy in exploring the possibilities of a porous and malleable border between the ordinary and secondary worlds to propose new interconnected futures for humans and non-humans without recourse to disaster or dystopia.

In this chapter I analyze how the Raven cycle repositions the YA quest fantasy narrative and its traditional hero within a complex network of human and non-human interrelations. I begin by outlining the YA quest fantasy narrative pattern and how the supernatural is used in the Raven cycle to de-center human characters, repositioning the teenage protagonists, Gansey, Blue, Adam, and Ronan, within dynamic networks of relations. In the subsequent sections, I turn to how multiple narratives and retellings of legends across vast timespans and spatial scales problematize humanist histories and emphasize the influence of past actions on twenty-first-century events. I conclude by discussing what happens to the typically liberal humanist YA quest fantasy narrative in the relational space of the Raven cycle.

UNSETTLING THE HERO: CONSTRUCTING RELATIONAL SPACE

I begin with the common narrative pattern of YA quest fantasy that typically asserts humanist constructions of history that are incompatible with more recent concepts of humans as "a self-conscious species that is actively transforming conditions" (Trexler 27) on an epochal scale. YA quest fantasy typically focuses on a single protagonist who encounters a series of increasingly challenging tests (and usually a death-like experience) before defeating the villain or evil forces, restoring things to how they "should" be, achieving personal growth while saving the world. This pattern of the quest, or hero's journey, remains markedly similar to the monomyth described by Joseph Campbell in *The Hero with a Thousand Faces* (1949/2008) and is by no means used only in YA quest fantasy. Repeated use of this familiar narrative pattern creates a sense of timelessness and inevitability, emphasized in quest fantasies that often conclude after the final conflict but "posit . . . the possibility of the reappearance of the Dark Lord, or of another, in the future" (Senior 190), simultaneously anticipating the reappearance of another hero. These cyclical patterns in fantasy texts enforce the separation of the human from the supernatural. In fantasy, supernatural characters and events are typically portrayed in "mythical time" (Nikolajeva 8) that is cyclical, repeating unchanging events and rituals, distinguishing it from the ordinary (primary) world's linear time. As such, when protagonists first encounter the magical or supernatural, they are drawn out of human "linear, chronological" (McCallum 169) history, including in YA quest fantasies where characters do not travel to a separate fantastical (secondary) world. In supernatural mythical time, both the Dark Lord/evil forces and the one special hero return to engage in the ritualistic sequence of tests and final conquest. This provides the dominant narrative pattern in YA quest fantasy.

Through these repeated patterns, the texts' fictional history is constructed in liberal humanist terms as a "system of universals which validate and authenticate experience in the present" (McCallum 168). As adolescent protagonists confront the same returning threats as previous generations, these YA fantasies retell the seemingly timeless and inevitable humanist story of progress through conquest. The pattern of a returning threat that requires periodic defeat, and the separation of mythical from historic time, is so common that many YA fantasies *begin* with a returning evil and the discovery of a new (adolescent) hero. In YA fantasy texts as varied as Susan Cooper's *The Dark is Rising* sequence (1965–1977), the first season of *Buffy the Vampire Slayer* (Whedon 1997), J. K. Rowling's *Harry Potter* series (1997–2007), and Cassandra Clare's *The Mortal Instruments* (2007–2016), the protagonists discover that they are a special individual whose fate it is to defeat a previously known and temporarily thwarted enemy. The repeated use of mythic narrative patterns and retellings of ancient myths and legends generates familiarity, even a sense of universality, which suggests these stories express enduring "truths" (Attebery 209) about humanity. Yet these "truths" are limiting: in all these texts it is only *after* encounters with the supernatural that the protagonists' futures become constrained as they learn that they alone are fated to re-tread the path of their predecessors and defeat the returning evil forces.

In the Raven cycle, the expected cyclical pattern of a YA supernatural quest and returning heroes is suggested at the beginning of *The Raven Boys* (*TRB*). The quest that provides the narrative arc for the Raven cycle is the teenage protagonists' search for the body of Glendower, a medieval Welsh king, whom they believe to be interred in Virginia. The quest is driven by the character Gansey who likens the teens' twenty-first-century quest to Arthurian legend and the more famous quest for the Holy Grail (*TRB* 279); and who names Glendower as well as Arthur as "heroes [. . . who] aren't really dead, but instead sleeping" (*TRB* 45). The goal of Gansey's quest is to find Glendower's tomb and wake him in order to achieve certainty of his own identity: Gansey "clung to the possibility that [. . . Glendower] would explain the intricacies of Gansey *to* Gansey" (*The Raven King* [*TRK*] 73, original emphasis). The mythical time of the supernatural quest is suggested as these heroes are only "sleeping," proposing the (white European male) hero as a figure of such enduring, universal importance to humanity that they cannot die but wait to be woken when the world needs them once again. The enduring appeal of Arthurian legends in new cultural contexts suggests a variety of "crossing-places" (McCausland 192) between the original stories and twenty-first-century retellings. Gansey's journey for his identity through seeking out a medieval king can be understood as a personal quest for certainty and predictability as he expects that the search for Glendower should follow a predictable sequence as "It was supposed to be a clue, and then another clue, and then another clue" (*Blue Lily, Lily Blue [BLLB]* 212), suggesting that Gansey believes that legends express enduring "truths" about humanity that "would explain" him. In the quest for Glendower, both the seemingly timeless pattern of the quest and the enduring figure of the king or hero guide Gansey's journey and hope for discovering his own stable sense of identity.

In continually promoting the seemingly inevitable patterns of humanist progress and conquest, YA quest fantasy narratives, even in twenty-first-century texts, may not respond "reflexively" (Marshall 531) to the ways in which human activity is altering life and planetary systems. Many YA quest fantasies assert the necessity of separation and enclosure, particularly in maintaining borders between the ordinary human world and the (supernatural) "other." In these texts, mythical time must be kept separate from the ordinary world's linear or "historic time" (Nuzum 207). There are numerous examples of texts in which a supernatural threat is due, at least in part, to the danger of a destabilized border between humans and "others": Muggles must be kept ignorant of the Wizarding world (in J. K. Rowling's *Harry Potter* series); Mundanes cannot know about Shadowhunters (Cassandra Clare's *The Mortal Instruments*); werewolves and vampires must hide their supernatural embodiments from humans (Stephanie Meyer's *Twilight* saga). The victories over the Dark Lord figure/evil forces conclude these narratives by restoring the separation between humans and "others," asserting the immutability of the existing social order and the necessity of enclosure. Although encounters with the supernatural challenge the protagonists' view of human knowledge and control, the dominant narrative pattern of tests, conquest, and a return to enclosure suggests that the human world is safe precisely because it is enclosed and separate, following "historic" time. In contrast, in the Raven cycle, the achievement of Gansey's quest would destabilize this boundary: if the teenagers succeed in waking Glendower, they will bring a medieval Welsh king alive into twenty-first-century Virginia and the supernatural will uncontrovertibly become a part of the primary world. In this twenty-first century novel, the goal of the quest challenges familiar narratives and inverts them to de-center human characters and humanist histories.

YA fantastic realism that responds to the Anthropocene can fruitfully explore dynamic interconnections between supernatural and ordinary space-times, rejecting the division between "mythical" and "historical" times that separates humans from non-humans. Gansey's belief that Glendower is sleeping and can be woken after 600 years positions the quest within supernatural space-time. In the Raven cycle, the supernatural occurs along the "ley lines" (e.g., *TRB* 24) that connect places of particular supernatural intensity in a grid that encircles the world. The image of a global network effectively exposes "the artificiality of cultural boundaries" (McCulloch 128) as the ley lines do not follow national borders or cultural territories, defying human divisions and demarcations imposed upon conquered space. As the ley lines are supernatural, they do not follow the rules of "historical" time. The ley lines defy all human attempts at knowledge or control: they have multiple names (*The Dream Thieves* 364) and cannot be precisely mapped or detected, even with special devices attuned to the supernatural (e.g., *TRB* 67). However, neither do the ley lines follow the repeating cycles and rituals of "mythical" time as they are open to communication with any other place or time (e.g., *BLLB* 4; *TRK* 8) and have no clear start or finish point as there were "[b]eginnings and endings as far as the eye could see" (*TRK* 4). The ley line grid fruitfully portrays a non-human system that confounds human understanding and control, but not through separate mythical time. The recognition of environmental systems that "cannot be encompassed by, controlled by, or even entirely known by human culture" (Alaimo, *Undomesticated* 183) is important to conceptualizing humans as embedded with non-humans in the Anthropocene. The portrayal of a global network that is vibrant with endless possibilities of communication and connection across all times and places proposes the productive potential of coexistence, instead of hierarchy, among humans, non-humans, and systems/processes.

In contrast to humanist constructions of space as a static backdrop, relational space is continuously being produced "as a simultaneity of stories-so-far" (Massey 9) in which there can be no dominant story, direction, or hero. The supernatural ley lines are portrayed as relational space along which there were "so many events and possibilities [. . .] that no single one stood out" (*BLLB* 2). However, the multiple trajectories that produce this supernatural relational space resist enclosure and, therefore, containment from the primary (ordinary) world in the Raven cycle. As such, the primary world is also portrayed through multiple heterogeneous stories as the four novels are narrated from various third-person points of view, not only by each of the teenage protagonists (Gansey, Blue, Ronan, and Adam) but also by various antagonists, as well as minor characters who may only appear for one brief chapter across the four novels. The multiple trajectories of different characters, many of which have nothing to do with Gansey's quest, increasingly complicate the ways in which the characters' "lives were twined together" (*TRK* 12). Multiple voices in texts present "opportunities for alternate readings" (Nodelman 18), and the reader and teenage protagonists are invited to consider possible new meanings created by different stories in relation to each other. The depiction of relational space in the text's primary world is important for suggesting the productive possibility of moving away from the dominant ontologies in response to the climate crisis. In the Raven cycle, Gansey's narrative and the quest for Glendower are de-centered within a more complex textual, shifting space-time co-produced through multiple simultaneous trajectories within the primary, recognizable, present-day world.

Supernatural space in the Raven cycle disrupts the idea of an enduring, repeated narrative pattern for Gansey's quest. The teenage protagonists, Gansey, Blue, Adam, and Ronan, conduct their search for Glendower along the supernatural ley lines that are always shifting as they are depicted as relational space. In dynamic space that is continuously being produced, there is the "chance of space" (Massey 111), an element of unpredictability "in precisely that possibility of being surprised" (116) by new encounters. Along the ley lines, the quest for Glendower diverges from the predictable path when the teenage protagonists venture into a cursed cave and Gansey repeatedly thinks that this is not how the quest is "supposed" (*BLLB* 206, 212, 217) to go. Gansey perceives the dirty cave as unsettling and unappealing, like following a "rabbit hole, down and down" (*BLLB* 207). The teenagers are in a new terrain as they travel an animal-made route unmapped by humans, suggesting an unknown non-human world. The allusion to Lewis Carroll's *Alice's Adventures in Wonderland* (1865) foreshadows that the protagonists' encounters in the cave will challenge and disrupt anthropocentric assumptions and expectations. When the teenagers find a tomb in the cave, they discover Glendower's daughter, the witch Gwenllian. When they find Gwenllian alive in the tomb, Gansey realizes, "It wasn't that his courage had left him; his certainty had" (*BLLB* 217). The accidental discovery of Glendower's daughter challenges the construction of timeless certainty in re-treading the path of legendary heroes. Through de-centering the hero and disrupting the hero's journey through the depiction of relational space, the possibility of new encounters and the importance of trajectories other than (male) humanist histories are opened up.

The coexisting heterogeneous trajectories of relational space deny a single dominant narrative, demanding a recognition that history "cannot be told [. . .] as the story of [. . .] that classic figure (ironically frequently itself essentialised) of the white, heterosexual male" (Massey 10). As such, after Gansey, Blue, Ronan, and Adam free Gwenllian from the tomb, she tells her own version of the events that Gansey has not been able to find in his research. The inclusion of multiple perspectives on narrative histories in YA texts can demonstrate how "dialogic and documentary approaches to the past work together to imply a history which is open and contestable" (McCallum 173). Instead of a cyclical, repeating history, the openness of the past repositions each narrative history as partial and subjective. The contrast between Gwenllian's story of her own experiences and Gansey's methodically researched history provides an alternative version of the Glendower legend that opens up new meanings that complicate Gansey's hopes that he can be guided by past heroes. Gwenllian's version of the Glendower legend proposes that the past is constructed through the coexistence of heterogeneous trajectories, not through the dominant narrative of the hero. As Gwenllian's story is not a quest, she does not follow that narrative pattern but instead sings "a furious little song about Glendower's poet Iolo Goch" (*BLLB* 269). Gwenllian's song de-centers Glendower, focusing instead on Iolo Goch, who incited Glendower to war, and on Gwenllian's own actions. Gwenllian's passionate and vivid song refuses the inevitability of the quest culminating in a final heroic conflict as she tries to stop the war: "as blood soaked into the ground of Wales, Gwenllian did her level best to stab him to death" (*BLLB* 269). In her song, it is Glendower's war and the influence of Iolo Goch that need to be stopped, rather than the threatening "other" of the English king, disrupting the supposedly inevitable course of progress through conquest.

Gwenllian's attempts to stop the war challenge the motif of reliance on one special hero to save the world. In the Anthropocene, there will be no single hero, no superhuman fight that saves the planet, no enemy that can be defeated to create a predictable world under human control. The figure of a special hero who saves the world in order to provide a satisfying conclusion to humanist narratives in novels cannot respond to "the enormity, urgency and indeterminacy of climate change" (Goodbody and Johns-Putra 11). The actions of all humans are important in shaping the future of the world and the complexities of these interactions in creating new pathways can be productively reimagined through the concept of relational space. It is in these terms that Gwenllian's attempt to stop the war can be understood: she tells Gansey, "I did *something* so that others would do *something*. That is kingly" (*TRK* 337–338, original emphasis). Both her recognition of the influence of Iolo Goch on Glendower and her understanding that others might be influenced by her own actions position Gwenllian as a character who perceives herself and others within complex networks of interrelations. Gwenllian also acknowledges that these networks do not follow set pathways as she hopes that others might "do *something*," emphasizing the openness of possibilities away from the well-trodden path of conquest. Gwenllian's perspective offers one trajectory among many, all of which are open-ended; there is no final conflict that restores stability, instead there exists the potential for action by multiple others in ways that are not yet determined. This recognition of the need for action by everyone, not just by the special hero who is fated to save the world, provides Gansey (and the reader) with an entirely different conceptualization of humans as interconnected and the open futures that unexpected encounters can produce. Gwenllian's version of the Glendower legend problematizes not only the predictable journey on which worthy knights become heroes but the idea of a known path at all.

BEYOND THE QUEST: EXPLORING TIME AND SPACE THROUGH NON-HUMAN HISTORIES

Gansey's version of the Glendower legend and the narrative pattern of the quest omits not only other human characters' perspectives and experiences, such as Gwenllian's, but also interactions between humans and non-humans. The anthropocentrism of the expected pattern of quest fantasy imposes itself upon narrative settings as "the land of the male hero" (Baker 246), sculpting mythic landscapes along the trajectory of the hero's journey. The enduring meanings of mythic landscapes construct the environment as backdrop, changing "so slowly as to make the history of man's relation to his environment almost timeless" (Chakrabarty, "The Climate of History" 204). Gansey's version of the Glendower legend describes the Welsh landscape as mythic and enduring, evoking familiar images of "the green swell of the Welsh foothills, the wide glistening surface of the River Dee, the unforgiving northern mountains that Glendower vanished into" (*TRB* 45). The pastoral greenery, rivers, and mountains of Gansey's story are commonplace fantasy "spatial stereotypes" (Carroll 85) that provide initial familiarity to the textual world. Children's and YA fantasies that draw on real places can invoke the "complex layers of history embedded" (Hunt 11) in the landscapes that inspire settings for the characters' journeys. In mythical landscapes shaped by "universal" journeys of conflict and conquest, legends and heroes endure: in the Welsh landscape of "Gansey's stories, Owain Glendŵr could never die" (*TRB* 45). However, the multiple versions and perspectives of the Glendower legend emphasize that the construction of mythic landscapes relies on the "denial and oppression of differences" (Heise, *Sense of Place* 6). In Gansey's story, there is no interaction between people and place; the landscape is a mere setting. Whether drawn from the real world or entirely fantastical, settings inscribed with the meaning of the hero's journey assert a humanist concept of progress that connects people to the environment only through conquest.

The idea of a timeless landscape given meaning by humanist narratives relies on the concept of a static natural world that needs to be revised in light of growing evidence about the ways in which human activity is altering life and planetary systems. Humans are continuously interacting with others, both human and non-human, in complex networks that propose a "different kind of encounter between humans, non-humans and the environment" (Heise, *Sense of Place* 91). The enduring meaning of mythic landscapes is at odds with the concepts of space as continuously produced through human and non-human interactions. In many fantasy texts, including the Raven cycle, sentient trees or forests are part of the supernatural world and, as such, trouble the notion of nature as a static backdrop to human endeavor and propose forms of non-human agency. Nonetheless, the humanist impulse typically reasserts itself in fantasy texts that often emphasize the need for human stewardship and control of agential (super)natural beings from J. R. R. Tolkien's *The Lord of the Rings* (Ekman 175) to Rowling's *Harry Potter* (Jaques 132). An animate environment or non-humans in fantasy texts are not sufficient to challenge dominant ontologies that place humans as superior to nature; even where humans are the stewards or protectors of nature, this hierarchical relationship denies the embeddedness of human and non-human within complex, dynamic relations.

In the Raven cycle, the entity Cabeswater is used to depict a shifting environment co-produced by humans, non-humans, and physical processes. Cabeswater exists along the ley line in the Virginia Mountains in a supernatural relational space. Through repeated encounters between the teenage characters and Cabeswater it becomes clear that "Cabeswater was not a forest. Cabeswater was a thing that happened to look like a forest right now" (*TRK* 424). Cabeswater is a conscious entity of its own, distinct from the forest, yet not separate from it. The supernatural forest environment is continuously being produced by interactions between Cabeswater, the living birds and plants, and the physical environment of the forests' trees, rocks, and watercourses. The dynamism of Cabeswater suggests the agency of non-human life forms and systems. As it becomes increasingly clear that humans do not have complete knowledge of or mastery over nature, non-humans and systems can be understood to have "'agency' as they shape the world in ways that are irreducible to human knowledge or construction" (Trexler 23). The agency of Cabeswater is expressed through the portrayal of the forest as always changing, which makes the teenagers realize that "they could emerge from the forest at an entirely different time or place than they had entered" (*TRK* 59). In relational space, each encounter becomes a *re*-encounter, open to the unexpected, as the teenage protagonists realize that Cabeswater "did follow rules, just not the linear ones they took for granted in the ordinary world" (*TRK* 59). The unpredictable climatic and environmental changes in the Anthropocene have exposed that "humans are not the sole makers of the non-human world" (Williams 171) and the depiction of the dynamic forest that changes in the absence of any human characters refutes the humanist construction of space as "empty" or static, waiting for human mastery. The open-endedness of relational space decenters human ways of knowing through the very dynamism of non-human relations.

In this supernatural space, the human protagonists are not separate from the environment as Cabeswater and the teenager characters interact *within* and *with* the forest, depicting how humans and non-humans co-produce environments. This co-production is always uncertain, never wholly shaped or directed by human endeavors and desires. Encounters between humans and non-humans in the text's supernatural forest can produce unintended consequences, such as when Cabeswater manifests hornets from Gansey's imagination because it "was such a good listener" (*BLLB* 25) but unaware that the swarm would kill him. However, Cabeswater does not only respond to Gansey's unspoken fear but also responds to his friends, Ronan, Adam, and Blue, who ask Cabeswater to make it safe, thus saving him. In space that is continuously co-produced through human and non-human encounters, there is always the possibility for the unexpected, whether wondrous or threatening, beneficial or destructive. Cabeswater's agency repositions the teenage characters as participants within dynamic networks, co-creating new trajectories in all possible directions. The open-endedness of interactions between humans and non-humans conceptualizes all life forms as "connected in a mesh without a center or an edge" (Morton 169). The absence of borders or enclosure to the "mesh" of coexisting life and physical processes extends through both time and space: this embeddedness of humans in co-producing relational space cannot be confined to the teenage characters' experiences of the supernatural forest.

The scale of impact of human activity on ecological systems that produced a new epoch requires reimagining narratives of history that respond to the knowledge that the "ecological overshoot of humanity does not make sense without reference to the lives of other species" (Chakrabarty, "Politics" 34). However, a complex mesh of non-human and human histories should not erase important differences and distinctions. Conceptualizing the simultaneous interconnection and heterogeneity of humans and non-humans is essential to retain "nature's otherness" (Alaimo, *Undomesticated Ground* 183) and avoid a return to the separation of humans from "nature" or homogenizing histories. Artemus (Blue's father) is a character who portrays the distinction and inseparability of humans and non-humans through his embodiment as a *tir e e'lintes* (*TRK* 326) or "tree-light." As a tree-light, Artemus can "wear" (*TRK* 327) either a tree or a "skin-house" (*TRK* 329). The transformation that Artemus undergoes is consistent with change through "overclothing" (Bynum 29) as he does not change into a tree or a human, only changes what he "wears." Through overclothing "radical difference is added to a core that is little if at all affected by the addition" (Bynum 21), thus overclothing "maintains the distinction" (Bynum 103) between "wearing" a tree or human form, while these states are simultaneously connected through the "core" of the supernatural tree-lights. The portrayal of Artemus's changes through overclothing emphasizes that he does not transform from one radically different state to another. Through the tree-light embodiment, the character retains important distinctions between trees and humans yet refuses to conflate distinction with separation. Artemus's embodiment is therefore crucial to reimagining humans' environmental embeddedness without hierarchy, simultaneously conceptualizing heterogeneity and connection.

The Anthropocene did not begin with the coining of the term at the dawn of the twenty-first century and, from his position of being neither tree nor human, Artemus's narrative history emphasizes the embeddedness of humans and non-humans over scales that exceed the experience of individual humans, or those of a few generations. Anthropocene literature, particularly science fiction and fantasy, can engage with the scalar challenges of an epoch by portraying "geological time through narrative experiments with non-human points of view" (Marshall 533). Artemus's tree-light perspective begins not with the war but "[w]hen Wales was young" (*TRK* 328), reaching far enough back in time not only to de-center Glendower but human activity as he tells Blue that when Wales was newly formed "there were trees" (*TRK* 328). Far from humans founding a new nation in an "empty" wilderness, Artemus emphasizes that, before humans, this was a living land of trees. The shaping of a nation by humans in Artemus's narrative suggests a humanist ideology of social progress defined through the "conquest and control of space" (Harvey 254). As the trees are pressed to human's service, "Wales turned from a place of forests to a place of fires and ploughs and boats and houses" (*TRK* 327–328). The fires and objects that Artemus mentions are all made of wood, that is, dead trees. As such, Artemus's narrative exposes human-centrism that values the environment "only in relation to its use to humanity (which includes wars against other humans)" (Jaques 113). As Artemus explains that Wales "became a place for all the things that trees could be except for alive" (*TRK* 328), his non-human perspective entwines human and natural history to evoke twenty-first-century readers' understanding of deforestation as habitat destruction implicated in species extinction. This hints at a further shared fate of tree and human through the potential destruction of our own habitat—the planet—and the possibility of human extinction.

Yet Artemus's story resists a straightforward narrative of human mastery as he emphasizes the agency of the natural world. The extreme and unpredictable shift in ecological systems in the Anthropocene "undermines the passivity of place, elevating it to an actor that is itself shaped by world systems" (Trexler 233). Artemus explains that the tree-lights chose to support Glendower in the war (*TRK* 328), problematizing the dominant ontology of humans over nature that is used to justify the exploitation of nature. The tree-lights' decision to join Glendower expresses the possibility of reciprocity and co-operation as Artemus explains that Glendower "could speak to us. He wanted his country to be a wild place of magic" (*TRK* 328). Artemus rejects human mastery or stewardship of the forest, proposing instead a return to interrelations through which human activity can bring about changes that benefit both humans and forests. This perspective from European deep history affirms the possibility of positive relations that actively co-produce forest environments to support biodiversity and beneficial processes, from pollination to water purification, through a relationship that is "symbiotic . . . [as] woodland flourishes under good human management" (Maitland 5). The alliance between Glendower and the tree-lights suggests the possibility of interrelations between humans and the environment that are mutually beneficial as their victory would return "powerful" (*TRK* 328) energies to Wales. This idea—that when humans and non-humans participate in complex networks, rather than hierarchies, there are possibilities for mutually beneficial futures—is important for resisting the inevitability of disaster in the Anthropocene without denying the scale of the climate crisis. However, as war participates in precisely the ideologies of conquest and mastery that pushes the tree-lights to near extinction, the alliance with Glendower does not lead to a new co-operative future and Artemus concludes, "We all lost everything. He lost everything" (*TRK* 328) as the English win the war. The emphasis on "we" and "he" expresses the entwined fates of humans and non-humans as well as the fatal dependence on one special individual to save the world.

The vast scale of Artemus's narrative decenters humanist histories, legends, and quests that propose "universals" about important individuals and "inevitable" patterns of progress and conquest. In light of Artemus's history of Wales' deforestation, the green foothills from Gansey's version of the Glendower legend are no longer a timeless backdrop to heroic adventures but denuded through humans' overuse of forest resources in pursuit of social progress and war. The dominant ontology that posits a non-human world as a resource to be used in the pursuit of human endeavors "requires and intensifies a blindness to the very nature upon which it relies" (Colebrook 272). The seemingly unchanging landscape, inscribed with heroic tales of conquest, denied the human activities that had produced the mythic "green swell of the Welsh foothills" from what was previously forest. Rather than an unchanging backdrop, the changing Welsh landscape is constructed within a narrative history that emphasizes that "humans have for a very long time helped to produce their environments" (Williams 165). But it is only relatively recently that humans as a species have become "geological agents" (Chakrabarty, "The Climate of History" 206), shifting the planet into the Anthropocene. Artemus's character describes the history of the Welsh nation as a continuous process of exploitation of woodland resources and extensive deforestation across timescales vast enough for each human generation to elide the cumulative effects of their own activities, constructing an "unchanging" environment.

The geological span of an epoch presents another challenge in Anthropocene literature that attempts "the articulation of connections between events at vastly different scales" (Heise, *Sense of Place* 206), made possible in the Raven cycle by its depiction of relational space co-produced by human and non-human characters. Artemus provides a non-human perspective that articulates the continuity between times, places, humans, and non-humans across geological scales: through this character, the distant past is not enclosed and separate from the present. Artemus's history of Wales does not mark time by the passage of years but presents a continuous narrative of the development of a nation. Past and present are not merely different points "in the historical queue" (Massey 5) as suggested by humanist teleological progress, but construct a continuous narrative beyond individual human experience. Artemus does not narrate a story of individuals, families, or localities but of a land, co-produced through human and non-human activity. And when Glendower, Gwenllian, and Artemus leave for Virginia after the war, the narrative continues as a transnational history that progresses into the twenty-first century as the teenagers find Gwenllian and Artemus still alive. Through its representation of continuous interrelations across these vast scales, Artemus's story ominously insists that the destruction of past human activities can no longer be safely parceled away in history.

In the final novel of the Raven cycle, the teenage protagonists must confront the threat of the unmaker demon that is destroying the supernatural forest of Cabeswater and everything attached to it in twenty-first-century Virginia. The unmaker demon is not a fantaseme that threatens the predictability and stability of the primary world but a present-day environmental threat produced by past human actions on the other side of the world. The unmaker demon's origins stand in stark contrast to the examples of Anthropocene fiction that focus on disruptions to (Western) human lifestyles to portray "climate change as a disaster that happens *to* us" (Colebrook 266), that is, as a destabilizing external event that leads to an unpredictable, dangerous future. Artemus reveals that Glendower's Welsh war had created the unmaker demon (*TRK* 328) by the rules of the secondary world that "was not just good for growing trees and kings. It was also good for growing demons" (*TRK* 285). The unmaker demon is a *"natural product of this environment"* (*TRK* 186, original emphasis), that is, an unintended consequence of humans co-producing space with non-humans when the war spilled "more than enough bad blood" (*TRK* 285) on the ley line to grow a demon. In the Raven cycle, interactions between human and non-human characters that co-produce space can be variously productive or destructive on either side, influencing each other across scales beyond individual human experience or control. The supernatural threat that the teenage protagonists face at the conclusion of the Raven cycle is produced not only by human activity but by war: the very activity of conflict and conquest that underpins supposedly victorious humanist histories of human mastery and control. In the depiction of the destructive force of the unmaker demon created by the Welsh-English war, the Raven cycle finally reveals that the enduring humanist narrative of the Glendower legend and Gansey's twenty-first-century hero's quest not only elide the multiplicity of meanings and trajectories that co-produce space but deny their own impact on others and the potentially devastating consequences for future generations.

WHAT IS A MEDIEVAL KING LIKE YOU DOING IN A PLACE LIKE THIS? YA QUEST FANTASY IN THE RELATIONAL SPACE OF THE RAVEN CYCLE

The relational space of the Raven cycle seems to be an inhospitable environment for a YA quest fantasy of a heroic (male) journey following universal patterns: when space is co-produced through interrelations it "must be predicated upon the existence of plurality" (Massey 9). Yet the Raven cycle is itself a retelling of the Glendower legend, although one in which the simultaneous stories and trajectories of multiple characters portray the complex entanglements of humans and non-humans across vast scales. In a relational space that refuses a dominant story, the authority of Gansey's perspective of Glendower as hero and his legend as guiding history is problematized by the ongoing stories of Gwenllian and Artemus, who are still alive in the novels' present timeline. Gwenllian and Artemus do not simply add new perspectives to the Glendower legend; the song of the witch and the geological perspective of the tree-light create a process of mythopoesis as "modern myth-making" (Attebery 4). This process draws on well-known characters, narrative patterns, and landscapes to reinvent them in new contexts, "inviting readers to revise their previous understanding" (Oziewicz 9). Gwenllian challenges the universality of the quest, highlighting the trajectories of people erased from legends of conquest and proposing alternative trajectories. Artemus embodies the interconnectedness of humans and the environment across vast temporal and spatial scales. Consequently, it is perhaps no surprise that when the teenage protagonists finally discover Glendower's tomb, they find him dead (*TRK* 380). The supernatural location of the tomb in the Raven cycle's relational space defies the ritual and repetition of patterns expected in "mythical time." However, the Raven cycle does not dismiss the importance of the textual history to the twenty-first-century teenage protagonists; rather, it insists that the ongoing influence of past stories and trajectories cannot be confined to the dominant story of the (white male European) hero, or its emphasis on separation and conquest. The multiple stories and open-ended possibilities that are constructed through the Raven cycle operate to question a timeless meaning of humanist histories in a dynamic, unpredictable world.

The Raven cycle rewrites the traditional YA quest fantasy within relational space that includes the quest narrative as only one of many possible, interrelated trajectories. In a relational space humanist histories are repositioned as part of an ongoing "complexity and not the universals which they have for so long proposed themselves to be" (Massey 11). As such, when Gansey discovers that Glendower is dead, he realizes that a medieval king cannot tell Gansey "who to be, or how to live" (*TRK* 382). Gansey comes to realize that it is his interconnections with others that make his actions meaningful as he stops the unmaker demon by sacrificing himself willingly according to the text's supernatural rules (*TRK* 330). Although Gansey is de-centered from being the special hero who saves the world, repositioning characters within complex networks does not diminish the significance of individual actions in the text. Gansey's friends, Blue, Adam, Ronan, and Cabeswater act together to bring Gansey back to life, not as a human but as "nearly human-shaped" (*TRK* 426), created from "the bits and bobs Cabeswater had assembled to give him life" (*TRK* 434). Gansey's quest finally ends when he begins a new life with this fluid human/non-human identity. By the end of the Raven cycle, the reader has learned that none of the four teenage protagonists are entirely human: Gansey is resurrected from his friends' memories and "dream stuff" (*TRK* 425), Ronan can manifest objects from his dreams, Adam is the magician, and Blue is half tree-light. These teenage characters are portrayed in stark contrast to the liberal humanist imperative of most YA quest fantasy that constructs its adolescent protagonist's development as "an individual quest to discover a stable sense of self in the face of unsettling" (Waller 55) encounters with the supernatural.

Instead, for Gansey, Blue, Adam, and Ronan, it is the realization of their fluid identities, shaping and shaped by complex interactions with human and non-human others, that constitutes their personal growth and maturation.

Responding to the Anthropocene demands new kinds of quests. Literature presents opportunities to reimagine narrative histories and futures in which humans are environmentally embedded, exploring how concepts of space and time influence narrative patterns and the types of stories that it is possible to tell. I have argued that concepts of relational space co-produced by humans and non-humans are helpful for reimagining the dynamism of complex networks in the Anthropocene. Through these multiple, heterogeneous trajectories, relational space is always changing and "there are always connections *yet to be made*" (Massey 107, original emphasis). This space of open possibilities destabilizes the certainty of the future, particularly a future informed by enduring patterns of humanist histories. Ultimately, the relational space of the ley lines and Cabeswater is not safely separated and demarcated from the "historic" time of the ordinary world in the Raven cycle, but integrated within the embodiments and between the ongoing trajectories of the adolescent protagonists, suggesting the potential of as yet unmade futures for coexisting life forms. Through these intertwined human and non-human narratives, histories, and embodiments, the Raven cycle proposes the openness of futures in the Anthropocene.

WORKS CITED

Alaimo, Stacy. "Ecology." In *The Routledge Companion to Literature and Science*, edited by Bruce Clarke and Manuela Rossini. Routledge, 2011.

———. *Undomesticated Ground: Recasting Nature as Feminist Space*. Cornell UP, 2019.

Attebery, Brian. *Stories about Stories: Fantasy and the Remaking of Myth*. Oxford UP, 2014.

Baker, Deirdre F. "What We Found on Our Journey through Fantasy Land." *Children's Literature in Education*, vol. 37, no. 3, 2006, pp. 237–251. doi:10.1007/s10583-006-9009-1.

Buell, Frederick. "Global Warming as Literary Narrative." *Philological Quarterly*, vol. 93, no. 2, 2014, pp. 261–294.

Buell, Lawrence. "Environmental Writing for Children: A Selected Reconnaissance of Heritages, Emphases, Horizons." In *Oxford Companion to Ecocriticism*, edited by Greg Garrard. Oxford UP, 2014, pp. 408–422.

———. *The Future of Environmental Criticism Environmental Crisis and Literary Imagination*. John Wiley & Sons, 2009.

Bynum, Caroline Walker. *Metamorphosis and Identity*. Zone Books, 2001.

Campbell, Joseph. *The Hero With A Thousand Faces*, 3rd ed. New World Library, 2008.

Carroll, Jane Suzanne. "Spatiality in Fantasy for Children." In *The Edinburgh Companion to Children's Literature*, edited by Clementine Beauvais and Maria Nikolajeva. Edinburgh UP, 2017, pp. 73–91.

Carroll, Lewis, and John Tenniel. *Alice's Adventures in Wonderland: &, Through the Looking Glass and What Alice Found There*. Macmillan Collector's Library, 2016.

Chakrabarty, Dipesh. "The Climate of History: Four Theses." *Critical Inquiry*, vol. 35, no. 2, 2009, pp. 197–222. doi:10.1086/596640.

———. "The Politics of Climate Change Is More Than the Politics of Capitalism." *Theory, Culture & Society*, vol. 34, no. 2–3, 2017, pp. 25–37. doi:10.1177/0263276417690236.

Clare, Cassandra. *The Mortal Instruments*. Margaret K. McElderry Books, 2015.

Clifford, James. *Routes: Travel and Translation in the Late Twentieth Century*. Harvard UP, 1997.

Colebrook, Claire. "The Future in the Anthropocene: Extinction and the Imagination." In *Climate and Literature*, edited by Adeline Johns-Putra. Cambridge UP, 2019, pp. 263–280.

Cooper, Susan. *The Dark Is Rising*. RHCP Digital, 2010.

Crutzen, Paul J., and Eugene F. Stoermer. "The 'Anthropocene'." *Global Change Newsletter*, vol. 41, 2000, pp. 17–18.

De Cristofaro, Diletta, and Daniel Cordle. "Introduction: The Literature of the Anthropocene." *C21 Literature: Journal of 21st-Century Writings*, vol. 6, no. 1, 2018, pp. 1–6. doi:10.16995/c21.73.

Ekman, Stefan. *Here Be Dragons: Exploring Fantasy Maps and Settings*. Wesleyan UP, 2013.

Farzin, Sina. "Saci Lloyd's "The Carbon Diaries 2015" (2008)." In *Cli-Fi: A Companion*, edited by Axel Goodbody and Adeline Johns-Putra. Peter Lang, 2019, pp. 187–192.

Goga, Nina, et al. *Ecocritical Perspectives on Children's Texts and Cultures: Nordic Dialogues*. Palgrave Macmillan, 2018.

Goodbody, Axel, and Adeline Johns-Putra. *Cli-Fi: A Companion*. Peter Lang, 2019.

Harvey, David. *The Condition of Postmodernity: An Enquiry into the Origins of Cultural Change*. Blackwell, 1989.

Heise, Ursula K. "Science Fiction and the Time Scales of the Anthropocene." *ELH*, vol. 86, no. 2, 2019, pp. 275–304. doi:10.1353/elh.2019.0015.

———. *Sense of Place and Sense of Planet*. Oxford UP, 2008.

———. "The Hitchhiker's Guide to Ecocriticism." *PMLA*, vol. 121, no. 2, 2006, pp. 503–516.

Hunt, Peter. "Landscapes and Journeys, Metaphors and Maps: The Distinctive Feature of English Fantasy." *Children's Literature Association Quarterly*, vol. 12, no. 1, 1987, pp. 11–14.

IPCC. *Climate Change 2014: Synthesis Report. Contribution of Working Groups I, II and III to the Fifth Assessment Report of the Intergovernmental Panel on Climate Change*. Intergovernmental Panel on Climate Change, Geneva, 2015.

Jaques, Zoe. *Children's Literature and the Posthuman: Animal, Environment, Cyborg*. Routledge, 2014.

Le Guin, Ursula K. *The Lathe of Heaven*. Scribner, 1971.
Levy, Michael, and Farah Mendlesohn. *Children's Fantasy Literature: An Introduction*. Cambridge UP, 2016.
McCallum, Robyn. *Ideologies of Identity in Adolescent Fiction the Dialogic Construction of Subjectivity*. Garland Pub., 1999.
Maitland, Sara, and Adam Lee. *Gossip from the Forest: The Tangled Roots of Our Forests and Fairytales*. Granta, 2013.
Markley, Robert. "Literature, Climate, and Time: Between History and Story." In *Climate and Literature*, edited by Adeline Johns-Putra. Cambridge UP, 2019, pp. 15–30.
Marshall, Kate. "What Are the Novels of the Anthropocene? American Fiction in Geological Time." *American Literary History*, vol. 27, no. 3, 2015, pp. 523–538. doi:10.1093/alh/ajv032.
Massey, Doreen B. *For Space*. SAGE, 2005.
McCausland, Elly. *Malory's Magic Book: King Arthur and the Child, 1862–1980*. Boydell and Brewer, 2019.
McCulloch, Fiona. *Contemporary British Children's Fiction and Cosmopolitanism*. Routledge, 2017.
Meyer, Stephenie. *The Twilight Saga Complete Collection*. Little Brown Books, 2010.
Morton, Timothy. "Coexistence and Coexistents: Ecology without a World." In *Ecocritical Theory: New European Approaches*, edited by Axel Goodbody and Kate Rigby. U of Virginia P, 2011, pp. 168–180.
Nodelman, Perry. *Alternating Narratives in Fiction for Young Readers: Twice Upon a Time*. Palgrave MacMillan, 2017.
Nikolajeva, Maria. *From Mythic to Linear Time in Children's Literature*. Scarecrow Press, 2000.
Nuzum, K. A. "The Monster's Sacrifice-Historic Time: The Uses of Mythic and Liminal Time in Monster Literature." *Children's Literature Association Quarterly*, vol. 29, no. 3, 2004, pp. 207–227.
Oziewicz, Marek. *One Earth, One People: The Mythopoeic Fantasy Series of Ursula K. Le Guin, Lloyd Alexander, Madeleine L'Engle and Orson Scott Card*. McFarland, 2008.
Senior, W. A. "Quest Fantasies." In *The Cambridge Companion to Fantasy Literature*, edited by Edward James and Farah Mendlesohn. Cambridge UP, 2012, pp. 190–199.
Stiefvater, Maggie. *Blue Lily, Lily Blue*. Scholastic, 2014.
———. *The Dream Thieves*. Scholastic, 2013.
———. *The Raven Boys*. Scholastic, 2012.
———. *The Raven King*. Scholastic, 2016.
Tolkien, J. R. R. *The Lord of the Rings*. HarperCollins, 1994.
Trexler, Adam. *Anthropocene Fictions: The Novel in a Time of Climate Change*. U of Virginia P, 2015.

Waller, Alison. *Constructing Adolescence in Fantastic Realism.* Routledge, 2011.
Wheddon, Joss, creator. *Buffy the Vampire Slayer.* Mutant Enemy Productions, 1997.
Williams, Justin. "Theorizing the Non-Human through Spatial and Environmental Thought." In *The Oxford Handbook of Environmental Political Theory*, edited by Teena Gabrielson et al. Oxford UP, 2016, pp. 160–177.

Chapter 3

The Forest as a Voice for Nature
Ecocriticism in Fantasy Literature
Britta Maria Colligs

For centuries, humanity has drastically altered the face of the world and so disturbed Earth's environmental systems, thereby introducing the new geological epoch of the Anthropocene. The concept of this epoch is based on the assumption that the transition from the previous geological epoch, the Holocene, is mainly due to humanity's negative impact upon the environment, indicating that "humankind has become a global geological force in its own right" (Steffen et al., 843). While initially introduced as a neutral comment on humanity's influence on geological developments, the application of the critical theory of the Anthropocene now highlights the fact "that our species has become a crucially significant factor in potentially cataclysmic climatological and biogeographical changes" (Garrard et al., 149). This idea is apparent in the current discussions in various fields about climatological as well as biological issues concerning mass population, deforestation, intensive farming, and so forth (cf. Lowenthal 54–55). As a result, "[t]he concept of the Anthropocene asks that we think and imagine on a wholly different scale, vastly more global in scope, vastly more historical in extent, in the course of making decisions about countless matters of environmental concerns. And it asks that we take seriously the specific responsibilities that arise from this shifting of perspectives" (Garrard et al., 150). Shifting the perspective toward an earth-centered point of view is a fundamental element within ecocriticism, which very broadly discusses the relationship between the human and the environment in various fields. This theoretical approach is relevant in literary theory for it offers a chance to reflect on literature from an ecocritical point of view and thus facilitates critical reading to serve a broader sociopolitical purpose—in this case, environmentalism. Ecocriticism thus forms a lens in literary theory that has great urgency in the era of the Anthropocene, even though these tropes have persisted in the study of nature in literature over time.

In this chapter, the forests of selected fantasy worlds will be analyzed as representatives for their respective ecosystems. Forests are vital components of our environment, and thus, the study of literary forests can contribute to the understanding of their significance in our current climate crisis. Operating as a voice for nature, the entire ecosystem of fantasy forests, as well as their individual tree characters, functions as memorials for nature and educators for the different humanoid races in the narratives, thus potentially serving this function for the reader at large. With the focus on the environment within the discipline of ecocriticism, these narratives are able to address environmental concerns covertly and overtly through their representation of the forests. Consequently, the fantasy forest as an entire ecosystem can become an active agent of and voice for the environment and so comment on its overall significance and the cataclysmic intrusions by human or humanoid characters in their respective narratives, as well as in the primary world of the reader.

ECOCRITICISM IN THE AGE OF THE ANTHROPOCENE

As a response to the increased awareness of humanity's negative impact on the environment within the Anthropocene, ecocriticism examines, very broadly, the relationship between the human and the environment; or, in terms of literary theory, it analyses the relationship between literature and the physical environment encouraging a new reading of nature (cf. Barry 238; Glotfelty xix; and Kerridge 530).[1] In general, nature or the environment represented in a text can be examined in two ways. On the one hand, the landscape can be seen as a mere setting or place where the events take place and is thus chiefly connected to the characters within the narrative (Kern 260). On the other hand, landscape and the environment can also become more than solely the background to the action where "its significance [is seen] as primarily symbolic, so that it becomes something essentially other than itself" (Kern 260). With their focus on the environment and the characters' interaction with and attitude toward it, ecocritics propose a paradigm shift, that is, a move away from an anthropocentric worldview toward an ecocentric perspective, with nature and the non-human, such as animals, at the center (Brawley 98). The emphasis lies on a balanced relationship between humans and nature, seeing them as equals or even elevating nature above human concerns, a notion that is strived for in the Anthropocene. Throughout the historical development of the field, different trends have been recognized and described as waves, beginning in the 1980s with a refocused close reading of nature in British Romanticism and American Transcendentalism and, later, including human presence within nature and expanding the study of rural landscapes and wilderness to suburban and urban places as well (Buell 18–28). In the late noughties, a third and fourth wave appeared simultaneously identifying, on the one hand, a "world citizenship" connecting everyone to the environment and global climate crisis and, on the other hand, a *material ecocriticism* which focuses on the "interchanges across human bodies, animal bodies, and the wider material world" (Alaimo, qtd. in Marland 855). Consequently, ecocriticism has become a wide-ranging form of environmental advocacy, which establishes a renewed reading of any given text to its orientation to the environment.

Analyses which draw upon this reading are particularly applicable to fantasy and speculative literature. Fantasy in general evokes a sense of wonder ranging from simple amazement at the marvelous to a sense of the numinous or mysterious, which is often evoked by magnificent landscapes and/or non-human entities. In this genre, encounters between human characters and sentient non-human "others" call into question the nature of the human and, simultaneously, the boundaries between the self and other. Such literatures often draw on the paradigm shift heralded by ecocriticism, namely a shift away from the anthropocentric bias toward a focus on the environment with its two principles: the idea of *animism* (the world around us is alive and all creatures/non-human entities are able to communicate with each other) and the idea of *interrelatedness* (all beings and things are connected) (Brawley 17). In fantasy and speculative literature, with often elaborate secondary worlds, nature and the environment can have a specific relevance because the authors of such texts are able to develop their specific nature deliberately. More than in most other genres, nature in fantasy literature can truly become an independent character with its own agency, such as Tolkien's mountain Caradhras, which seemingly hinders the fellowship on their journey across its mountain range (Tolkien, *Fellowship* 375–383).[2] Fantastic worlds therefore estrange the reality we know, which may concomitantly foster an active examination of our world (Manlove 16–26). Due to "the feeling of awe which is experienced in a fantasy [fantasy literature] has the ability to reshape our perceptions of the natural world and can challenge us to rethink our relations with the natural world" (Brawley 6). Consequently, an ecocritical approach to the texts of fantasy and speculative fiction provides relevant observations on the understanding of nature and the environment in the current climate crisis.

THE FOREST AS A VOICE FOR NATURE

As a vital part of the natural environment, the forests of the world have been subject to the change of humans' attitude toward the concept of nature.

Various ideas of the forest are part of our (Western) cultural knowledge and align themselves with the general idea of nature developed throughout history. As a classical wilderness and a contrast to places of civilization, as a mythical realm for supernatural creatures, or as a safe haven and recreational area, the idea of the forest has changed in the course of the history of culture and society. Forests therefore cannot only be seen as a natural environment of trees, various plants, and wildlife, but are also "important archetype[s], symbolically reflecting the basic structure of the unconscious, the undefinable, and the essence of life and existence" (Konijnendijk 19). With their differing associations, forests form a space described by Michel Foucault as heterotopia, that is, "real places" that have more layers of meaning or relationships to other places than the obvious one (24). As discursive and institutional or cultural spaces, heterotopias thus constitute a transforming space that is more than the initially observed "physical" place. Consequently, Foucault establishes that "we do not live in a homogeneous and empty space, but on the contrary in a space thoroughly imbued with quantities and perhaps thoroughly fantasmatic as well" (23). In our current climate crisis, the cultural and historical layer, the forest as a wilderness, safe haven, and/or recreational area, has to be extended to the value of the forest for the environment at large.

With the rise of ecocriticism and a growing awareness of humanity's negative impact on nature, forests in general "have become metonymies for the earth as a whole" (Harrison 199). As a complex and interconnected living ecosystem, forests hold a vital position within the wider context of the environment for the reason that they are the most crucial provider of habitats allowing biological diversity and offering a wide range of genetic information. Furthermore, forests act as regulators for the global and local climate and can prevent soil erosion, hill slope failure, and downstream sedimentation (CBD 1). Therefore, protecting and understanding the forest's intricate biological network has become a major focus of ecological activism. The German forester and author Peter Wohlleben, for example, explains the forest's elaborate *social* network and describes its trees as families living together in his groundbreaking international bestseller *The Hidden Life of Trees* (in the original *Das Geheime Leben der Bäume*, 2015).[3] Trees in a forest system communicate with each other, support struggling or sick trees by sharing nutrients, and warn each other of impending dangers via chemicals. By an anthropomorphized comparison of the forest's and the individual tree's social life to human life, Wohlleben manages to give his reader a better understanding of the forest, which seems necessary in order to protect the sensitive ecosystem. As a result, the forest and its multiple associations have assumed a powerful symbolic status as a complex integrated system—one that has to be protected in order to protect Earth as a whole, as both are interconnected and share a complex system that influences each other.

UNDERSTANDING THE FOREST ECOLOGY

In her novella *The Word for World is Forest* (1972), Ursula K. Le Guin discusses the value of the forest for the environment at large. Within her narrative, Le Guin portrays a world where humans have already destroyed the entire environment on Earth and are now expanding beyond it to capitalize on colonies within the wider planetary systems. On the fictional planet of Athshe, a military logging colony has been established in order to exploit the indigenous population and obtain their local timber, due to the fact that wood has become a scarce commodity and a "necessary luxury" (178) on Earth. The forest on Athshe is the central habitat as well as a cultural foundation for its indigenous people. The deep connection and coexistence between the forest and its inhabitants is made explicit here and so establishes the Athsheans as part of their natural world: "the substance of their world was not earth, but forest. Terran man was clay, red dust. Athshean man was branch and root. They did not carve figures of themselves in stone, only in wood" (240). The connection between man and forest is expanded to the interdependency between the forest and the overall environment. The Terran anthropologist, Raj Lyubov, tries to explain the significance of the forest for the entire environment by stating that "[a] forest ecology is a delicate one. If the forest perishes, its fauna may go with it. The Athshean word for *world* is also the word for *forest*" (227, original emphasis). The equalization of forest and world through the use of the same expression "Athshe" indicates the interrelatedness and conformity between the two, "the soil and the planet, two meanings and one" (240). The health of the forest—or destruction of it as in the case of Earth—reflects the state of the whole world; what happens to one will also affect the other. Thus, Le Guin's narrative, published almost half a century ago, reflects on the ecological crisis through the exploitation of nature, as well as a lack of respect for the rights of indigenous cultures.[4] Le Guin states that

> it was becoming clear that the ethic which approved the defoliation of forests and grainlands and the murder of non-combatants in the name of "peace" was only a corollary of the ethic which permits the despoliation of natural resources for private profit or the GNP, and the murder of creatures of the Earth in the name of "man." The victory of the ethic of exploitation, in all societies, seemed as inevitable as it was disastrous. ("Introduction" 8)

Nearly fifty years later, not much has changed and problems of deforestation and the exploitation of nature have increased over the last few decades with, for example, the dwindling of the once dense and widespread ancient forests in almost all parts of the world for the sake of human progress (cf. Syvitski).

In *The Word for World is Forest*, the Athshean Selver and, to an extent, Lyubov function as mediators between a healthy forest and the colonizing Terrans in order to protect the delicate environment. As previously mentioned, the Athshean see themselves as part of the natural environment with a direct connection to trees (Hovanec 89). Their natural habitat is the forest with their lodges built beneath particular trees, which then also constitute their families/clans, such as the Ash, Birch, and Holly (Le Guin, *Word* 192). The idea that Athsheans are made out of wood is mirrored in the human-like qualities attributed to the trees: "They all lay broken and uprooted. [Selver] picked up the silvery branch of one and a little blood ran out of the broken end" (200–201). In this passage, the reader is introduced to a powerful image of bleeding trees that have been violated by mankind. An intact forest is a place of health for the Athsheans and deeply connected to their peace of mind within their collective subconscious. In her novella, Le Guin depicts a "vivid presentation of the dynamics of a sane society which lives in harmony with its natural environment because its members are themselves in psychological equilibrium" (Watson 231). The forest is a therapeutic landscape, a place which has positive psychological and physical effects on the individual Athshean realized in their ability to consciously control their dreams. Within the environmental movement, this beneficial effect of nature/the natural environment on mental health has been widely realized and then utilized, for example, in the widespread Shinrin-yoku movement. "Forest bathing," coined and established by the Japanese Ministry of Agriculture, Forestry and Fisheries in 1982, describes the benefits of "making contact with and taking in the atmosphere of the forest" (Park et al., 18). Simultaneously, madness is closely connected to the absence of trees in *The Word for World is Forest*. When Athsheans go mad, they are "taken to Rendlep where nobody lives any more, and left there. [. . .] There's nothing to kill on Rendlep. No trees, no people. There were trees and people, but now there are only the dreams of them" (295). The loss and destruction of the forest that is experienced throughout the narrative has a deep effect on the indigenous people, who begin to change their formerly peaceful behavior in order to retaliate against the destruction of the forest. In the end, the Athsheans violently revolt against the Terrans and end their logging exploits on Athshe. Le Guin thus "*has* been able to define nature as an essence which is both physical and mental, a vital element, not only in the American experience, but in the consciousness of all humankind" (Hovanec 90, original emphasis). Reflecting on the interconnectedness of the forest and the entire environment and linking it to the mental state of the individual, Le Guin's work, set against the upcoming environmental movement of the 1960s and 1970s, attempts to shift the reader's perspective toward nature and highlights the significance of the forest for the reader in a world dominated by profit and war.

With the help of fictional mediators, such as Selver and Lyubov, facilitating between the environment and the humanoid characters within the narrative, the shift toward an ecocentric perspective and an understanding of the intricate global network of the forest is recognized. A similar mediating character is J. R. R. Tolkien's Tom Bombadil, whose clarifications help the hobbits, and thus in extension the reader, understand the forest's position within a human-dominated world. When stepping into the Old Forest in *The Fellowship of the Ring* (1954), the four hobbits enter a dark and dangerous realm in which they encounter their first real antagonist, the Old Man Willow (Flieger, "Trees" 148–149). After almost being strangled and buried alive by the willow (Tolkien, *Fellowship* 162–163), the hobbits naturally develop a feeling of animosity against the trees and the Old Forest. However, through the words of Bombadil, safe in his house, the hobbits start "to understand the lives of the Forest, apart from themselves, indeed to feel themselves as the strangers where all other things [are] at home" (178–179). Bombadil functions as a neutral educator for the hobbits by giving rational motives for the forest's malevolent nature against humanoid characters: "Tom's words laid bare the heart of trees and their thoughts, which were often dark and strange, and filled with a hatred of things that go free upon the earth, gnawing, biting, breaking, hacking, burning: destroyers and usurpers" (179).[5] The anthropomorphized hatred of the forest is vividly illuminated by the humans' exploitation of the forest, "destroyers," and their domination of nature, "usurpers." Bombadil moves between the two parties (nature and mankind) helping them understand each other. The significance of Bombadil as a mediator was stated by Tolkien himself, declaring that Bombadil "represents something that [he] feel[s] important" (Tolkien, *Letters* 178). It becomes clear that Bombadil reflects Tolkien's own understanding of nature as numinous and humans' non-appropriation approach to the environment as particularly destructive (Brawley 105). In this case, Bombadil becomes a valuable character, commenting on the maltreatment of the forest within the world of Middle-earth, as well as extending this point of view to the world of the reader, so serving as a lens through which an ecocritical understanding of the forest and nature can be developed in the characters and the reader.

Whereas Bombadil is positioned between nature and the characters/reader, Tolkien's Ents and especially Treebeard are a more immediate voice of and for the forest and thus nature. The tree-like Ents were once created by Ilúvatar, the supreme deity of Tolkien's cosmology, as "Shepherds of the Trees" in order to protect them from the axes of the dwarves and to "speak on behalf of all things that have roots, and punish those that wrong them" (Tolkien, *Silmarillion* 41, 52). They are thus the oldest of all living races (Kocher 109). As stewards, they are part of the natural environment of the Fangorn Forest and are closely interconnected with it: they share, for example, the same physical attributes with trees. However, they are able to walk freely and have their own language and poetry, a characteristic usually reserved for humanoid characters; thus, they are a literate complex culture and represent "nature voiced" (Jeffers 23). Treebeard, who is simultaneously called *Fangorn*, represents the entire forest and functions as an educator for the understanding of and respect for nature for the two hobbits, Meriadoc Brandybuck and Peregrin Took. Their meeting in *The Two Towers* (1954) corresponds with Bombadil's story, full of stimulating passages, creating an emotional response for the hobbits while affecting the reader as well. Treebeard's language is alive with touching imagery lamenting the loss of a once dense and widespread forest where he "could walk and sing all day and hear no more than the echo of [his] own voice in the hollow hills" (84). In addition, he tells the gloomy story of how they lost the Entwives (93–96). Reminiscing about an untroubled past full of plenty set against the present destruction of the forest to fuel the war industry, Treebeard demonstrates once again Tolkien's distress about the maltreatment of nature, and, additionally, generates an emotional relationship between the forest and the characters/reader. Treebeard represents the ecocritical lens for the reader by focusing on nature and, initially, not taking part in the affairs of men, "because nobody is altogether on [his] *side*, [. . .] nobody cares for the woods as [he] care[s] for them" (89, original emphasis). Understanding the forest as a complex place with its own history and memory filled with prosperity, but also prone to violence from within (such as from Old Man Willow) and outside, is vital in order to step away from the forest as a plain commodity for mankind and appreciate nature as something more profound.

The value of a healthy forest has been highlighted, yet it is the absence of forests and their devastation due to deforestation and human maltreatment that exacerbate the feeling of loss and alarm for an endangered environment within the narratives. By contrasting devastated areas to a healthy ecosystem, the abrupt encounter with deforestation is usually considered destructive in the literature and is frequently compared to graveyards, battlefields, or wastelands. Tolkien presents his reader with exactly this concept when illustrating the highly industrialized valley of Isengard:

> Once it had been green and filled with avenues, and groves of fruitful trees, watered by streams that flowed from the mountains to a lake. But no green thing grew there in the latter days of Saruman. The roads were paved with stone-flags, dark and hard; and beside their borders instead of trees there marched long lines of pillars, some of marble, some of copper and of iron, joined by heavy chains. [. . .] The plain, too, was bored and delved. Shafts were driven deep into the ground; their upper ends were covered by low mounds and domes of stone, so that in the moonlight the Ring of Isengard looked like a graveyard of unquiet dead. (Tolkien, *Two Towers* 197–198)

Tolkien's aversion to the maltreatment of nature and excessive industrialization is explicit here and stimulates the reader to reflect on the devastating geographical changes made in the era of the Anthropocene.[6] The turning of a once green and prosperous valley into a "graveyard of unquiet dead" depicts an unnatural man-made industrial landscape and suggests the decay of nature with "burned and axe-hewn stumps of ancient groves" (196) along the way. Further shocking images of deforestation can be found in C. S. Lewis's *The Chronicles of Narnia* (1950–1955), where the characters come across "a hideous lane like a raw gash in the land, full of muddy ruts where felled trees had been dragged down to the river" (Lewis, *Last Battle* 679). The significance of the forest as an ancient living organism that has been brutally violated is also discussed in Christopher Paolini's *Inheritance Cycle* (2003–2011), where teams of humans venture into the Elven forest Du Weldenvarden to cut down ancient trees for their war engines (Paolini, *Brisingr* 84–85). In all of these examples, the characters of the fantasy worlds know that humans need wood for various reasons, yet it is the extreme logging of the forest for war machinery without any regard to the wider environment that is criticized. Consequently, the violent destruction of nature is intensified by its connection to further devastation through war, and thus the feeling of loss and sorrow is amplified and stretched beyond the realm of the forest, linking it to the wider world again.

The brutal violation of nature is also deployed in T. A. Barron's novel *The Ancient One* (1992), where a comparison of a deforested area to wastelands and battlefields underlines humanity's arrogance toward nature and signals the forest's cultural position as a simple commodity. Barron's entire novel focuses on the protection of an ancient grove with some of the oldest trees, the coastal redwoods, against the local logging company, with the grove being turned into a national park at the end of the novel. The redwoods are represented as God's first temples and one in particular is "the most majestic tree of all. It stood taller and broader than the rest, older than anything else in the forest" (71). The tree's link to history is relevant, hinting at the fact that nature, and especially ancient trees, have existed for a very long time and should thus be respected in their own rights.[7] With the rise of civilization, forests have been logged to provide timber and space and this exploitation is an emotionally charged issue in Barron's narrative.[8] While hiking through the forest, the main protagonist, Kate, suddenly stumbles into a felled forest area. Kate's haunting description comes as a complete contrast to the wholesome forest described previously, shocking her and the reader alike. The scene is compared to "old photographs of trenched battlefields in World War One. An entire section of the forest, a square about a mile on each side, had literally vanished. Nothing remained but a wasteland of torn limbs, uprooted trunks, slashed bark, and mangled branches strewn across the pockmarked terrain" (43). By comparing the clearing to old photographs of the trenches in World War I, a time of extensive devastation, Barron heightens the horror of ruin and desolation after a catastrophic event. In this context, the "torn limbs" describe the trees' branches scattered around the terrain as well as referring, metaphorically, to the actual limbs of fallen soldiers during the War—an image that has already been discussed in Le Guin's novella. The physical connection or even similarity between a tree and a person is a common motif and often the tree is used to represent humans (Bloch 42; Rival 17). Additionally, Barron's graphic description of the wasteland with the use of violent adjectives (torn, uprooted, slashed, mangled, and pockmarked) triggers a feeling of despair and, consequently, this emotional and horrific imagery is potent in conveying Barron's ecocritical message of protection. The devastating images heighten the necessity for protecting the forest and present the destroyed balance between the forest, nature, and life as such.

On a similar note, the negative impact of extreme deforestation is discussed in Ali Shaw's novel *The Trees* (2016), an apocalyptic ecocritical fantasy thriller. After the entire world has been afforested overnight, various groups try to make their living within a primal forest space; however, most of them seem to lose "their battle to survive in the woods" (297). The largest settlement the main protagonists discover shows humans' incapability to learn from previous mistakes as they disregard the idea of living in harmony with the environment. A large group of people come together to log an entire valley in order to build a rudimentary village with "thirty or forty crude shelters constructed along the grid of muddy tracks. Mud, in fact, fleered the entirety of the valley and glistened in the sun" (349). The village represents the modern model of massive urbanization and intensive farming and stands, again, in clear contrast to the previous lush and green forest. The idea of a settlement where people can safely live together and start anew should be a welcoming sight. However, the reader is presented with a negative image of nature being violated. The settlers turned the "whole valley into a wasteland" (349) with only dull colors present. With stumps of felled trees, Shaw, like Barron, evokes the notion of a battlefield. The corruption of nature into an inhospitable environment is accompanied by a subtle corruption of the individual's and the community's moral code as the villagers are led by unscrupulous men who do not back away from violence and suppression. As a contrast, a healthy forest, and therefore healthy nature, seems to be an indicator of a positive interconnection between all life forms. Shaw, similarly to the previously analyzed narratives, establishes an emotional link to a nourishing forest by providing a disturbing picture of violated nature. In this way, the authors are able to address environmental issues within the Anthropocene and encourage a shift in perspective and the validation of nature as something more than a simple resource.

THE FOREST AND ITS TREES AS ACTIVE AGENTS

In the fantasy narratives discussed here, forests act as one collective entity reacting consciously to the negative interference of the humans and humanoid characters and can thus be seen as active agents for nature. The concept of agency has commonly been associated with the capacity of individuals to act independently and make their own free choices, even though those might be determined by social factors (Barker 240). In general, agency is attributed to humans and its transfer onto other life forms, most prominently animals, is debated in literature with the study of animal narratives or within the philosophy of posthumanism pondering the question whether posthuman characters, such as Philip K. Dick's androids in *Do Androids Dream of Electric Sheep?* (1968), have similar abilities and agency as humans. The question of whether plants overall have any form of agency or are only capable of reacting to their specific environmental situation is a debate this chapter does not have the scope to discuss. The focus here is on the literary worlds where nature, in particular the forest, is able to act individually as an agent. The particular image of nature reclaiming abandoned places is a powerful image, one that can be found in fictional worlds of literature or film but also in real life exhibited in photography such as the collection *Naturalia: Reclaimed by Nature* (2018) by photographer Jonathan Jimenez. Jimenez photographed various deserted man-made constructions, such as hotels and scenes from the Chernobyl Exclusion Zone, to show how nature is reclaiming those places. In an interview with *Lonely Planet*, he clearly makes a reference to humanity's climatological and geographical impact in the Anthropocene and establishes the strength of nature: "We turned the earth inside out. Now we're just waiting for her to spit us out. Every civilization in human history has fallen, ours will too, and if you look in the right places you can see it starting to happen" ("See How"). This idea is portrayed, for example, in Lewis's *Prince Caspian* (1951), where the abandoned ruins of Cair Paraval, the seat of the high kings and queens of Narnia, have been reconquered by a dense forest (318–328). Whereas nature reclaims abandoned places through time and natural progression in these examples, the forests in fantasy literature can additionally reconquer space in a more direct way by becoming active agents for the environment.

The forest as an agent and driving force against the maltreatment of nature is evident in Shaw's novel, whose title, *The Trees,* hints at their significance for the narrative. As previously mentioned, an entire primal forest springs out of the earth in an instant, covering the entire world. In his opening chapter, Shaw depicts an apocalyptic world where the forest violently reclaims its ancient space:

> The forest burst full-grown out of the earth, in booming uppercuts of trunks and bludgeoning branches. It rammed through roads and houses alike, shattering bricks and exploding glass. It sounded like a thousand trains derailing at once, squealing and jarrings and bucklings all lost beneath the thunderclaps of broken concrete and the cacophony of a billion hissing leaves. Up surged the tree trunks, up in a storm of foliage and lashing twigs that spread and spread and then, at a great height, stopped.
>
> In the blink of an eye, the world had changed. There came an elastic aftershock of creaks and groans and then, softly softly, a chinking shower of rubbled cement. Branches stilled amid the wreckage they had made. Leaves calmed and trunks stood serene. Where, not a minute before, a suburb had lain, there was now only woodland standing amidst ruins. Some of the trees were flickeringly lit by the strobe of dying electricity, others by the fires of vehicles that had burst into flames. The rest stood in darkness, their canopy a gibbet world hung with all the things they'd killed and mangled as they came. (6)

It is not a subtle and peaceful takeover, but a destructive and vigorous outburst of nature. As an entire ecosystem, the forest becomes a force to be reckoned with, destroying everything in its way. The reader is presented with a ferocious and deafening chaos due to the rapid growth of trees, creating a sense of urgency and dire need for nature to change the face of the world. This abrupt and forceful eruption of a forest indicates nature's seemingly loss of patience after "[i]t had been silent for a long, long time" (Shaw 325). In this one-time event, nature sets the advancements of humanity back to primitive times to provide an answer to "all the things going wrong" (34). Narrated as a one-time event, Shaw primarily focuses on the aftermath of the forest's invasion and the humans' struggle to comprehend their new living situation.[9] During their travels through the primal forest, the three main protagonists come across further devastation and destruction of cornerstones of modern civilization: the communication systems have been brought to standstill without any electricity, roads have been ruined and made impassable, and houses have been demolished so that there are no longer comfortable and safe places for humans. The primal forest in *The Trees* does not seem to be a reaction to individual characters' maltreatments but nature's ultimate reply after "[s]he sent us more warnings than anyone could count" (87). Shaw overtly links his narrative to the issues of the Anthropocene, where problems of global warming, deforestation and "messages from nature," such as the expansion of the hole in the ozone, massive extinction, and higher frequencies of great floods (cf. Syvitski), are being discussed but only gradually worked against on a global scale. In his narrative, the forest has one enormous outburst of agency in order to change the course of time to give nature some peace and time to recover.

The forests of Tolkien's Middle-earth, particularly the Old Forest and Fangorn, represent a collective agency as well as accommodating individual tree agents. Both forests are considered dangerous and act as obstacles and antagonists for those characters who maltreat them. After leaving their familiar environment of the Shire behind, the four hobbits feel threatened by the dark and ominous Old Forest which is "consciously menacing [and] consciously ill-intentioned toward those humans who invade it" (Flieger, "Trees" 148). Stories of the forest's mischievousness circulate among the hobbits living close to its borders, speaking of trees that "may drop a branch, or stick a root out, or grasp at you with a long trailer" (Tolkien, *Fellowship* 153) or actively move around to conceal the traveler's path. Furthermore, the forest is said to have attacked the hedges which shut out the wilderness from the Shire by planting themselves right next to it and leaning over it. Here, the reader is first presented with the idea of wild nature creeping into cultivated landscapes trying to reclaim space, which is portrayed as an active and conscious choice and thus gives agency to the forest. Because of the hobbits' counterattack (they cut and burn down hundreds of trees to clear a space between the hedge and the forest) and Bombadil's education, the shift from a human/humanoid-centered perspective to an environmental perspective is established here and the forest is transformed into a sentient space with a collective consciousness and agency.

Whereas the Old Forest solely acts within its own forest space, the Ents of the Fangorn Forest reveal a more advanced form of forest agency by actively going to war against their enemies. The Ents, who have already been established as educators and memorials for the forest, as well as the Huorns, animated non-talking trees living in Fangorn Forest and looked after by the Ents, can be seen as individual agents. Nevertheless, they act as a collective forest unit to protect their environment and decide consciously in an Entmoot, a gathering of Ents, to participate in the overall war in *The Two Towers* (97–101). The Ents are aware of their own position within Middle-earth and the changing times, knowing well that this will be their final revolt against the destruction of nature:

> Of course, it is likely enough, my friends" [Treebeard] said slowly, likely enough that we are going to our doom: the last march of the Ents. But if we stayed at home and did nothing, doom would find us anyway, sooner or later. That thought has long been growing in our hearts; and that is why we are marching now. It is not a hasty resolve. Now at least the last march of the Ents may be worth a song." (Tolkien, *Two Towers* 108)

Once more, Tolkien employs a highly emotional narrative to underline nature's cornered position in a world that is slowly changing. The idea of the Ents coming together for the last time to face their oppressors presents a gloomy picture of the self-sacrifice of nature and the world as a whole. Yet, at the same time, it also shows nature's self-empowerment by taking matters into their own hands. Saruman's enterprise, turning the once green valley of Isengard into an industrial area by cutting down major parts of the forest creating massive wastelands, is the ultimate threat to the forest and this is precisely what arouses the Ents into action: Their lives are in danger and it is "the orc-work, the wanton hewing without even the bad excuse of feeding the fires, that has so angered [them]" (Tolkien, *Two Towers* 107). Treebeard's statement here unmistakably reflects Tolkien's own thoughts on the subject. In his letters he states that he is "(obviously) much in love with plants and above all trees, and always ha[s] been; and [he] find[s] human maltreatment of them as hard to bear as some find ill-treatment of animals" (Tolkien, *Letters* 220). This love is clearly represented in his entire world of Middle-earth. The Ents and Huorns, who themselves march against the hosts of Isengard at Helm's Deep and so crush Saruman's hosts there (Tolkien, *Two Towers* 174), are clearly capable of thinking and evaluating their situation and from this make their own choices on how to act.

Tolkien's Ents marching collectively against industrialization and the destruction of nature is one of the most widely known examples of a forest's agency in literature. Pippin considers this imposing picture of trees on the move: "Could it be that the trees of Fangorn were awake, and the forest was rising, marching over the hills to war?" (Tolkien, *Two Towers* 102–103) Nature awakening and actively working against their suppressors is a common image in literature, one that is also depicted in Lewis's *Prince Caspian*. The mythical people of Narnia, that is, the talking animals, the Dryads (tree nymphs or tree spirits), and Naiads (water nymphs/ spirits), have been in hiding or fallen into a deep sleep after the Humans (Telmarines) came to Narnia and started felling trees. The talking animals are aware of nature's strength and the forest's importance for the overall world of Narnia. They know that when the Dryads and Naiads rise again, nature will be a force strong enough to expel the Telmarines, who are "horribly afraid of the woods, and once the Trees moved in anger, [their] enemies would go mad with fright and be chased out of Narnia as quick as their legs would carry them" (Lewis, *Prince Caspian* 353). The trees, or more precisely the Dryads, are awoken in the course of the narrative and soon join the final battle against the Telmarines. Similar to the Ents, the Awakened Trees of Narnia are depicted as characters somewhere between human and tree (406); nevertheless, they work as a collective forest unit in this situation. The reader is presented with "woods on the move. All the trees of the world appeared to be rushing towards Aslan" (387). Therefore, the entire forest acts as an agent for nature and the talking animals in Lewis's world.

So far, the focus has been on the forest as a collective unit; however, the beauty of fantasy and speculative fiction allows individual tree characters, sentient non-human others, to act as agents for the environment as well. Tolkien's Treebeard, as previously discussed, is a walking, talking tree character with a distinct agency, acting as a literate educator for an understanding of and respect for nature from the characters and reader. The Ents as individual tree characters, together with Lewis's moving trees, are the most advanced agents of the environment for they are able to communicate and move around freely, not being bound to one particular place. Rooted trees, appearing therefore even more like real-life trees, might not have the same kind of agency as the walking and talking tree characters; nevertheless, we find individual trees in literature that show agency. An example of a rooted tree as protector of the entire ecosystem is introduced in Paolini's *Inheritance Cycle*. The Menoa Tree is the central and sacred tree in the Elven forest Du Weldenvarden and the guardian of the forest. It is described as a massive pine tree with roots stretching out into the forest "as if it were the heart of Du Weldenvarden itself. The tree presided over the woods like a benevolent matriarch, protecting its inhabitants under the shelter of her branches" (Paolini, *Eldest* 305). The tree's main concern is the affairs of the forest, taking into consideration everything that flourishes and grows within her ecosystem. As a sentient being, the tree has her own consciousness and is able to communicate with her surroundings and the humanoid characters through telepathy. Shocked by the sheer presence and awareness of the tree, Eragon, the main protagonist, exclaims: "It's awake! [. . .] I mean [. . .] it's intelligent" (306). Being able to communicate, having a consciousness, and a form of intellect are part of the attributes of an agent. Acting upon a divination that they will find a weapon underneath the tree that will help them overthrow the tyrant in Alagaësia, Eragon and especially his dragon Saphira attack the Menoa Tree to get to the sword. They are subsequently threatened by the enclosing forest around them and are smothered by the Menoa Tree, defending herself and the entire forest. Trying to reason with the tree, Eragon pleads with her by making her aware of the consequences, also for her forest, if he cannot defeat the tyrant Galbatorix. Answering this, the Menoa Tree states that: "*If [Galbatorix] tries to kill my seedlings, then he will die. No one is as strong as the whole of the forest. No one can defeat the forest, and I speak for the forest*" (658, original emphasis). Direct agency in the form of defense is portrayed, yet she also hints at the overall strength of the forest and its endurance against maltreatment. As the central figure and representative of the entire forest, the Menoa Tree displays the concepts of interconnectedness and animism which are so valuable within the theory of ecocriticism.

In contrast to trees that act as guardians of their ecosystem and thus of the environment as a whole, some other prominent tree characters in fantasy narratives are only slightly animated and are primarily concerned with their own well-being. As previously mentioned, Old Man Willow in Tolkien's Old Forest is a character who pushes Frodo Baggins into the river and traps Merry and Pippin within his roots purely out of malice (Tolkien, *Fellowship* 163). The Whomping Willow in J. K. Rowling's *Harry Potter* novels (1997–2007) is another example of an animated tree that punishes its surroundings. The willow tree, initially planted on the grounds of Hogwarts to disguise and guard a secret tunnel, lashes out at everyone who comes too close, with or without ill-intentions. In their second year of school, Harry Potter and his best friend Ronald Weasley are confronted by the Whomping Willow after they fly their magical Ford Angelica into the tree. The tree starts "attacking them. Its trunk was bent almost double, and its gnarled boughs were pummelling every inch of the car it could reach" (Rowling, *Chambers* 78). Obviously infuriated, the tree reacts by assaulting the intruders. The question of whether the reactions of the various rooted trees are consciously performed or whether they are merely an automatic reaction to variant forms of stimuli is debatable. In the case of the Menoa Tree and the Whomping Willow, the implications concerning the agency of the trees might be diverse; nevertheless, the trees seem to consciously react to the characters and can therefore also be seen as agents in their own rights.

CONCLUSION

As has been indicated, fantasy and speculative narratives can shift the general perspective away from an anthropocentric point of view by giving its tree characters an individual voice and agency. The forests mentioned are not inanimate places but, as heterotopias, present the reader with more layers of meaning and substance. They are conscious entities with individual sentient tree characters that are able to think and act on their own behalf and are thus elevated to something larger than the physical space. As representatives for the entire environment, the forests and individual trees become memorials for a healthy environment and educators for the characters and the reader, making them understand the forest's significance and value for their world, and Earth in general. By frequently concentrating on poignant imageries, especially in regard to the destruction of the forest, the authors are able to establish an emotional link between humans/humanoid characters and the wider natural environment. As active agents, the forests and trees guard their ecosystem and act vigorously against the maltreatment and destruction of nature by human/humanoid races. Their actions often seem to be the ultimate response to all the wrongdoings, which can be seen as a direct comment on the current climatological issues tackled within the Anthropocene, even if some of the texts have been published earlier. Protecting the forest and the environment at large, the forests of the narratives become a force to be reckoned with, displaying their inner strength and endurance to eventually overcome their oppression. Due to the fact that fantasy literature is primarily concerned with the idea of the past and contains otherworldly creatures and exaggerated scenarios (see Shaw's answer, for example), it is understandable that the narratives offer no solutions to the prevailing climate crisis. However, they do raise awareness of the maltreatment of nature and suggest a shift in interpretative perspective and reading practice, focusing on nature's point of view to complement the current urgency and advocacy of environmentalism. Consequently, they manage to establish a positive attitude toward nature within the narrative, which can ultimately be transferred onto the reader, establishing a critical reading. Additionally, the forests' narratives comment on as well as criticize our own behavior toward nature and the environment.

NOTES

1. A similar theoretical background is already published in the article "The Loss of Ancient Forests: An Ecocritical Reading of T. A. Barron's *The Ancient* One" in the annual *Inklings – Jahrbuch für Literatur und Ästhetik* (*Yearbook for Literature and Aesthetic*), vol. 37, 2010, pp. 65–80.

2. This particular scene is open for debate: The fellowship does hear "eerie noises [and] sounds [. . .] of shrill cries, and wild howls of laughter" (Tolkien, *Fellowship* 377) which could suggest someone else is controlling the weather at Caradhras; Tolkien's book suggests Sauron as a potential agent of the storm, whereas Peter Jackson's adaptation (2001) clearly shows Saruman casting his spells. Nevertheless, Aragon "call[s] it the wind" (Tolkien, *Fellowship* 377) and so dismisses the question of human agency in this passage. However, the storm is consistent with the behavior of actual storms within the mountains and the reader is only presented with the fellowship's experience and perception of it so that a clear agency of the mountain Caradhras might actually not be given (cf. Flieger, "Forest and Trees" 101).

3. Wohlleben is criticized by more than one fellow forester for a fairy tale narrative and for anthropomorphizing trees and the forest system, as well as for focusing highly on blaming forestry for the dwindling of the forest. A petition was launched in 2017 by a diverse group of scientists who, although acknowledging the raising awareness of the problematic situation of European forests, disapprove of the fact that "so many people obtain a very unrealistic understanding of forest ecosystems because the statements made here are a conglomerate of half-truths, biased judgements, and wishful thinking derived from very selective and unrepresentative sources of information" (Open Petition, "Even in the Forest"). Nevertheless, Wohlleben manages to raise awareness of the significance of preserving the forest in times of ecological activism and, consequently, his bestseller has been adapted into a documentary shown in cinemas in 2020.

4. With Rachel Carson's *Silent Spring*, published 1962, modern environmental writings as well as literary research has its beginning (cf. Garrard 1; Marland 847). The study discussed frequent instances of the negative interaction of humans with nature and demanded a shift in perspective. In addition to the ecocritical aspect of the time, Le Guin also indicates in her introduction that her novella was a comment on the political situation and American involvement in the Vietnam War (Le Guin, "Introduction" 7–8).

5. This exact statement is spoken by Treebeard in Jackson's *The Two Towers* (2002). By excluding the character of Tom Bombadil from the film adaptation, Jackson added his speech and position toward nature to the character of Treebeard. Although simply due to character reduction, the idea that Treebeard provides the hobbits, and the viewer, with an explanation of the forests' aversion toward anything able to move is a powerful image. Treebeard's anger is visible in his facial expression and his voice when he speaks about the "gnawing, biting, breaking, hacking, burning: destroyers and usurpers." His deep and earthly voice is more rapid and louder, showing an outburst of painful emotions and long suffering by the hands of mankind.

6. A similar depiction of the negative consequences for nature due to industrialization is shown in *The Return of the King* (1954) when the four hobbits return to their Shire only to see it being turned into a chaotic and industrial country. Here as well, witnessing the loss of trees and especially seeing the Party Tree (the center and heart of the Shire) cut down, is the utmost blow for the hobbits and highlights the special place trees have in Tolkien's world and in culture in general (Tolkien, *Return* 360).

7. The tallest coastal redwood, which is also the tallest tree in the world, is Hyperion, with a height of 115.72 m, standing in Redwood National Park, California; the oldest living redwood, which is believed to be around 2,500 years old, has been nicknamed General Sherman and can be found in the Sequoia National Park, California. (Breyer, Lima 15, NPS).

8. The logging of trees and destruction of forests for the benefit of "progress" is not only discussed in Barron's novel but in other texts as well. Tolkien, Lewis, and Paolini repudiate exaggerated industrialization for war industry, Le Guin condemns industrialized logging for powerful corporations on the expanse of nature and the indigenous population, and Shaw equates, as highlighted later in the chapter, the clearing of a forest area for human habitat with the moral corruption of some of his characters.

9. The structure of the novel is interesting as it is divided into four parts which all but one start with three different perspectives on the outburst of the forest the same night. Two of these chapters, all called "The Night the Trees Came," present the reader with the forest's forceful annexation, whereas the last part begins with the perspective of nature in the form of the fantasy creatures, the "whisperers," telling the reader that it was time to act. The third part of the novel, however, focuses on a completely contrasting landscape and idea. The chapter "The Coast" presents the reader with the open sea and signals this part's discussion of their particular differences (especially openness vs. confinement).

WORKS CITED

Barker, Chris. *Cultural Studies: Theory and Practice*, 4th ed. Sage, 2012.
Barry, Peter. *Beginning Theory: An Introduction to Literary and Cultural Theory*, 3rd ed. Manchester U P, 2009.
Barron, T. A. *The Ancient One*. The Berkley Publishing Group, 2004.
Bloch, Maurice. "Why Trees, Too, Are Good to Think With: Towards an Anthropology of the Meaning of Life." In *The Social Life of Trees: Anthropological Perspectives on Tree Symbolism*, edited by Laura Rival. Berg, 1998, pp. 39–55.
Brawley, Chris. *Nature and the Numinous in Mythopoeic Fantasy Literature*. McFarland, 2014.
Breyer, Melissa. "11 Facts about Coast Redwoods, the Tallest Trees in the World." In *Tree Hugger*. Dotdash Publication, 21 May 2020. www.treehugger.com/natural-sciences/11-facts-about-coast-redwoods-worlds-tallest-trees.html. Accessed 04 August 2020.
Buell, Lawrence. *The Future of Environmental Criticism: Environmental Crisis and Literary Imagination*. Blackwell, 2005.
Flieger, Verlyn. "The Forest and the Trees: Sal and Ian in Faerie." In *Tolkien: The Forest and the City*, edited by Helen Conrad-O'Brian and Gerard Hynes. Four Courts Press, 2013, pp. 107–122.
———. "Taking the Part of Trees: Eco-Conflict in Middle-earth." In *J. R. R. Tolkien and His Literary Resonance: Views of Middle-Earth*, edited by George Clark and Daniel Timmons. Greenwood Press, 2000, pp. 147–158.
Foucault, Michel. "Of Other Spaces." *Diacritics*, vol. 16, no. 1, 1986, pp. 22–27.
Garrard, Greg. *Ecocriticism*. Taylor & Francis, 2011.
Garrard, G., et al. "Imagining Anew: Challenges of Representing the Anthropocene." *Environmental Humanities*, vol. 5, 2014, pp. 149–153.
Glotfelty, C. "Introduction: Literary Studies in an Age of Environmental Crisis." In *The Ecocriticism Reader: Landmarks in Literary Ecology*, edited by C. Glotfelty and H. Fromm. U of Georgia P, 1996, pp. xv–xxxvii.
Harrison, R. P. *Forests – Shadows of Civilisation*. U of Chicago P, 1992.
Hovanec, Carol. "Visions of Nature in *The Word for World is Forest*: A Mirror of the American Consciousness." *Extrapolation*, vol. 30, no. 1, 1989, pp. 84–92.
Jeffers, Susan. *Arda Inhabited: Environmental Relations in The Lord of the Rings*. Kent State UP, 2014.
Kern, Robert. "Ecocriticism: What Is It Good For?" In *ISLE Reader*, edited by Michael P. Branch and Scott Slovic. U of Georgia P, 2003, pp. 258–281.
Kerridge, Richard. "Ecocriticism and Environmentalism." In *Literary Theory and Criticism*, edited by Patricia Waugh. Oxford UP, 2006, pp. 530–543.
Kocher, Paul H. *Master of Middle-earth – The Achievement of J. R. R. Tolkien*. Allen and Unwin, 1972.
Konijnendijk, Cecil C. *The Forest and the City: The Cultural Landscape of Urban Woodland*. Springer, 2008.
Le Guin, Ursula K. "Introduction." In *The Eye of the Heron & The Word for World is Forest*. Ursula K. Le Guin, Cox & Wyman, 1991, pp. 5–11.

———. "The Word for World is Forest." In *The Eye of the Heron & The Word for World is Forest*. Ursula K. Le Guin, Cox & Wyman, 1991, pp. 171–301.
Lewis, C. S. *The Chronicles of Narnia*. Harper Collins, 2011.
Lima, Manuel. *The Book of Trees: Visualizing Branches of Knowledge*. Princeton Architectural Press, 2014.
Lowenthal, David. "Origins of Anthropocene Awareness." *The Anthropocene Review*, vol. 3, no. 1, 2015, pp. 52–63.
Manlove, C. N. "On the Nature of Fantasy." In *The Aesthetics of Fantasy Literature and Art*, edited by Roger Schlobin. Notre Dame UP, 1982, pp. 16–35.
Marland, Pippa. "Ecocriticism." *Literature Compass*, vol. 10–11, 2013, pp. 846–868.
National Park Service. "The General Sherman Tree." *National Park Service*, 22 June 2020. www.nps.gov/seki/learn/nature/sherman.htm. Accessed 04 August 2020.
Open Petition. "Even in the Forest, It's Facts We Want Instead of Fairy Tales." *Open Petition*, 14 August 2018. www.openpetition.de/petition/online/even-in-the-forest-its-facts-we-want-instead-of-fairy-tales. Accessed 04 August 2020.
Paolini, Christopher. *Eldest*. Corgi Books, 2011.
———. *Brisingr*. Corgi Books, 2009.
Park, Bum Jim, et al. "The Physiological Effects of Shinrin-yoku (Taking in the Forest Atmosphere or Forest Bathing): Evidence from Field Experiments in 24 Forests across Japan." *Environmental Health and Preventive Medicine*, vol. 15, 2010, pp. 18–26.
Rival, Laura. "Trees, from Symbols of Life and Regeneration to Political Artefacts." In *The Social Life of Trees: Anthropological Perspectives on Tree Symbolism*, edited by Laura Rival. Berg, 1998, pp. 1–36.
Rowling, J. K. *Harry Potter and the Chamber of Secrets*. Bloomsbury, 2014.
Secretariat of the Convention on Biological Diversity (CBD). "The Value of Forest Ecosystems." *CBD Technical Series*, no. 4, 2001.
"See How Nature is Reclaiming Abandoned Spaces Around the World." *Lonely Planet*, 15 March 2018. www.lonelyplanet.com/articles/see-how-nature-in-reclaiming-man-made-spaces-around-the-world. Accessed 04 August 2020.
Shaw, Ali. *The Trees*. Bloomsbury, 2016.
Steffen, Will, et al. "The Anthropocene: Conceptual and Historical Perspectives." *Philosophical Transactions of the Royal Society*, vol. 369, 2011, pp. 842–867.
Syvitski, James. "Anthropocene: An Epoch of our Making." *Global Change*, vol. 78, 2012, pp. 12–15.
Tolkien, J. R. R. *The Letters of J. R. R. Tolkien*, edited by Humphrey Carpenter. Harper Collins, 2006.
———. *The Fellowship of the Rings*, 4th ed. Unwin Paperbacks, 1981.
———. *The Two Towers*, 4th ed. Unwin Paperbacks, 1981.
———. *The Return of the King*, 4th ed. Unwin Paperbacks, 1981.
———. *The Silmarillion*, edited by Christopher Tolkien. Unwin Paperbacks, 1979.
The Two Towers. Directed by Peter Jackson, 2002. New Line Cinema, 2003.
Watson, Ian. "The Forest as Metaphor for Mind: 'The Word for World Is Forest' and 'Vaster than Empires and More Slow'." *Science Fiction Studies*, vol. 2, no. 3, 1975, pp. 231–237.
Wohlleben, Peter. *The Hidden Lives of Trees*. Greystone Books, 2015.

Chapter 4

The Fantasy of Wilderness

Reconfiguring Heroism in the Anthropocene, Facing the Age of Ecocentrism

Lykke Guanio-Uluru

This chapter discusses how the Anthropocene reconfigures the interpretation of heroism in speculative fiction, based on close readings of Stephenie Meyer's *Twilight* series (2005–2008) and Scott Westfield's *Uglies* (2005). Both works compare and contrast a lifestyle in consumerist opulence with an alternative "myth of the wild," making them interesting texts for comparison from an ecocritical perspective. In *Twilight*, Meyer's vampires are both dangerous predators and high-end consumers—a lethal combination that the series' heroine aspires to. In Westerfield's dystopian *Uglies*, human nature is subdued as teenagers are surgically modified to enjoy life as an endless party. However, the protagonist escapes surveillance and control by joining a dissident group that survives in the wild. In the course of Westerfield's series, the habitual dystopian critique of totalitarian regimes acquires an ecocritical spin as life in the wild is both glorified and problematized, while governmental agency is justified on the grounds of wilderness conservation.

Drawing on ecocriticism, and particularly on Greg Garrard's (2012) discussion of the topos of wilderness as it is formulated in American environmentalism, this chapter examines the deployment of the wilderness topos in the two narratives. In both works, the wilderness is posited as an ideal that is sought and embodied by the stories' main characters, and their larger-than-life heroism is formulated in terms of their relationship to wilderness. With reference to the transhumanist ideas of Nick Bostrom (2003; 2005; 2013), the chapter further discusses the conversion of both series' protagonists to superhuman in regard to the concept of the Anthropocene.

CLARIFYING THE TERM "ANTHROPOCENE"

The past fifty years have seen the gradual development and expansion of the field of ecocriticism, with Rachel Carson's *Silent Spring* (1962) as an often-cited seed of origin (Garrard 1). Equally important has been Arne Naess's formulation of deep ecology in the 1970s, made more widely available in English in the 1980s (Naess 1989). Critical posthumanism, with Donna Haraway as an early and important theorist (1991; 2008; 2016), has contributed significantly to a still ongoing rethinking of the concept of the human, in relation both to gender and to technology, as have Rosi Braidotti (2013) and N. Katherine Hayles (1999; 2017).

By now, ecocriticism and deep ecology have established that anthropocentrism, the placing of humans at the center of the universe, is not an ideological position that tends to promote care for the wider environment. Central to Western culture, anthropocentrism has allowed us to treat land, plants, and animals as subservient to human needs and interest. The result is that humans have multiplied to the detriment of other species. Due to rapid and ongoing industrialization, the pollution of land, water sources, and the atmosphere has now reached a level where it affects the planetary ecosystems, causing widespread species extinction (Kolbert 2014; Wilson 2017). The situation has led to the proposal that we have entered a new geological epoch, the Anthropocene, where human impact is such that it alters the global environment. The term *Anthropocene* was first used by ecologist Eugene Stormer in the 1980s and adopted by atmospheric chemist Paul Crutzen, who in the early 2000s proposed it as the name of a new geological epoch, marked by human geological influence (Haraway, *Staying with the Trouble* 44). While widely adopted, the term has its critics, not least because it manages to yet again place humanity center stage in the story of the earth's evolution. While Haraway prefers the term *Capitalocene*, identifying capitalism as a driving force behind the current environmental destruction, she concedes that the term *Anthropocene* is already well established and that it is, to some, less controversial than the term Capitalocene (Haraway, *Staying with the Trouble* 47). This chapter adopts the term Anthropocene, which is now in common use, while acknowledging its problematic aspects.

While both these terms, the Anthropocene and the Capitalocene, identify large-scale problems that we are currently facing, they also subtly direct our thinking in relation to these problems. Both terms are anthropocentric in that they establish humans as the main agents of global and geological change. Additionally, as noted by Adam Trexler, "Anthropocene" is "*anticipatory*, indicating humanity's *probable impacts* on geophysical and biological systems for millennia to come" (1, my emphasis). Thus, the use of the term

Anthropocene projects a vision of the earth as deeply impacted by human activity into the far future.

Clearly, our choice of terms matters to our respond-ability, since it impacts how we conceptualize our present situation. Thus, an appellation that subtly directs us toward potential solutions rather than toward perpetuation of the same doom might be more constructive than the two terms discussed above, even if they are diagnostically accurate. Relabeling the present epoch as the Age of Ecocentrism challenges us to imagine our world as one where all living organisms have intrinsic value, regardless of their value or importance to humans. It redirects our focus and prompts us to remember that all biological organisms have an *umwelt* (Uexküll) that we need to consider in day-to-day activities as well as in long-term plans. This label thus feeds into Haraway's view of the earth as a symbiogenetic "becoming-together" of all kinds of creatures and critters (*Staying with the Trouble*), while reminding us that humans are but a part of the intricate web of life on earth.

Departing from an analysis of Garrard's conception of wilderness as it plays out in the *Twilight* series, this chapter goes on to discuss how the valuation of the central heroic transformation of Meyer's series, as Bella turns into a vampire, is reconfigured when read through an anthropocentric lens. While *Twilight* is a paranormal romance (Kaveney 215), borrowing from both gothic literature and the romance genre, *Uglies* is best classed as dystopian science fiction. Even if the novels belong to different subgenres of fantasy, the value arguments of both works are formulated in relation to the white American conception of the wilderness as discussed by Garrard (2012). In *Uglies*, the protagonist, Tally, is already a transhuman subject at the start of the series, and the chapter proceeds to examine how the transformed identities of the female main characters of both series neatly map onto Bostrom's transhumanist vision. Discussing the problematic aspects of transhumanism from an environmentalist viewpoint and in relation to the Anthropocene, the chapter ends by considering both narratives from the (future) perspective of an Age of Ecocentrism.

TWILIGHT AND "THE TAMING OF THE BEAST"

According to Garrard, wilderness, construed as "nature in a state uncontaminated by civilization," is a potent figure of American environmentalism (66). Discussing the concept, Garrard contrasts the topos of the pastoral, pertaining to long-settled, domesticated landscapes, with the trope of wilderness that "fits the settler experience in the New Worlds—particularly the United States, Canada and Australia—with their apparently untamed landscapes and the sharp distinction between the forces of culture and nature" (67). This conception of the landscapes of the "New Worlds" as marked by a "sharp distinction" between culture and nature is, of course, framed from a colonialist perspective that masks the already established presence of indigenous populations in these territories, all with their differing nature–culture relationships.

Tracing the historical origins of the concept of wilderness and its development from a Western cultural perspective, Garrard notes that the word "wilderness" is derived from the Anglo-Saxon "wilddeoren," an expression that originally designated a place replete with untamed beasts "beyond the boundaries of cultivation" (67). Such a distinction is meaningful to people with an agricultural economy and while its basic meaning has changed little in the course of time, it has more recently "attracted new connotations" (67). In the Anthropocene, a reversal of the conception of the wilderness as threatening is becoming apparent, since wilderness areas are now under threat from human civilization rather than the other way around. As Stephenie Meyer's *Twilight* series draws heavily on the American conception of wilderness, this recent Anthropocene reversal affects the value connotations of the series in a way not anticipated by Meyer.

Given the development of the settler-defined concept of wilderness as "a touchstone of American cultural identity" (Garrard 74), the importance of wilderness to the articulation of the heroine's reconfigured sense of self in the *Twilight* series is hardly surprising. The question is just whom this American sense of cultural identity includes—and excludes. The saga is set in the rain-drenched town of Forks in western Washington, located on the Olympic Peninsula that stretches across the Puget Sound from Seattle. The Peninsula hosts temperate rainforests and several national salmon rivers and national parks. Thus, Meyer locates her vampire series in a national "wilderness," her story involving a version of the local conflict between the indigenous American Indian population, the Quileute, and the area's white settlers. The Quileute tribe currently lives on reservation land on the western coast of the Peninsula, and the main town of this area, La Push, features in Meyer's fiction. Several critics have pointed to racially problematic aspects of Meyer's series relative to the working out of the narrative's conflict over land (Jensen; Leggatt and Burnett; B. Burke; Guanio-Uluru). Arguably, a cross-cultural conflict is deeply embedded in the American cultural conception of the term "wilderness." The historical sediments of this conception are revealed through Meyer's fiction that is configured in terms of a dichotomy between "civilization" and "wilderness."

The story is narrated in the first person and focalized through Bella Swan (or "beautiful swan"). It draws on several fairy tale templates. Its protagonist falls in love with a centuries-old vampire who desires to draw her blood, thus alluding both to the Dracula myth and the story of the beauty and the beast. Conceiving of herself as an "ugly duckling," Bella eventually finds her true beauty with wealthy vampire Edward Cullen as her Prince Charming. This sparkling prize is not handed to her on a plate, however. As Sara Buttsworth points out, quoting Jacques Zipes (27), this is a "survival tale with hope" (Buttsworth 49). Staying at home in Forks, modestly running her father's household in true Cinderella fashion, Bella must fend off waves of vampire attacks and the romantic advances of Quileute suitor Jacob, whom she considers her best friend but whom she does little to care for. All her attention is vested in the mesmerizing but paternalizing Edward Cullen, who has the wealth, looks, and immortality that Bella aspires to. While Jacob is seemingly her equal, mending motorbikes and taking care of his invalid father at the Quileute reservation, he obviously cannot compete with Cullen's fairy tale glory.

Judith Leggatt and Kristin Burnett note how the romantic rivalry between Edward and Jacob over Bella is entwined with an ancient dispute over land rights, where "the supernatural treaty in Twilight is a literary parallel to the historic Treaty of Olympia, and the saga offers a lens through which to examine the treaty, its historical significance and the present-day implications and understandings of such an agreement" (27). In the playing out in the *Twilight* saga of this historical treaty negotiation, "Bella represents the land, Jacob embodies the Quileute people, and Edward Cullen stands in for the newcomers" (27). Reading the saga thus, as a historical allegory, Leggatt and Burnett argue that while Meyer's saga falsifies historical realities in having both parties respect their treaty (which in reality was broken by the white settlers), it accords with reality in that the newcomer usurps the land and the Quileute must transfer his affections elsewhere (27–28).

The battle between "civilization" and "wilderness" in the *Twilight* saga rages both between and within each character, however. While Edward Cullen and his vampire coven take pride in their ability to choose a "vegetarian" diet, consisting of wild game rather than human beings, they must all struggle with their "inner beast" in order to control their instincts and their urge to draw human blood. Battling his desire to bite Bella, Edward consequently roams the American wilderness, killing and draining animal prey. In *Twilight*, he goes to Alaska (237) specifically to this end. While he does not, on that occasion, disclose what species he feeds on, he elsewhere notes that his favorite prey is the mountain lion, which, according to the Alaska Department of Fish and Game, is rare in this area (Woodford). The mountain lion is registered globally in the category "least concern" on the IUCN Red List of Threatened Species. However, Edward's hunting takes on a new meaning in the Anthropocene, as it constitutes a threat to a wilderness increasingly under pressure.[1] Isla Myers-Smith has calculated the environmental cost of vampire predation more exactly as:

> Immortal predators will exact a continuous predation pressure on populations of large mammals along the West Coast. If each Cullen vampire is feeding on 4-12

cougars or grizzly bears per year (a conservative estimate based on the novels, I might add), this is a substantial annual harvest. (Myers-Smith, qtd. in McElroy and McElroy 86)

Since in the Anthropocene humans rather than "wilddeoren" constitute the greatest threat for survival on a global level, the Cullens' dietary preferences, while perhaps humane, do not come across quite as ethically admirable as Meyer intends. Rather, the changing connotations taken on by the concept of wilderness in the Anthropocene undermine her ethical argument, which is founded on a now outmoded construction.

Bella's contending suitor Jacob must also strive to reign his inner beast, as he starts to "phase" into a gigantic wolf to protect the Quileute territory—a transformation sparked by the entrance of the Cullens into the area. Reading the series as a historical allegory, the region's local Quileute inhabitants are reframed as "wild beasts" by the (deadly white) newcomers, thus highlighting the colonial perspective embedded in the (white) American concept of wilderness. Before he learns to control his shape-shifting, Jacob too represents a potential danger to Bella—but this is an "old-fashioned" danger: the danger of the "wilddeouren" living outside the boundaries of the white civilization that Edward Cullen, with his grand piano and expensive mansion, represents. Living closer to the land, Jacob, like the local environment, suffers from the presence of vampires in Forks.

TWILIGHT'S JET-SET HEROISM

In ecological terms, Jacob is less of a threat than the fashion-forward Cullens, who are cast as high-end consumers. Living in relative poverty on indigenous reservation land, Jacob's carbon footprint is considerably smaller than that of the Cullen clan, who own a garage full of fast cars that they like to drive as an "indulgence." While Edward says things such as "the wasting of finite resources is everyone's business" (*Twilight* 71) and "we have to be careful not to impact the environment with injudicious hunting" (188), his general, opulent lifestyle displays few traces of environmental concern. In practice, his environmental attitudes seem but skin deep. As James McElroy and Emma Catherine McElroy have pointed out, the Cullens "feature as speciate vamps with insouciant, middle-class values and tastes. The fact that they purchase but never eat generous servings of cafeteria food is just one more no-no when it comes to looking at their carbon footprints" (85). This practice also looks bad from the viewpoint of food waste reduction.

The bulk of the *Twilight* narrative is concerned with Bella's negotiation and choice between the different sets of values and lifestyles represented by

Edward and Jacob—without acknowledging that the choice has environmental consequences. Discussing the way in which Meyer has appropriated and reworked Quileute Indian legends, Kristian Jensen notes: "Meyer's vampires and shape-shifter mythology reconstitutes the Enlightenment dialectic of the mentally advanced and providentially dominant Europeans, and the primitive, though pure and noble, indigenous man" (101). From an environmentalist perspective, Jacob is definitively more advanced than Edward, whose wealth allows him to indulge his penchant for fast and expensive cars.

Trexler has pointed out how suspense novels are "all but unimaginable without fast cars and jets, which are some of the most efficient engines invented for generating greenhouse gas emissions" (13) and the Cullens' high-end lifestyle, which is so attractive to Bella, is made up in equal measure from old-style colonial wealth (with its problematic connotations of exploitation of labor and racism) and of a celebration of James Bond-like adventure, where the power of fast engines is a central trope.

Bella's gradual conversion from a stay-at-home, domesticated Cinderella to a fast, lethal, and wealthy vampire may read as an empowering female coming-of-age story (Guanio-Uluru 231), but Bella's empowerment, and subsequent transition from a moderate to a high-end consumer lifestyle, take on a different meaning in the Anthropocene. While Trexler concedes that "it is difficult to condense the distributed, impersonal causes of global warming into a climate villain" (14), this might be where Meyer, unintentionally, has succeeded. Even as Bella's Cinderella-script transformation from an underprivileged to an affluent lifestyle may previously have seemed like a desirable empowerment, her shift is formulated through the patterns of overconsumption that drive climate change. This, to the environmentally conscious reader, repositions Meyer's vampire heroes, despite her intent, in their classical role as villains.

UGLIES: THE ECOLOGICAL EXPENSE OF FREE WILL

While *Twilight* may be read through an ecocritical lens, Scott Westerfield's *Uglies* much more explicitly engages with posthuman and environmental concerns. The story's main characters are literally reconfigured—through biotechnology and cosmetic surgery. A science fiction story, the setting in *Uglies* is fictional, with the main locations named Uglyville, New Pretty Town and, further afield, the Smoke, a forested wilderness area. Uglyville is where everyone lives until the age of sixteen, when they undergo surgery, having their faces crushed and remodeled with plastic composites to become Pretties. Pretties all live in New Pretty Town, attending perpetual parties. In fact, the whole population is age-segregated, with separate areas assigned for the middle-aged Middle Pretties and the older Late Pretties. The boundaries between the separate sections are under surveillance so that the perimeters of one's world are clearly defined.

The story is narrated in the third person and focalized through Tally, initially an "ugly" looking forward to having the remodeling operation so she can rejoin her friends across the river, in New Pretty Town. Sneaking out one night to spy on the Pretties, she befriends Shay, who teaches her to hoverboard and shows her a world beyond the perimeters of the city: "The forest to either side was a black void full of wild and ancient trees, nothing like the generic carbon-dioxide suckers that decorated the city" (*Uglies* 54). Thus, the story pits the well-groomed and carefully controlled environment of Tally's world against a conception of wilderness as existing "beyond the boundaries of cultivation" (Garrard 67). Following Tally, the reader gradually becomes acquainted with this wilderness, sharply segregated from the controlled and modeled environment of the city. In contrast, the wilderness allows beings—be they humans, plants, or animals—to *take their own shape*. The story's ethical argument thus echoes a Romantic view of nature as the true educator, a view influentially developed by Jean-Jacques Rousseau in *Emile—or On Education* (1763), where the child ideally is kept away from the city to grow up in free interaction with pastoral nature (Nyrnes 77). Shay tries to convince Tally that the runaway society of the Smoke, situated in this wider wilderness, is the better place to be:

> "It's not like here, Tally. They don't separate everyone, uglies from pretties, new and middle and late. And you can leave whenever you want, go wherever you want."
>
> "Like where?"
>
> "Anywhere, Ruins, the forest, the sea. And . . . you never have to have the operation." (*Uglies* 86)

Tally is not convinced, leaving Shay to run away without her. However, on the day that Tally is about to have her operation, she is called in for interrogation by Special Circumstances (SC), who control the movements of everyone in the city. Thus, *Uglies* develops an ecological twist on the classical dystopian set-up where the protagonists must combat a totalitarian regime. While the head of SC is frightening, her rationale for the policing is based on concern for the environment:

> Dr. Cable narrowed her eyes, her face becoming even more like a predator's. "We exist in equilibrium with our environment, Tally, purifying the water that we put back, in the river, recycling the biomass, and using only power drawn from our own solar footprint. But sometimes we cannot purify what we take in

from the outside. Sometimes there are threats from the environment that must be faced." (*Uglies* 103–104)

Thus, surveillance and government control work within the story to curtail individual freedom in order to preserve an environmental equilibrium, maintained by keeping people and wilderness strictly separated—just as sharply divided as they are in the (white) American cultural imagination. Told that she will stay ugly until she cooperates, Tally eventually agrees to go after Shay to help SC locate the rebel society of the Smoke that is conceived of as an environmental threat. Following the cryptic instructions on a note left by Shay, Tally consequently travels into the wild in pursuit, passing the ruins of the "Rusties," which are traces of our contemporary civilization—a culture described as "wasteful" (139) in its love of metal and concrete, the remnants of which are still scarring the countryside centuries later. Making her way through unknown territory, Tally learns to respect and love the wilderness:

> Mountains rose up on her right, tall enough that snowcapped their tops even in the early autumn chill. Tally had always thought of the city as huge, a whole world in itself, but the scale of everything out here was so much grander. And so beautiful. She could see why people used to live out in nature, even if there weren't any party towers or mansions. Or even dorms. (*Uglies* 147)

Besides invoking Burke's (1757) notion of the sublime, the description here actualizes Garrard's remark that "the ideal wilderness space is wholly pure by virtue of its independence from humans, but the ideal wilderness narrative posits a human subject whose most authentic experience is located precisely there" (78). Coasting across the landscape on her hoverboard, subsisting on dehydrated foods, her survival aided by her advanced technological equipment, Tally's journey exemplifies the kind of wilderness experience that Garrard argues is central to deep ecological philosophy—an experience that "risks identification with privileged leisure pursuits that sell authenticity while mystifying the industrialized consumerism that makes them possible" (78). If wilderness is nature devoid of human presence—as is, according to Garrard, the case in much American nature writing—then how can humans survive sustainably in the wild? In *Uglies,* this question is played out in relation to the inhabitants of the Smoke.

When she first arrives, after a strenuous journey, Tally finds that "[t]he Smoke really was smokey" (*Uglies* 186). The valley community comprises around twenty-one story wooden buildings, some with solar panels. There are wooden walkways and several open fires, as well as numerous garden plots. When Tally spots tree stumps at the edge of the settlement she is horrified: "Trees. . ," she whispers in horror. "You cut down trees" (187). Shay assures her that the damage is local: "It seems weird at first, but it's the way the pre-Rusties lived too, you know? And we're planting more on the other side of the mountain" (187). Tally is only half convinced and imagines all the people in her city "let loose in the countryside below, cutting down trees and killing things for food, crashing across the landscape like some risen Rusty machine" (199). This image of human destruction of the environment echoes an Anthropocene perspective and justifies the words of the SC head that "Humanity is a cancer and we are the cure" (263)—a stance that may be labeled as a preservationist view of the wild.

Notably, only certain species seem worthy of Tally's consideration. She soon takes part in prising loose old railroad tracks from masses of vines, without ever flinching as these plants are pulled out of the ground and cast aside. Arguably, this harms the vines as much as cutting down trees harms trees. The difference is that vines are smaller plants—and that they are not used for anything, as is the wood, but simply discarded. Later, Tally learns that the people in the Smoke act like conservationists, "killing only species that didn't belong in this part of the world or that had gotten out of control thanks to the Rusties' meddling" (220). This is an anthropocentric position in the sense that it implies that humans are the agents responsible both for altering the environment and for bringing it back to its "rightful" state. Furthermore, it suggests a somewhat static view of environmental processes that in reality depend on continual adaptation and change.

Tally is unaccustomed to the use of animals for food and clothing—practices she observes in the Smoke. In regard to the treatment of animals, Ursula Heise distinguishes between the approach of the animal welfare movement that is concerned with individual animals at risk and that of environmentalists, who are "generally committed to species rather than individuals" and seek to protect a wide range of species, plants, fungi, and microorganisms included, up to complex ecosystems (135–136). The inhabitants of the Smoke take an environmentalist approach in that they are concerned about protecting the species of trees, planting new trees when they cut down individual trees. They also hunt with reference to species: "only species that didn't belong in this part of the world" (*Uglies* 220). Heise notes: "To environmentalists, sustainable hunting is merely the human variant of predation, one of the most basic processes in ecological food webs" (136). Tally's environmental views initially are at odds with such a species-oriented outlook.

Tally is conditioned to exist in a carefully controlled environment. Her initial reaction to the use of wood and of animals for food in the Smoke suggests that she is habituated to consider human violence toward (certain) other life forms problematic. Her orientation is thus not fully anthropocentric. Her reluctance to harming individuals of (certain) plant and (most?) animal species aligns her with the focus on individuals identified by Heise as typical of the animal rights movement. For Tally, however, this sensitivity toward harming others extends to trees. The recognition that individuals of (certain) other species are valuable in themselves, and not just there for humans to use as they see fit, moves her outlook toward an ecocentric perspective, as framed from an Age of Ecocentrism. However, choosing to stay on, she soon falls in with the ways of the Smoke community.

The novel does not disclose or discuss in any detail what the basis of subsistence is in Tally's city, except that she seems used to a vegetarian diet—the "meat" in her dehydrated travel food is "soy-based" (*Uglies* 231). At the same time, her city is clearly dependent on a lot of sophisticated technology, the material basis of which is never explained. Thus, her civilization's practical relationship to nature and natural resources is hard to pin down. However, it seems to operate with a conception of wilderness where any human activity represents a "contamination" of the natural space. The premise of Tally's city culture is that humans are akin to a pest, which must be kept under careful control so as not to take over. Hence the operation at sixteen, which stunts human reasoning to make everyone content with an existence in carefully controlled small enclaves or cities, leaving the rest of the world "uncontaminated by civilization" (Garrard 66). As the doctor who discloses the truth about the mind-altering operation to Tally puts it, the Rusties were clearly "crazy" as they almost destroyed the world, something that "convinced people to pull the cities back from the wild, to leave nature alone" (*Uglies* 254). Considering the destructive behavior of the Rusties, that is, contemporary humanity, the argument seems persuasive. Still, during her stay in the wild Tally adopts the conservationist views of the Smoke community, and the book ends as she commits to undergoing the operation so that the Smoke's doctor can test a cure she has developed for reversing its effects. The ending thus suggests that human freedom of mind trumps the preservation of an untouched wilderness, presenting human freedom as the highest good. In other words, Tally seems to move from an ecocentric to a more anthropocentric attitude in the course of *Uglies*.

TRANSHUMAN HEROINES

Elsewhere (Guanio-Uluru), I have argued that Bella's transformation from a slow and clumsy human to a fast and hyperaware vampire quite neatly maps onto Bostrom's transhumanist vision—except that her means of transformation is vampire venom rather than biotechnology. According to Bostrom, transhumanism is a loosely defined movement seeking to understand and evaluate "the opportunities for enhancing the human condition and the human organism opened up by the advancement of technology" ("Human Genetic Enhancements" 493). The posthuman subject of Bostrom's vision has "greater clarity of mind," more vivid experiences, and feels "a deeper warmth and affection" for those they love ("Why I Want" 31), all thanks to technological enhancements.

Francesca Ferrando places transhumanism under the umbrella term of the posthuman, while arguing that transhumanism does not "fully engage with a critical and historical account of the human" (28). Such a revision of the concept of the human has been undertaken by critical posthumanism, with Haraway (1991; 2008), Wolfe (2010), and Braidotti (2013) as notable contributors. Bostrom agrees that he is not revisionist in this sense: "I see my position as a conservative extension of traditional ethics and values to accommodate the possibility of human enhancement through technological means" ("Why I Want" 32). His position is further conservative in the sense that it advocates access to privilege based on wealth, while dismissing issues of social inequality: "The non-privileged would remain as people are today but perhaps deprived of their self-respect and suffering occasional bouts of envy" ("Human Genetic Enhancements" 500). Survival of the wealthiest, in other words, and with unlimited funds, Edward Cullen certainly fits the bill.

The transhumanist longing for "superpowers" is probably as ancient as humanity, since the oldest surviving work of literature, the *Epic of Gilgamesh*, portrays a king with unrivaled strength that defies death. The acquisition of superhuman abilities is a staple of fantasy and superhero fiction, and Bostrom traces the sources of transhumanist inspiration all the way from *Gilgamesh*, via the alchemist tradition, Enlightenment thinking, and Friedrich Nietzsche's Übermensch to science fiction ("History"). Transhumanism thus very consciously taps into this rich and storied vein of human longing, from whence its persuasive and mythical force derives. Bostrom speculates that technology now allows us to "overcome some of our basic biological limits" ("Human Genetic Enhancements" 494) and this is precisely Bella's aim in *Twilight*. According to Bostrom:

> The enhancement options being discussed [by transhumanists] include radical extension of human health span, eradication of disease, elimination of unnecessary suffering, and augmentation of human intellectual, physical and emotional capacities. ("Human Genetic Enhancements" 493)

While this sounds enticing, Bostrom fails to offer any specification of what kinds of suffering he considers unnecessary but calls for a discussion of "which parts of ourselves we might be willing to sacrifice" (495) on our way to embodying the transhuman ideal, since it will involve becoming someone radically other than a current human being.

Drawing heavily on Anne Rice's *Interview with the Vampire* (1976), Meyer envisions Bella's vampire awakening as the acquiring of augmented sensory capability and superhuman speed and strength (Guanio-Uluru 201–202). Tally, too, undergoes a similar transformation. In the third volume of Westerfield's series, Tally is forced to join SC and is surgically modified to perform as a Special. Thus, she too ends up super strong, superfast, and lethal, with augmented senses: "From her training, Tally knew that she could close her eyes and use the merest echoes to navigate the forest blind, like a bat following its own chirps" (*Specials* 6). As humanity continually is pushing against new technological boundaries, the border between speculative fiction and real possibility is becoming fuzzier. But what is the environmental cost of the transhumanist vision—how does transhumanism relate to the realizations of the Anthropocene?

TRANSHUMANISM IN THE ANTHROPOCENE— AND IN THE AGE OF ECOCENTRISM

The short answer is that it does not. The word "Anthropocene" is not mentioned a single time in *The Transhumanist Reader* (More and Vita-More), despite its relatively recent publication date in 2013, nor is the word "environment." The only two (out of forty-two) contributions that discuss "nature" consider it to be nothing but a metaphor. Roy Ascott writes: "Nature is, of course, all metaphor: the good, the pure, the unadulterated, the whole. It speaks of innocence, a kind of blessed naivety, as well as the wild, the unspoilt, and the instinctive" (438).[2] Max More addresses "Mother Nature" as: "Mother nature, truly we are grateful for what you have made us. No doubt you did the best you could. However, with all due respect, we must say that you have in many ways done a poor job with the human constitution" (449). In transhumanist terms, nature is either illusionary or something that needs improving upon. Transhumanism has no time for frailty but regards the human body like a machine that may be tinkered with to boost its performance, much like Jacob tinkers with his motorbikes. To transhumanists, the wider environment is a non-issue, as they look past organic reality to ground their sense of self in technological possibility. They still need to eat and breathe, however. While they dream of the future, their ideas of the human are not up to date, but map onto the Renaissance ideal man, long since exposed as blinkered, gender- and ethno-centric by feminist and postcolonial thinkers. Transhumanists seem to devalue nature, as well as their own human nature, and fail to acknowledge the cost of technological development to the natural world (mining, overexploitation of natural resources, pollution). Projecting an image of the human as the master of biological processes, transhumanists close their eyes to their own biological vulnerability, even as they are still members of the human species, dependent upon the natural environment.

While sharing the transhumanist vision of the superhuman, both *Twilight* and *Uglies* remain in touch with organic realities, which are represented above all by the concept of the wild. In *Twilight*, Bella must choose between the "man of the land" Jacob, and her sparkly fantasy hero Edward. While she chooses the latter, it is not without a struggle. In *Uglies*, too, the technologically enhanced characters must make sense in and of the natural world—the wilderness that exists outside of human control and that which represents true freedom. Thus, in both *Twilight* and *Uglies* the world remains larger than the human and is, to some extent, unpredictable. It is this unruly dimension that is lost in the transhumanist representation of reality, rendering it rather sterile.

Thus, transhumanism is completely at odds with the Age of Ecocentrism—its field of vision encompasses only the human. The literary views of the human potential represented in *Twilight* and *Uglies* are richer and more complex than those of academic transhumanism because they encompass other species as well as environments that are not human made and controlled. Consequently, the characters remain in dialogue with the natural world, deriving their self-understanding from the basis of this interaction of the human and other-than-human that is fundamental to an ecocentric perspective.

NOTES

1. Adam Trexler (2015) has pointed out how the staples of genre fiction take on new meanings in the Anthropocene, without problematizing the term.
2. The premise must be that if consciousness can exist apart from the organic body, the organic body is dispensable.

WORKS CITED

Ascott, Roy. "Back to Nature II: Art and Technology in the Twenty-First Century." In *The Transhumanist Reader*, edited by Max More and Natasha Vita-More. John Wiley & Sons, 2013, pp. 438–448.

Bostrom, Nick. "A History of Transhumanist Thought." *Journal of Evolution and Technology*, vol. 14, no. 1, 2005, pp. 1–25.

———. "Human Genetic Enhancements: A Transhumanist Perspective." *Journal of Value Inquiry*, vol. 37, no. 4, 2003, pp. 493–506.

———. "Why I Want to Be a Posthuman When I Grow Up." In *The Transhumanist Reader*, edited by Max More and Natasha Vita-More. John Wiley & Sons, 2013, pp. 28–53.

Braidotti, Rosi. *The Posthuman*. Polity Press, 2013.

Burke, Brianna. "The Great American Love Affair: Indians in the Twilight Saga." In *Bringing Light to Twilight: Perspectives on the Pop Culture Phenomenon*, edited by Giselle Liza Anatol. Palgrave Macmillan, 2011, pp. 207–220.

Burke, Edward. *A Philosophical Enquiry into the Origin of Our Ideas of the Sublime and the Beautiful, 1757*, 2nd ed., edited by Paul Guyer. Oxford World's Classics, 2015.

Buttsworth, Sarah. "Cinderbella: Twilight, Fairy Tales, and the Twenty-First Century American Dream." In *Twilight and History*, edited by Nancy R. Reagin. John Wily & Sons, 2010, pp. 47–69.

Carson, Rachel. *Silent Spring, 1963*. Penguin Classics, 2000.

Epic of Gilgamesh. Translated by Andrew George. Penguin Classics, 2003.

Ferrando, Francesca. "Posthumanism, Transhumanism, Antihumanism, Metahumanism, and New Materialisms: Differences and Relations." *Existenz*, vol. 8, no. 2, 2013, pp. 22–32.

Garrard, Greg. *Ecocriticism*. Routledge, 2012.

Guanio-Uluru, Lykke. *Ethics and Form in Fantasy Literature: Tolkien, Rowling and Meyer*. Palgrave Macmillan, 2015.

Haraway, Donna J. *Simians, Cyborgs and Women: The Reinvention of Nature*. Routledge, 1991.

———. *Staying with the Trouble: Making Kin in the Chthulucene*. Duke UP, 2016.

———. *When Species Meet*. U of Minnesota P, 2008.

Hayles, N. Katherine. *How We Became Posthuman: Virtual Bodies in Cybernetics, Literature and Informatics*. U of Chicago P, 1999.

———. *Unthought: The Power of the Cognitive Nonconsious*. U of Chicago P, 2017.

Heise, Ursula. *Imagining Extinction: The Cultural Meanings of Endangered Species*. U of Chicago P, 2016.

Jensen, Kristian. "Noble Werewolves or Native Shape-Shifters?" In *The Twilight Mystique: Critical Essays on the Novels and Films*, edited by Amy M. Clarke and Marijane Osborn. McFarland & Company, 2010, pp. 92–106.

Kaveney, Roz. "Dark Fantasy and Paranormal Romance." In *The Cambridge Companion to Fantasy Literature*, edited by Edward James and Farah Mendlesohn. Cambridge UP, 2012, pp. 214–223.

Kolbert, Elizabeth. *The Sixth Extinction. An Unnatural History*. Bloomsbury Publishing, 2014.

Leggatt, Judith, and Kristin Burnett. "Biting Bella: Treaty Negotiation, Quileute History, and Why 'Team Jack' Is Doomed to Lose." In *Twilight and History*, edited by Nancy R. Reagin. John Wily & Sons, 2010, pp. 26–46.

McElroy, James, and Emma Katherine McElroy. "Eco-Gothics for the Twenty-First Century." In *The Twilight Mystique: Critical Essays on the Novels and Films*, edited by Amy M. Clarke and Marijane Osborn. McFarland, 2010, pp. 80–91.

Meyer, Stephenie. *Breaking Dawn*. Atom, 2012.

———. *Eclipse*. Atom, 2012.

———. *New Moon*. Atom, 2012.

———. *Twilight*. Atom, 2012.

More, Max, and Natasha Vita-More, eds. *The Transhumanist Reader*. John Wiley & Sons, 2013.

More, Max. "A Letter to Mother Nature." In *The Transhumanist Reader*, edited by Max More and Natasha Vita-More. John Wiley & Sons, 2013, pp. 449–450.

Naess, Arne. *Ecology, Community and Lifestyle*, translated and edited by David Rothenberg. Cambridge UP, 1989.

Nyrnes, Aslaug. "The Nordic Winter Pastoral." In *Ecocritical Perspectives on Children's Texts and Cultures: Nordic Dialogues*, edited by Nina Goga et al. Palgrave Macmillan, 2018, pp. 75–90.

Rice, Anne. *The Vampire Chronicles Collection, 1976*. Random House, 2002.

Rousseau, Jean-Jacques. *Emile – Or on Education, 1763*. Translated by Allan Bloom. Penguin Classics, 1991.

Trexler, Adam. *Anthropocene Fictions: The Novel in a Time of Climate Change*. U of Virginia P, 2015.

Uexküll, Jacob von. "The Theory of Meaning." In *Essential Readings in Biosemiotics: Anthology and Commentary, 1920*, edited by Donald Favareau. Springer, 2010, pp. 81–114.

Westerfield, Scott. *Specials*. Simon & Shuster Children's UK, 2011.

———. *Uglies*. Simon & Shuster Children's UK, 2011.

Wilson, Edward O. *Half Earth: Our Planet's Fight for Life*. Liveright Publishing Corporation, 2016.

Woodford, Riley. "Mountain Lions in Alaska." *Alaska Department of Fish and Game*, February 2004. www.adfg.alaska.gov/index.cfm?adfg=wildlifenews.view _article&articles_id=26. Accessed 20 September 2020.

Zipes, Jack. *Why Fairy Tales Stick: The Evolution and Relevance of a Genre*. Routledge, 2006.

Part II

(POST)APOCALYPTIC WORLD AND THE ANTHROPOCENE

Chapter 5

Anthropocene vs. Plague

Disastrous Diseases and Their Impact on Society as Seen in Literature from Thucydides to Modern Speculative Fiction

Jiří Jelínek

It would seem that a catastrophic pandemic belongs to the brief list of occurrences which could shatter human superiority or at least loosen the grip humankind has on the world. This chapter, however, intends to show that this fact does not turn the concept of a disease or a plague into the antithesis of the Anthropocene. On the contrary, an uncontrollable malady challenging the boundaries of human power may even serve as one of the vital parts of the anthropocenic imagery, with the very possibility of a pandemic being a direct consequence of the Anthropocene. Shortly after Crutzen and Stoermer had introduced the term in 2000, Anthropocene entered the popular discourse and became a widely used cultural concept (Trischler 312). In accordance with the cultural history view, this chapter will understand the Anthropocene not only as an era in which humanity has caused massive environmental changes (Trischler 323) but also as a cultural period governed by anthropocentric discourses, hopes, and fears.

Even though the epidemics, both real and fictitious ones, thrive in large societies and civilizations, we should not assume that the global epidemic fictions have come to the spotlight only with the emergence of the Anthropocene or with the outbreak of COVID-19. The modern era has indeed seen a rise in their numbers; the disease though, being one of the greatest fears of both the individual and the society as a whole, has always been a subject of literary narratives, regardless of whether we speak of myths, historiographical writing, or fiction. Various types of plagues and maladies, real or fictitious, have been sometimes used literally, and sometimes as a metaphor for another type of tragedy or profound change. David Bevan, the editor of *Literature and Sickness* (1993), has put together in the publication's introduction some of the most telling examples—melancholy in romanticism, syphilis in post-romanticism, tuberculosis in modernism, nausea in the Sartrean existentialism, and AIDS in the narratives of the 1980s and 1990s (3). We can also very well expect an emergence of "coronavirus fiction" which will appear not only in the form of memoirs, documentaries, and novels of realism but also speculative fiction. While this list reminds the reader of some of the most fascinating illnesses from the viewpoint of an individual struggle and while for some even the term *epidemic* or *pandemic* could be used, the image of an irreversible tide of plague that consumes (or regenerates) a whole civilization or even humankind in its entirety can be found in modern literature mostly in genre fiction—especially in the popular catastrophic and post-apocalyptic subgenre of speculative literature.

The various works of fiction in this field have made use of many topics and plot variants, but only a few are as enduring and ever returning as the idea of catastrophic plague. Elizabeth Rosen has written in her take on the apocalyptic literature that the story of plagues killing off humanity, while being as old as storytelling itself, continues to grip the literary imagination (48). Mary Shelley's *The Last Man* (1826), generally regarded as the first modern manifestation of the apocalyptic disease genre, is based on the idea of a world-wiping plague, and we can find it in some well-known subsequent works of the late nineteenth and early twentieth centuries, such as Jack London's *The Scarlet Plague* (1912) (Rosen 69). Some of the successful novels of the apocalyptic and post-apocalyptic genre from the last decades of the twentieth century, such as Stephen King's *The Stand* (1978) or Robert McCammon's *Swan Song* (1987), utilize this theme as well.

While the depiction of war or natural disasters has changed to a greater or lesser degree through history, with nuclear warfare or an asteroid hitting the Earth being presented as new threats in contemporary literature, the image of a catastrophic disease has still remained practically unchanged—an invisible, often undetectable, antagonist of the human civilization. To examine the roots of the subgenre and their influence on modern literature, we must dive rather deep into the history of literature. Probably the most famous cases in the ancient literatures are the description of the plague in Athens in *The History of the Peloponnesian War* (fifth century BCE) by Thucydides, one of the oldest Greek historiographers, and the same event described by the Roman writer Titus Lucretius Caro (first century BCE) in his didactic epic *Of Nature*. These two works, although conceived as historiographic and didactic, contain many elements which came into prominence in modern fiction.[1] This chapter does not aim to analyze them, as they both have already been examined in detail in many studies and papers,[2] but to show that some aspects important for the modern literature utilizing the topic of apocalyptic disease, most importantly the issue of the plague's origin, have a surprisingly long tradition and are present in ancient texts, albeit in a different hierarchy.

In Thucydides's *History of the Peloponnesian War*, we may perceive the gradually changing opinion of the plague-stricken Athenians on what caused their struggle. All three basic views on the possible origins of an epidemic are present here. The historian describes how the Athenians blamed their Peloponnesian enemies first: "It fell on the city of Athens suddenly. The first affected were the inhabitants of the Peiraeus, who went so far as to allege that the Peloponnesians had poisoned the wells" (96). Later they evidently switch to the theory that the disease must have natural causes, arguably because it is too great of a catastrophe to be caused deliberately. Thucydides presents this as common knowledge, with attention directed mostly at the path the plague has taken: "The original outbreak, it is said, was in Ethiopia, the far side of Egypt: the plague then spread to Egypt and Libya, and over much of the King's territory" (96). Finally, some of the Athenians end up remembering the prophecy and link the illness with supernatural causes:

> Those who knew of it also remembered the oracle given to the Spartans, when they enquired whether they should go to war and the god answered that they would win if they fought in earnest, and said that he himself would take their side. The general surmise was that the facts fitted the oracle. The plague has indeed begun immediately after the Peloponnesians had invaded, and it never reached the Peloponnese to any significant extent, but spread particularly in Athens and later in other densely populated areas. (100)

Even though Thucydides lists divine intervention as a possibility that was spoken about during the plague, he presents it mostly as an unlikely or even absurd scenario.

This inclination to seek natural causes is present in other ancient texts as well. Three centuries later, the Roman poet Titus Lucretius Caro based his description of the plague in Athens on Thucydides's report, altering it in some points for it to fit better into his Epicurean doctrines (Commager Jr. 105); and though he mentions Death, he describes the origins of the catastrophic pestilence in a strictly materialistic manner:

That seeds there be of many things to us
Life-giving, and that, contrariwise, there must
Fly many round bringing disease and death.
When these have, haply, chanced to collect
And to derange the atmosphere of earth,
The air becometh baneful. (Lucretius 230)

Even in premodern texts, the disease is surprisingly rarely seen as a result of demonic or diabolic entities acting to harm humanity. This interpretation is absent from Thucydides and Lucretius. In other famous half-fictionalized accounts of a plague, such as Giovanni Boccaccio's *Decameron* (1353) or Daniel Defoe's *A Journal of the Plague Year* (1722), the blame is put either on the stars (or natural causes in general) or on God's plan. *Decameron*, for instance, offers both possibilities, as it is shown in the following harrowing passage:

> Whether it was owing to the action of the heavenly bodies or whether, because of our iniquities, it was visited upon us mortals for our correction by the righteous anger of God, this pestilence, which had started some years earlier in the Orient, where it had robbed countless people of their lives, moved without pause from one region to the next until it spread tragically into the West. (Boccaccio 6–7)

The uncertainty not only about the origin but also about the very sense of the pestilence adds to the atmosphere of chaos and insecurity, conveyed by Boccaccio's introduction. It could be also argued that in Boccaccio's take on the plague, the catastrophe brings not only destruction but also a new chance for creation—after all, it is the reason to hide in the countryside, tell stories, and invent new fictional worlds—and perhaps that way, it is given some sense.

The premodern inclination to perceive a world-shattering plague as a new start for the world—forest-fire style, a catastrophe, but with positive connotations—is present even more strongly in some of the most successful and best-known contemporary apocalyptic works of fiction. Robert McCammon's *Swan Song* (1987), a novel depicting the world after the nuclear war, has its characters struggle with "Job's masks," that is, tumorous fleshy helmets growing over around their heads, thereby making seeing, breathing, and talking almost impossible. However, they work more like cocoons than anything else. Eventually, the helmets fall off and reveal a new face, in accord with the true nature of its owner—for instance, the girl called Swan, who serves as a champion for goodness and growth, gets a lovely face with "the most beautiful hair" (620). For this reason, the phrase "transformative power" would seem more appropriate than "destructive power" when discussing the role of the disease in the story.

Modern apocalyptic literature utilizes all of the mentioned ancient concepts of the origin and justification of the plague; however, it usually expands them or approaches the old ideas in new distinct ways. First, the idea of a man-made catastrophic disease or the idea of a pestilence caused by divine or magical influences is no longer seen as outlier theories; they have entered the popular discourse. The artificially created disease features in some of the best-known novels, such as Justin Cronin's *The Passage* (2006) or Stephen King's *The Stand* (1978), in which a deadly virus breaks loose from a scientific laboratory—a very real fear for a contemporary reader. In *The Stand*, an allusion to conspiracy thinking is also present: "The guard said he wouldn't be surprised to find out that the longhaired comsymp pervos had done it by putting something into the water" (King 268). However, in later works, a bioterrorist attack is not mere speculation anymore but an objective fact in the fictional world.

At the same time, the relation of the catastrophic disease to the supernatural in modern fiction can be described as ambiguous in most cases, the unearthly influence being one of the more plausible explanations for the outbreak of a malady. This relation works in both ways, however: not only is the origin of the disease often explained as supernatural, but in some cases the intended supernatural danger—such as zombies or vampires—is introduced to the plot as a disease. According to Nancy Traill's theory presented in her *Possible Worlds of the Fantastic* (1995), this usually happens in the paranormal mode, meaning that the "natural world" is extended by new phenomena, formerly seen as supernatural, but now objectively observable and verifiable (67–72). In the aforementioned and influential Max Brooks's *World War Z* (2006) a zombie virus appears; in novels such as Dan Simmons's *Children of the Night* (1992), Richard Matheson's *I am Legend* (1954), or Justin Cronin's *The Passage* (2010)—all three being quite popular works of speculative fiction—the existence of vampires is explained in more or less scientific terms.

In all three texts, the characters are unsure how to perceive the changes happening in the world around them. In Richard Matheson's *I am Legend* (1954), the protagonist examines the possibility of the "supernatural" vampiric disease being caused naturally until the text finally states: "He sat in the kitchen staring into a steaming cup of coffee. Germs. Bacteria. Viruses. Vampires. Why am I so against it? he thought. Was it just reactionary stubbornness, or was it that the task would loom as too tremendous for him if it were germs?" (Matheson 75) In this passage, two key explanations can be identified: a supernatural explanation (which is actually basic and less scary than in premodern texts) and a natural, biological one (which induces terror). Based on this turnaround, it would seem that, instead of anything supernatural, nature itself represents the most formidable opponent for humankind in the anthropocentric, post-Enlightenment "disenchanted world."

The poetics of such catastrophic fiction is built around two basic discourses: the modern scientific and sci-fi catastrophic thought on the one hand, and the Western Gothic tradition on the other. It could be argued that the image of a disease is what binds those two points of view together, as it is prevalent in both of these—the plague being both one of the most important and influential apocalyptic elements in modern fiction and one of the key aspects connected to the premodern and Gothic revenant mythos.

Important as the problem of where the disease comes from is, the real question is what it actually does to people who are affected by it. This issue goes far beyond a simple medical description, as it is usually connected to the very philosophy of the work and its narrative strategy. One of the most typical ways to demonstrate the transformative power of a disease is inversion, which can be in some aspects similar to the carnivalesque "world upside down," examined and popularized especially by Mikhail Bakhtin. Both bodily and social aspects of human civilization are completely reversed by the grotesque—the lower body, bound to materiality, excretion, and childbirth, comes out on top, while the noble and spiritual is debased. Bakhtin even mentions the plague itself when thinking back to Boccaccio's *Decameron* and states that the time of plague in the fourteenth century creates new, unique conditions for the creation of frank, unofficial words and images, offering a "general turnover" (272–273). A key point of Bakhtin's theories is the proximity of life and death, with the decay being a part of life itself, enabling its continuation: "But thanks to degradation the world is renewed; one might say reborn" (309). Michael Gardiner sums up the regenerative power of the carnival by saying that through parodic inversions the arbitrariness of human conceptions (including, for instance, the approach to time) is revealed (35).

As stated, the inversion, caused in this case by the disease, can be either physical or social, in some cases both. Physical inversion is probably less interesting in this context—it can be summarized as corporeal changes, marking the disease's victims, often relying on aesthetics similar to that of the already mentioned modern zombie fiction. The carnivalesque nature can be shown in two examples from the early nineteenth-century writing, John Wilson's "The City of the Plague" (1816) and Alexander Pushkin's *Feast in the Times of Plague* (1830).

In John Wilson's epic poem "The City of the Plague" (1816), an old man talks to the protagonist about the horrors he has seen in the plague-stricken London:

Over your heads from a window, suddenly
A ghastly face is thrust, and yells of death
With voice not human. Who is he that flies,
As if a demon dogg'd him on his path?
With ragged hair, white face, and bloodshot eyes. (14)

The major source of horror is not the disease itself, as the germs are invisible, but the changes it inflicts, turning the normal and familiar inhabitants of the city into the images of Otherness. It should be noted that while the poem occasionally depicts "piles of corpses" and other grim scenery, seeing the dead is not presented as the worst possible experience during the times of pestilence. Instead, it terrifies the reader with a "ghastly" man, neither truly living nor truly dead, transgressing the boundaries between the worlds. The text is not clear about whether the man is sick and dying or if he has simply succumbed to madness from the gruesome situation. He retains, however, some of the typical features of a corpse or a demon—such as the whiteness of his face or the inhuman voice.

Alexander Sergeyevich Pushkin has further developed this inversive plague aesthetics in his famous play *Feast in the Times of Plague* (1830), an edited translation of Act one from Wilson's work. In one of the scenes, a character called Louisa speaks about her half-dream, after a cart with dead bodies driven by a black man passes the house outside. The passage is inspired by a similar scene depicting a cart of human bodies in "The City of the Plague" (Wilson 15), the otherworldly and grotesque atmosphere is, however, even more intense:

Some dreadful thing—all black . . . white-eyed . . .
That called me to its cart . . . and there
The dead lay deep . . . and babbled words . . .
Some strange and unfamiliar tongue. (Pushkin 170)

The basic opposition of the dead and the living is further boosted by color symbolism and the fact that the dead are blabbering in an incomprehensible language, making them even more exotic and weird. To put it in other words, death by some common cause would produce a familiar corpse, but the plague turns its victims into strangers and populates the city with disconcerting "others," their depiction being similar to the contemporary view of foreigners from outside the civilized world, speaking their peculiar languages.

The social inversion caused by catastrophic diseases in some stories is usually subtler, but it may set the tone of a subversive narrative in the same way as the material inversion, if not more effectively. In some cases, the social inversion applies just to one aspect of human civilization, highlighting it. The following paragraphs will discuss some of the components of human culture that may be inverted: the concept of physical closeness, the concept of family or kinship, gender roles, language, or the idea of time and social progress. A number of possibilities in this field is, however, much larger, and the aspects discussed should be perceived only as examples.

In some cases, the disease turns the society into "anti-society"—human society, usually defined by the contact and interaction of its members, becomes extremely divided because of the plague and the fear it rouses. Most readers have probably experienced the quarantine measures and the social distancing rules during the COVID-19 pandemic. In some works of fiction, former members of the society could now be described as "the others," this time not just because of the changes in their physique, but mainly as a consequence of fear; the catastrophic disease is an agent of new social division and exclusion, bringing in societal boundaries that could be described as xenophobic.

In Peter Heller's *Dog Stars* (2012), the protagonist, a pilot called Hig, knows about a nearby colony of Mennonites, but even though he wants to help them and occasionally drops supplies for them, he is afraid to come too close as members of the group suffer from a blood disease, which may be dangerous. Even though the condition is rare and unknown, the narrator could not help himself from linking it to other illnesses he knows: "Like a plague but slow burning. Something like AIDS I think, maybe more contagious" (7). For most of the novel, the narrator maintains an exact distance of 15 feet, whenever he is in contact with the Mennonites: "The families know to stay fifteen feet back. I've trained them" (19). Even though it is just a precaution, it shapes Hig's perspective of his relations with the Mennonites, injecting it with military language and thinking: "Always that bit of mutually respected demilitarized zone across which words can be flung followed maybe by bullets and arrows and death. That's what we called it, the DMZ. Awkward at first, but not now" (138). This rejection of physicality returns several times as a motif and can even be pinpointed as one of the governing aspects of Heller's post-apocalyptic world. As Barbara Fass Leavy noted, the fear of contagion brings the "I" and "not-I" into heightened conflict (8).

Catastrophic disease speculative fiction often describes the inversion of core social values in the world. The collapse of states and human communities, in general, would seem obvious; however, the "sacred" institution of the family is sometimes challenged as well. In John Christopher's *The Death of Grass* (1956), a virus is destroying all kinds of grass, including most of the crop; and even though the disease does not directly kill people, it does so indirectly, through famine and chaos. The protagonist's brother, David, is killed after he refuses to let the group of people led by the protagonist into a sheltered valley (Christopher 192). The main character then contemplates how, in the new order of social hierarchy, fratricide is unavoidable. The viability of the concept of always putting family first is disputed, as many family members are forced to see one another as direct competition.

Robert Merle's *Les Hommes protégés* (1974, translated into English as *The Virility Factor*) utilizes the catastrophic disease called Encephalitis 16 as a plot device to reverse gender roles in society. The main aim of this novel is to show the current (as of the 1970s) state of society and the problematic treatment of women by switching the social status of the two binary genders. For example, men are banned from inheritance in the story, and one of the last scenes depicts the protagonist walking down the street, being cat-called and almost kidnapped by some female masons (341). The reader could expect a complicated situation with a more complex dynamic between genders, their constantly shifting hierarchy, and striving for equality or the emergence of new genders. However, the novel offers no treatment of said issues—it simply switches the masculine and feminine roles. The work thus serves more as a case for proving a point than a way to tell a "realistic" narrative; the simple inversion enables the author to comment on the contemporary society, while the catastrophic illness itself serves as nothing but a plot device. The author could have, naturally, used any method to explain the complete turnover—his choice of disease as the main factor does not seem to be, however, completely arbitrary. It could be argued that he used pestilence exactly because it is generally regarded and traditionally presented in both fiction and non-fiction as a key aspect of social change, and therefore using it to show that one very special type of social inversion would strengthen the novel's plausibility.

The next major aspect of human society addressed in this chapter is the way people communicate; the transformative power of catastrophic disease can be illustrated by the changes it imposes on language. Jack London's novella *Scarlet Plague* (1912) depicts the world a few generations after a pandemic wiped out most of Earth's human population. The youngest generation of "new people" is presented as entirely uncivilized and even demeaning when listening to their old grandfathers' account of the era before the disease and the coming of the catastrophe. While all their actions are almost parodic in their simplicity and their degeneration encompasses "their code of behavior, values, abstract thinking, and even sense of humor" (Luczak 88), the language they use serves, as the narrator himself notices, as the most apparent evidence of the uncivilized state in which the humankind finds itself now:

> They were very quick and abrupt in their actions, and their speech, in moments of hot discussion over the allotment of the choicer teeth, was truly a gabble. They spoke in monosyllables and short jerky sentences that was more a gibberish than a language. And yet, through it ran hints of grammatical construction, and appeared vestiges of the conjugation of some superior culture. Even the speech of Granser was so corrupt that were it put down literally it would be almost so much nonsense to the reader. This, however, was when he talked with the boys. (London 314)

It could be debated, of course, whether the opposition of civilized language is barbaric and uneducated language, or rather no speech at all; but, as the text itself states, the author did not seek to show an inversion of any random language, but specifically the corrupted form of the once-mighty English. This should be read as a colonial take on the difference between the "Aryan language" and the "gibbering" of "lesser" cultures. Fascinated by the pseudo-scientific racial and degeneration theories penned by Dr Charles Edward Woodruff, Jack London described through the decline of language what he saw as an inevitable fall of complicated "Aryan civilization" with all its modernity (Luczak 89). We may, however, compare it to the image of the babbling dead in Pushkin's *Feast in the Times of Plague* as well—while the writers' motivations were completely different, the similarity of the imagery proves how deeply ingrained the idea of inversion is in the catastrophic disease fiction.

The last of the aspects the catastrophic diseases invert is the human concept of time and purposeful history, and especially the idea of progress. In catastrophic and apocalyptic fiction, the modern Western notion of time can be deconstructed, as the fictitious disease puts the human civilization back to its very beginning, basically reversing the known history and bringing an end, sometimes temporary, to the Anthropocene. We can trace this line of thinking back to Thucydides's account, in which the sick lose all hope for the future: "The most dreadful aspects of the whole affliction were the despair into which people fell when they realized they had contracted the disease (they were immediately convinced they had no hope, and so were much more inclined to surrender themselves without a fight)"(98). This despondency described by the Greek historiographer is primarily individual; however, judging from the following passages, it would seem it stems as much from the chaos, lawlessness, and the distortion of the "natural order" the Athenians had been living in until the coming of the plague. It could be therefore closely linked to the frightening uncertainty the catastrophic disease brings, and not only in a singular human life but also in the life of human cultures and nations, or even humanity as a whole.

We may find an almost identical passage in P. D. James's novel *The Children of Men* (1992): "But those who lived gave way to the almost universal negativism, what the French named *ennui universel*. It came upon us like an insidious disease; indeed it was a disease, with its soon-familiar symptoms of lassitude, depression, ill-defined malaise, a readiness to give way to minor infections, a perpetual disabling headache" (12). The connection between disease, negativism, and the feeling of a lost future is much clearer here. However, as the novel itself states, people are behaving this way only because they know there will be no future generations of humans to inherit the Earth. The anthropocentric thinking of people born in the Anthropocene comes into conflict with the fact that they are no longer living in it.

The concept of time can be inverted or reversed even in those cases in which humans are not to be completely extinct. Most of the apocalyptic and post-apocalyptic fiction describing the destruction of civilization by nuclear warfare (such as Merle's *Malevil* (1972) or McCarthy's *The Road* (2006)) uses a straightforward plot composition—either the greatest peril for the characters (the great catastrophe itself) is present at the very beginning or the characters remember it as a past event. The plague, on the other hand, usually presents a menacing presence throughout the whole plot and is usually resolved only at the end, if at all. That is the case with *The Scarlet Plague* (1912), *The Dog Stars* (2012), *The Virility Factor* (1974), *The Stand* (1978), and many other novels. Even Daniel Defoe starts his *Journal of the Plague Year* (1722) with a mention that the plague "was returned again in Holland" (1), after it went away after a period of epidemics last year; and while it disappears from London at the end of the novel, the possibility of it returning yet again at some moment seems to be implicitly present in the text (as well as it has been present in the media coverage of the COVID-19 pandemic). In Albert Camus's *The Plague* (1947), this fact is even reflected by the characters, seeing the uncertain temporality as the worst aspect of the disease:

> Tarrou agreed that he'd predicted a disaster, but reminded him that the event predicted by him was an earthquake. To which the old fellow replied: "Ah, if only it had been an earthquake! A good bad shock, and there you are! You count the dead and living, and that's an end of it. But this here damned disease, even them who haven't got it can't think of anything else." (114–115)

It may be argued, though, that some other catastrophes, for example, a slowly rising flood, possess a similar quality, as Barbara Fass Leavy has proven by citing a *New York Times* report on floods in Texas. However, she also states that diseases can be singled out as unique in their effects on human lives and interactions (Leavy 17–18).

Of the most common tropes in post-apocalyptic fiction is the human inability to raise future generations in a "civilized" way. This can be caused by a considerable decrease in human population (as shown in *The Scarlet Plague*), but it can be also linked to the inability to produce children, often because of genetic disorders caused by pollution—such as depicted in Brian Aldiss's *Greybeard* (1964), Philip K. Dick's *Do Androids Dream of Electric Sheep?* (1968), or Margaret Atwood's *The Handmaid's Tale* (1985), to name just a few examples. The novel *Greybeard* (1964) depicts a world in which nuclear testing and resulting toxic waste have made people barren. Most of the human population is old and ageing, and when the reader learns that there are some children actually present in the world, they are described as savages living in the woods, avoiding the disease by going back to prehistoric human ways and starting the civilization again. The seemingly unshatterable Anthropocene is weakened, even undone, in those types of plot, and the biosphere is permitted to thrive again. It does not, however, condemn the very idea of Anthropocene as a wrong way for the planet to take, as it almost never describes an absolute end of civilization. Rather, it usually presents humanity with a second chance to create a more functional society.

This regress to living in the forest is probably in accord with the idea of a "Golden Age" or a "Golden Race," known in the Western context mainly from the Greek mythology (Livingstone 130); various ideas about the past can be used, however. John Christopher's *The Death of Grass* (1956), for example, does not only corrupt relations between relatives, as stated above; it also draws examples directly from the biblical rendering of ancient times. After the destruction of most grass, humans are forced to fight for scarce food. The events described in the novel lead, with a sense of unavoidable destiny, to the scene in which the circumstances force the protagonist to fight his own brother—which, evidently, mirrors Cain's murder of Abel, as the protagonist himself realizes. When he is talking about the valley which his son will eventually inherit, he states: "He will own it. It's a nice bit of land. Not as much as Cain left to Enoch, though" (Christopher 192). *The Stand* can also be mentioned in this context. The novel is generally regarded as the most religious of King's works, but its portrayal of God shifts from the modern religious views to those of the Old Testament, specifically the Book of Job (Mustazza 92). The popular novel *The Handmaid's Tale* (1985), in which the society deals with the problem of human infertility, centers its plot around a return to biblical manners and traditions as well, this time deliberately; the ensuing hardships for women being arguably the worst of the disease's effects, even more disastrous than the infertility itself—"recessive and limiting in every conceivable way" (MacArthur 64). The inversion of time may be closely linked to the social inversion.

The return to the past is, however, seldom seen as an unambiguously negative turn of events, but neither is it painted as something completely positive in itself. If we go back to London's *Scarlet Plague*, we can see that the uncivilized state, although the text presents it as a new beginning, is not conceived as something desirable; but neither is the overly cultivated time before the Scarlet Plague. Human history is constructed as an oscillation between two extreme points in this prose: barbarism and civilization. The ideal state of society can be reached only for a short time, when going from one state to another, and from this point of view, the plague can be seen as an essentially beneficial occurrence.

Similar views on the inversion the disease brings are presented in many other of the mentioned works—the disease in *Swan Song* reveals the true faces of people and brings redemption; in other works of fiction, the rapid decrease of the human population gives the next generation a chance of starting anew or even introduces a whole new form of intelligent life (*I am Legend*). The catastrophic diseases are, above all, presented as an element of change, and while the premodern texts describe it mostly as a terrible (yet inevitable) calamity, the modern catastrophic genre has created a much more intricate view on the topic. As Elizabeth Rosen stated in the introduction to her monograph *Apocalyptic Transformations* (2008), the postmodern version of the apocalypse replaces the idea of End of Time with a notion of an end of one time, thus marking a return to the cyclical view of time (Rosen xxiv).

It could be argued that catastrophic speculative fiction, while drawing major inspiration from premodern takes on the topic, seeks ways to cope with the very real danger of a pandemic in the modern world, and with the hypothetical end of human dominion over the Earth. In many novels, the fictitious disease, be it a force of nature or intervention of supernatural powers, takes the responsibility out of human hands and offers a complete turnover of everything the society considers unchangeable—and in doing so, the inversion caused by the disease becomes almost an act of salvation. This does not mean, however, that the concept of the Anthropocene is somehow weakened by these inclinations. It could even be argued that this deconstruction of human infallibility forms the natural next step in the development of the anthropocenic thought. After all, one of the chief concerns of the Anthropocene is undoubtedly the fact that humankind, becoming its own master, has lost its innocence regarding its own fate and is expected to carry the heavy burden of godlike responsibility. Various fictitious plagues offer a solution: macabre fantasy of an unfightable natural or divine destruction of everything the people have built.

The Anthropocene, even though directly linked to reason and planning, can be infused this way by the elements of unpredictability and randomness. The catastrophic disease brings the possibility of constant inversion and change to the table, taking away the obligation of constant progress. Thus, the Anthropocene does not need to be seen as something essential and eternal; and the prospect of a substantial change gives comfort to those who live in the troubled modern times. The boundaries are still there, the human race is told, and the responsibility for the state of the world, however burdensome, is not absolute.

The consequences this weakening of human responsibility has for the Anthropocene in the fictional worlds of speculative fiction can be various; some of them, however, seem to be more prominent than others. Once the malaise has been overcome, there is an infusion of optimism, as seen in *Greybeard*, *The Virility Factor*, or *The Stand*. This, ironically, is permitting the Anthropocene to continue, demonstrating the regenerative power of the catastrophe. Another impact the pandemic usually has is a reassessment of human relations to the natural and the supernatural: both the environment and the metaphysical entities are once again seen as forces to be reckoned with, even bargained with, as in *Do Androids Dream of Electronic Sheep?*, *The Swan Song*, *The Stand*, and others. The human society in the Anthropocene becomes more self-aware, which leads to a more intellectual and thought-provoking climate and enables the very idea of the Anthropocene and its ramifications to become more prominent.

NOTES

1. It is even possible that *The History of the Peloponnesian War* has had a direct influence on modern catastrophic disease fiction. Catherine Rubincam has closely compared Thucydides's work and Daniel Defoe's *A Journal of the Plague Year*, commonly named the first modern fictionalized description of a pestilence; she has then expressed the idea that Defoe knew Thucydides's description of the plague and was inspired by it (Rubincam 194).

2. See Robin Mitchell-Boyask's *Plague and the Athenian Imagination* (2007), James Longrigg's "Epidemic, ideas and classical Athenian society" (1992), Charles Segal's *Lucretius on Death and Anxiety* (1990), and others.

WORKS CITED

Bakhtin, Mikhail Mikhaïlovich. *Rabelais and His World*. Translated by Hélène Iswolsky. Indiana UP, 1984.

Bevan, David. "Introduction." In *Literature and Sickness*, edited by David Bevan. Rodopi, 1993, pp. 3–4.

Boccaccio, Giovanni. *The Decameron*. Translated by Guido Waldman. Oxford UP, 1998.

Camus, Albert. *The Plague*. Translated by Stuart Gilbert. Vintage International, 1991.

Commager Jr., H. S. "Lucretius' Interpretation of the Plague." *Harvard Studies in Classical Philology*, vol. 62, 1957, pp. 105–118.

Defoe, Daniel. *A Journal of the Plague Year*, edited by Louis A. Landa. Oxford UP, 1998.

Christopher, John. *The Death of Grass*. Penguin Books, 2009.

Gardiner, Michael. "Bakhtin's Carnival: Utopia as Critique." In *Bakhtin: Carnival and Other Subjects*, edited by David Shepherd. Rodopi, 1993, pp. 20–47.

Heller, Peter. *The Dog Stars*. Alfred A. Knopf, 2012.

James, P. D. *The Children of Men*. Penguin Books, 1994.

King, Stephen. *The Stand*. Signet, 1990.

Leavy, Barbara Fass. *To Blight with Plague: Studies in a Literary Theme*. New York UP, 1993.

Livingstone, Niall. "Instructing Myth: From Homer to the Sophists." In *A Companion to Greek Mythology*, edited by Ken Dowden and Niall Livingstone. Blackwell Publishing, 2011, pp. 125–140.

London, Jack. *The Science Fiction of Jack London: An Anthology*. Gregg Press, 1975.

Longrigg, James. "Epidemic, Ideas and Classical Athenian Society." In *Epidemics and Ideas: Essays on the Historical Perception of Pestilence*, edited by Terence Ranger and Paul Slack. Cambridge UP, 1992, pp. 22–44.
Luczak, Ewa Barbara. *Breeding and Eugenics in the American Literary Imagination: Heredity Rules in the Twentieth Century*. Palgrave Macmillan, 2016.
Lucretius Carus, Titus. *On the Nature of Things*. Translated by William Ellery Leonard. Dover Publications, 2004.
MacArthur, Sian. *Gothic Science Fiction: 1818 to the Present*. Palgrave Macmillan, 2015.
Matheson, Richard. *I am Legend*. Fawcett Publications, 1957.
McCammon, Robert. *The Swan Song*. Pocket Books, 2009.
Merle, Robert. *The Virility Factor*. Translated by Martin Sokolinsky. Weidenfeld and Nicolson, 1977.
Mitchell-Boyask, Robin. *Plague and the Athenian Imagination: Drama, History, and the Cult of Asclepius*. Cambridge UP, 2007.
Mustazza, Leonard. "Repaying Service with Pain: The Role of God in *The Stand*." In *A Casebook on The Stand*, edited by Anthony Magistrale. The Borgo Press, 1992, pp. 89–108.
Pushkin, Alexander. *Boris Godunov and Other Dramatic Works*. Translated by James E. Falen. Oxford UP, 2009.
Rosen, Elizabeth. *Apocalyptic Transformation: Apocalypse and the Postmodern Imagination*. Lexington Books, 2008.
Rubincam, Catherine. "Thucydides and Defoe: Two Plague Narratives." *International Journal of the Classical Tradition*, vol. 11, no. 2, 2004, pp. 194–212.
Segal, Charles. *Lucretius on Death and Anxiety: Poetry and Philosophy in De Rerum Natura*. Princeton UP, 1990.
Thucydides. *The Peloponnesian War*. Translated by Martin Hammond. Oxford UP, 2009.
Traill, Nancy. *Possible Worlds of the Fantastic: The Rise of the Paranormal in Fiction*. U of Toronto P, 1996.
Trischler, Helmut. "The Anthropocene: A Challenge for the History of Science, Technology, and the Environment." *NTM Zeitschrift für Geschichte der Wissenschaften, Technik und Medizin*, vol. 24, 2016, pp. 309–335.
Wilson, John. *The City of the Plague and Other Poems*. Edinburgh, George Ramsay and Company, 1816.

Chapter 6

Fantasy, Myth, and the End of Humanity in M. R. Carey's *The Girl with All the Gifts*

Maria Quigley

The Anthropocene epoch has seen humans dominate and exert tremendous influence on the Earth's ecosystems. Unfortunately, the power of humanity as a geological force has had disastrous implications for our environment as we are confronted with the calamitous reality of our actions daily. As sea levels and temperatures rise, air and land pollution increase, and entire species of plant and animal life disappear, we cannot ignore the imminent threat that is being posed for future generations. Moreover, although we are aware that numerous species are on the brink of extinction, and the environment that we call home is being irreparably altered, we are primarily concerned with the implications that these changes pose for the future of humanity. The anthropocentric worldview, which places humanity in a privileged position apart from other species, ignores the interdependency of species in an ecosystem. Despite the need to widen our responsibility beyond our own species, our self-interest appears to win out time and time again.

Our anxiety surrounding the continuation of the human species is being played out continually in cultural spheres, particularly in the post-apocalyptic genre. Images of disaster and destruction are reflected and processed in these post-apocalyptic imaginings. The first decade of the twenty-first century has seen a dramatic surge in the production of these texts, and the sustained popularity of the genre in the years after 9/11 is a testament to the fact that we now understand how quickly life as we know it can be destroyed. Natural disasters, such as Hurricane Katrina, and pandemics, such as SARS, Ebola, and Covid-19 have added to the apocalyptic sense of doom that seems to have pervaded the twenty-first century. Climate change has become one of the most important issues of contemporary life, and many apocalyptic and post-apocalyptic texts feed off this real-life concern. However, almost all of the films, TV shows, and literature within this genre posit the belief that even after life as we know it has ended and civilization has been destroyed, some humans still survive. These narratives propose that the world cannot exist without humanity; it seems that nothing can annihilate the human race entirely and put an end to the Age of Anthropocene. This chapter will examine the fantasy of human survival even after the end, in the post-apocalyptic genre. Tracing the origins of the genre from religious tradition right up to its present-day popularity, I will then analyze M. R. Carey's *The Girl with All the Gifts* (2014), a text that challenges the anthropocentric point of view as it goes against the grain of the mythic endurance of humanity and instead proposes an alternative view of a future without human beings at its center.

Post-apocalyptic texts tell of the fall of civilization after a catastrophic event, focusing on the attempts of survivors at rebuilding and restoring society. The post-apocalyptic genre focuses on the aftermath of the end. This paradox, of a narrative that goes beyond the end, has a long history, prior to it being adopted by science fiction. Originating in one of the world's oldest religions, Zoroastrianism, the apocalypse occurs after a 3,000-year struggle between good and evil, when the destructive Aziz Dahaka, son of Angra Mainyu, reigns terror on the world. Saoshyant, the savior, raises the dead for final judgment and ultimately brings about Frashokereti, a state in which good triumphs as the wicked are returned to hell and evil is defeated. Although each tells their own different story of the end of days, apocalypticism can be seen in Christian, Judaic, and Islamic eschatology.[1] Religious apocalypse is formed when an intervention by God results in a cataclysmic event, all men are judged, evil is punished, and the good and faithful are saved as life on Earth is renewed. In their analysis of the origins of apocalyptic literature Christian Hoffstadt and Dominik Schrey point out that "the Greek word *apokálypsis* translates as 'lifting the veil' or 'revelation.' In the Christian tradition the apocalypse is understood as the foreseeable and necessarily tragic end of all history that nevertheless has a cathartic or purifying function" (28). The cataclysmic apocalypse, brought about by God, clears the world of the wicked, evil, and unfaithful. It brushes away all that is wrong or bad, leaving the humble, faithful elect who may now return to a peaceful existence. Apocalypticism, as portrayed in religious texts then, can be said to be for-the-most part concerned with the distinction between good and evil, the sinners and the faithful, heaven and hell. As the apocalypse began to be used in non-religious texts, most notably the science fiction genre, the cataclysmic event was now not caused by the hand of God but some other, either natural or man-made, disaster. The publication of Mary Shelley's *The Last Man*, in 1826, signals a move in the nineteenth century "from the notion of purgatory and paradise towards the more profane image of a post-cataclysmic world in ruins" (Hoffstadt and Schrey 28). Non-religious apocalypse tales were not interested in the judgment of man, and the distinction of good and evil, so much as they were solely concerned with the survival of humanity in any form. Although many pieces of apocalyptic and post-apocalyptic literature were published in the years after, it was not until after World War II that the genre gained perceptible popularity among readers. The advent of the nuclear bomb made it clear to the world that human beings were now in possession of what Jonathan Schell describes as "instruments of the most radical evil imaginable—the extinction of the human species" (34). Schell's statement exemplifies the anthropocentric viewpoint as all concern and responsibility for anything non-human, other species, and the biosphere itself are neglected as humans are prioritized. Nuclear tension, the threat of communism, and the possibility of mutually assured destruction culminated in an atmosphere of anxiety so absolute that M. Keith Booker has dubbed the Cold War period "the Golden Age of nuclear fear" (5). These fears and anxieties were expressed in many novels and films within the period. In her seminal essay "The Imagination of Disaster," Susan Sontag analyses the appeal of disaster movies of the 1950s,

> The lure of such generalized disaster as a fantasy is that it releases one from normal obligations. The trump card of the end-of-the-world movies [. . .] is that great scene with New York or London or Tokyo discovered empty, its entire population annihilated. Or [. . .] the whole movie can be devoted to the fantasy of occupying the deserted metropolis and starting all over again, a world Robinson Crusoe. (121)

This escape from a society characterized by fear and apprehension, into a "hopeful fantasy of moral simplification" (126), could also be used to explain the renewed popularity for everything post-apocalyptic in the twenty-first century. The post-9/11 landscape has seen not just a revival of post-apocalyptic imaginings, but also a dramatic increase in the production and popularity of post-apocalyptic zombie narratives.

Inspired by Richard Matheson's *I Am Legend* (1954),[2] the post-apocalyptic zombie narrative presents an ever-increasing zombie horde engaged in an attack on the surviving humans. Within these texts we see how the spread of the zombie virus, or plague, results in the breakdown of civilization. Governments fall, law enforcement agencies disintegrate, and military organizations and health care infrastructures are swamped. Services such as electricity and water are cut off, mass media and news outlets stop broadcasting, and the internet and other modes of communication stop working until all that is left are isolated groups of survivors that band together in this new non-technological, hostile environment. The groups either hole up in a sort of shelter or journey toward safe zones, scavenging for food, water, and supplies such as weapons. The zombie apocalypse is one of the most popular end-of-the-world scenarios within the genre. As Kim Paffenroth notes, "more than any other monster, zombies are fully and literally apocalyptic ... they signal the end of the world as we have known it for thousands of years. Also, in the original meaning of 'apocalyptic,' they 'reveal' terrible truths about human nature, existence, and sin" (13). The zombie horde lends itself well to the destruction and downfall of civilization as society becomes more aware of the real-world outbreaks of infectious disease. The zombie challenges our understanding of what it is to be human, and the place of humans in the world. As Paffenroth noted, they often reveal harsh truths about human nature, as these stories are less focused on the actual zombies but more concerned with how the survivors react to the catastrophe and how the situation influences their actions, opinions, and morality. Steven Shaviro describes zombies as "the obscure objects of voyeuristic fascination" (104). The explosion of the zombie across multimedia platforms, including literature, film, television, and video games, in the last twenty years is a testament to this fascination. Infecting every corner of culture, the zombie has become prolific in contemporary society, popularizing the concept of the zombie apocalypse and representations of its post-apocalyptic aftermath. This resurgence prompts the question: What is it that keeps the audience returning, time and time again, to these tales of catastrophic destruction and the subsequent rebuilding of society?

In *Sense of an Ending*, Frank Kermode explains that our attraction to the apocalypse can be related to our need to relate our being, at one point in time, to a beginning and an end. Without an endpoint, with which we can organize other events in our life, we are lost in chaos. He states that "we project ourselves—a small, humble elect, perhaps—past the End, so as to see the structure whole, a thing we cannot do from our spot of time in the middle" (Kermode 8). When discussing the long history of apocalyptic tradition, he asserts that, "the great majority of interpretations of Apocalypse assume that the End is pretty near. Consequently, the historical allegory is always having to be revised; time discredits it. And this is important. Apocalypse can be disconfirmed without being discredited. This is part of its extraordinary resilience" (8). Although predicted visions of the end have come and gone, prophecies have been proven false, and the world is still turning, people are still drawn to the idea of the world suddenly ending. In our contemporary world, the end is "no longer imminent, the End is immanent" (25). The end is a pervasive theme in society. We are attracted to the apocalypse, to this total destruction, to the End. However, as already noted, the end is never truly the end. Ira Chernus affirms this, "we accept the lure of annihilation, only to discover that it is a temporary condition, a gateway to renewal and rebirth. This is perhaps the most pervasive theme in all the world's religious myth and ritual. It may also be the most pervasive theme in the symbolism of nuclear weapons" (85). The apocalypse is only the beginning; the real story begins after it. With society decimated, the only thing to do is rebuild, start again. In "The Manhattan Phone Book (Abridged)," John Varley writes,

> We all love after-the-bomb stories. If we didn't, why would there be so many of them? There's something attractive about all those people being gone, about wandering in a depopulated world, scrounging cans of Campbell's pork and beans, defending one's family from marauders. Sure, it's horrible, sure we weep for all those dead people. But some secret part of us thinks it would be good to survive, to start all over. Secretly we know we'll survive. All those other folks will die. That's what after-the-bomb stories are all about. ("Manhattan Phone")

This renewal, rebirth, and starting over appear to be at the core of post-apocalyptic texts. Berger notes that "[t]he end itself, the moment of cataclysm is only part of the point of apocalyptic writing. The apocalypse as eschaton is just as importantly the vehicle for clearing away the world as it is and making possible the postapocalyptic paradise or wasteland" (6). The focus is placed on the survivors of the apocalypse, whether the cause was viral, nuclear, ecological, or technological, and the hardships they encounter, as they navigate through this new world. The post-apocalyptic landscape is usually non-technological, forcing survivors into a simpler, feudal, agrarian way of life. Although there are obvious difficulties adjusting to life in this kind of society, it is often an underlying assumption that regression to this simpler existence is in many ways better than the lives the characters were living before.[3] Fredric Jameson has called this type of text "a Utopian wish fulfilment wrapped in dystopian wolf's clothing" (384). An apocalyptic event releases its survivors from the toils of their everyday life. Mick Broderick describes this desire as "the fantasy of nuclear Armageddon as the anticipated war which will annihilate the oppressive burdens of (post)modern life and usher in the nostalgically yearned-for less complex existence" (362).

To facilitate the creation of this new world, and to portray it as a better way of life, most texts also provide a critique of society before the cataclysmic event. Often society before the event, within the text, is the contemporary world that the text was created in. Peter Skult posits that the post-apocalyptic narrative forces us to confront the normal landscape and environment as we know it being turned into "an uncanny wilderness," adding that the "the majority of stories that belon to the post-apocalyptic canon are set in a post-catastrophic version of our own recognizable Earth, and thus comment on our own reality, and it is largely from this immediate connection that the genre derives its strength: through the imagined destruction of our world" (104). As we are confronted with more and more images and news items that detail the very real destruction and changes the Earth is undergoing due to human activity, we turn more to fiction where we can critique this scenario from a safe distance while not making any real changes. Issues like climate change seem to be so overwhelming that it is safer to mirror and amplify the issue in a fictional universe to meditate over our fears and concerns. As Roger MacFarlane points out, we acknowledge the crisis "if at all, as an ambient hum of guilt, easily faded out. Like other unwholesome aspects of the Anthropocene, we mostly respond [. . .] with stuplimity: the aesthetic experience in which astonishment is united with boredom, such that we overload on anxiety to the point of outrage-outage" ("Generation Anthropocene"). The post-apocalyptic narrative allows us to engage with the crushing imminence of Earth's destruction from a safe space. These narratives allow us to play out the fears of the collective unconscious by critiquing our current predicament, and in a way solving the problems in a fictional setting, as this is easier than solving the problem in reality. Berger points out that although apocalyptic and post-apocalyptic texts serve many functions, the most prevalent is "a total critique of any existing social order. [. . .] visions of the end and its aftermath emphasize that no social reform can cure the world's diseases. Every structure of the old world is infected, and only an absolute, purifying cataclysm can make possible an utterly new perfected world" (7). The post-apocalyptic zombie narrative utilizes this social critique of contemporary life, allowing us to interrogate the cultural anxieties of our times. Academics such as Kyle Bishop and Elizabeth Aiossa have argued that in addition to feeding into survivalist fantasies, zombie narratives can be read as allegories of real-world concerns such as rampant consumerism, global terrorism, biological warfare, outbreaks of infectious diseases, corrupt government organizations, and mass immigration.[4] Although zombie narratives often posit the source of the zombie outbreak as a man-made virus, M. R. Carey's 2014 novel *The Girl with All the Gifts* instead presents us with a naturally occurring fungal infection that affects not only human beings but also the very landscape of Earth.

Carey's post-apocalyptic zombie novel is set twenty years after what the novel terms the Breakdown. A huge percentage of the British population was infected by the fungal contagion, which turned them into zombie-like creatures, called hungries. The hungries have lost all mental faculties and feed on the flesh of living humans, spreading the infection by biting. The novel establishes that the "hungry pathogen is an old friend in a new suit, *Ophiocordyceps unilateralis*" (Carey 59). A scientist in the novel, Dr Caroline Caldwell, explains that this parasite was first discovered on ants. She goes on to detail,

> How *Ophiocordyceps* spores lie dormant on the forest floor in humid environments such as the South American rainforest. Foraging ants pick them up,

without noticing, because the spores are sticky. They adhere to the underside of the ant's thorax and abdomen. Once attached, they sprout mycelial threads which penetrate the ant's body and attack its nervous system. The fungus hot-wires the ant. (59)

As the fungus takes control of the ant, it makes it climb to the highest point it can reach. The fungus then "spreads through the ant's body and explodes out of its head—a phallic sporangium skull-fucking the dying insect from the inside. The sporangium sheds thousands of spores and falling from a great height they spread for miles. Which of course is the point of the exercise" (60).

The Cordyceps fungal infection has now "jumped the species barrier, then the genus, family, order and class" (60), infecting human beings. This Cordyceps infection exists in the real world, and Carey is not the only author to produce a fictionalized account of it jumping the species barrier. In the Naughty Dog video game, *The Last of Us* (2013), we are presented with a world in which a huge percentage of the population has succumbed to this same infection and turned into zombie-like creatures. Presenting an infection that already exists in nature as the cause of the apocalypse pushes both texts past the boundary of science fiction, and further into the realm of possibility. The core belief that the human species is at the top of the evolutionary ladder is challenged as these texts question our unwavering conviction that we dominate and control the environment around us. As Amy Green points out,

> Advances in science, such that the very code of DNA has been categorized and understood, coupled with the infiltration of technology into nearly every aspect of life in recent years have allowed for a resurgence of this previous infallibility, the sense of absolute certainty of human dominance that existed before the first scientific revolutions began to question that place. (753)

She goes on to ask, "What would it take for humans to once again feel that repulsion, that sense of feeling exposed as less, perhaps even unworthy of any place of prominence in the natural order of the world?" (753) Even though Green's analysis is focused on *The Last of Us*, her question can also be applied to Carey's novel, which is based around the premise that survivors of the apocalyptic event should not try to rebuild society as it was, placing themselves in a place of dominance over all, but instead must recognize their frailties, and make way for a new species to come to power.

The Girl with All the Gifts centers around a group of human survivors including army personnel, a scientist, and a teacher, occupying a military base in the country and trying to find a cure for the infection. Their research involves experimenting on second-generation human-hungry hybrid children. These creatures can think and speak like humans but have an insatiable urge to consume flesh. The novel opens with our protagonist Melanie, a human-hungry hybrid being held captive at the base. We learn that Melanie has never seen the outside world. Her whole life has been spent in a cell, with occasional trips to the shower and lessons in a classroom. From the outset Melanie's knowledge of Greek myth provides a means for her understanding of the world. She tells us that her name "means 'black girl,' from an ancient Greek word, but her skin is actually very fair so she thinks maybe it's not such a good name for her. She likes the name Pandora a whole lot, but you don't get to choose" (Carey 1). Myth, stories, and fairy tales have given her a sense of self. Karen Armstrong notes that from the beginning humans have "invented stories that enable us to place our lives in a larger setting, that revealed an underlying pattern, and gave us a sense that, against all the depressing and chaotic evidence to the contrary, life had meaning and value" (2). Humans are mythmakers, and in a post-apocalyptic world where chaos reigns, it seems only natural that Melanie would fall back on this time-honored tradition to gain some understanding of herself, and her place in this world. She tells us that "she's ten years old, and she has skin like a princess in a fairy tale; skin as white as snow. So she knows that when she grows up she'll be beautiful, with princes falling over themselves to climb her tower and rescue her" (2). Melanie's understanding of herself is painfully at odds with the reality of her situation. This is made clear very early in the novel when she is being retrieved from her prison cell by two army personnel. As one man trains his gun on her, the other restrains her in a wheelchair. This precautionary treatment seems strange and overdramatic as Melanie smiles, greets the soldiers politely, and complies with all their orders. She is then escorted into a classroom, where she joins numerous other children in similar restraints, all under the tutelage of Miss Justineau. Miss Justineau is the only character that treats these hybrid children as human. Melanie's adoration of her teacher is highlighted when she muses that, "when Miss Justineau teaches, the day is full of amazing things. Sometimes she'll read poems aloud, or bring in her flute and play it, or show the children pictures out of a book and tell them stories about the people in the pictures. That was how Melanie got to find out about Pandora and Epimetheus and the box of all the evils in the world" (12). Her humane treatment of the children is ridiculed by Sergeant Parks, the man in charge of running the base. He believes that she does not understand the monstrosity of these creatures, which he refers to as "frigging little abortions" (5). We later learn that these creatures were not born into this world but instead ate their own way out of their mothers' wombs, killing their mothers in this process of birthing themselves. To prove his point, he removes a blocker cream, which masks the scent of his flesh, from his arm, and hovers in front of one of the restrained children. In a split second the child turns feral, growling, salivating, and struggling to break free of his restraints. This feral response soon spreads to all the other children in the room, who are subject to their base need to consume human flesh. Melanie is the only exception as she seems to be able to somewhat control her instincts. This demonstration shows that despite appearing as children, these creatures are dangerous and threatening, and the restraints are necessary for the safety of the human survivors.

After this event, Melanie begins to question not just who but what she is. She realizes that her sense of self is at odds with how she is perceived by others. However, her feelings for Miss Justineau never waver, in fact they become even stronger. She says,

> There can't be anyone better or kinder or lovelier than Miss Justineau in the world; Melanie wishes she was a god or a Titan or a Trojan warrior, so she could fight for Miss Justineau and save her from Heffalumps and Woozles. She knows that Heffalumps and Woozles are in Winnie-the Pooh, not in Greek myth but she likes the words, and likes the idea of saving Miss Justineau so much that it becomes her favourite thought. (18)

Melanie writes a story about Miss Justineau, beginning with "Once upon a time," weaving elements of Greek myth into the tale in which she saves Miss Justineau from a monster, "and they lived together, for ever after, in great peace and prosperity" (20). She acknowledges that "the last sentence is stolen word for word from a story by the Brothers Grimm . . . and some of the other bits are sort of borrowed from . . . Greek myths . . . or just cool things she's heard people say. But it's still Melanie's story" (20).

Melanie places herself in the hero role in her story, she wants to protect and save Miss Justineau from danger, so the pair can live happily ever after. As the protagonist of the novel, she is expected to become a kind of hero, and as the novel progresses, we see her evolve into that role. However, as she is defined as something other, something monstrous, by other human survivors, including Sergeant Parks and Doctor Caldwell, the reader recognizes that they are identifying with a hybrid protagonist. Melanie is part human, but she is also something other, something different, something new. She has evolved beyond the human into a kind of posthuman being.[5]

Melanie draws on fantasy, myth, and storytelling to understand her own identity and to discover where her place is in this strange post-apocalyptic world. However, Melanie is not the only one trying to figure out her place in the world. The scientist of the group, Dr Caldwell, has been tasked with finding a cure for the fungal infection. Instead of examining how Melanie and the other hybrid children fit into this new world, she uses them as nothing more than specimens in her experiments. Although the world has changed beyond recognition and humans are clearly in decline, she is still adamant that this world rightfully belongs to human beings and she will stop at nothing to regain control of Earth. Melanie's demonstration of self-restraint, and her exceptional intelligence, is what makes her an exceptional specimen for study for Dr Caldwell. Her experiments involve killing the hungry children to examine their brains. Just as the army personnel treat the children as an othered monster, she treats them as an othered specimen. Although the soldiers are ultimately fearful of the hungry children, Dr Caldwell's scientific inquiry into finding a cure leads to her interest in them as a type of sub-human animal to experiment on. She has no qualms about killing them, as she believes her work is for the greater good, that is restoring humanity to its former place of power in the world. The novel overtly depicts the scientist as cold, calculating, and monstrous in her treatment of the hybrid children. Although Melanie has been defined as the monstrous other, Caldwell's attitudes and actions signal that her behavior is even more monstrous. As all prior experiments have failed, Caldwell sets her sights on Melanie, as she again stands out from the other hungry children. She believes that Melanie is just mimicking human emotion, as she does not believe a creature like her is capable of anything more. Just as Melanie is brought into Caldwell's lab, the army base is overrun by hungries, which saves Melanie from being the next victim of the scientist's scalpel.

After their base is destroyed, Melanie is the only hybrid child to survive. As she recounts the journey that she takes with the remaining human survivors to London, we gain a clearer insight into how this fungal infection has not only made changes to humanity but also transformed the landscape and environment. We see the world through Melanie's eyes as she helps the group to navigate through the post-apocalyptic landscape, despite their treatment of her at the base. This is the first time that Melanie has ever been free of confinement, as she spent most of her life imprisoned. We see her try to make sense of this outside world and we are told that she "builds the world around her as she goes" (166). The countryside is described as "overgrown with weeds," with "ragged hedges" and "crumbling walls" (166). Melanie describes the road as a "faded black carpet pitted with holes, some of them big enough for her to fall into" (166). Her eyes see "[a] landscape of decay—but still gloriously and heart-stoppingly beautiful" (166). We are presented with descriptions of houses in ruin, with "windows broken or boarded up. Doors hanging off their hinges" (167). Melanie astutely comments that "this world she's seeing was built by people, to meet their needs, but it's not meeting their needs anymore. It's all changed. And it's changed because they've retreated from it. They've left it to the hungries" (167). In a town they enter on their journey they find "waist-high weeds have smashed and grabbed their way up between tilted flagstones, mature brambles throwing up fist-thick stalks like the tentacles of subterranean monsters" (203). The fungal infection has altered the landscape that was once dominated by humans. These tentacles grow from the bodies of the hungries once the fungal infection has ravaged them, and as it continues to evolve. This is most clearly seen in London, where Dr Caldwell encounters tentacles that have wound together to create a "grey wall, forty feet high" (400). The urban center created by humans has been totally reclaimed by nature. Coming face to face with the power of nature, and humanity's inability to control it, Caldwell's belief in the superiority of man falters. She sees it as a "gauntlet, flung down by a bullying, contemptuous universe that allowed human beings to grope their way to sentience just so it could put them in their place that bit more painfully" (406).

Caldwell is not the only one to question the place of man in this new environment. As Melanie sees more of this new world, it becomes clear to her that the human survivors are unable to adapt to this new post-apocalyptic landscape. She knows that without her help they would not have been able to make it as far as they did. When the group reaches London, she understands that the fungal infection, which is a part of her, has reclaimed the environment too. She challenges the assumption that humanity's survival, at the cost of her own life, is for the greater good. In the end, Melanie figures out how the fungal infection works and how it is evolving. Just like Eve and Pandora before her, she can be said to cause the downfall of man as she opens a Pandora's Box, unleashing evil on the world, when she creates an airborne strain of the infection, effectively eliminating all humanity. Melanie understands that humans can never coexist with the hybrid children, who are better suited to this new environment. Humans have become obsolete. By releasing the airborne strain of the infection, she effectively wipes out humanity, creating a drastically alternative view of the future.

Carey's unusual post-apocalyptic world is also detailed in the prequel *The Boy on the Bridge* (2017), which was published after *The Girl with All the Gifts*. Although the main action takes place before the events of *The Girl with All the Gifts*, the epilogue is set twenty years later and reintroduces Melanie, now a young woman. She takes a group of human hybrids to one of the last outposts where humans have miraculously survived the airborne infection. Melanie points out to their leader that they will not survive for long as their crops are failing and offers them help. She does this just because she can. She tells them her reasoning,

> "Because we thought you were all gone and we're so happy that we were wrong. That your people and my people can meet, and talk, and learn from each other. You'd just have been legends to us, otherwise." She smiles, as though that

thought strikes her as funny. "I know how legends work. In a few generations, there'd be a thousand wild stories about you, and the truth . . . well, the truth would just be a story a little less interesting than the rest." (*The Boy* 455)

This epilogue seems to be a revision of the alternative future proposed in *The Girl with All the Gifts*. It eliminates some of the subversive potential of *The Girl with All the Gifts* as it harks back to that mythic fantasy of human survival even after the apocalypse, attempting to discount the powerful alternate viewpoint that was created in the first novel.

However, if we take *The Girl with All the Gifts* as a standalone text, although Melanie's human traits are celebrated, the novel appears to send the message that the future of the world is not human as we have always presumed in post-apocalyptic fiction. As the pre-title caption for *The Boy on the Bridge* points out, "A human being . . . is a very hard thing to be." Although this prequel points out that humans have survived, yet again, they are seen to be barely existing in a harsh outpost, where it seems that without help, they will peter out.

The Girl with All the Gifts points to the end of the Age of Anthropocene. Humans are no longer in control; they no longer hold dominion over their environment; nature has retaliated. The new inheritors of this earth are human-hybrid creatures that display the best traits of humanity, while existing in a symbiotic relationship with the fungal infection that has reclaimed the earth. The fittest have survived. For humanity to endure, it has had to evolve beyond what we think of as human. This new post-apocalyptic world is now ruled by a posthuman hybrid species, creating a radical and subversive view of the future of humanity.

NOTES

1. For a general overview of eschatology in Judaism see John W. Bailey's "Jewish Apocalyptic Literature" (*The Biblical World*, vol. 25, no. 1, 1905, pp. 30–42), in Islam see Norman O. Brown's "The Apocalypse of Islam" (*Social Text*, no. 8, 1983, pp. 155–171), and J. P. Filiu and M. B. DeBevoise's *Apocalypse in Islam* (University of California Press, 2012). For further discussion of apocalypse see J. M. Court's *Approaching the Apocalypse: A Short History of Christian Millenarianism* (I. B. Tauris, 2008).

2. Matheson's novel tells the story of one man trying to survive in a world that has been destroyed by a pandemic that turns people into infectious vampire-like creatures. A commercial success upon release, the novel was adapted into the films, *The Last Man on Earth* (1964), *The Omega Man* (1971), and *I Am Legend* (2007). The novel has been a major influence on not just the vampire genre but also the zombie genre. George Romero has also credited the novel as being an inspiration for his seminal

film, *Night of the Living Dead* (1968), as it popularized the concept of an apocalypse as the result of disease and paved the way for the concept of the zombie apocalypse.

3. It should be noted that not all post-apocalyptic texts follow this narrative. Some novels, such as Cormac McCarthy's *The Road* (2006), portray a much bleaker outlook for the future of mankind that can be read as nihilistic.

4. See Kyle Bishop's *American Zombie Gothic: The Rise and Fall (And Rise) of the Walking Dead in Popular Culture* (McFarland, 2010) and Elizabeth Aiossa's *The Subversive Zombie: Social Protest and Gender in Undead Cinema and Television* (McFarland, 2018).

5. The posthuman has been theorized as a state in which a human being exists beyond the human. The posthuman state is almost always achieved with the use of some form of technology. However, I read the posthuman as a blurring of the boundary between the human and other, where the other may take the form of technology or nature. The monster has long represented the threat of the other, the them that threatens the us. The zombie itself is a monster that blurs this boundary between human and monster. The hybrid nature of Melanie in Carey's novel can be read as posthuman as she is part human, but she also exists in a state that is beyond human as she is part hungry. See Elaine L. Graham's *Representations of the Post/Human: Monsters, Aliens and Others in Popular Culture* (Manchester UP, 2002) for more on how the relationship between human and monster can be read as posthuman.

WORKS CITED

Aiossa, Elizabeth. *The Subversive Zombie: Social Protest and Gender in Undead Cinema and Television*. McFarland, 2018.

Bailey, John W. "Jewish Apocalyptic Literature." *The Biblical World*, vol. 25, no. 1, 1905, pp. 30–42.

Berger, James. *After the End: Representations of Post-Apocalypse*. U of Minnesota P, 1999.

Bishop, Kyle. *American Zombie Gothic: The Rise and Fall (And Rise) of the Walking Dead in Popular Culture*. McFarland, 2010.

Booker, M. Keith. *Monsters, Mushroom Clouds, and the Cold War: American Science Fiction and the Roots of Postmodernism, 1946–1964*. Greenwood Press, 2001.

Broderick, Mick. "Surviving Armageddon: Beyond the Imagination of Disaster." *Science Fiction Studies*, vol. 20, no. 3, 1993, pp. 362–382.

Brown, Norman O. "The Apocalypse of Islam." *Social Text*, vol. 8, 1983, pp. 155–171.

Carey, M. R. *The Boy on the Bridge*. Orbit, 2017.

———. *The Girl with All the Gifts*. Orbit, 2014.

Chernus, Ira. *Dr. Strangegod: On the Symbolic Meaning of Nuclear Weapons*. U of South Carolina P, 1986.

Court, J. M. *Approaching the Apocalypse: A Short History of Christian Millenarianism*. I. B. Tauris, 2008.

Filiu, J. P., and M. B. DeBevoise. *Apocalypse in Islam*. U of California P, 2012.

Graham, Elaine L. *Representations of the Post/Human: Monsters, Aliens and Others in Popular Culture*. Manchester UP, 2002.

Green, Amy M. "The Reconstruction of Morality and the Evolution of Naturalism in the Last of Us." *Games and Culture*, vol. 11, no. 7–8, 2016, pp. 745–763.

Hoffstadt, Christian, and Dominik Schrey. "Aftermaths: Post-Apocalyptic Imagery." In *British Science Fiction Film and Television: Critical Essays*, edited by Tobias Hochscherf and James Leggott. McFarland, 2011, pp. 28–39.

Jameson, Fredric. *Postmodernism or, The Cultural Logic of Late Capitalism*. Verso, 1995.

Kermode, Frank. *Sense of an Ending*. Oxford UP, 2000.

MacFarlane, Roger. "Generation Anthropocene: How Humans Have Altered the Planet Forever." *The Guardian*, 1 April 2016. www.theguardian.com/books/2016/apr/01/generation-anthropocene-altered-planet-for-ever. Accessed 8 November 2019.

Paffenroth, Kim. *Gospel of the Living Dead: George Romero's Visions of Hell on Earth*. Baylor Press, 2006.

Schell, Jonathan. *The Unfinished Twentieth Century: The Crisis of Weapons of Mass Destruction*. Verso, 2003.

Shaviro, Steven. *The Cinematic Body*. U of Minnesota P, 1998.

Skult, Petter. "The Role of Place in the Post-Apocalypse: Contrasting the Road and World War Z." *Studia Neophilologica*, vol. 87, sup. 1, 2015, pp. 104–115.

Sontag, Susan. "The Imagination of Disaster." In *Science Fiction: A Collection of Critical Essays*, edited by Mark Rose. Prentice Hall, 1976, pp. 116–131.

Varley, John. "The Manhattan Phone Book (Abridged)." 1984. www.varley.net/Pages/Manhattan.htm. Accessed 10 April 2019.

Chapter 7

Beyond the Anthropocene

Human Enhancement, Mythology, and Utopia in James Patterson's Maximum Ride *Cycle*

Anna Bugajska

INTRODUCTION

Anthropocene as a term has been gaining popularity since the beginning of the twenty-first century when it was used by Paul J. Crutzen to denote an era in the Earth's history significantly marked by the activity of human beings (Crutzen). The impact of humanity on the natural environment has been remarkable, and has been differently conceptualized, medialized, and assessed. Nowadays, it forms a part of the general awareness about the global state of environment, as a part of not only academic discussion but also political risk assessment, popular culture, and everyday concern. The very name "Anthropocene" points to its focus on the role of human beings in the world, their responsibilities, and crimes (Truccone Borgogno), and seeks to provoke the idea of a modification of the role of humanity that will bring a benefit to the whole system.

It has to be noted that in the popular imagination posthumans and transhumans are usually portrayed negatively; however, of late, this is being reassessed (Bugajska, *Engineering Youth*; Clarke and Rossini; Hauskeller et al.). Vampires, werewolves, mutants, and monsters have consistently been cast in the role of villains, and becoming one of these creatures was seen as degradation from the "natural" human form, with the result that human–animal hybrids and chimeras have been demonized. Despite much of the anthropocentric imagery, positive presentation of such beings started to appear sometime during the 1970s,[1] an example being the Marvel comic series. However, with a closer look one can notice that those enhanced beings that are more human-like are less conflicted than those that undergo a transformation as a result of biochemical experiments or of being bitten by a spider. The strong bias against human–animal beings possibly comes from what Leon Kass (2003) calls the "yuck factor" (known as repugnance in the bioethical literature of the subject) and lends itself to the generally negative, or at least problematic, presentation of hybridization and chimerization in culture.

The general problems of anthropocentric bias have found reflection in literature, significantly the so-called cli-fi, for example, Kim Stanley Robinson's *2312* (2012), Cormac McCarthy's *The Road* (2006), and Ian McEwan's *Solar* (2010). In juvenile literature the themes connected with the Anthropocene and related to Nature are frequent; some examples that can be mentioned are Nancy Farmer's *Matt Alacrán* series (2002; 2013), Eoin Colfer's *Artemis Fowl* series (2001–2012), Marie Lu's *Legend* series (2011–2013), Dan Wells's *Partials Sequence* (2012–2014), Marcus Sedgwick's *Floodland* (2000) and *Saint Death* (2016), and Calavarro's *Decelerate Blue* (2009). Zoe Jaques has observed that there is a remarkable phenomenon where frequently young audiences are posited as heroes to save the world, and are burdened with anthropocentric responsibility for the state of the environment (115–116, 198). An example of this approach is certainly the *Maximum Ride* cycle (2005–2015), a complex action-adventure story about young siblings confronting the Anthropocene. A mixture that combines features of dark medical thriller, science fiction, and cli-fi, it amplifies the current anthropological and ecological crises, hyperbolizing the problems of humans plagued with the fear of their own extinction and with the guilt for the disasters they have brought to the world.

Ultimately, James Patterson sees the principle of responsibility (Jonas) not in geoengineering or in some other kind of human-made remedy to the climate change directed at Nature. He confronts his readers with posthumanization as the answer to the challenges of the Anthropocene and to anthropocentric drive to manage the issues it entails. Posthumanization as a motif in juvenile fiction has been discussed among others by Victoria Flanagan, Zoe Jaques, Anita Tarr and Donna White, Anna Bugajska, and Jennifer Harrison. These authors survey a variety of problems connected with the increasingly invasive presence of biotechnologies in everyday life and the heightened incidence of positively valued changes in the anthropocentric model. In comparison to what Noga Applebaum described in *Representations of Technology in Science Fiction for Young Adults* (2009) as technophobic narratives, contemporary fiction seems to have experienced a wave of scenarios in which humans are attracted to and bond with technologically or artificially created biological beings, and—what is more—seek to introduce ameliorative, fundamental changes in their own bodies. While the posthuman may be simply perceived as a fictional representation of Otherness that is reflected in our everyday life and in our relations with people who do not fit the current norm for "humanity," these beings are more and more frequently an authentic ethical playground of real decisions: to use or not to use new technologies, to enhance or not to enhance. It is true, as Harrison writes, that the contemporary posthumanizing narratives challenge the strong version of Enlightenment humanism (1–34); however, more fundamentally, they challenge the existence of human nature as such. Nevertheless, neither of these challenges to posthumanism are the answer: rather, they are a symptom of a profound anthropological crisis that leads us to rethink our relations to other, non-human beings.

In the case of Patterson's cycle, utilizing the elements of Christian mythology allows the author to tacitly signal a challenge to world religions to accept or reject enhancement and the notion of anthropogenic climate change. This perspective forms the focus of this chapter and the background for an investigation of the following thesis: the Christian mythology used by Patterson serves to reinforce the message of posthumanism and to encourage a weak version of transhumanism, which is based on such human enhancement that reaches out to the surrounding world rather than transhumanist detachment from it. As such, it undertakes an advocacy for the new post-Anthropocene humanism.

In the first part of the text the motif of human enhancement in the *Maximum Ride* cycle is discussed. The second part is devoted to an analysis of mythological tropes underlying the human enhancement philosophy and biopolitcs. The tensions between myth and utopia are investigated, and a general diagnosis is made as far as the mythological underpinnings of human enhancement rhetoric are concerned. Further, the study explores the specific influence of hybrid and chimera mythology on the popular culture and especially juvenile dystopias, with a subsequent more detailed discussion of the reworking of the images of Angels and Horsemen by James Patterson to contrast two types of human enhancement plans meant to answer the challenges of the Anthropocene. The final part examines the notion of a utopia of human enhancement, referring to the theory of evantropia and to the scholarship on human enhancement utopia. It is well known that there exist tensions between myth and utopia, which create the challenge not only for the present study but also for a more broadly taken evantropian biopolitical plan. The investigation of these dimensions of Patterson's narrative allows one to see the series as an anthropological experiment, remaining in opposition to the overwhelming anthropological pessimism, usually connected with the Anthropocene discourse. Patterson makes an interesting attempt to show that it is possible to build a new concept of human on the basis of the models provided by mythological and religious archetypes and the contemporary science and culture.

ENHANCEMENT AND OTHER EXTREME SPORTS

The *Maximum Ride* cycle was written over the decade that can be identified as one during which we could witness fundamental changes in the reception of biotechnological development not only in children's literature (Bugajska, *Engineering Youth*) but above all socially and politically. The accelerating biomedical progress, with such achievements as three-parent babies or bioprinting, was accompanied and fueled by the philosophico-ideological movement called initially as transhumanism, and later on (since 2008) as Humanity+. For the last few decades, this movement has been propagating human enhancement via advanced biotechnology in four spheres: physical, cognitive, emotional, and moral. The ultimate goal is supposed to be the achievement of the posthuman status (Bostrom), that is, one that significantly differs from and surpasses the current human condition. We can speak especially of the immortality research, cognitive enhancers, and advanced prostheses, but also about the work on the human genome, recently crowned with the discovery of "protein scissors," CRISPR-Cas9, which allows for genetic modification even in adults.

The cycle seems to reflect the social anxieties resultant from the mixture of ideological discourse and the progress in science, especially the debate between bioconservatives and technoprogressivists. Much of the rhetoric used by Patterson, especially imparted on the level of imagery, derives from the general anti-eugenics front, and more specifically falls back on and reacts to the famous report authored by the American bioethicist Leon Kass. Rather than slavishly subscribe to this or that party in the quarrel between those that profess the Proactive Principle (Steve Fuller) or the Precautionary Principle (Hans Jonas), the author elects his own way, focusing not so much on whether or not we should enhance human beings, but how such enhanced humans would fit in the society. His exploration encompasses nine volumes, at times presciently predicting the actual events we are witnessing now (e.g., the rise of young climate activists or actual human–animal hybrids).

The basic premise of the *Maximum Ride* series is the successful creation of human–animal hybrids, that is, beings modified on the DNA level.[2] The protagonists are Avians: children taken from or given up by their parents, with the exception of Angel, a wholly lab-created child. They do not differ much from other human beings in their behavior or in their psyche; they are, however, equipped with physical changes that influence their daily life and result from human experiments. The cycle begins with *The Angel Experiment* (2005), which introduces the Flock: Max, Fang, Iggy, Nudge, Gasman, and Angel. The children live alone, after they escaped from School, as the medical experiments facility is called in the cycle. All of them are winged, super-strong, and have fast metabolism:

We're—well, we're kind of amazing. Not to sound too full of myself, but we're like nothing you've ever seen before.

Basically, we're pretty cool, nice, smart—but not "average" in any way. The six of us—me, Fang, Iggy, Nudge, the Gasman, and Angel—were made on purpose, by the sickest, most horrible "scientists" you could possibly imagine. They created us as an experiment. An experiment where we ended up only 98% human. That other 2 percent has had a big impact, let me tell you. (Patterson, *Angel Experiment*, 1–2)

We were created by scientists, whitecoats, who grafted avian DNA onto our human genes. (26)

The beginning of the novel sets up the stage for the dramatic dichotomy that forms the background of Patterson's enhancement narrative. On the one hand, the "mutants" are "amazing," but on the other—they were created by "the sickest, most horrible scientists." The nature of the experiments is left to be imagined, but additional information given by Max, the narrator, allows us to expect the worst; the children were kept in cages and treated in a dehumanizing manner. In spite of this treatment, the Avians form a healthy family with strong bonds. Max and Fang, the eldest, take care of the remaining children, especially those who suffer the consequences of medical experiments: Iggy is blind and Gasman has a damaged digestive system. The youngest, Angel, is special, and throughout the story her powers, including telepathy, evolve. In both the initial volume and the following ones—*School's Out Forever* (2006) and *Saving the World and Other Extreme Sports* (2007)—the Flock is hunted by the Erasers: lupine–human hybrids, later on further cyborgized, which remain in the service of the medical scientists, attempting to build programmable superstrong beings. At the same time, Patterson unfolds the existential dilemmas of ALife: separation from biological parents, rejection by their "technological" parents, the status of a person, and so on.

These three initial books can be said to form a closely connected trilogy, and from the fourth volume, *The Final Warning* (2008), the cycle changes narrative tone and focus. The title references rhetoric familiar from the environmental discourse, and from this volume on human enhancement is presented as inevitably entwined with the problems of climate change, and it seems that in itself human enhancement is a larger plan for humanity's survival (a topic undertaken also by Wells in the *Partials Sequence*, 2009–2014). What is more, Patterson sensitizes his young audience to anti-speciecist openness: the Flock is joined by an enhanced dog Total, whose uplifted[3] existence within a predominantly human society proves full of difficulties (the author addresses the right to marriage between enhanced and non-enhanced dogs, for instance). It further destabilizes the anthropocentric perspective characteristic of the society the Avians are living in. The later volumes of the cycle are very clear about the catastrophic consequences of anthropogenic climate change and present human enhancement as the only possibility to survive violent climate events. Especially two scientists, Dr Janssen and Dr Gunther-Hagen, are prominent proponents of modifying humanity in accordance with transhumanist precepts. Janssen chooses hybridizing humans with animals, while Gunther-Hagen goes further with the creation of Horsemen, deprived of any human features save for augmented biological traits. Both scientists are presented as unethical, despite the rational reasons they provide for human experiments they are performing. Their only interest is genetic perfection; Gunther-Hagen is actually glad for the apocalyptic events on the Earth as they save him the trouble of removing imperfect people. He loses sight of the fact that the Avians are already prepared for survival in hostile conditions: besides their initial skills, they develop the ability to breathe underwater and to communicate with animals.

The propositions to biologically alter humans for survival in a hostile environment, whether on Earth or in outer space, have already appeared (Almeida and Diogo; Lehmann; Liao; Savulescu; Persson and Savulescu). They have been accompanied by perhaps more vocal groups of extinctionists and anti-natalists, postulating that humans should simply die out. Caught between posthumanism and anti-humanism, Patterson chooses the survival of humanity, albeit in a modified form: one, however, that does not respond fully to the anthropocentric ideals of transhumanism. Rather, what he portrays is a kind of connective posthumanism, familiar from Rosi Braidotti's *The Posthuman* (2013) and David Roden's *Posthuman Life: Philosophy at the Edge of Human* (2015).[4] His posthumans form a "scrap of untainted sky" (Moylan) in the dystopian world. However, the author seems to make a distinction, not entirely clear-cut and sharp, between a positive myth-based image and a negative eugenic utopian image, forcing the readers to rethink the entanglement of myth and utopia in general, and their unique interplay within the human enhancement plan.

THE MYTHOLOGY OF HUMAN ENHANCEMENT

The fact that myth somehow forms the underpinning and the final goal of utopia has been noticed by numerous scholars, who also draw attention to the inherent tension between the world of the sacred (*mythos*) and the secularized (*ou/eu topos*). In his classical *The Shape of Utopia: Studies in a Literary Genre* (1970), Robert C. Elliott points out that, often as it might be seen as opposite to utopia,[5] myth provides the inspiration and stirs a longing for what utopia is trying to concretize and to subject to rational analysis. And while in his assessment, utopia is the most appropriate fictional answer to the development of science, it reposes on the founding myths and imaginations. The sacred sensed and experienced through myth becomes the subject of the actions of human as a creator. In this way, we arrive at a secularized version of a mythological image, which is reenacted in the realm of science and technology. Like human technological creations, it is imbued with external, usually anthropocentric, telos.

In a similar fashion to Elliott, Lucas E. Misseri claims that the human enhancement plan is the secularization of the idea of creation, perfectly fitting Elliott's analysis (34). The secularization in utopia, which originated in a Catholic milieu (Thomas More's *Utopia*, 1516), usually refers the reader back to Christian mythology.[6] The idea of human enhancement utopia has been discussed by scholars of religion and theology as deriving in a straight line from Christianity, building on its images and the longings it evokes (Mercer and Trothen). Naturally then, the technological and biopolitical utopias that transhumanism constructs are rooted in mythological imagery of Christianity and implicated in its religious significance.[7]

Here, however, it is necessary to reach out beyond Christianity to establish the departure point for further analysis, and to understand how Patterson's series resonates with human enhancement discourse. The focus of the analysis is a specific type of extreme enhancement, namely, hybridization and chimerization of people. As of now, few countries allow the creation of recombinant human–animal embryos for experimentation purposes that are usually destroyed under the fourteen-day rule (Cavaliere; Chan; Cyranoski; Koplin and Savulescu; Koplin and Wilkinson). However, more and more often in recent years the call for lifting the ban on growing human–animal creatures has been heard, and now, the genetic modification of humans is a fact (Barash; Carretero; Cyranoski). Patterson starts from a point in children's literature where a technophobic narration is still dominant (Applebaum); however, his cycle continues into an era that has been called Biotechnical Revolution (Stripling 24). The tensions between the visions rooted in the generally accepted mythological images of human–animal beings and the utopia of the salvation of humanity through posthumanization are very clear in the story about Maximum Ride and her siblings.

It can be observed that Patterson achieves this tension through the use of different devices. First, both mythical and utopian images are used in his novels with ambivalent value. As stated before, myth-based images are generally described as being "optimistic"; nevertheless, this is only partially true. Some of the mythological images seem to be positive, and some—also referencing enhancement—negative. Even a superficial look at the plot makes it clear that the Avians are positive (reinforced in the last volume by the image of Phoenix), and the lupine Erasers negative. In addition, the Horsemen are simply killing machines. The latter image in the books is appropriated by the Nazi-like project of a eugenic utopia; thence: it acquires a very negative value.

Second, the tension is created by contrasting two familiar figures of mythology: a winged man and a wolf-man. When it comes to the winged man, it is of prime importance for the H+ movement. Transhumanists reach to Icarus, with detachable technological wings, as a figure of the aspirations of human enhancement (Hauskeller, *Mythologies of Transhumanism* 4). The soaring hopes this image represents are nevertheless tied more closely to wearables than to the actual ability to fly that is genetically inherent to new creatures. It is also not reported that avian–human hybrids would be an area of interest for embryo experimentation. This, if performed, would represent a clear case of radical enhancement, not justified with practical needs. Bearing this in mind, it can be claimed that Patterson purposefully turns to mythology, rather than actual technological background, to introduce new aspects into the human enhancement debate. He moves beyond the myth of Icarus to imagine an actual combination of man and bird on the genetic level: an irreversible change that ultimately impacts the pattern of functionally modified humans.

The trope of flight, going back to the unique powers claimed by shamans in primitive societies, is one of the signs of transcending human condition and entering the realm of the divine (Campbell 257; Eliade, *Rites* 64; Eliade, *Myths* 102; Eliade, *Szamanizm* 185). It is not, however, equivalent to saying it is a positively charged trope. Creatures like harpies or sirens are associated with danger for humans, ugliness, and monstrosity. The deep mythical rooting of Patterson's Avians is therefore ambivalent. Wings symbolize their capability to—at least symbolically—perform an ascent to heaven, and their connection to the sacred. At the same time, though, winged human-avian creatures in mythology are presented sometimes in such a way as to raise instinctive fear. It is especially important to notice that those creatures that do not speak human language seem to pass beyond humanity into monstrosity; and Patterson keeps this distinction in his moving presentation of creatures like Harry-Huryu, a kid that in *Maximum Ride Forever* joins Max:

> Then it hit me: They looked like the flock—tall and lean human bodies with wings attached behind the shoulders—but they behaved . . . differently. As I spoke, they cocked their heads in sharp little movements and made clicking sounds in the back of their throats.
>
> And . . . they were naked. Not naked as in acres of skin, but naked as in without clothes. These kids were covered with feathers *all* over—thick, downy feathers, everywhere but their heads.
>
> Between my cracked lips and matted hair, I'd been feeling pretty feral, but these kids were straight-up *wild*. They flew like birds because they actually were more like birds than humans. (Patterson, *Maximum Ride Forever* 179)

The wildness of the "imperfect" Avians, and their presentation as more animal than human beings, may be at first perceived as the failure of scientific experimentation. In the latter part of the book, the relationship between Harry and Max is shown as difficult: Harry's actions resemble ones of a mentally disabled person or a stage between a primate and a human (what could be termed a prehuman (Clarke 141–145)). What is symptomatic, though, Patterson is careful to show that Harry is accepted by the Avians despite his imperfections or "disabilities," and that he is able to bond with the Flock, choosing Maximum as his "Max Mum."

In contrast, the transformation into a wolf seems to symbolically bring humans closer to animals, unbridled instincts, and predatory power. It is this trope that Patterson chooses to link with the monstrosity of human enhancement efforts, focused on the functionality of thus created beings as killing machines, and not on any other aspect of their life. Cannibalism and the motif of killing humans and children strongly tied to the images of wolves, werewolves, and anthropomorphized wolves in general, here are reworked in the portrayal of intrinsic hatred the Erasers bear for the Avians. It is best visible in an inter-species, inter-sibling rivalry that seems to motivate the actions of one of the Erasers, Ari:

> He felt his heart speed up with anticipation, his fingers itching to close around a skinny bird-kid neck. Then he started to *morph*, watching his hands. The frail human skin was soon covered with tough fur; ragged claws erupted from his fingertips. Morphing had hurt at first—his lupine DNA wasn't seamlessly grafted into his stem cells, like the other Erasers'. So there were some kinks to be worked out, a rough, painful transition period he'd had to go through.
>
> But he wasn't complaining. It would all be worth it the moment he got his claws on Max and choked the life right out of her. He imagined the look of surprise on her face, how she would struggle. Then he'd watch the light slowly fade out of her beautiful brown eyes. She wouldn't think she was so hot then. Wouldn't look down on him or, worse, *ignore* him. Just because he wasn't a mutant freak like them, he'd been nothing to her. All she cared about was the flock this and the flock that. That was all his father, Jeb, cared about too.
>
> Once Max was dead, that would all change. And he, Ari, would be the number-one son. *He'd come back from the dead for it.* (Patterson, *School's Out* 11–12; original emphasis)

Although Ari retains his senses and is able to direct his actions and motivations in the way Harry is unable to, this rationality in a transformed body is shown as leading him to evil, while the "bird kid's" instincts tend toward the patterns of healthy bonding. His transformation is described with words evoking the audiences' horror and disgust, connected with pain, violence, and death. It is in accordance with the cultural trope chosen by Patterson as the basis, and remains in agreement with the negative imagery surrounding such phenomena that is especially characteristic of the Christian cultural circle. Typically, wolves are associated with the underworld and the descent into hell (Campbell; Szynkiewicz), and these associations are to be confirmed by the above description (e.g., an allusion to coming back from the dead). However, shape-shifting is also one of the shamanic powers, and signifies a kind of transcendence. Thus, it can be seen that Ari becomes better in some way: the frailty of the Avians is juxtaposed with his toughness, their weakness with his determination. If adaptability was based solely on brute force, he is portrayed through evolution as fitter and more likely to survive the struggle. The lack of the ability to fly, though, seems to put the Erasers at a disadvantage; nevertheless, later on they are equipped with mechanical wings that bring ridiculous results.

These two examples of hybrids, although familiar to many world mythologies, are deeply imbued with Christian meanings, as well as linked to the popular appropriation of these images. The frequent, although not justified, the representation of angels from Biblical stories is one of men with wings. The image is so strong as to create an archetype in the general imagination, making it possible to claim, at least for the Western audiences, an immediate association between the Avians and angels. At the same time, the Biblical image of the wolf is usually one that is negative, as it associates wolves with the powers of spiritual evil and destruction (e.g., Ezekiel 22:27; Jeremiah 5:6; Matthew 7:15, 10:16; John 10:12, Acts 20:29). This association is especially strong in the rhetoric of the New Testament: the apostles are sent "as sheep" to face the wolves of pagans and false prophets, who seek to destroy the Kingdom of God (e.g., Matthew 7, 10, 26; Luke 10). An especially relevant picture comes from the Acts, where the disciples are warned that "wolves" shall try to destroy the "flock" (Acts 20). The direct parallel that can be spotted between this passage and Patterson's novels allows the reader to interpret the struggle between the two types of enhanced humanity as the confrontation between the "meek" Avians that "shall inherit the earth" and their enemies that shall perish. In this way, Patterson weaves into his story a subliminal message that a certain type of enhancement is better than others: the one tending toward posthuman connectivity with the world, rather than the one relying on the amplification of brute strength.

This point is pursued in the finale of the series, where Patterson makes a direct reference to the Bible in his creation of Horsemen. In the Book of Revelations, St. John writes about a vision of four Horsemen seated on four differently colored horses: a white horse, a red horse, a black horse, and a pale horse (Rev. 6). They are unnamed and not clearly described, apart from the last Horseman, whose name is Death. The first Horseman is traditionally seen as a conqueror and sometimes interpreted as Jesus Christ, coming to the Earth for the second time. The second Horseman symbolizes war and destruction, and he is tasked with provoking conflicts between people. The third Horseman has scales in his hand, and symbolizes famine (Rev. 6:5). From this allusion it can be expected that Patterson's Horsemen are apocalyptic beings that are issued on the world to destroy it.

However, this is not the case. The Horsemen are actually the embodiment of the eugenic dream of Dr Gunther-Hagen. For the reader unfamiliar with the Book of Revelations, the image Patterson's creation evokes is rather horrific (a combination of a horse and a man), while in the text they are perfect people in terms of biological enhancement: in a sense, a reworking of the first Horseman of the Apocalypse. In this manner, Patterson introduces powerful disruptive tension to the original myth. Fundamentally, the transhumanist overmen Gunther-Hagen creates are powerful but also programmed human "biobots" (Kriegman et al.): supersoldiers obedient to the will of their creator. The powers issued by God on Earth to make an end to the old world and introduce it to the new order of things are here replaced by killing machines that target the actual posthumans: Avians, posthumanized, enhanced hybrids. God, in this reading, is on par with Gunther-Hagen, a Nazi-like German doctor, inspired by and referencing a well-known German anatomist, the creator of plastination and the initiator of Body Worlds events. The associations are very clear: "It was Goebbels," says Gunther-Hagen in *Maximum Ride Forever*, "with his understanding that nothing human could be sacred, and the Hulk, with his appetite for complete and total destruction, who laid the foundation for our current revolution" (224). In this way Patterson ties together Christian mythology, twentieth-century history, bioethics, and popular culture.

This deeply postmodern narration, while deconstructing and challenging the basic cultural and religious tenets, attempts at the same time to bring into agreement the various systems from which it borrows. It is not so much to form an eclectic picture as to show that the posthuman world can be a dystopia, but can be a utopia all the same, and that shared values that are professed by various religions, traditions, and races remain a basis for the new posthuman world. This role of fiction finds confirmation in the literature of the subject. As we can read in Hughes,

> Popular culture both reflects and shapes political culture. The depiction of the posthuman in popular culture is therefore not only a running commentary on the political concerns of the time, with posthumans as stand-ins for everything from communists to immigrants, but also a potent shaper of attitudes towards extant and future varieties of humanity. [. . .] Speculative fiction can cultivate respect for transhuman difference and democratic possibility on the one hand,

or reinforce speciesist "human racism" on the other, by drawing the reader or viewer into a deep, empathetic connection with a human protagonist who is forging solidarity with posthumans or beleaguered by posthuman threats, or with posthuman heroes or sympathetic posthuman victims. (Hughes 235–236)

This complex picture is further combined with the one of ecological disaster. All of the above mythological tropes are inscribed into the Anthropocene narration. While the Avians are clearly modified for survival in hostile climate conditions, this is inscribed in a bigger plan, which assumes removing the surplus of humanity, in accordance with the famed "humanity is cancer of the Earth" discourse. In the *Maximum Ride* cycle, the scientists of Itex, a biotechnological organization, attempt to work out a solution that will reduce the number of unenhanced humans (the Remedy) and replace them with possibly the finest posthumans. In the words of Dr Janssen:

"I was thinking that the world's population is destroying itself," she said in a steely tone I recognized. (I have one just like it.) "I was thinking that someone had to stand up and take drastic action before this entire planet is incapable of supporting human life. Yes, you're my daughter, but you're still just part of the big picture, part of the equation. I was thinking I'd do anything to make sure the human race survives. Even if it seems awful in the short term. In future history books, I'll be heralded as the savior of humanity." (Patterson, *Saving the World* 283)

By employing the point of view of Max, a modified human being, Patterson shows that this plan is far too idealistic, and that the pursuit of an ideal human for an ideal world never ends: no version is ever final and satisfying, and the older versions are treated, ultimately, as models to be removed. However, overall, he finishes his cycle on a note that may be seen as threatening for the unenhanced humanity: only the chosen ones survive the natural disaster that eventually comes, and few are admitted to live with the Avians in Paradise. What is more, it is expected that only the offspring of the enhanced humans will remain to, perhaps, repopulate the Earth (like the child of Max and Fang: Phoenix).

The myths evoked by Patterson to a degree remain in line with the imagery employed by the transhumanist movement. The reliance on the trope of flight is typical for transcendence and strongly tied with the belief in the power of technology (Tatar 22; Schmeink), and this is repeated in the aforementioned Icarus, and the images of popular mythology for other types of enhancement: Iron Man, Hulk, or vampires (Hauskeller et al.). Nevertheless, the interplay between the two most important mythological references utilized by transhumanist rhetoric, Prometheus and Lucifer, retains anthropomorphic imagery, riddled, however, with internal paradoxes. The non-human Titan brings fire to the people and acts out of concern for their well-being, and for this he suffers his punishment. The angel, on the other hand, is at least ambiguous, if not downright villainous in the story of the rise of humankind, and is connected with the hatred of people and the intent to kill them. This shows that the transcendence proposed by human enhancement discourse is locked in the dilemma of improvement, bringing survival only to the enhanced, "sicut deus" beings (Bugajska, "Religia"; Hauskeller, *Mythologies of Transhumanism*). Eventually, a darker shade is brought to the interpretation of Patterson's novels: semi-angels inherit the Earth, making one think of Lucifer rather than Prometheus. The restoration of the power of flight after the Fall signifies, perhaps, that the "peaceable kingdom" will not be as imagined in the Bible: the glorious city, New Jerusalem, is replaced with eco-paradise. However, it is the ascent of ambivalent creatures: this ambiguity is visible in Angel, the youngest Avian, who is manipulative and, at times, ruthlessly pursues her plans because she trusts in her "better" understanding.

What can be concluded from the section about mythology is that Patterson frequently challenges the forbidding power of myth relating to the creation of hybrids and chimeras. In general, though, the author relies strongly on the cultural associations of mythological images and, with their help, makes a case for a type of human enhancement that would lead to the survival of posthumans in a new world. What is more, with the employment of religious allusions he complicates the Christian vision of the paradise.

THE UTOPIA OF HUMAN ENHANCEMENT

In recent years, with the rise of transhumanism as a serious social and political power, human enhancement started to be seen in the academic circles as a result of a new type of utopian thought, derived from the eugenic utopias originating in the nineteenth century. These utopias concentrated on designing such a biopolitical organization of the society so as to arrive at a perfectly healthy and biologically most viable population. Infamously, the extremes of such utopianism found realization in initiatives such as the Ugly Laws (1867–1914) in the United States and the Nazi attempt to create a perfect race (1930s–1940s). No wonder then that bodily utopianism is burdened with many negative associations, which results in homologizing it with dystopia. However, the latest research into the biotechnological utopias and a thorough look into the transhumanist thought provide a more refined theoretical background.

In the literature of the subject the references to the utopia of human enhancement are frequent, to the degree that the proponents of the movement, like Max More, feel it necessary to defend themselves against the negative associations that come with the term (More 14–16; Pilsch 17). However, there are only a limited number of studies that are devoted specifically to the description of this type of utopia. In his numerous publications, Michael Hauskeller has demonstrated how transhumanists rely on deeply ingrained cultural patterns, and how the thought of Bostrom and Pearce is permeated with utopian dreaming. However, the definition of *utopia* he accepts is very broad: he considers utopia simply a "better place" and sees its function in reminding humans that "the world doesn't have to be as it is: that there are other possible worlds that we could live in" (Hauskeller, "Utopia" 101).[8] What is more, he does not make much distinction between and does not rigidly define *myth* and *utopia*; he provides an overview of certain cultural tropes that seem to underlie the transhumanist project. Nevertheless, this distinction does not reach into the actual biopolitics and utopian theory. More specific studies are those of Patricia Stapleton and Andrew Byers, and Andrew Pilsch. In their volume on biopolitics and utopia, Stapleton and Byers provide the reader with a particular perspective on the scientific development and its underlying ideology as a kind of utopia, hinged on the belief in progress and situated within the body (1–9). Pilsch, relying on Jameson's utopian theories, claims that transhumanism is "the only discourse today actively imagining a radical future as radically alien as communism's idea of a classless society was in the late nineteenth century" (3), and singles out evolutionary futurism as the driving force of what he calls the human technologies of utopia.

The theory that is used here was outlined by Lucas E. Misseri, and developed further for the literature studies (Bugajska, *Engineering Youth*), specifically for the context of young adult dystopias. In relation to the existing sources, here it will be given new consideration. Misseri called the type of human enhancement/transhumanist utopianism outlined above evantropia (eu+anthropos) and related it to Bostrom's ideal of a perfect body. However, evantropia is contextualized in the social health plans of twentieth-century Latin America (Misseri 34); therefore, it encompasses much more than simply the enhancement of an individual body. It also possesses a biopolitical aspect, thus being a versatile tool that can be refined for specific purposes. Within this theory, we can distinguish evantropia, which would roughly correspond to positive types of enhancement, and dysantropia, the undesirable effects of the same practice.[9]

In the *Maximum Ride* cycle it is evident that both evantropia and dysantropia appear significantly, and that their juxtaposition, and the later interplay between the shades of evantropia, are fundamental to the novels. At first glance, though, the typology suggested here does not correspond well to the complex patterns of the books: it seems that in the majority of sources the human enhancement utopia is understood as a synonym of a transhumanist utopia, and the latter is usually seen as opposite to posthuman utopia if only in terms of the anthropocentrism of the former and anti-anthropocentrism of the latter (e.g., Harrison). Nevertheless, even within the discussion on anthropocentrism, the distinctions are not so obvious, and in the human enhancement debate it is clearly stated that the goal of transhumanist practices is arriving at the posthuman status, that is, radically different from what is now proposed as human and connected with deliberate choice, whether it be one of weakness, suffering, or death. A number of transhumanist theorists do not reject the human body as redundant; on the contrary, they make it the site of the realization of the posthuman dream (to mention Sandberg's morphological freedom).[10]

In this manner, in Patterson's cycle we can speak about the evantropia of the Avians. They arise as a realization of a certain ideal, an embodiment of a staple of the imagination of transcendent humans: angels. This heavenly ideal is realized in the flesh, and is part of a bigger plan that is supposed to lead to the creation of the society of enhanced humans living in Paradise (the name of a safe place in the world touched by the lethal Remedy). The Avians are both the site of experimentation, and the concretization of utopian thought. They are also the ones that are going to build the new world, and thus, we can speak of evantropia as a realized dream of enhanced humanity. Although the bird children differ radically from what today is considered human, even in their DNA, they retain a certain continuity on the level of shared values. This seems to suggest that Patterson believes in the existence of universal axiology: love, friendship, solidarity, life, and loyalty can be found both in humans and in posthumans. However, the general presentation of unenhanced humanity in the books is rather to the disadvantage of humans. Max and her siblings show more discernment, sensitivity, altruism, and ecological awareness than non-Avians. Through their modification and merging with non-human people, they seem to have obtained an enhanced moral sensitivity, which should lead to building a better world that is not simply based on the biological survival of the fittest, as is the plan of Dr Gunther-Hagen, but true to the best in all aspects of being human. Importantly, Patterson leaves space for fallibility, vulnerability, disability, and non-normativity, as crucial aspects of a future posthumanity.

Dysantropia, on the other hand, can be identified using the example of the Erasers. The description of Erasers leaves no doubt that the experiment with human–lupine hybrids was wrong both in its intention and in its result. In comparison with the Avians, they are crude, awkward, and ridiculous, mixing the negative werewolf trope with the fairy tale image of a wolf-villain that gets outsmarted by the protagonists. The tragedy of thus modified children is shown only by the example of Ari; and, together with the "degradation" of his body, his psyche is also succumbing to hate, vengeance, and overwhelming suffering. The reader is led to assume that Erasers do not share in the axiological makeup of humans or Avians, and their only goal is destruction. They are presented as flawed because they cannot be easily controlled and cannot control their own instincts: thus, they are ineffective in combat, which is their only purpose.

The scientists are more successful when it comes to the Horsemen. Readers might wonder if the Horsemen belong to evantropia or dysantropia. On the one hand, they are the very embodiment of the transhumanist project: perfect, superstrong beings—although "with fur, wings and wolfish features" (Patterson, *Maximum Ride Forever* 244). They, however, are not going beyond human limitations by seeking connectivity and reaching out to the outside world. They are simply enhanced in their humanity, and the name "Horsemen" is nothing more than a linguistic marker, an index that points to an image of humanity taking its dominion over nature, domesticating, taming, and using it for battle. Just like horsemen use horses for their own—sometimes evil—purposes, the posthuman Horsemen are created with the purpose of serving humans in exerting power on the world. They are the expression of the ultimate anthropocentrism. The reader, thus, is offered a disturbing picture of a eugenic utopia come true, at least on a small scale.

It is clear that the Horsemen do not belong in the new world. An enhanced ecotopian Paradise is juxtaposed with Himmel: an underground laboratory of Dr Gunther-Hagen, in which he creates the Horsemen that are supposed to mete out death. Even if he says, "The earth is my primary patient" (Patterson, *Maximum Ride Forever* 350), he seems not to be interested in Nature and does not care for the preservation of life as the highest value. As Patterson writes, "Dr. Gunther-Hagen might have been a philanthropist, an environmentalist, and a brilliant scientist. But he was also a rich, manipulative extremist with a God complex—never a good combo. [. . .] He is plague, and war, and famine, and death" (*Maximum Ride Forever* 268). The technological paradise, then, the man-made utopia, brings an apocalypse in the sense of annihilation of life, and ironically the human enhancement heaven is powerfully presented as hell. It is, though, a type of human enhancement that remains fully anthropocentric and masks a lust for power under the guise of concern for the environment. It also tacitly links Christian religious views to such anthropocentrism that legitimizes the human dominion over the world and shows the negative effects of such an interpretation of the Christian doctrine for all beings in the world.

Patterson, then, seems to promote an evantropia that leads to a posthumanization that is similar to the one promoted by Donna Haraway, Rosi Braidotti, and Thomas Morton: one which entails opening oneself to the Otherness of non-human people, and renouncing rigid claims about human exceptionality in relation to the world. However, questions arise as to the way in which the evantropian ideal is created. Evantropia as a goal, as a bodily utopia, transpires as a desirable dream. Still, the evantropia as a social project is shown to be a flawed and potentially highly dangerous idea, riddled with difficulties, which more often than not bring about dystopian, eugenic totalitarian results. Finally, it can be seen that, this way or another, Patterson does not see the survival of humanity in any other way than accepting some kind of radical enhancement. However, he does not seem to believe that the extinction of humanity as we know it is something to be afraid of. The utopian hope resides in the idea of achieving a posthuman status, which here is enhanced with angelic imagery and juxtaposed with the strictly anthropocentric utopia of the Horsemen, and with the dysantropia of the Erasers. Thus, the overall ending of the cycle can be perceived as ambiguously positive.

CONCLUSION

In conclusion, the analysis above proves that James Patterson, despite representing a rather traditionally conservative group (Catholics), propagates radical enhancement for the survival and peaceful coexistence with the world. By using the imagery borrowed from myths, folktales, popular culture, and Christianity, he makes a case for the posthumanization of humans. Further, Patterson focuses on the advantages of hybridization and chimerization, despite the overall negative evaluation these biotechnologies have obtained in today's world. This allows one to suspect that public opinion would be ready to support experiments of scientists such as Juan Carlos Izpisúa Belmonte or Hiromitsu Nakauchi, and consequently genetically modify their children (Bugajska, *Engineering Youth*; Carretero; Cyranoski).

What is especially important is situating enhancement within the environmental crisis context. Patterson seems to go along the same line of reasoning as Savulescu and Liao, in that he sees the necessity for more than just emotional connectivity with other species. In fact, the modified DNA outlined in the series seems to enhance the morality of the Avians. This appears to be a reaction to the anthropogenic climate change discourse, on the one hand, blaming people for harming the environment, and on the other, placing on them the responsibility to act and amend the damage done to Nature. It is clear in the novels that the majority of human enhancement effort is motivated by the "ecological" need only on the surface. By getting rid of the "cancer of the Earth," that is, people, this effort does not actually seek new ways of interacting with the environment, but focuses only on the augmentation of human strength, on making profit, and satisfying scientific curiosity. Both Avians and Erasers fall victim to an instrumental approach to Nature; yet, the former manage to create a new egalitarian family, leading the world into a post-Anthropocene era. What transpires from the novels is a romanticized belief in a new Noble Savage: made up of both human and animal parts that "physically" go beyond the idea of an inter-species boundary, which allows the protagonists to understand the needs of the environment as their own.

Various types of utopianism are at play in the novels, coming in complex relations with mythologies and religions. We can speak about eugenic utopia, transhumanist utopianism, ecotopianism, evantropia–dysantropia dyad, and possibly more. Through a heavy reliance on myth and fantasy in their rhetoric the advocates of transhumanism complicate their message. The statement that utopia actually is myth in action could not be more apt: Patterson combines familiar images to create his own narrative about humanity plus beyond the Anthropocene, a concurrent narrative to one of transhumanist "religions" and apocalyptic Christianity, as well as the dystopian and catastrophic visions connected with the twentieth-century totalitarianisms. While utilizing dystopian settings and typical dystopian elements, Patterson moves beyond the anthropocentric apocalyptic imagery and presents an opportunity to build an after-Anthropocene world by implementing the hybridization of humanity and the humanization of animals. His narrative remains humanistic while rejecting anthropocentric Enlightenment humanism and provides an interesting exploration of what may be called a successful evantropia: such body modification that restores the balance between the environment and humanity.

NOTES

1. Arguably earlier (since the 1940s) or later (since the recent adaptations of the Marvel comics at the beginning of the twentieth century). For more information see e.g., Applebaum; Bugajska, *Engineering Youth*; Hauskeller et al., Schmeink.

2. It needs to be mentioned that Patterson is neither consistent nor precise in his biotechnological terminology. There is a clear distinction between hybrids and chimeras; Patterson, however, often calls his protagonists simply "mutants" or "recombinants."

3. The term popularized in philosophy by Georg Dvorsky, to talk about enhanced, usually humanized animals.

4. By connective posthumanism we can understand one distinct from other posthumanisms, e.g., transhumanist posthumanism. It underlines the connection with the body but also the connection between humans and different types of beings on the principle of zoe, that is, a life force. Thus, it is fundamentally anti-racist and anti-speciecist. Roden even writes about the concept of "wide humanity," wherein humans are connected in one system with other things which can be considered human as well as long as they do not form a separate system. Thus, humans are connected not only biologically with Nature but with objects like a toothbrush.

5. See also Sorel's classical distinction in *Réflexions sur la violence* (2013), and its discussion by Levitas in *The Concept of Utopia* (1990).

6. On the discussion of the complex tensions between myth and Christianity see, e.g., Łaszkiewicz.

7. In fact, transhumanists create their own religious or pseudo-religious organizations, e.g., the Godhead cult, or prometheism (Bugajska "Religia"; Hauskeller, *Mythologies of Transhumanism*; Mercer and Trothen).

8. One of the questions that can be posed in relation to this type of utopia is what is meant by the "world" and how the innovators that push the posthumanist and transhumanist agenda relate to non-human nature. In a general understanding, posthumanism tends to be seen as non-anthropocentric, and transhumanism as anthropocentric. This means that the non-human world for transhumanists would likely mean Nature of which they think as of a blind force that needs to be directed by technology: thence the drive to either human domination over Nature, tending to humanize the non-human world via, e.g., animal enhancement, or to separate from the world, as in ecomodernism. On the other hand, posthumanism tends to oppose human uniqueness and seeks connectivity with the world of non-human beings; it can be said that it sometimes tends toward flat ontology and panpsychism. However, such a brief commentary does not give justice to the existent debate, as we can distinguish, e.g., transhumanist posthumanism among the many conceptualizations within posthumanities. For more information on the debate see, e.g., More and Vita-More; Roden.

9. Dysantropia still remains not clearly defined and can be understood in various ways. For example, Misseri believes it is an abuse of the human enhancement ideal which can lead to harm, and even to the extinction of humanity as a species (to be replaced with some kind of non-human or radically posthuman beings that have no ethically significant connection to humans). I see it more broadly: as any practice of human enhancement that leads to undesirable consequences, i.e., to the intended or unintended creation of monsters, bringing harm to human or posthuman beings, unleashing disease on the world, creating a "zombiecracy," etc.

10. "We favor morphological freedom—the right to modify and enhance one's body, cognition, and emotions. This freedom includes the right to use or not to use techniques and technologies to extend life, preserve the self through cryonics, uploading, and other means, and to choose further modifications and enhancements" ("Transhumanist Declaration (2012)" in More and Vita-More 55; cf. Sandberg).

WORKS CITED

Almeida, Mara, and Rui Diogo. "Human Enhancement. Genetic Engineering and Evolution." *Evolution, Medicine, and Public Health*, vol. 1, 2019, pp. 183–189.

Applebaum, Noga. *Representations of Technology in Science Fiction for Young Adults*. Routledge, 2009.

Barash, David P. "It's Time to Make Human-Chimp Hybrids." *Nautilus*, 8 March 2018. http://nautil.us/issue/58/self/its-time-to-make-human_chimp-hybrids. Accessed 20 November 2019.

Bostrom, Nick. "The Future of Humanity." In *A Companion to Philosophy of Technology*, edited by Jan K. Berg Olsen et al. Blackwell Publishing, 2009, pp. 551–557.

Braidotti, Rosi. *The Posthuman*. Polity Press, 2013.

Bugajska, Anna. *Engineering Youth: The Evantropian Project in Young Adult Dystopias*. Ignatianum UP, 2019.

———. "'Religia' ulepszania: od evantropii do nieśmiertelności" ["The 'Religion' of Enhancement: From Evantropia to Immortality"]. In *Ulepszanie człowieka – perspektywa filozoficzna* [Human Enhancement: A Philosophical Perspective], edited by Piotr Duchliński and Grzegorz Hołub. Ignatianum UP, 2018, pp. 261–280.

Campbell, Joseph. *The Masks of God: Primitive Mythology*. Penguin Books, 1979.

Carretero, Nacho. "Juan Carlos Izpisúa: 'Avances así permiten la vida'." ["Juan Carlos Izpisúa: 'Such developments favor life'."]. *El País*, 22 August 2018. www.elpais.com/elpais/2017/08/22/ciencia/1503411254_955787.html. Accessed 22 August 2018.

Cavaliere, Guilia. "A 14-Day Limit for Bioethics: the Debate over Human Embryo Research." *BMC Medical Ethics*, vol. 18, no. 38, 2017. doi:10.1186/s12910-017-0198-5.

Chan, Sarah. "How and Why to Replace the 14-day Rule." *Current Stem Cell Reports*, vol. 4, 2018, pp. 228–234.

Clarke, Bruce. "The Nonhuman." In *The Cambridge Companion to Literature and the Postuman*, edited by Bruce Clarke and Manuela Rossini. Cambridge UP, 2017, pp. 141–152.

Clarke, Bruce, and Manuela Rossini, eds. *The Cambridge Companion to Literature and the Posthuman*. Cambridge UP, 2017.

Crutzen, Paul J. "The 'Anthropocene'." In *Earth System Science in the Anthropocene*, edited by Eckart Ehlers and Thomas Krafft. Springer, 2006, pp. 13–18.

Cyranoski, David. "Japan Approves First Human-Animal Embryo Experiments." *Nature*, 26 July 2019. www.nature.com/articles/d41586-019-02275-3. Accessed 23 April 2020.

Dvorsky, Georg. "All Together Now: Developmental and Ethical Considerations for Biologically Uplifting Nonhuman Animals." *Journal of Evolution and Technology*, vol. 18, no. 1, 2008, pp. 129–142.

Eliade, Mircea. *Myths, Dreams and Mysteries: the Encounter Between the Contemporary Faiths and Archaic Realities*. Harper and Row Publishers, 1967.

———. *Rites and Symbols of Initiation: the Mysteries of Birth and Rebirth*. Harper and Row Publishers, 1965.

———. *Szamanizm i archaiczne techniki ekstazy* [Shamanism: Archaic Techniques of Ecstasy]. Translated by Krzysztof Kocjan. Wydawnictwo Naukowe PWN, 1994.

Elliott, Robert C. *The Shape of Utopia: Studies in a Literary Genre*. Chicago UP, 1970.

Flanagan, Victoria. *Technology and Identity in Young Adult Fiction: The Posthuman Subject*. Palgrave Macmillan, 2014.

Haraway, Donna. "Anthropocene, Capitalocene, Plantationocene, Chthulucene: Making Kin." *Environmental Humanities*, vol. 6, 2015, pp. 159–165.

Harrison, Jennifer. *Posthumanist Readings in the Dystopian Young Adult Fiction: Negotiating the Nature/Culture Divide*. Lexington Books, 2019.
Hauskeller, Michael. *Mythologies of Transhumanism*. Palgrave Macmillan, 2016.
———. "Utopia in Trans- and Posthumanism." In *Posthumanism and Transhumanism*, edited by Stefan Sorgner and Robert Ranisch. Peter Lang, 2014, pp. 101–108.
Hauskeller, Michael, et al. *The Palgrave Handbook of Posthumanism in Film and Television*. Palgrave Macmillan, 2015.
Hughes, James J. "Posthumans and Democracy in Popular Culture." In *The Palgrave Handbook of Posthumanism in Film and Television*, edited by Michael Hauskeller et al. Palgrave Macmillan, 2015, pp. 235–245.
Jaques, Zoe. *Children's Literature and the Posthuman: Animal, Environment, Cyborg*. Routledge, 2015.
Jonas, Hans. *The Imperative of Responsibility: In Search of an Ethics for the Technological Age*. U of Chicago P, 1984.
Kass, Leon. *Beyond Therapy. Biotechnology and the Pursuit of Happiness*. A Report of The President's Council on Bioethics. Harper Collins, 2003.
King James Bible. www.kingjamesbibleonline.org/. Accessed 24 April 2020.
Koplin, Julian, and Dominic Wilkinson. "How Should we Treat Human–Pig Chimeras, Non-Chimeric Pigs and Other Beings of Uncertain Moral Status?" *Journal of Medical Ethics*, vol. 45, no. 7, 2019, pp. 457–458.
Koplin, Julian J., and Julian Savulescu. "Time to Rethink the Law on Part-Human Chimeras." *Journal of Law and the Biosciences*, vol. 6, no. 1, 2019, pp. 37–50.
Kriegman, Sam, et al. "A Scalable Pipeline for Designing Reconfigurable Organisms." *PNAS*, vol. 117, no. 4, 2020, pp. 1853–1859.
Łaszkiewicz, Weronika. *Fantasy Literature and Christianity: A Study of the Mistborn, Coldfire, Fionavar Tapestry and Chronicles of Thomas Covenant Series*. McFarland, 2018.
Lehmann, Lisa S. "Is Editing the Genome for Climate Change Adaptation Ethically Justifiable?" *AMA Journal of Ethics*, vol. 19, no. 12, 2017, pp. 1186–1192.
Levitas, Ruth. *The Concept of Utopia*. Syracuse UP, 1990.
Liao, Matthew S. "Talking Climate Change Through Human Engineering?" *TedTalk*, 2013. www.youtube.com/watch?v=AcaKMu7I6vU. Accessed 14 February 2020.
Mercer, Calvin, and Tracy J. Trothen, eds. *Religion and Transhumanism: The Unknown Future of Human Enhancement*. Praeger, 2014.
Misseri, Lucas E. "Evantropia and Dysantropia: A Possible New Stage in the History of Utopias." In *More after More: Essays Commemorating the Five-Hundredth Anniversary of Thomas More's Utopia*, edited by Ksenia Olkusz et al. Facta Ficta Research Centre, 2016, pp. 26–43.
More, Max. "The Philosophy of Transhumanism." In *The Transhumanist Reader*, edited by Max More and Natasha Vita-More. Wiley-Blackwell, 2013, pp. 3–17.
More, Max, and Natasha Vita-More, eds. *The Transhumanist Reader. Classical and Contemporary Essays on the Science, Technology, and Philosophy of the Human Future*. Wiley-Blackwell, 2013.
Morton, Timothy. *Humankind: Solidarity with Non-Human People*. Verso, 2017.

Moylan, Thomas. *Scraps of the Untainted Sky: Science Fiction, Utopia, Dystopia*. Westview Press, 2000.
Patterson, James. *The Angel Experiment*. Headline, 2006.
———. *School's Out—Forever*. Headline, 2007.
———. *Saving the World and Other Extreme Sports*. Headline, 2008.
———. *The Final Warning*. Arrow, 2009.
———. *Maximum Ride Forever*. Arrow, 2015.
Persson, Ingmar, and Julian Savulescu. *Unfit for the Future: The Need for Moral Enhancement*. Oxford UP, 2012.
Pilsch, Andrew. *Transhumanism: Evolutionary Futurism and the Human Technologies of Utopia*. U of Minnesota P, 2017.
"Proactionary Principle." www.extropy.org/proactionaryprinciple.htm. Accessed 12 February 2020.
"Revelations 6:5." *The Bible Hub*. www.biblehub.com/revelation/6-5.htm. Accessed 24 April 2020.
Roden, David. *Posthuman Life: Philosophy at the Edge of Human*. Routledge, 2015.
Sandberg, Anders. "Morphological Freedom: Why We Not Just Want It, but Need It." In *The Transhumanist Reader*, edited by Max More and Natasha Vita-More. Wiley-Blackwell, 2013, pp. 56–64.
Savulescu, Julian. "New Breeds of Humans: The Moral Obligation to Enhance." *Reproductive Biomedicine Online*, vol. 10, supp. 1, 2005, pp. 36–39.
Schmeink, Lars. *Biopunk Dystopias. Genetic Engineering, Society and Science Fiction*. Liverpool UP, 2016.
Sorel, Georges. *Réflexions sur la violence*. Entremonde, 2013.
Stapleton, Patricia, and Andrew Byers, eds. *Biopolitics and Utopia: An Interdisciplinary Reader*. Palgrave Macmillan, 2015.
Stripling, Mahala Y. *Bioethics and Medical Issues in Literature*. Greenwood Press, 2005.
Szynkiewicz, Sławoj. *Herosi tajgi. Mity, legendy, obyczaje Jakutów* [Heroes of the Taiga: Myths, Legends and Customs of the Yakuts]. Iskry, 1984.
Tarr, Anita, and Donna R. White, eds. *Posthumanism in Young Adult Fiction: Finding Humanity in a Posthuman World*. UP of Mississippi, 2018.
Tatar, Maria. "Introduction." In *The Annotated Peter Pan. Centennial Edition*, by J. M. Barrie, edited by Maria Tatar. W. W. Norton and Company, 2014, pp. 22–46.
Truccone Borgogno, Santiago. "Postericidio como en crimen intergenerational" ["Postericide as Intergenerational Crime."]. *En Letra: Derecho Penal*, vol. 5, no. 8, 2019, pp. 55–77.

Chapter 8

At the Crossroads of Ideas

The Russian View on the Anthropocene in Metro *Series by Dmitry Glukhovsky*

Joanna Krystyna Radosz

Written in 2002 and published three years later, the prospective utopia *Metro 2033* by Dmitry Glukhovsky has become a phenomenon both in Russia and abroad, and the foundation of the *Metro Universe*—a project in which a wide range of authors from different countries have contributed their ideas about the world, where survivors of the nuclear war were forced to live underground. The primary books are currently recognized so commonly that Glukhovsky's project has become a benchmark of the post-apocalyptic speculative fiction genre, for instance, for Lech M. Nijakowski, who refers to the series at the very beginning of his work regarding post-apocalyptic fiction culture (9).

According to Paweł Wiater, writing on *Metro 2033*, "[m]ore and more frequently does our imagination lead us to wondering what the consequences of a sudden catastrophe would look like" (249). Hence, the researcher points out the crucial plot of Glukhovsky's series: the consequences of human-induced disaster following the nuclear war and, moreover, the fact that Earth no longer remains in human control. The transmedial shared universe which has evolved around the series, in fact, addresses the problem of a sudden and vicious end of the Anthropocene, perceived as an accomplished shift in narration "from human generations and history to species' emergence and deep time" (Colebrook 1).

The aim of this chapter is to discuss the Anthropocene as presented in Glukhovsky's trilogy within the context of the Russian tradition of portraying human-induced disasters in speculative fiction as well as picturing Moscow Metro and its symbolic meaning in literature. It is argued that *Metro 2033* trilogy fits the Western anthropocenic discourse, especially as far as Sverre

Raffnsøe's statement that "the human species has become too big to fail, especially from its own point of view, but also in a wider sense as our goal now is to survive" (23) is concerned. Yet, the consequences of the specifically Russian view on the Apocalypse and the end of human dominance over the Earth are also discussed. Accordingly, the structure of the chapter is: first, to follow the post-apocalyptic tendencies in Russian speculative fiction as well as to present "the subway plot" in Russian literature, its genesis, and development; then, to implement the results of both tendencies in the case study of particular parts of Glukhovsky's trilogy, discussing the end of the Anthropocene period.

The term "Anthropocene" was introduced in 2000 by Paul Crutzen as the way to describe a human-dominated geological period following the Holocene (23), and then popularized by Jan Zalasiewicz and his co-researchers in the paper entitled "Are We Now Living in Anthropocene" (Zalasiewicz et al.). The researchers explained the necessity of introducing a new term with the irreversible change of Earth caused by human activity, especially the rapid increase in population, development of megalopolis, and the excessive use of fossil fuels. Thereafter, the Anthropocene became the subject of interest not only for geologists but also for philosophers such as Raffnsøe or Christian Schwägerl, along with specialized studies on various aspects of the topic as in the monograph *Anthropocene Feminism* (2017), edited by Richard Grusin.

The term appealed also to Russian researchers. Nikolay Drozdov et al. argue that the idea of the Anthropocene equalizes the human-induced changes in the environment with the force of nature and that it leads to a pessimistic conclusion of the negative human influence on Earth (17). In the popular interpretation, presented by Erle C. Ellis, the Anthropocene is the period of increased destructive human activity resulting in the environmental collapse of Earth, and leading directly to the sixth mass extinction (130). On the other hand, Alexandr Sheshnyov underlines the interdisciplinary nature of anthropocenic studies. Accordingly, apart from the impact on the natural sciences, the newly described term is also vital for social studies. This sociocultural dimension of the Anthropocene can provide an opportunity to gather people around the idea of environmental salvation. Moreover, the anthropocenic awareness calls for finding a different perspective on Earth than the anthropocentric one. In order to achieve this goal, Drozdov suggests "transforming the scientific discourse into the common dialogue with a guarantee of the feedback" (10). Such an approach requires cooperation from researchers, politicians, and activists as well as culture-makers, regarding their impact on the awareness of the society.

By the same token, the Anthropocene has become an interesting subject for writers. This resulted in the emergence of ecologic tendencies in speculative fiction, noticed in contemporary literary studies. Notwithstanding the current trend to raise environmental awareness, Elena Ivanova denies the existence of such a genre as ecologic speculative fiction, observing rather a range of common motifs referring to the subject: "1) the nuclear disaster and its radioactive consequences [. . .]; 2) the triumph of the AI, which eventually leads to the exhaustion of natural resources, and the dying out of the planet; 3) progressive, purposeful, human-induced reduction to zero of all the environmental indicators" (193). These three motifs are common in contemporary speculative fiction, yet they can be observed, along with other post-apocalyptic visions, even before the Anthropocene was proclaimed. Although the intense awareness of the approaching environmental disaster and its consequences came to speculative fiction in Russia only after the Soviet Union had collapsed, the post-Soviet authors seem to have been inspired by previous works concerning the topic. In order to understand the background of the post-apocalyptic layer of Glukhovsky's novels, it is essential to follow the development of such ideas in Russian speculative fiction from the genre's very beginning.

The history of speculative fiction in Russia dates back to the nineteenth century, when the first works of the genre were created. Among the most popular of them is the unfinished novel *Year 4338* (*4338-й год*, 1840) by Vladimir Odoyevsky, part of which was published as *The Petersburg Letters* (*Петербургские письма*) in 1835. The plot of Odoyevsky's work revolves around the life on Earth on the eve of a huge disaster: Biela's comet is going to crash into Earth. The idea is based on the real astronomical calculations according to which the comet should wipe out the life on the Earth's surface exactly in the year 4338 and thus reflect the Russian *intelligentsiya*'s apocalyptic fears. The "comet theme" gained enormous popularity during the first half of the nineteenth century; it was used by such authors as Faddey Bulgarin, who even created a fictive journal consisting of correspondence between the Earthmen and the inhabitants of the comet—in order to calm down the fear of the crash. Thus, both Bulgarin and Odoyevsky laid the foundations for the main purpose of post-apocalyptic fiction: warning the readers and simultaneously reducing their fear of the future. The "comet theme" literature aimed at presenting the world which mankind no longer controls and as such it can be perceived as the first approach to the problem of the Anthropocene.

Post-apocalyptic fiction gained popularity among both writers and readers only at the beginning of the twentieth century, which can be perceived as a result of the decadent movement spreading over Europe at the turn of the centuries. Among the fiction concerning natural disasters one can find Alexander Kuprin's novel *The Liquid Sun* (*Жидкое солнце*, 1911). The story's anthropocenic undertone is already visible in a short summary made by Anindita Banerjee in her book on pre-revolutionary Russian speculative fiction: "Alexander Kuprin's story *The Liquid Sun* [. . .] culminated in a futile battle with the forces of entropy. Although its protagonist devises a method to store solar energy for the impending cold and darkness, the subterranean tank he fills with light explodes at the last moment" (67). The battle between the solitary man and the forces of entropy indicates the context of terminating the era of human control over Earth. Despite being neglected for years, nowadays Kuprin's story has become a source of inspiration for writers who present individual human attempts to preserve the Earth.

Having begun after World War I and the civil war, the Soviet era forced another approach, denying the writers' right to write explicitly about the fear of the inevitable, irreversible natural disaster. Soviet ideology implied the power of communists and their will to make Earth dependent on every level. As the ideologists expected, this was not achievable with common people and their tendency to fail. Thus, the idea of turning humans into machines found expression in literature of the period, for instance, in *Jealousy* (*Зависть*, 1927) by Yuri Olesha, in which it is explicitly stated: "I want to become a machine" (Olesha 70). However, it was not only the will of writers themselves to suit the new type of thinking and show "the new man" (soon to be mockingly called: *homo sovieticus*). Among the recommendations for young speculative fiction writers, coming from the era when the socialist realism was introduced as the official trend in art, the following ones can be found: "to subject to mankind all the forces of nature," "to restrain finally all the natural disasters," "to artificially create in the factories all the necessary substances, including proteins" (qtd. in Prashkevich 650–651).

For some decades, the ideological restraints were preventing writers from addressing the side-effects of such an approach to the problem of relations between the Earth and mankind. Only after Stalin's death and the proclamation of Khrushchev's "secret report" on Stalinism with its cult of personality, it was possible to present the "pessimistic" views in literature, although in a range narrower than in Western works. Khrushchev's report, however, enabled the anthropological turn in Russian speculative fiction, which resulted in turning to the problems of mankind. Publishing the novel *Andromeda: A Space-Age Tale* (*Туманность Андромеды*) in 1957, Ivan Yefremov acted as the first writer to break with the primacy of the anthropocentric idea, with his colleagues to follow. The cult of the machine was replaced with the cult of the human organism. Controlled by censorship demanding to maintain the Soviet optimism, in contrast to the more fear-inducing orientation of Western speculative fiction, the majority of writers focused on praising the human power over Earth. The approach mostly put mankind before nature, yet it also enabled a wider perspective for the few writers who were worried about not only the communist system but also Earth's fate. Such were, for example, the Strugatsky brothers, who debuted with the science fiction novel *The Land of Crimson Clouds* (*Страна багровых туч*, 1959). Already in their first works one could see the anxiety resulting from the unknown nature of the future and the worry about human condition. Because of their denial to believe in the omnipotence of the Soviet people, among their fellow writers and researchers the Strugatskys gained the reputation of writers who—due to the lack of ability—constantly perceive the humans of the future with all their shortcomings (in contrast to, for instance, Yefremov, whose people of the future would have got rid of both negative personal traits and emotions in general).

Notwithstanding the critical reviews, the Strugatskys were constantly focusing on the threat mankind posed to the world and the future. Probably the most adequate example in the context of this chapter is the novel *Definitely Maybe* (*За миллиард лет до конца света*), first published in 1974, which is concerned with the problem of entropy and the universe attempting to prevent a scientist from making a discovery that might irreversibly alter the Earth's life. Decades before the Anthropocene was defined and received its name in scientific discourse, Soviet writers seem to have predicted its dangerous potential. Moreover, the Strugatskys' fiction in general refers to the problem of interdependence of mankind and the environment, and indicates dangerous ethical principles in the Soviet vision of people conquering the universe, in such works as *Far Rainbow* (*Далекая Радуга*, 1962) or *Noon: 22nd Century* (*Полдень, XXII век*, 1962). Entropy, the term inseparably connected with the problem of the Anthropocene and its perspectives, after being introduced in Russian literature by Evgeniy Zamyatin, appeared repeatedly in the Strugatskys' works, combined with a related issue: the chosenness. Its most widespread form was the unwilling chosenness, resulting in a number of moral dilemmas: should the individual intervene in the turns of history? Is it possible (and, paramount, is it beneficial) to jump at once from the wilderness to the civilization (Tarasevich et al.)? The problem addressed by the Strugatskys is not the possibilities of the individual attempting to transform the reality, but the moral responsibility for every single change that is likely to interfere with the entropy. As one can observe, the issues raised by the brother writers already in the 1960s remain current and crucial in the times of anthropocenic awareness. Furthermore, the Strugatskys have provided a background for their successors dealing with similar problems during and after the *perestroika* period, when *glasnost* ("openness" of the political and media discourse) enabled the presence of apocalyptic themes in speculative fiction. Hence, the tropes provided by the pre-Soviet and Soviet authors were developed right after the Soviet Union collapsed in 1991. As during the epoch of decadence, the authors became afresh overwhelmed by apocalyptical moods, which resulted in the publishing of such fiction as E. Filenko's *Gigapolis* (*Отсвет мрака*, 2002), demonstrating the danger of the technicized world, or N. Gaydamaka's *Lullaby* (*Колыбельная*, 1988), in which a mother soothes her child, yet as it falls asleep she herself fears the new world, in which mankind has gained absolute control over Earth. The negative consequences of technological progress and human development, resulting in, ironically, dehumanization, are also the leitmotiv of short stories and novel by Anna Starobinets.

In the 1990s and at the beginning of the 2000s, the dread of technology and human power with all its consequences was combined with the fright of the new era and the omnipresent chaos, which dominated the post-Soviet territory. As Eugeniy Goldschmidt observed:

> along with the globalisation, there goes the powerful process of the destabilisation and degradation of the multiple areas of mutual relations [. . .], on which there lays more and more common weather anomalies. The increasing pace of the changes, their low predictability results in the uncertainty, fears, aggression, the threat of losing one's identity and entity on both individual and governmental level. It is the most explicit on the example of the 1990s, when the governmental, national, cultural and economic roots of our country and other Eastern European countries were destroyed. (61)

Such position, rather common in the Russian discourse on the issue of social and political aspects of the Anthropocene, is widely reflected in literature, combining the global problem of human-induced degradation of Earth with rapid geopolitical changes. Whether the question lies in the dread of troubles technology can bring, as it is to be observed in the works mentioned above, or in fear of nature attempting to regain its primal position, speculative fiction in the post-Soviet space is nowadays mostly underpinned with the local context or, at least, the mentions of the specifically local problems: political, ecological, economic, and others. This note is crucial for understanding the anthropocenic background of Glukhovsky's series, along with the fact that virtually in none of the works mentioned above the natural environment plays a role different than being the reason for a catastrophe. Moreover, speculative fiction authors draw far more frequently from the fear of technology than from the ecological awareness, and even if the latter is demonstrated as a significant element of future anxieties, it remains almost undescribed. Such are the frames of the history of speculative fiction in Russia, which will provide the necessary background for the analysis of the Metro series in terms of the awareness of the influence of human activity on the environment.

Another context frame for interpreting Glukhovsky's works is the Russian cultural symbolic system concerning the subway (especially the Moscow Metro). Discussing the possible reasons for the series' popularity, Mariya Galina notes:

> the novel abounds in the underground mythology" in its contemporary appearance, beloved by the tabloids. According to such a mythology, anything can be

found in the Metro: the mutant rats, the actual mutants, the beast-like chthonic creatures, another—the secret—subway, the shadow speleologists" and even, as it is believed . . . other secret passages, this time—to Hell. (Galina)

This brief summary of the widespread Moscow Metro mythology indicates its value for the contemporary Russian collective awareness and, subsequently, popular culture. However, the myths evolving around the pop-culture motifs cannot be perceived as the product of modern times, globalization, and popularization of the cultural symbols, insofar the Moscow Metro had been inspiring writers long before it was raised from the tales of the underworld life of Moscow. Matvey Grechko states that the underground city was being built since 1780 and embraced passages, cellars, wells, underground rivers and streams, and finally, dungeons (243). As in the case of other European cities (for instance, Paris in Victor Hugo's *Les Miserables*), Moscow underworld had the structure of a labyrinth and simultaneously a palimpsest, consisting of consecutive layers of buildings and city life. Any labyrinth, however, needs its Minotaur—thus, at the turn of nineteenth and twentieth centuries the traveler Vladimir Gilyarovsky observed that below the Moscow ground one can find "drunk, dirty people, who had not bathed for a long time and have little in common with the actual people" (qtd. in Grechko 276–277). Then the collective subconscious turned the image of the "underground people" into the legends of "the guardians of the underground"—present also in contemporary Moscow Metro folklore.

The idea of the subway stimulated literary imagination even at the stage of construction plans. Although the Moscow Metro opened only in the 1930s, the first plans for building a net of underground transport in the city had been made already at the end of the nineteenth century, as the population of Moscow increased to the extent when it became necessary to structure public transport so as to avoid crowded streets. Yet the first project, proposed in 1902 and concerning the "flying" public transport, was rejected and the idea forgotten until 1913, when two concepts of the first Russian underground railway were developed (Romanov 7). The construction began, but already in 1914 it was suspended due to the outbreak of the Great War and then remained unfinished. However, already at the stage of the first plans, information about the upcoming public transport breakthrough had spread and become a starting point for one of the first Russian science fiction writers, Alexandr Rodnykh. Inspired by the existing underground railways and the laws of physics, Rodnykh wrote an amusing story about the subway spreading between Moscow and Saint Petersburg. Written as a joke, *Automatic Subway between Moscow and Petersburg* (*Самокатная подземная дорога между Москвою и Петербургом*, 1902) sometimes is still mistaken for a popularizing brochure or an unfinished novel (see Banerjee 60). Due to the war and the Bolshevik Revolution, followed by the civil war and the period of regaining stabilization at the governmental level, the building of an underground railway was postponed until the Stalin era, when the project emerged again and was eventually completed, with the first line (the Sokolnicheskaya line) opened for public use in 1935 and the second in 1938, already before World War II. Notwithstanding the pragmatic Soviet spirit, when religious beliefs were considered as "opium for masses," the mysterious atmosphere surrounding the implementation of the project was still observed, as the builders—mostly prisoners—found such objects as the well-preserved house from the eighteenth century, which was said to cause illness to all builders trying to demolish it. However, similar stories were not to be published until the perestroika period, contrary to the educational Soviet stories from the builders of the Moscow Metro collected in books such as *The Stories of the Metro Builders* (*Рассказы строителей метро*, 1935). Nevertheless, the particular conspiracy of silence around the building process raised speculations resulting in the appearance of a wide range of urban legends. Most of them were inspired by a certain behavior of the Metro employees. As Oleg Divov and Maksim Rublev explain:

> A real Metro legend can be distinguished by possessing three features. Firstly, its existence was caused by metro employees themselves. Secondly, it is based on a real event, either incorrectly interpreted or transformed into speculative fiction through oral transmission. Thirdly, such a legend can be commented on by a person who, deliberately or involuntarily, became its cause and source. Then, one can follow the "legendation" process. (308–309)

Such a mechanism triggered the emergence of a number of urban myths, some of which might be easily explained with the real events, for instance, a legend of "the burnt driver" who turned out to be an actual metro driver of Ethiopian origins (Grechko 282), whereas the source of other stories remains unknown. Interestingly, in either case, the legends continue to live their own lives, now and again becoming the background for fictional plots.

Only during the final stage of the Soviet Union's existence were the number of casualties and the facts concerning the inhumane conditions of the construction process revealed. They would have remained partially unknown if it had not been for the help of the so-called "diggers"—amateurs exploring the underground city structures, including railway tunnels. Inspired by these discoveries, a digger named Vladimir Gonik decided to write a pamphlet accusing the Soviet government at the beginning of the 1980s. As it was widely practiced, he disguised his criticism of the system in the fictional plot, in which soldiers are dispatched into the metro tunnels, where they eventually discover a group of people living in the underground for decades. Portraying the "Metro tribe" as a sect following Stalin's doctrine long after the dictator's death, the novel entitled *The Hell* (*Преисподняя*, published in 1992) draws on the Old Believers' tradition,[1] which leads the followers of the religion to bury themselves under the ground to survive the upcoming Apocalypse. To create a convincing background, the author uses his rich experience as an underground explorer, sharing with the reader the secrets of the Moscow Metro tunnels, such as the existence of the so-called Metro-2, the system built as an escape route for the government and the president. Notwithstanding the lack of official information on such a system, its existence was not denied by the governmental press officers either. Hence, the "legend" became indirectly confirmed.

The Metro-2, which received its name only in Gonik's novel, became one of the most widespread Moscow Metro myths ever since and fueled the belief that the underground railway can function as a nuclear shelter on a long-term basis. In fact, it is impossible due to the complicated power system designed to keep the water level in the underground low—as soon as the power was cut off, the Moscow Metro would be inundated over a period of two to four days (Divov and Rublev 305–306). The awareness of the way the underground railway functions did not, however, silence the rumors of it being suitable for a shelter for years and even decades. Although Gonik's novel is no longer popular, it nevertheless initiated a certain manner of representing the Moscow Metro in literary texts, resulting in a wide range of works, from short stories to the whole *Metro 2033* project.

Since Gonik, the Moscow Metro has become an object not only of admiration but also of fear. It symbolized the threat posed to society by interfering with the underworld, developed in Russian speculative fiction during the early 2000s. Such is, for instance, the Metro portrayed in *The Hell*, yet a similar approach can be observed also in the short story "The Living Ones" ("Живые," from the collection *Переходный возраст*, 2005) by Anna Starobinets, where the underground corridors serve as a bastion for the living people in their battle against androids. The contrast between the old human world, put underground—that is, according to Yi-Fu Tuan's typology, at the least prestigious level (65)—and the new one developing on the surface, should be perceived as an important theme for the extensive Moscow Metro mythology, as far as Glukhovsky's series is concerned. Starobinets's interpretation of the battle between the under- and the overworld resembles the one proposed by Igor Pronin in the novel *Witnesses of the Rat-Catcher* (*Свидетели Крысолова*, 2004), in which the rats hiding in the underground become a new plague to the dying Moscow.

As one can observe from the examples mentioned above, the Metro is recognized for bringing death to the world above the ground. It is presented similarly in Oleg Ovchinnikov's novel *ProMetro* (*ПроMetro*, 2006), published only after the *Metro 2033* trilogy was launched, yet influencing the second and third volumes of the series. Ovchinnikov uses the Moscow Metro as a device to develop the protagonist, telling a universal story of the search for the meaning of life and forgiveness. Drawing on the atavistic fear of the underworld as the land of death, Ovchinnikov's novel focuses on the tension resulting from the prolonged stay underground.

The literary image of the Moscow Metro is not limited to the works referred to here, yet a discussion of a wider range of works referring to the topic appears unimaginable within the scope of this chapter. Insofar, the works described above provide a set of certain characteristics of the underground railway in Russia and, in particular, in Moscow, for the city—in contrast to Saint Petersburg—symbolizes the wild and uncontrollable element of Russian nature. Many of these recurrent motifs, such as a variety of underground legends, the link between the Metro and the underworld, the theme of death, the reversal of the world's order, and Moscow context along with the concept of Metro-2, have become a background for Glukhovsky's narrative as well.

The two traditions of Soviet and Russian speculative fiction definitively affected Glukhovsky's series. As it will be demonstrated in the second part of the analysis, *Metro 2033* trilogy addresses the Anthropocene and its tragic consequences in a particularly Russian way and within the framework of the underground theme. First of all, at the beginning of the first book the world which has collapsed due to a nuclear war is seen by the reader through the eyes of the protagonist, a young man named Artyom. The first chapters of the story adopt a very personal tone, and as such they serve to raise the reader's interest instead of explaining the condition of the world built by Glukhovsky. In contrast, *Metro 2034* begins with a general description of the damages and the assertion that twenty years after the catastrophe "the human is no longer the lord of Earth" (Glukhovsky, *Metro 2033 Trilogy* 361). The statement remains the key point for the whole trilogy, especially as far as the mutant discourse is concerned. In Russian tradition of mercy and compassion for the Other in any of their forms, mutants (in the trilogy called the *Shadows*), initially perceived as a threat, turn out to be a new race striving for the salvation of mankind. As the author explains, he aimed at creating a world different from many other post-apocalyptic works by its premise that the mutants ought not to be eliminated but engaged in a dialogue (qtd. in Wiater 257). Notwithstanding being the new lords over Earth (the upper world), they remain ready to help people restore civilization. Nevertheless, their effort proves futile as mankind is ready neither to accept the loss of power nor to establish a dialogue with the so-called *homo novus* (Glukhovsky, *Metro 2033 Trilogy* 32–33). The history of the mutants' striving for the connection with the involuntary chosen one—Artyom—as a mediator resonates with a universal myth of a misunderstood Savior coming from the Otherworld (in its most popular Western variant—Jesus Christ), yet not only. He can be as well compared to the typically Russian figure of the "new human" from the Soviet age, associated with the concept of the *homo sovieticus*—a sarcastic term denoting a collective human being with the collective mind, no individual traits, characterized by its inertia and indifference. Glukhovsky's *Homo novus* might be perceived as an enhanced post-nuclear *homo sovieticus*, with a perfectly collective mind and a will to serve the common welfare. Yet, due to its visual dissimilarity from the human, it is doomed to misunderstanding and, subsequently, exodus. The only one capable of communication with the Shadows, Artyom, fails to convince the Metro authorities that the dialogue is necessary. Thus, the protagonist fulfills the fate of the Strugatskys' chosen one.

Another instance of indebtedness to the tradition of Russian speculative fiction is the implementation of political discourse. The reasons and course of the nuclear war remain unknown in order to convince the reader that the outbreak of another world war might be provoked by anything (Wiater 255), even considering the fact that from a scientific perspective a range of effects of a nuclear attack exclude the massive radiation forcing living organisms to stay in shelters for decades (see Lasik 136–137). Yet, what is paramount, Glukhovsky explicitly informs the reader that the nuclear attack was aimed precisely at Russia and that even long after the catastrophe, the Moscow wireless communication is being drowned by the undefined West (Glukhovsky, *Metro 2033 Trilogy* 578). Notwithstanding the generally universal and transnational appeal of the trilogy, which will be discussed below, Glukhovsky did not avoid a specific Russian connotation, suggesting a special status of Russia within the universe of the trilogy. The open end of *Metro 2035* leaves some degree of uncertainty. It remains unclear whether all mankind was removed from power over the whole Earth or only the Russian people are put through this experience by either their own authorities—making it easier to control the whole population—or the outer world. Thus, one cannot be certain about the extent to which the hell, raised—as Zywert observes (173)—without the participation of God, that is, entirely human-induced, is the hell concerning the global community. This specifically local accent corresponds with the tradition of self-centered perception of reality and global disasters in Soviet and Russian speculative fiction.

Addressed in the previous point, the problem of an egotistical narrative is also present at the level of ecological and environmental awareness within the text. Whereas the entropic motif (especially popular in Russian speculative fiction since the Strugatskys) gains repetitive frequency throughout the trilogy and can be observed, for instance, in Artyom's laconic statement: "Life has no plot" (Glukhovsky, *Metro 2033* 191), it should be underlined that besides the triumph of entropy—also at the environmental level—the novels contain no obvious, or at least distinct, ecological background. In these terms, Glukhovsky's trilogy lies within the framework proposed by the post-Soviet speculative fiction concerning the warning for the future. The author may focus on technologies or detailed descriptions of everyday life (known in Russian literature as a tradition of *byt*) in the Moscow underworld, yet he omits the problem of climate and environment changing due to the nuclear war. Although the protagonists—either Artyom in *Metro 2033* and *Metro 2035* or Sasha in *Metro 2034*—manage to travel to the surface, the landscape they see is described in terms of their feelings, as in the following paragraphs:

> There was a mind-boggling, inconceivable amount of space here, to the right and to the left and in front. This boundless space was both spellbinding and strangely depressing at the same time. [. . .] The sun had already set, and the city was gradually descending into a dingy twilight. The skeletons of low apartment houses, dilapidated and pitted by decades of acid rainstorms, stared at the travelers with empty orbits of broken windows.
> The city . . . It was a dismal, yet magnificent sight. Hearing no calls, Artyom stood still, looking about as if mesmerized; he could finally compare reality with his dreams and with nearly equally blurry childhood memories. (Glukhovsky, *Metro 2033* 164)

The consequences of the nuclear disaster for natural environment are scarcely mentioned in the phrase "acid rains," yet their effect remains visible only on the surface of the houses. Artyom, and along with him other characters, demonstrates interest first and foremost in the remains of the city: architecture and landmarks remembered from childhood. Although the Moscow botanical garden is one of the most important places for the plot, Glukhovsky does not describe its appearance either before or after the war. Significantly, the narrative perspective concerns primarily the characters' feelings and emotions, which serve to stress the tension.

Curiously enough, the environment plays a sufficient role within the semantic layer of the text. Namely, the surroundings over the surface are perceived as a living organism and, therefore, personified. As it can be observed in the quoted paragraphs, the buildings are embodied as the ones having literally "eye-holes," (translated, though, as "empty orbits") whereas the city in general is described with the epithets indicating its vivid nature, despite the post-nuclear entourage. Such impression is evoked, for instance, by the image of Moscow "crying" over the head of a character named Elena (Glukhovsky, *Metro 2033 Trilogy* 382). Since crying is the exclusive attribute of living creatures, the use of such a metaphor by Glukhovsky not only personifies the city but also confirms its ontological status as a being neither yet dead nor already resurrected. The possibility of a new beginning for Moscow and the whole world (even if the term addresses only the limited zone) brings hope, thus fulfilling the primal task of post-apocalyptic speculative fiction.

With respect to its ontological status, the Moscow Metro itself is in the *Metro 2033* series similar to the city. Glukhovsky presents the structure as a living organism capable of not only communicating with mankind—by, for instance, "the whispers of the tunnels" (*Metro 2033 Trilogy* 33), heard by Artyom from the beginning of his peregrination—but also giving birth to its distinct creatures, the Shadows. Being specifically Metro beings, they resemble both Gonik's sect from the Moscow underworld and the Living Ones from Starobinets's story, despite their initial status as non-humans. As soon as the human characters have an opportunity to meet the Shadows, they start perceiving them as "the people inside-out" (Glukhovsky, *Metro 2033* 339). By their nature, the Shadows are mutants, but their origins remain unknown. What appears more important is their position in the chthonic space of the Metro, where they are primal inhabitants, in contrast to the people. Being a natural tissue of the underground tunnels, the Shadows are created to both guard the Metro from excessive human activity and guide the people to make progress from mere vegetation to satisfactory life. However, mankind turns out deaf to the voice of Metro messengers: Artyom, the only one who is able to communicate with the Shadows, understands their actual role too late and can only witness the process of their annihilation by rackets. Then, the Metro becomes an even more silent and unfriendly milieu, which ought to be left as soon as possible. Although its children were destroyed by people, it is still alive and the mere difference is the manner in which it treats human, now clearly unwanted, guests. Subsequently, the characters start becoming ill and feeling claustrophobic, and yet, due to fear, the majority of them do not feel ready to try living on the surface again.

The Russian tradition of "Metro literature" is also continued within the trilogy by referring to the particular metro legends mentioned above, for instance, the one about mutant-rats, with which the series actually begins, or the half-legend concerning the existence of Metro-2. Perceived as a shelter for the "Soviet Gods," the secret underground railway structure appears in Glukhovsky's books as the realization of a certain myth, allowing one to believe that the other myths are real as well. Furthermore, the motif of coming to the underworld in order to save lives can be found in most basic myths of all times and cultures. In Western culture, grounded in the tradition of Ancient Greece and Rome, the motif is associated with the narrative about Demeter and Persephone or the story of Orpheus and Eurydice. Identified with the Land of the Dead, the underworld refers to darkness, fear, degradation, deficient existence, and merely space—not a place, using the typology proposed by Yi-Fu Tuan (16). It stands in opposition to the prestigious high floor. The observations of the spatial anthropology lead to a conclusion that the inhabitants of the Moscow Metro in Glukhovsky's series are degraded due to their position on the lowest level. Moreover, they should be considered the living dead ones, since they have inhabited the area traditionally dedicated to the deceased. Thus, they function in opposition to the structures that are explicitly alive—the Metro in particular and Moscow in general.

The Metro's inhabitants in *Metro 2033* resemble the dead ones already in their appearance, being presented as unnaturally pale, frail, skinny, and chronically sick. Such description refers especially to the children who were born underground. Furthermore, they cannot lead a full-fledged existence because of the overpopulation in Metro tunnels, applying, for instance, to the home station of Artyom, inhabited by about 200 people. The alarmingly high population density forces collectivism more than any Soviet edict would do, turning the inhabitants of the station into actual screws of the para-state machine. They are, therefore, compelled to obey a daily routine of the station and made to live in massive groups, which minimizes the likelihood of developing deeper relationships and starting a normal family. Deprived of privacy, the people are forced to share the area of the railway station—designed, as Agnieszka Bednarek underlines, neither as a house nor as a public space but as something in-between where *oiko* interferes with *polis* (78). As far as the term "home" and its Greek origins are concerned, one should not forget that "Polis" is also the name of the half-legendary union of Moscow Metro stations, where life mostly resembles the erstwhile existence on the surface. The chosen toponym indicates the basic values of Polis: the privacy and home-like atmosphere—the associations which lead the inhabitants of other fractions to leave other stations and embark on a dangerous expedition in search of more of the previous life.

However, for Artyom, who manages to reach Polis, the name of the fraction turns out to be delusive and brings merely disappointment in the existence which only faintly resembles life on the surface. Being as overpopulated as any other station, Polis cannot offer the space for solitude, the *sine qua non* condition for the sustainable development of the individual (Tuan 81, 89) even in a collective society. The fact troubles in particular the people who remember life before the catastrophe, such as Miller, who strives to convey its appearance to his daughter Anya, Artyom's wife (Glukhovsky, *Metro 2033 Trilogy* 541). However, it turns out impossible not only due to the forced collectivism—since the collective activity can be perceived as a distinct trait of Russian national character and as such, even in its degenerated form is bearable—but also because of the chthonic nature of Metro existence.

Perpetual darkness, the lack of perspectives, the world stripped of culture with merely quasi-cultural ventures, such as staging plays (Glukhovsky, *Metro 2033 Trilogy* 654) are the signs of vegetation in the whole Metro community. As the narrator observes, before the nuclear war, death was pushed aside and the bones of the dead were "disturbed" in spite of the so-called "eternal rest" (456), yet after mankind came down to the underworld, death took its revenge, turning their living space into its own kingdom. This interpretation corresponds with the reading of the Metro underworld provided in other literary works, including the primary source—Gonik's *The Hell*.

Galina considers the increasing popularity of the chthonic metro-theme as an alarming tendency that indicates a rising demand of returning from the linear to the circular time and, hence, into the vicious circle of repetitive history (Galina). According to the researcher, interest in the stories set in the actual land of death signals the unbearable uncertainty of real life and a desire to lead safe and expectable existence even at the cost of losing the right to solitude and, subsequently, freedom. Such interest, which can be observed in post-apocalyptic post-Soviet works analyzed above, can be seen as typical for Russian speculative fiction of the 1990s and early 2000s. The reason behind this seems to be the chaos of the so-called "wild nineties" (лихие девяностые), the decade of economic experiments, constant crises, and uncertainty about the closest future. Significantly, Glukhovsky already started to write *Metro 2033* during the decade and, as far as the atmosphere and tension are concerned, he explicitly considers the setting of his first novel a tale about the 1990s in Russia (qtd. in Nijakowski 290). This indirectly verifies the hypothesis set by Galina and situates Glukhovsky's series in the context of Russian post-apocalyptic speculative fiction in general.

Apart from the problem of contemporary culture and everyday life along with its chthonic subtext, Glukhovsky's books nevertheless revolve around searching for the solution. As pointed out by both Leonid Fishman and Andrzej Niewiadomski, post-apocalyptic speculative fiction serves to comfort the readers, and the authors ought to propose an optimistic plot or, at least, imply a hope of redemption (Fishman; Niewiadomski 193). So does Glukhovsky, as he suggests communicating with the Shadows as a solution (in *Metro 2033*) and then, when the Shadows are already annihilated—searching for the new beginning on the surface. The trilogy ends with Artyom and Anya planning to start a new life away from the underworld, although no one of the station inhabitants is willing to follow them. The statement made by Grigorovskaya about the first two novels that "[Glukhovsky] does not propose anything capable of breaking the vicious circle of Russian history" (68) becomes outdated as soon as one reads the last chapters of *Metro 2035*. The proposal is simple: to restore the bond with nature and, as the author himself claims, not to "destroy the mutants" but to destroy the monsters hidden within people themselves and to learn to live on the surface once again (qtd. in Wiater 257). To conclude, there exists a wide range of arguments verifying the hypothesis standing at the beginning of the chapter—that Glukhovsky draws richly from the tradition of representing the Anthropocene and the inevitable Apocalypse in Russian speculative fiction. He also follows the tradition of presenting the Moscow Metro in a certain manner, linking the structure with the chthonic world, yet simultaneously making it the only shelter for "old" mankind. Thus, the trilogy is worth a careful reading for its specifically Russian context, which is a significant addition to global tendencies.

NOTE

1. The Old Believers were originally the Orthodox believers which had not accepted the reforms introduced by patriarch Nikon of Moscow in 1666. The changes in the liturgy and religious tradition (such as different spelling of Jesus' name) lead to the schism of the Russian Orthodox Church, which lasts until today (see Kowalska 383–391).

WORKS CITED

Banerjee, Anindita. *We Modern People*. Wesleyan UP, 2012.
Bednarek, Agnieszka. "Dworzec—wykolejony dom. Próba oikologii z domieszką heterotopologii." ["Railway Station—the Derailed House: An Attempt at Oikology with Some Heterotopology."] In *Przestrzeń—literatura—doświadczenie. Z inspiracji geopoetyki*, edited by Tomasz Gęsina and Zbigniew Kadłubek. Wydawnictwo Uniwersytetu Śląskiego, 2016.
Colebrook, Claire. "We Have Always Been Post-Anthropocene: The Anthropocene Counterfactual." In *Anthropocene Feminism*, edited by Richard Grusin. Minnesota UP, 2017, pp. 1–20.
Crutzen, Paul J. "Geology of Mankind." *Nature*, vol. 415, no. 23, 2002, p. 23.
Divov, Oleg, and Max Rublev. *Ne prislonât'sâ. Pravda o metro* [Please, Don't Lean: The Truth about the Metro]. Eksmo, 2011.
Drozdov, Nikolay, et al. "Voprosy formirovaniâ nauki antropocena." ["Issues of Forming the Science of Anthropocene."] *Aktualnye problem ekonomiki i prava*, vol. 10, no. 2, 2016, pp. 5–21.
Ellis, Erle C. *Anthropocene. A Very Short Introduction*. Oxford UP, 2018.
Fishman, Leonid. "V sisteme 'dvojnoj antiutopii'." ["In the System of the 'Double Antiutopia'."] *Magazines.Gorky.Media*, Druzhba Narodov, 2008. www.magazines.gorky.media/druzhba/2008/3/v-sisteme-dvojnoj-antiutopii.html. Accessed 12 May 2019.
Galina, Mariya. "Mir bez solnca." ["The World Without the Sun."] *Magazines.Gorky. Media*, Novyi Mir, 2010. www.nm1925.ru/Archive/Journal6_2010_8/Content/Publication6_129/Default.aspx. Accessed 12 May 2019.
Glukhovsky, Dmitry. *Metro 2033*. Translated by Natasha Randall. Gollancz, 2009.

Glukhovsky, Dmitry. *Metro 2033. Trilogiâ pod odnoj obložkoj* [Metro 2033: The Trilogy under One Cover]. AST, 2017.
Goldschmidt, Eugeniy. "Metafizičeskij podhod k koncepcii noosfery i ee roli v razvitii sovremennoj nauki, kul'tury, civilizacii." ["The Metaphysical Approach to the Concept of the Noosphere and its Role in the Development of Modern Science, Culture and Civilization."] *Vestnik KemGU*, vol. 4, 2017, pp. 61–66.
Gonik, Vladimir. *Preispodnââ* [The Hell]. Moskva: Slog, 1992. *RoyalLib*. www.r oyallib.com/book/gonik_vladimir/preispodnyaya.html. Accessed 5 May 2017.
Grechko, Matvey. *Zasekrečennye linii metro Moskvy* [Secret Lines of the Moscow Metro]. Eksmo, 2012.
Grigorovskaya, Anastasiya. "Fenomen ikličnosti istorii v rossijskoj antiutopii 2000-h godov." ["The Phenomenon of Cyclization of History in Russian Antiutopia of the 00's."] *Vestnik Leningradskogo gosudarstvennogo universiteta im. A.S. Pushkina*, vol. 4, 2011, pp. 63–70.
Ivanova, Elena. "Èkologičeskaâ fantastika. Metaforizaciâ prirodnyh âvlenij." ["Ecological Science Fiction: Metaphorization of Natural Phenomena."] *Politicheskaya lingvistika*, vol. 46, 2013, pp. 192–195.
Kowalska, Hanna. "Old Belief." Translated by Witold Liwarowski. In *Ideas in Russia*, edited by Andrzej de Lazari. Semper, 1999, pp. 383–391.
Lasik, Marta Magdalena. "Post-atomowe place zabaw." ["Post-Nuclear Playgrounds."] *Fenix*, vol. 5, no. 1, 2019, pp. 135–140.
Niewiadomski, Andrzej. *Literatura fantastycznonaukowa* [Science Fiction]. PWN, 2012.
Nijakowski, Lech M. *Świat po apokalipsie* [The World after the Apocalypse]. Scholar, 2018.
Olesha, Yuriy. *Zavist'* [Jealousy]. FTM, 2008.
Prashkevich, Gennadiy. *Krasnyj Sfinks. Kniga vtoraâ* [The Red Sphinx. Second Volume]. Svinin i synovya, 2009.
Raffnsøe, Sverre. *Philosophy of the Anthropocene*. Palgrave Macmillan, 2016.
Romanov, Alexandr. "Moskovskoe metro – načalo istorii." ["Moscow Metro – The Beginning of History."] *Vestnik universiteta*, vol. 4, 2012, pp. 1–6.
Sheshnyov, Alexandr. "Čto takoe 'antropocen'?" ["What Is 'the Anthropocene'?"] *Izvestnik Saratovskogo universiteta*, vol. 17, no. 3, 2017, pp. 200–206.
Schwägerl, Christian. *The Anthropocene*. Synergetic Press, 2014.
Tarasevich, Grigoriy, et al. "Sčast'e dlâ vseh. Darom." ["Happiness for All. For Free."] *Expert-Online*, Expert.ru., 2012. www.expert.ru/russian_reporter/2012/47 /schaste-dlya-vseh-darom/. Accessed 28 January 2018.
Tuan, Yi-Fu. *Space and Place*. Minnesota UP, 2001.
Wiater, Paweł. "Słowiańskie zamiłowanie do postapokalipsy. Uniwersum Metro 2033 jako zwiastun nowego rodzaju literatury fantastycznej." ["The Slavic Love for the Post-Apocalypse. The Metro 2033 Universe as the Omen of the New Speculative Fiction."] In *Fantastyka w literaturach słowiańskich. Idee—koncepty—gatunki*, edited by Andrzej Polak. Wydawnictwo Uniwersytetu Śląskiego, 2016, pp. 249–264.

Zalasiewicz, Jan, et al. "Are We Now Living in the Anthropocene?" *GSA Today*, vol. 18, no. 2, 2008, pp. 4–8.

Zywert, Aleksandra. "Witajcie w piekle (Dmitrij Głuchowski, 'Metro 2033')." ["Welcome to Hell (Dmitry Glukhovsky, 'Metro 2033')."] In *Rosyjska fantastyka dawniej i dziś*, edited by Andrzej Polak. Wydawnictwo Uniwersytetu Śląskiego, 2013, pp. 159–176.

Part III

SOCIETY AND POLITICS IN THE ANTHROPOCENE

Chapter 9

Apocalyptic Visions

N. K. Jemisin's The Stone Sky *and the Sociocultural Origins of the Anthropocene*

Keygan Sands

INTRODUCTION

Whether or not the Anthropocene is recognized as an official unit of geologic time, certain human activities and processes have left a stamp that will be recorded in layers of stone for millions of years. As we confront the expanse of deep time, as we reckon with the origins of our stratigraphic autobiography, so our stories must follow. N. K. Jemisin's *Broken Earth Trilogy*, published each year from 2015 to 2017, uses the techniques of fantasy to expose the roots of systems, particularly energy extraction and colonialism, that catalyze and propagate the Anthropocene Epoch. Through the final book in the trilogy, *The Stone Sky*, Jemisin examines Syl Anagist, the civilization that enacted a prolonged assault on the human and natural worlds and ultimately brought about serial apocalypses. Jemisin uses the "Fifth Seasons" of the trilogy to reveal the hidden systems that lead to inequality, injustice, and environmental harm; and through all this, she explores what it means to possess geological agency.

The Broken Earth Trilogy begins with the volcanic end of the world and an orogene woman—a person with the ability to magically control geologic forces—who discovers her son dead and her daughter stolen away. These cataclysms, both global and personal, happen cyclically and repeatedly, but the unknown narrator notes that this time, the world is ending "for the last time" (Jemisin, *The Fifth Season* 14). In *The Stone Sky*, the third and final volume of the trilogy, Essun, the orogene woman who tried to escape the enslavement and oppression of orogenes, is still searching for her daughter, Nassun, but has also learned that she might be the only orogene with enough power to open the Obelisk Gate, return the stolen Moon to the angry and very-much-alive Earth, and end the periodic, civilization-ending Fifth Seasons forever. Nassun, meanwhile, learns of her own orogenic ability to control the earth, heat energy, and the magic produced by living things; and she wants to use it to crash the Moon into Earth and end everything: a permanent closure to the suffering of the oppressed orogenes. While the two storylines of mother and daughter collide, the reader learns about the origin of the Fifth Seasons and Earth's anger through a character from Syl Anagist, the original civilization that tried to harvest magic from living things, including Earth itself, resulting in cataclysmic disaster.

Through the lenses of different disciplines, this chapter will examine how Jemisin uses the fantasy and science fictional elements of her plot, world, and characters to illuminate real-world systems. What perspective can fantasy provide in studying and thinking about the Anthropocene? What, in particular, does Jemisin accomplish through this text, and what does she reveal? The Anthropocene changes how we think about humanity in terms of time scales and agency, and it requires new modes of discourse and analysis to understand.

First, the chapter will outline the background of the scientific underpinnings of the proposed Anthropocene Epoch and what we know about our power over geology. The geosciences provide an important context to the incitement of the Anthropocene discussion, and notably, planetary sciences provided a "germination point" for Jemisin's trilogy: as she explains in the first volume's Acknowledgments, she attended the NASA-funded Launchpad workshop, a program to improve astronomy literacy among writers (Jemisin, *The Fifth Season* 467). Crucially, humanities and literary scholars have complicated the scientific narrative. Second, this chapter will utilize postcolonial and ecocritical perspectives, beginning with Dipesh Chakrabarty's much-cited 2009 article on the Anthropocene and climate change "The Climate of History: Four Theses," to dive into the text. Chakrabarty examines important challenges of thought that climate change and the Anthropocene entail: our current understandings of history are insufficient in thinking about humans as geological agents. This chapter will next explore Alexa Weik von Mossner's (2016) response to Chakrabarty, "Imagining Geological Agency: Storytelling in the Anthropocene," thus engaging *The Stone Sky* in a multilayered conversation to further unravel how it can help in understanding the Anthropocene. Weik von Mossner deals with the particular challenges and problems that storytelling faces in the Anthropocene. According to her, storytelling is crucial for human understanding of the self and the world, so it can also help in imagining the experience of being a geological force. Weik von Mossner uses some examples of speculative fiction as lenses through which to examine human-geologic agency, but her scope is limited. It will be explained how important fantasy literature is for communicating knowledge and understanding of the world. Finally, this chapter will examine expansions to these ideas from the environmental humanities, specifically ethnography and non-human studies, with special note of potential solutions to human disconnection from the rest of the planet. Jemisin's text offers the perspectives of non-human characters as a complicating factor. Environmental humanities scholars Marisol de la Cadena, Thom van Dooren, and Deborah Bird Rose examine what these perspectives can accomplish in terms of human–non-human relations.

As we recognize the immense transformations of the world and come to understand our own myriad roles in them, our storytelling must necessarily change as well to grapple with a new epoch. This chapter will explore what storytelling, particularly in Jemisin's Hugo Award-winning trilogy, can tell us about the origins of this epoch, our agency over geologic forces, and opportunities to correct wayward cultures' relationships to the non-human world. The *Broken Earth Trilogy* is a fantasy with science fictional elements, which, as this chapter will demonstrate, makes it an ideal source for critical evaluation. Before evaluating the text, it is important to first understand the context of the Anthropocene, a concept that elicits a sense of the fantastic and science fictional in our own real world. In an Anthropocene Epoch, we must understand and apprehend our own power as geologic agents.

THE ANTHROPOCENE EPOCH AND HUMANS AS AGENTS OF GEOLOGY

Tens of thousands of years ago, human migrations began the first of the human-driven animal extinctions we are now so familiar with: those of the Ice Age megafauna (Barnosky 11546). In the nineteenth century, wealthy Europeans revolutionized industry with the mass extraction and burning of fossil fuels, thus commencing the unbalancing of Earth's climate (Waters et al., 6–7). In the 1940s and 1950s, nuclear-capable nations dropped atom-breaking bombs, thus circulating distinctive radioisotopes through the global atmosphere and oceans such that they can still be found in sediment layers today (Waters et al., 9–10). These processes and events, among others, are part of a growing recognition that one species has had outsized impacts on global Earth systems, including, notably, the long system of geology.

In the early 2000s, atmospheric chemist Paul Crutzen began deliberation over adopting a new unit of geologic time into the official lexicon of stratigraphers. The International Commission on Stratigraphy, the body which defines *deep time* for scientific understanding, has been considering whether to officially define the *Anthropocene* as a distinct geological unit from our current geological epoch, the Holocene. The Commission, specifically its Subcommission on Quaternary Stratigraphy, established a Working Group on the "Anthropocene" in 2009 to investigate the evidence. This Working Group has published dozens of papers from its various members as of early 2019, ranging from definitions to broad reviews. The picture formed by the research indicates that the proposed Anthropocene is, indeed, geologically distinct from the original Holocene epoch in detectable ways. According to a 2016 publication by the Working Group, humans are creating, discarding, and polluting in such magnitude that our activities are already being stratified. Human activities are leaving behind synthetic materials such as plastics and aluminum, future "technofossils." Fossil fuel burning is depositing ash and carbon in layers. Various industries are leaving behind signatures of hydrocarbons, pesticide residues, lead isotopes from leaded gasoline, nitrogen and phosphorus from fertilizers, and radionuclides from atomic bombs. Climate change is altering the isotopes of carbon and oxygen present in global biogeochemical cycles (Waters et al., 3–7). Thus, it is revealed, piece by piece, that humans are agents of geology itself.

The scientific evidence shows that certain human activities have already led to a permanently altered geology of the planet. Scientifically speaking, we clearly know the sources of these novel stratigraphies, stratigraphies which each come with a profound and devastating story of ecological destruction. This scientific notion, since it is so vast in scope, has been rippling outward through other disciplines such as literature and the environmental humanities. Notably, many of these scholars work to complicate the simplified scientific narrative, in particular Andreas Malm and Alf Hornborg along with Donna Haraway. Malm and Hornborg directly challenged the notions of a global humankind or "anthros" by investigating the (Western, wealthy, patriarchal) origins of fossil fuel burning and steam engines, calling it "sociogenic" rather than "anthropogenic" (Malm and Hornborg 66). Haraway also probed the origins of the "Anthropocene" with her renamings: "Capitalocene, Plantationocene, Chthulucene" (Haraway 159). Haraway, at a basic level, wants her readers to realize that the "Anthropocene" is multifaceted: a transformation point in our relations not only with the natural world but also with each other and our own pasts and futures, especially as they relate to systems of colonialism and conquer. These systems, though ultimately ephemeral in the face of geologic time, are nevertheless crucial to breaking the "Anthropocene" into its many components. This reintroduces N. K. Jemisin's masterful trilogy and its perspective of marginalized and oppressed voices. True to the legacy of science fiction, her work explores new spaces of thought, in particular spaces where the forces of geology and history collide.

COLONIAL HISTORY ENTANGLED WITH DEEP TIME

In *The Stone Sky*, the final volume of *The Broken Earth Trilogy*, Jemisin reveals the crucial originating effect of the resource-consuming, imperial-derived civilization that started the Fifth Seasons of her world. In this far-past narrative, visited only in a few chapters of the novel, Syl Anagist is described as an intensely globalized system of interconnected cities which all have "the same infrastructure, the same culture, the same hungers and fears" (Jemisin, *The Stone Sky* 3). It arrived at that point via oppression and imperial takeover. Jemisin narrates that "all became Syl Anagist" when it desired land "occupied by many small and nothing peoples" (208). Syl Anagist expanded on an international scale, colonizing in a clear parallel to the historical empires of our world.

Syl Anagist does not just desire land, of course, but energy, which it extracts in the form of magic produced by living things. Just as its militaristic conquest parallels historical empires, its energy extraction parallels modern extractive industries in our world. Jemisin's fuel source, though, is fuel extracted from living beings rather than now-dead, inert fossil fuels: a streamlined metaphor in which bodies are directly drained. Syl Anagist's culture considers life sacred, but this masks the darker side: life is "sacred, and lucrative, and *useful*" (314). Life is a commodity because it is an energy source. The Fifth Seasons were actually the result of Syl Anagist's unending hunger for magic—it tried to extract magic from the (living) Earth, to "feed upon the life of the planet itself, forever" (322). But "Syl Anagist is ultimately unsustainable. It is parasitic; its hunger for magic grows with every drop it devours" (334). This ultimately led it to a catastrophic end—but not before it scarred the world for eons to come. Characters throughout the volumes of the trilogy discuss and encounter impossibly deep boreholes and floating obelisk-like crystals, later revealed to be of concurrent origin during the Syl Anagistine age. Jemisin thus provides another parallel between her world and modern fossil fuel extractive industries: drills and wells burrow into the skin of the planet to hollow out ancient stratigraphic layers. Syl Anagist's tuning crystals perhaps magnify this ever-deepening boring and extraction to impossible but logically consistent extremes. Would fossil fuel industries burrow straight through the crust of the Earth if they had the technology to do so and an economic reward? Jemisin's story of Syl Anagist offers an answer. It is primarily through the chapters, "Syl Anagist Five" through "Zero," that Jemisin investigates how humans experience geological agency and how systems of oppression and environmental destruction entwine.

Understanding the geologic life and agency of humans is crucial to apprehending the Anthropocene. The postcolonial historian Dipesh Chakrabarty asserts that many current understandings of history are insufficient in thinking about humans as geologic agents. Specifically, he points out that the anthropogenic explanations of climate change collapse the false humanist distinction between human history and natural history (Chakrabarty 201). Jemisin puts the species perspective, a perspective of humanity in terms of evolutionary and geologic time, in conversation with forces of colonialism, globalization, and capitalism: the perspective of historical time. Chakrabarty insists that both perspectives are necessary for understanding what climate change really means. The species perspective of humans gives us the scale to explain climate change as a crisis to humanity beyond its cultural systems; however, historical studies, in particular his postcolonial studies of globalization and capitalism, provide context for how climate change and the Anthropocene were instigated in part through oppression and marginalization. Kathryn Yusoff, writing about the geologic life of humans both as a collective and as individual subjects and using fossils as her guide, notes that "the Anthropocene defines a new temporality for the human as a being situated in geologic time"; it "folds geologic time into human corporeality" (Yusoff 781). This everyday-level awareness of geologic time is omnipresent in Jemisin's world: in fact, she begins her trilogy by making readers aware of deep time. The world of *The Stone Sky* is 40,000 years removed from the incitement of the Fifth Seasons. This is embodied by the character's language with the term "deadciv," used to denote ruins or artifacts belonging to one of the countless civilizations that were destroyed by previous cataclysms. Such artifacts litter the continent and sky, confronting characters routinely with the lost history of their species and the ephemerality of civilization itself. It takes just one destructive civilization to create this kind of crisis, though.

Only by disproportionately valuing growth and consumption can a human civilization commence a true Anthropocene. The postcolonial scholarship of Chakrabarty, Haraway, and Malm and Hornborg, as touched on above, discuss the necessary role of the expansion and globalization of Western economic structures, particularly capitalism's values of unending growth, in extracting and polluting on a scale large enough to alter the entire planet. The original civilization of Jemisin's world, Syl Anagist, was the origin of a fictional post-apocalyptic age. A culture built on resource and energy extraction without a check to feed a growth machine, representative of modern capitalism's tenet of insatiable development, leads to environmental destruction and what Rob Nixon calls a "displacement without moving": a loss of land while it is still inhabited (Nixon 19). Indeed, extraction economies throughout history have affected people disproportionately, for example, the pollution due to oil extraction in Nigeria. One of Rob Nixon's goals in his book, *Slow Violence and the Environmentalism of the Poor* (2011) is to demonstrate how writers respond to slow violence and displacements due to environmental injustice. He writes at length about Ken Saro-Wiwa, the late Nigerian writer and member of the Ogoni Tribe, whose homeland on the Niger Delta has been overtaken by oil interests and devastatingly polluted; oil and noxious gases enter the air, water, and soil through a network of pipelines, gas flares, and careless spills (Nixon 103–108). Jemisin writes about environmental injustice, too. During the Fifth Seasons in Jemisin's world, the orogenes are culled and the "commless" are left to die outside settlements, showing unequal impacts of disaster even as the displacement occurs over a global scale. Along with this global scale, climate change in our real world and the Fifth Seasons of Jemisin's deal with both short and long spans of time.

Jemisin's world reflects the potential global and deep-time catastrophe of climate change already underway on Earth. Climate disasters will, of course, displace some people first and more severely. Sea level rise, for example, is already threatening small island nations such as the Marshall Islands with flooding, erosion, saltwater intrusion, and inundation—effects that may be severe enough to remove entire populations from the islands. Climate change will produce climate refugees: widespread forced migrations and diasporas like the more rapid versions of human migrations that have played out over evolutionary time. Jemisin's world also combines both rapid and evolutionary migrations. Essun and her allies become refugees of climate change and violence when "something beautiful and wholesome," the fortified residence of their community, is destroyed; in the aftermath, Hoa guides them to a presumably empty city to the north because "they've got nothing else to hope for" (Jemisin, *The Stone Sky* 25, 24). The home of their budding cooperative culture, one in which the orogenes were treated as equally human as everyone else, is taken, threatening to take with it the culture they worked for. Migrations like these must have happened during previous Fifth Seasons as well. The world's primary continent, the Stillness, includes ethnic groups that have evolved adaptations to volcanic disasters since the long-removed Syl Anagistine age, notably ashblow hair. The people associated with this genetic trait, the Sanze, are the current ruling class, having spread themselves and their culture across the Stillness. Jemisin's world accesses both future and past, small-scale and large-scale movements of individuals and peoples. Through energy extraction, displacement, and migrations, Jemisin therefore demonstrates what Chakrabarty posits: scholars and writers need to think in both terms—deep *and* cultural history—to understand the climate crisis and ultimately to try and rectify wrongs.

Jemisin comments on how the cycle of oppression and extraction may be broken. In an interview with *The Guardian* about the series, she states that "sometimes survival requires change" (Berlatsky). In *The Stone Sky*, she tells the reader that "cooperation presents opportunities," (394) that we should not "lament when [worlds built on a fault line of pain] fall" (7). This message of change applies to our environmental situation. Opportunities exist for destructive cultures to change course, to rethink values such as growth and consumption. Some crises can still be diverted. By describing origins and solutions to environmental harm, *The Stone Sky* expands perspectives to investigate the roots and effects of an Anthropocene epoch, thus melding deep time and human time. This is only possible because of the power of the fantastic.

GENRE CONVENTIONS AS A VEHICLE FOR UNDERSTANDING

Fantasy and science fiction genre conventions can help in clarifying the Anthropocene. Jemisin creates her own systems of oppression and colonialism that, because they are entirely removed from our world, clarify understandings of real systems. Alexa Weik von Mossner's response to Chakrabarty's "Four Theses" describes the particular challenges that storytelling faces in portraying humans as a geologic force, and she provides speculative fiction and science fiction, particularly that of Kim Stanley Robinson and Dale Pendell, as a possible solution (Weik von Mossner 86). Fantasy like Jemisin's is uniquely situated beyond speculative fiction: by moving parallel rather than forward or backward in time, we can speculate at a greater remove.

Processes become clearer without other societal complications masking them. For example, Syl Anagist uses living things as energy sources, thus combining energy extraction and plant and animal commodification systems. There are very real entanglements in both systems: both lead to dehumanizing human groups and both fuel overconsumption. Jemisin wraps oppression and imperialism up with energy extraction technology through Hoa and his kin, the tuners—the bioengineered people meant to commence the process of magic harvesting from Earth. Much like many real indigenous peoples who were made out by colonizers to be subhuman, the dehumanization starts with the colonization of the Niess, a magically adept people who were viewed as "not the same kind of human as everyone else. Eventually: not *as* human as everyone else. Finally: not human at all" (Jemisin, *The Stone Sky* 210). In a convolution of bioengineering and colonial oppression, the tuners were made to be caricatures of the now dispersed and culturally extinct Niess. The Niess were not just oppressed, though: many of them were eventually placed in a kind of living–death state in the briar patch, a magic-harvesting system designed to keep them comatose indefinitely as energy sinks. Someone explains the system to Hoa and the other tuners with technical jargons such as "generative cycle," "need to reprime," "sink reservoir," and "thirty-seven lammotyrs stored" (263). The ruling system refers to groups of people as machinery. Hoa is incredulous, realizing that it is "as if these stored, componentized lives mean nothing to [them]" (263). And in our world, the componentized lives of livestock and crop plants are intensely commodified. Our extraction and processing of fossil fuel energy frequently dismisses the value of people and other living things in its way, turning them into disposable elements or workers for the extraction machine. Tying these systems together reveals an overarching path of prioritizing growth and extraction over living agency. The work of fantasy narratives—worlds one step removed from our own—exposes the collusion of these systems. Working through these systems, of course, are individuals—individuals who are, thanks to their status as fantastical, able to reveal much about their world and ours.

Some of Jemisin's individual characters, critically the narrator, Hoa, are geology-based, ageless transhumans and so have directly experienced the deep time and historical processes that led to the trilogy's present—thus they act as ambassadors for the reader's understanding. This was a specific challenge detailed by Weik von Mossner: individual agency is limited by human lifespans. Hoa and the other tuners start with a measure of geologic awareness: they have a shared communication ability they call "earthtalk," which allows them to send tactile vibrations to each other in a novel form of language; it utilizes phrases such as *cracked geode taste of adularescent salts, fading echo* (Jemisin, *The Stone Sky* 46, original emphasis) as a name and *shiverstone micaflake glimmer* as laughter (329). They speak and think in terms of geologic strata. Eventually, Hoa and the other tuners gain a true awareness of geologic time, as they are transformed into inorganic living beings (392). In the story's present, Hoa has trouble telling smaller units of time apart. His exclusive perspective allows insight into how harms play out over deep time.

As Kathryn Yusoff and Jennifer Gabrys profess, "the arts and humanities play an important role in thinking through our *representations of environmental change* [original emphasis] and give tangible form to the imagination of different worlds outside of the constraints of a given present" (Yusoff and Gabrys 518). Using characters only possible in the fantastic, Jemisin brings together massively different timescales—something necessitated by the Anthropocene idea and its generational effects. Jeffrey Jerome Cohen points out that "stone becomes history's bedrock as lithic agency impels human knowing" (Cohen 4). Stone, geology, and the geologic Earth become focal points of Jemisin's work, catalysts for and recorders of history: this last is represented quite literally by "stonelore," ancient wisdom detailing how to survive the Fifth Seasons and referenced often by characters in Jemisin's world. Beyond even the age of the stonelore, the geologic minds of the tuners provide a transitional space between physical, stratigraphic record, and written or remembered history. Thus, the tuners become a tangible method of apprehending collective human agency. Besides the temporal experience of geology, there is also the physical experience. The lithic agency of Jemisin's orogene characters, as with the tuner characters, allows the reader to experience vast time and human sociocultural systems in a way that might be otherwise impossible.

Jemisin's main characters possess geological agency in a way that only systems and centuries do in our world, thus providing a metaphor for our own understanding of our geologic agency: an inroad to imagining and experience. Jemisin defies Chakrabarty's assertion that we "may not experience ourselves as a geological agent" (Chakrabarty 221). Like other orogenes, Essun, Nassun, and Alabaster exert direct influence over the strata of the Earth, but these three change the fate of all humans on the planet: Alabaster by cracking open the continent, and then Essun and Nassun by trying to end the Fifth Seasons for good. Still, the characters are shaped by the oppressive systems they are part of, which complete the circle of deep time to historical time. In the present of the story, the ruling systems oppress and enslave the orogenes. The characters deal with these (now collapsing and transforming) systems extensively in the first two books of the trilogy, and *The Stone Sky* narrates the origin and the (hopeful) end of the oppression of the orogenes. In a *New York Times* interview, Jemisin professed, "I tend to write society as I see and understand it . . . I decided to focus on an oppressive society at the macro scale and what that society does to individuals" (Alter). This oppression is rooted in fear. Jemisin writes, "There are none so frightened, or so strange in their fear, as conquerors" (*The Stone Sky* 210). Conquerors fear losing control and being colonized—this has led to prevalent nationalism and anti-immigration stances amid the historic colonizers in our world. Colonial systems twist perceptions, attempting to turn the oppressed into monsters to fear. This is represented in a multifaceted way by Jemisin's work and does not translate exactly into a metaphor for geologic agency, but it provides places to connect thoughts and perspectives, forcing environmental humanities scholars to think about nationalism and oppression as mingling with issues of environmental justice. Important to all perspectives is the role of fear.

In Jemisin's world, the orogenes inspire fear because of their power—*because* of their geologic agency. A fear, manifested as denial, of our own collective geologic agency has produced chronic inaction and inequality. Fear roots and contaminates when those in power allow it to grow. Casting this premise through the prism of the fantastic breaks it apart into individual systems, actions, and histories that we as scholars can examine and parse for meaning. Jemisin explores agency in greater depth, particularly non-human agency, and this is the final revelation she sparks about the origins and consequences of the Anthropocene.

NON-HUMAN AGENCY AND MULTISPECIES ETHNOGRAPHIES

The presence of Earth as a character in the narrative and the actions of the bioengineered tuners in Syl Anagist illustrate the eco-cultural potential of non-human agents with interests in human affairs. The Earth of Jemisin's story has its own desires and perspectives. To it, all of humanity is viewed with what we would call a species perspective: "the Earth sees no difference between any of us [. . .] to it, humanity is humanity" (Jemisin, *The Stone Sky* 335). To the people of Jemisin's world, the Fifth Seasons are an unexpected consequence of their disregard for the Earth's agency. To us, climate change is a result of our own interference in Earth systems, reflected punishingly back on us. But then, "the Earth does not fully understand us. It looks upon human beings and sees short-lived, fragile creatures" (341). A fundamental disconnect in understanding between two living systems, one short-sighted and one far, creates terrible consequences for both. Spurred by the increasingly recognized presence of indigenous voices and goals in South American politics, the cultural anthropologist Marisol de la Cadena grapples with the theoretical implications of considering "earth beings" as political agents: "not simply nonhumans, they are also sentient entities whose material existence [. . .] is currently threatened by the neoliberal wedding of capital and the state" (de la Cadena 342). Jemisin asks the reader to perform a similar assumption, since Earth has direct, unimagined impacts on human society based on its own interests. Our own Earth progresses according to natural processes, moving with an unrelenting momentum that we need to comprehend in order to coexist.

There are potential solutions to humanity's tragic misunderstandings. Thom van Dooren and Deborah Rose emphasize the importance of storytelling in representing ways of living, being, and behaving—a "multispecies ethography." In fact, they even state that "many entities usually considered to be non-living are key parts of an ethographic account," and we must "remain deliberately open [. . .] to the possibility that the liveliness of such beings might itself become the *central* [. . .]focus of an ethographic account" (van Dooren and Rose 262; original emphasis). Jemisin's Earth represents both an Earth Being from de la Cadena and also a geologic liveliness from van Dooren and Rose—this clearly animates it in the reader's mind. Both of these theoretical considerations, when applied to *The Stone Sky*, can help us think about our place in a multispecies, pluriversal web of beings. Indeed, understanding Earth as truly animate is what finally gives Jemisin's characters the knowledge and motivation to repair their relationship with it. Although this provides a hopeful allegory for our real human–Earth relations, we must also keep in mind that the presence of non-human agency implies a lack of human control over the Anthropocene.

In particular, Jemisin illustrates the potential of commodified life-forms to behave in unpredictable ways despite efforts to control them. The handlers of the tuners firmly believe that "creations of Sylanagistine magestry cannot possibly have abilities that surpass it" (Jemisin, *The Stone Sky* 315). However, the tuners try to take control over their own fates, have emergent abilities like earthtalk, and still have a full emotional spectrum despite attempts to remove it. Hoa states, "I am powerful in ways they did not expect. They made me but they do not *control* me" (214; original emphasis). Bioengineered life-forms display unexpected properties—this is true in our world as well: from genetic drift between crops and wild plants to antibiotic-resistant bacteria developing in livestock. Attempting to exert complete control over living systems is a folly of imperialism. Put in a larger context, the Anthropocene may be anthropogenic, but it is not controlled or directed by humanity. On the opposite side of denying our geologic agency is the assumption of our geologic dominance.

CONCLUSION

Through this chapter, disciplines in the humanities, literature, and the sciences have revealed a depth and breadth of meaning in N. K. Jemisin's award-winning science fantasy trilogy, particularly the third volume, *The Stone Sky*. Jemisin's work provides an anchor, or "germination point," for us to examine how the forces of colonialism and capitalism interweave with geologic time to create global crises. She expresses the power both of energy-extraction-driven civilizations and of environmental disasters. The familiarity created by existing mentally within this intimate story space is crucial for human apprehension of geologic agency: we use stories to understand our world and our places in it. The imaginative power of fantasy and science fiction, in particular, were crucial tools for Jemisin's work: they freed her to explore characters-as-geologic agents, entangled energy and commodification systems, and non-human agency in ways that reveal metaphorical guidance for our real-world cultures. The critical success of the trilogy is especially hopeful: it shows writers and scholars both that there is ample room for stories of the Anthropocene.

The world of the Stillness, like Earth, exists in a state of human-geologic determinism. In her *Broken Earth Trilogy*, particularly in *The Stone Sky*, N. K. Jemisin asks us to both accept and challenge the Anthropocene's assumptions: while human civilization may have irrevocably altered the planet, it must not be considered dominant; other factors—other forces—are also at play. Fantasy acts as a vehicle of understanding and enacts social criticism. Contemporary fantasy with broad themes of ecology and injustice, such as *The Stone Sky*, urges us to examine what the Anthropocene might mean for our own future. As Yusoff and Gabrys point out, "the work of the imagination is a will to become; in many different ways the imagination extends, pushes, challenges, and confides to us what the human is" (Yusoff and Gabrys 529). Jemisin imagines for us a world spurred into environmental disaster by a colonialist, energy-hungry empire, where individuals possess geologic agency, where bioengineered beings defy the wills of their creators, where understanding and cooperation provide an exit from recurring oppression and environmental harms. Jemisin shows us that even after apocalypse, there is hope.

WORKS CITED

Alter, Alexandra. "N. K. Jemisin on Diversity in Science Fiction and Inspiration From Dreams." *New York Times*, 6 September 2016, p. NA(L). *Academic OneFile*. www.link.galegroup.com/apps/doc/A462580811/AONE?u=iastu_main&sid=AONE&xid=e20668cb. Accessed 28 April 2018.

Barnosky, Anthony D. "Megafauna Biomass Tradeoff as a Driver of Quaternary and Future Extinctions." *PNAS*, vol. 105, 2008, pp. 11543–11548.

Berlatsky, Noah. "NK Jemisin: The Fantasy Writer Upending the 'Racist and Sexist Status Quo'." *The Guardian*, Guardian News and Media, 27 July 2015. www.theguardian.com/books/2015/jul/27/nk-jemisin-interview-fantasy-science-fiction-writing-racism-sexism. Accessed 15 September 2020.

Chakrabarty, Dipesh. "The Climate of History: Four Theses." *Critical Inquiry*, vol. 35, no. 2, 2009, pp. 197–222.

Cohen, Jeffrey Jerome. *Stone: An Ecology of the Inhuman*. U of Minnesota P, 2015.

de la Cadena, Marisol. "Indigenous Cosmopolitics in the Andes: Conceptual Reflections beyond 'Politics'." *Cultural Anthropology*, vol. 25, no. 2, 2010, pp. 334–370.

Haraway, Donna. "Anthropocene, Capitalocene, Plantationocene, Chthulucene: Making Kin." *Environmental Humanities*, vol. 6, 2015, pp. 159–165.

Jemisin, N. K. *The Fifth Season*. Orbit, 2015.

———. *The Stone Sky*. Orbit, 2017.

Malm, Andreas, and Alf Hornborg. "The Geology of Mankind? A Critique of the Anthropocene Narrative." *The Anthropocene Review*, vol. 1, no. 1, 2014, pp. 62–69.

Nixon, Rob. *Slow Violence and the Environmentalism of the Poor*. Harvard UP, 2011.

van Dooren, Thom, and Deborah Bird Rose. "Lively Ethography: Storying Animist Worlds." In *Environmental Humanities: Voices from the Anthropocene*, edited by Serpil Oppermann and Serenella Iovino. Rowman & Littlefield International, 2017, pp. 255–271.

Waters, Colin N., et al. "The Anthropocene is Functionally and Stratigraphically Distinct from the Holocene." *Science*, vol. 351, no. 6269, January 2016, pp. aad2622-1–aad2622-10.

Weik von Mossner, Alexa. "Imagining Geological Agency: Storytelling in the Anthropocene." In *Whose Anthropocene? Revisiting Dipesh Chakrabarty's "Four Theses,"* edited by Robert Emmett and Thomas Lekan. *RCC Perspectives: Transformations in Environment and Society*, vol. 2, 2016, pp. 83–88. doi:10.5282/rcc/7421.

Yusoff, Kathryn. "Geologic Life: Prehistory, Climate, Futures in the Anthropocene." *Environment and Planning D: Society and Space*, vol. 31, 2013, pp. 779–795.

Yusoff, Kathryn, and Jennifer Gabrys. "Climate Change and the Imagination." *WIREs Climate Change*, vol. 2, no. 4, 2011, pp. 516–534.

Chapter 10

The Politics of Language and Culture in China Miéville's Novel *Embassytown*

Aleksandr Kolesnikov

China Miéville is one of those authors whose science fiction is less related to prognostication and more to real political and social issues. A typical example is his novel *The City & The City* (2009), written at the crossroads of genres (noir and urban fantasy are the primary dominants). The split city becomes a metaphor for cultural and political separation, allowing the writer to explore the questions of cultural and ethnic identity, to break the social and political mechanisms of self-determination and identification with the Other in the spirit of Roland Barthes. In this novel Miéville formulates the critical challenges of European society and touches upon the matters of interethnic communication, bringing the conversation into the sphere of political and civil identity. Thus, cultural constructs are essential to him, as they reassemble the natural state of things and form a hierarchical system (cf. Kuehmichel).

In the novel *Embassytown* (2011), which is the main subject of this chapter, Miéville further develops these ideas, drawing attention to language and culture and their role in forming the politics of opposing ourselves to Others. Nevertheless, "the book's real focus being human natural language [. . .] and the essence of humanness" (Głaz 337), it is important to keep in mind the power of language and its role in cultural politics. In the conclusion of his paper on Miéville's novel, Adam Głaz notes that

> the move from Language to language, from the yoke of thought imprisoned to the freedom of thought-as-interpretation, i.e. from anti-humanity to humanity, is good. But this opens the door to more experimentation: can the shift from a truth-based asemantic code to a prevarication-allowing semantic and symbolic language be a tragic one? (348)

Thus, Głaz seems to interpret the transition to a human-like mode of mentality as beneficial to the indigenous Hosts of the planet of Arieka, albeit notes a potential menace of such a change. Such reading of *Embassytown* presumes the postcolonial perspective. I start out where Głaz finishes. I will demonstrate how Miéville points out the political capabilities of language when it is included in or excluded from culture. Since the pivotal topic of Miéville's novel, among others, is interaction and communication of human (or at least of human-origin) and non-human creatures, it can no longer be read only as the postcolonial narrative, but as the narrative of the Anthropocene.

In her influential essay "The Promises of Monsters: The Regenerative Politics for Inappropriate/d Others" (original publication 1992, cited here from the 2004 edition that appeared in *The Haraway Reader*), which preceded the Anthropocene criticism, Donna Haraway suggests we should:

> "articulate" with humans and unhumans in a social relationship, which for us is always language mediated (among other semiotic, i.e., "meaningful," mediations). But, for our unlike partners, well, the action is "different": perhaps "negative" from our linguistic point of view, but crucial to the generativity of the collective. (89)

and

> articulation with those humans and non-humans who live in rain forests and in many other places in the semiotic space called earth. (92)

That is where the linguistic and cultural challenge for the Anthropocene comes from. As it is argued in Daniel Hartley's essay "Anthropocene, Capitalocene, and the Problem of Culture," the Anthropocene as a critical paradigm and environmental practice is "cultureless" (164). He insists that "we must also attack those elements of capitalist civilization which appear to have no immediate relation to ecology, but *which are in fact internal conditions of its possibility*" (165, original emphasis). Haraway seems to move even further, as her concept of the Chthulucene, and related to it "sympoiesis," implies "naturalcultural assemblages" and involves culture and language into the discussion of the Anthropocene (cf. Haraway, *Making Kin*).

In these circumstances the role of language, as not only a medium of culture but also a political mechanism, is increasing; thus the teaching of a different language goes beyond a strictly linguistic problem and becomes part of a broader range of problems, revealing the potential for political action. By teaching our language, we not only gain the opportunity to communicate with others but also impose our cultural paradigm, eliminating the alien, original culture, making our human view of the world the only possible one, thus limiting and subordinating the world to ourselves.

The problem, as addressed in Miéville's novel, seems inadequate in the Anthropocene era (Capitalocene, Chthulucene). The Terre (those of Earth origin) try to teach indigenous people of the planet Arieka not only to speak their language but to produce false statements (the language of the Ariekei is based solely on true statements, which makes, for example, metaphorical speech impossible). Such training has specific emancipatory potential, because it can put the Ariekei on the same level as people by providing an opportunity to communicate on an equal footing. That leads to Arieka's natives getting out of the colonial control of the Terre. On the other hand, the fact that political freedom will not only lead to the liberation from humans and the influence of the human space empire but also lead to severe cultural changes in the lives of the Ariekei themselves, is slipping away from the sight of Miéville.

That is what my thesis develops from. I suggest that although *Embassytown* succeeds as a piece of postcolonial fiction, it fails as the narrative of the Anthropocene. I will demonstrate what science fiction of the Anthropocene (and more specific—the Chthulucene) might look like in relation to cultural and linguistic challenges and how it could shape our understanding of Otherness in a slightly different way than postcolonial science fiction. I will then discuss the politics of language and culture as addressed in the novel and show that Miéville's handling of the problem is quite inadequate to the Chthulucene criticism. I want to argue that SF goes beyond the postcolonial narrative and provides not only the image of the Other that is not silent, inactive, cultureless, devoid of language and creativeness, and in need of enlightenment and inclusion in human political and cultural spaces, but also the image of the Other which is a companion to "articulate with."

HUMAN, NON-HUMAN, AND UNHUMAN: CULTURAL POLITICS, THE ANTHROPOCENE, AND SCIENCE FICTION

The opposition of the Same and the Other is one of the most fundamental and ancient in human culture and defines our behavior in the world around us. Being a derivative of society and culture, once opposed to nature, people define themselves not through their characteristics, but as a counterposition to the Other. Even if we are unable to answer the question of what is the essence of human nature, we can specify the difference that separates us from other animals, plants, and the world in general. The distinction becomes our identifying mark, while similarity ensures evolutionary security and the survival of the species. While mythological consciousness was incapable of distinguishing objects, fictional and real (and by extension, representation and its referent), the logical, rational type of thinking, developed by humankind at the beginning of the first millennium, is entirely determined by the ability to analyze, that is, to separate one from another (cf. Donald; Mithen). Otherness becomes not only an epistemological but ontological category, thus defining the modes of our interaction with the world around us. Throughout human history, Otherness has been the unknown, and the unknown carries unpredictability and danger. The whole world was the space of Otherness. That is why humankind is afraid of others: it is possible to protect oneself only by mastering the unknown, assimilating it, making it a fact of human culture. As Emmanuel Lévinas says: "Culture can, first, be interpreted—and this is the privileged dimension of the Greco-Roman West (and its possibility of universalization)—as an intention to remove the *otherness* of Nature, which, alien and previous, surprises and strikes the immediate identity that is the *Same* of the human self" (179).

Human–Nature relations are of particular interest to the Anthropocene criticism proposed at the beginning of the new millennium (cf. Schwägerl; Glikson; Satgar). As Bruno Latour notes in his recent essay, it is crucial for the Anthropocene to propose "a completely new definition of 'otherness'" ("Anthropology" 48), which would allow the transition from modernity to the contemporary to be completed (the distinction between "being modern" and "being contemporary" is crucial for Latour's comprehension of the Anthropocene and goes back to his influential book *We Have Never Been Modern,* published in English in 1993). Since the Anthropocene concentrates on human agency, it is extremely important to redefine our understanding of culture, to get rid of human exceptionalism. We need to recognize "that we share the planet with other life forms upon which our own biophysical make-up depends—even microbes" (Schlosser 288), we need to accept "a world beyond ours in which nature has become culture" (Schwägerl 172).

Since science fiction, fantasy, Gothic, and weird fiction, among other genres, can be considered as narratives of Otherness, which show the knock-on effects of a meeting with the Other (cf. Beaumont; Thacker; Trigg), it is hardly surprising that this kind of fiction now represents the narrative of the Anthropocene. Before any further discussion of the matter, a few points should be made about culture in its connection with language, as it is extremely important for the analysis of China Miéville's novel.

On a higher level, the process of removal of Otherness can be considered not within Culture–Nature relationship but as intercultural exchange. The basis of such an interaction is communication through language. Linguistic identity becomes not only a marker of alienation but the mechanism of cultural homogenization, implemented through language. As language is one of the main factors in identity formation, the preservation or destruction of a language, which is different from the "default language," is directly linked to the politics of the protection or elimination of another culture: "It may be that these languages never become languages of power per se, languages of economics or politics, but for this particular community, it's really important" (Clapperton). In this case, language can be considered as a mechanism of constructing various "symbolic forms" (the concept coined by a German philosopher Ernst Cassirer)—"the images, narratives, and theories through which we make sense of facts" (Tygstrup 87). On the basis of the ideas of Cassirer, Antonio Gramsci, and Jacques Rancière, Frederik Tygstrup demonstrates that symbolic forms are also the forms of power and domination and therefore are politically significant (93–96). As Tygstrup clarifies Cassirer's statement, "a culture should be assessed on the basis of its explicit performative linguistic practice" (93), hence language diversity becomes a guarantee of the cultural one. Taking into account the constant transformation of communicative practices, it is important to protect different languages as part of linguistic policies for cultural diversity. Nowadays, it is one of the most remarkable challenges for humanity (cf. Schlosser 137–142).

Donna Haraway claims that SF (which she defines as "speculative fabulation, science fiction, science fact, speculative feminism, so far" ("Staying" 36; cf. "SF")) is "the patterning of possible worlds and possible times, material-semiotic worlds, gone, here, and yet to come" ("Staying" 36). In the new geological era of human impact, science fiction, as well as science fantasy, or speculative fiction, or weird fiction, or Gothic tales, become the genres that are most fitting to the epoch. What is more important, there is a need for fiction, or broader aesthetics, which is capable of providing the images of "those significant others that are the silent recipients of violence in an era of anthropogenic-induced climate change" (Yusoff, "Biopolitical Economies" 76). Kathryn Yusoff, an attentive and thoughtful reader of Bataille, Haraway, Foucault, Rancière, and others, argues that today's aesthetics is the aesthetics of political action. She claims that "re-categorizing of aesthetics as a practice rather than representative of some other socio-political 'thing' considers aesthetics in terms of what it does in the world rather than what other experiences or thoughts it might give space or time to" (Yusoff, "Biopolitical Economies" 79). Thus, literature, as well as other forms of arts and humanities, must respond to this.

For a long time, science fiction was on the periphery of the literary process and aesthetic practice because many researchers and recipients considered the genre as unrelated to urgent social and political issues (Bould). In some respect this criticism was fair and appropriate (cf. Le Guin). On the other hand, it was these literary trends which shaped our view of the Other, and thus, through the opposition of the Self and the Other allowed us to better understand what humanity as a species is (Beaumont). It was a human being, with a human view of the universe, who was most often in the center of the early science fiction narratives (and that is why it was the object of Le Guin's criticism). After the withdrawal of the paradigm of anthropocentrism, such literature has increasingly begun to redefine the concept of human and non-human (un-human and inhuman), criticizing the well-established cultural and social paradigm (Moore).

Proposing images of non-human and un-human, science fiction invites one to see oneself in very striking images of what we, as a species, are used to dealing with. In this way, science fiction does not only provide us with images of the Other that make us change our perception of our place in the world but also takes on a method of defamiliarization (or estrangement) that changes our understanding of ourselves, allowing us to think of ourselves as the Other (cf. Beaumont; Davidson). As Eugene Thacker points out in the philosophical context, these topics are becoming evident in the contemporary world as a political reality: "one of the greatest challenges that philosophy faces today lies in comprehending the world in which we live as both a human and a non-human world—and of comprehending this politically" (2).

These ideas overlap largely with the problems associated with the concept of the Anthropocene, which highlights the irreversible changes in the environment that have been provoked by human activity. Both environmental issues and biopolitics are in the center of the Anthropocene. However, while traditional Anthropocene criticism focuses on the impact that humans have on Earth and its species (Bignall et al.; Glikson; Hamilton et al.; Steffen et al.), science fiction and fantasy can offer a different perspective.

By extrapolating human handling of the planet to the universe, such literature points to the fact that the human impact on the world around is not limited to the Earth alone, but actually (or potentially) affects the entire Universe. Chris Pak develops this idea further as: "Narratives of terraforming and geoengineering are, at their core, narratives about the Anthropocene" (500). The practices and habits that humankind has developed over the years could (and will) be applied on a very different level, creating a new colonial future, when more and more planets will be colonized. That is what science fiction attentive to ecological, environmental, and geosociological challenges of the new era develop from. Climate fiction, as well as ecological and environmental science fiction, is now a key subgenre "as a popular response to climate change" (Evans 484). Milner et al. explain that "these fictional responses run roughly parallel to the options available in real-world discourse" (19). On analyzing five different novels Alexandra Nikoleris et al. claim that these narratives put different kinds of effects "into focus, and they are viewed and interpreted from different geographic, social, and cultural points of view" (73).

As I have mentioned before, human influence will not only be geological (or ecological), but also sociopolitical, and the challenges of the Anthropocene are not limited to the environmental problems but extended to a broader complex of issues, particularly, as Kathryn Yusoff points out, "politics as we have known it shifted" (Yusoff, "Politics" 256). Just as humans have conquered and enslaved this planet throughout their history, adapting it to their own needs, so new outer spaces will be conquered in accordance with this well-established paradigm. As the subjugation of the aboriginal cultures of Africa and America was justified by the Enlightenment, so the exploration of the cosmos and cosmic cultures could be treated in the same Enlightenment-like manner. However, such "enlightenment," as demonstrated by the history of the interaction of Western civilization with the indigenous populations of Africa and America, is highly questionable and is more like a conquest. Humanity, in this sense, can be perceived not as much as a species that carries the holy fire of knowledge but rather as a source of threat on a universal level. The challenges of imperialism, colonialism, and their connection to power and dominance are traditionally associated with those of postcolonial literature, as well as with other forms of the postcolonial narratives.

An illustrative example of this new colonial policy can be found in the 1960s classic series *Star Trek* (NBC, 1966–1969). Through the idea of a frontier as a flexible boundary, this kind of fiction shows how colonial and imperial policies of humankind, with the rise of technical possibility, can be deployed on a cosmic level. In other words, such science fiction does not differ much from literature showing the relationship of the Western world with the indigenous population of America during the time of its conquest. Despite the intention to provide more diverse image of human and humanness, *Star Trek* "promotes an anthropocentric position in the representation of animals as much as in the representation of other alterns" (Neuwirth; cf. Hoagland and Sarwal 7–8).

Postcolonial science fiction depicts this situation more delicately, without giving humanity the status of a source of cultural and technological enlightenment. Postcolonial science fiction "explores the nature of Otherness and Futurity, and what happens when these ideas are expressed by those who were the *subjects* of earlier versions" (Sawyer 3, original emphasis). As Ericka Hoagland and Reema Sarwal point out in the introduction to *Science Fiction, Imperialism and the Third World* (2010), "the 'Other' is one of the most well-known markers that science fiction and postcolonial literature share in common" (10).

The concept of the Other becomes part of the philosophical agenda of the twentieth century as part of the project of the phenomenological analysis introduced by Edmund Husserl in his groundbreaking book *Cartesian Meditations* (Fr. *Méditations Cartésiennes*, 1931). Husserl focuses on the concept of the Other in the "Fifth Meditation," constituting its transcendental and inaccessible status (89–151). He defines *Otherness* as an ontological category. The concept of the Other as formulated by Husserl is the Absolute Other. It implies the solitude of the Self in the world around and presumes idealistic or even, to some extent, solipsistic interpretation of the Being. In turn, Emmanuel Lévinas defines the *Other* as a rather ethical category which is universal for a human being. As far as "ontology cannot account for other" (Treanor 15) any attempts to account for the Other by ontology reduce Otherness to Sameness. Brian Treanor formulates the essence of Lévinas's point of view as: "to be Other is to be incomprehensible, infinite" (17). Thus, radical Otherness cannot display itself to the world. Human vision, imagination, and language cannot deal with the pure alterity. The autonomy of the Other resists any conceptualization. As Bernhard Waldenfels points out, "the experience of the alien as alien resists every form of totalizing and universalizing" (355).

Lévinas claims that the Otherness of the world around establishes itself through language. Ludwig Wittgenstein describes this as follows: "The limits of my world are the limits of my language" (*Tractatus* 115). We are struggling to allow objects which slip away from our definition to exist in reality. Absolute Otherness is transcendental to human language and thus cannot be conceptualized. The limit of language is not so much the limit of the world, in which we live, as the limit of human vision. Language plays "the powerful role in forming our minds" (Palmer 95), serving as a cognitive mechanism, as well as a communicative tool. In other words, language does not only limit our knowledge but also sets a framework beyond which our imagination cannot go—to think of something that would be beyond our language (the Absolute Other). Although this limit is not absolute and the boundaries of the world as they appear to us are permanently shifting, the role of the language in shaping our mind is significant (cf. investigations in the field of cognitive linguistics—Lakoff and Johnson; Gibbs; Fauconnier and Turner; Turner et al.; Turner). Language in this case reflects the specificity of human conceptual and cognitive apparatus.

Thus, on the one hand, language connects the Self and Otherness of the world. On the other hand, it constitutes the gap between the two. It turns out that in the process of exploring the universe where a person always encounters the unknown (strange) and continuously appropriates this unknown, making it his or her own (cf. Cassirer's interpretation of the Culture–Nature relations in the quote above). In this case, there is a threat of destruction of the identity, which makes this unknown object unique. Inclusion in one's own (dominant) culture is associated with the threat of destruction of the other culture. The arising problem does not only have a political aspect but also poses some ethically ambiguous questions.

The problem of the Alien/the Other can be solved in two different ways. First, it is the acceptance of the autonomy of the Other and the impossibility of translating the other language into one's own without loss. The impossibility of such a translation was pointed out, in particular, by Willard Quine in his works on the logical analysis of language (cf. Quine), or in the phenomenology of language in its relation to the Other proposed by Lévinas in *Otherwise than Being, or beyond Essence* (1974). The recognition of the autonomy of the Other leads to the withdrawal of the notion of the existence of a single view on the world, which would adequately describe the reality in which we live. Moreover, such recognition should be followed by the rejection of the hierarchy of different models of the world, where one model of the world could be recognized as better describing the world than the other one. Imposing one's own culture on the Other through language could be interpreted in this case as an attempt to relieve this Otherness from its self-sufficiency.

Alternatively, recognition of the Other could appear to be the starting point in the search for common ground for different cultures. This model, which involves the inclusion of the Other in a shared space, has been developed and promoted primarily by Jürgen Habermas (*The Inclusion of the Other* 1996). It implies not only inclusion but also an attempt to take into account the interests of different groups through the formation of a discourse area. At the heart of such inclusion lies the possibility of establishing communication and common ground for discourse. Such a model presupposes the communicative equality of the negotiators, which can be only achieved, first, in the conditions of a single speech model, and, second, in the conditions of the honesty of the negotiators. For Habermas, this is a question that primarily affects the political and moral aspects. However, the question of honesty is not limited to the question of true and false statements but is turned into the question of moral honesty.

Phenomenological comprehension of the Other, enriched by the ideas of Jacques Derrida, Jacques Lacan, and Michel Foucault, becomes the basis for postcolonial criticism provided by Homi K. Bhabha. His criticism follows the ideas of Edward Said and transforms it into the discussion of the present forms of colonialism, multiculturalism, and hybridity. He draws special attention to the concept of cultural otherness standing up for its constructed nature. Thus, cultural otherness loses ontological absoluteness emerging not as a relative but an unstable and thus translatable phenomenon. Bhabha's discourse is based on the idea of the impossibility of pure cultures, of radical autonomy, and closeness to external influence. Bhabha's solution of cross-cultural communication lies in the fact that keeping in mind cultural differences one can adopt a position in-between. This assumption "leads to a transparency of culture that must be thought outside of the signification of difference" (Bhabha 127). That turns the problem from the representation of the Other to searching for such forms of culture that are in-between: "designations of cultural difference interpellate forms of identity which, because of their continual implication in other symbolic systems, are always 'incomplete' or open to cultural translation" (162–163). Bhabha calls for "a cultural temporality that is both disjunctive and capable of articulating, in Lévi-Strauss's words, 'forms of activity which are both at once ours and other'" (163).

That forms a hybridity, Bhabha holds on, which keeps the Otherness of the Other as far as "the 'difference' of cultural knowledge that 'adds to' but does not 'add up'"—this difference being "the enemy of the *implicit* generalization of knowledge or implicit homogenization of experience" (163, original emphasis). Subverting "hegemonic 'normality'" (171), Bhabha calls for a critical paradigm that "resists the attempt at holistic forms of social explanation" (173). That notion turns down the project of assimilating minorities through inclusion and elimination of Otherness. The challenge is to put into practice "a new collaborative dimension, both within margins of the nation-space and across boundaries between nations and people" (175) by keeping the cultural differences and apprehending alienation of cultural and political practices.

To a great extent, the postcolonial Other is the cultural and, in this sense, human Other. Bhabha's criticism articulates the necessity of inter- and intra-cultural activities which are subverting the limits and borders of nations and cultures. Since science fiction often depicts the interrelations of human and non-human beings, its subject matter connects the postcolonial perspective with that of the Anthropocene. This is a considerable extension of the postcolonial discourse since "transhistorical postcolonialism has been concerned with avoiding anthropocentric projection by respecting the incommensurability of aliens and alterity with the self" (Gaylard 24).

As "postcolonialism is a theoretical lens through which any literature may be read – from the epics, the Bible and Shakespeare through to spy thrillers, westerns and pulp romance" (Hoagland and Sarwal 5), the Anthropocene can be considered as a critical tool or specific narrative rather than a genre. Taking into account the ethical and ontological status of the Other and its relations to communicative practice allows the Anthropocene perspective to be broadened to focus not only on environmental issues and biopolitics but also on rethinking humanity's relationship with the image of the Other, regardless of whether it is considered subjective from the human perspective or not. Meanwhile, if postcolonial criticism focuses on the forms of representation of the Other to "foreground their position, heritage and interests in order to avoid eliding the voice of the other, the subaltern, the indigenous, the oppressed" (Gaylard 26), the narrative of the Anthropocene and the Anthropocene-foregrounded science fiction must provide the image of what Donna Haraway calls sympoiesis. Postcolonial science fiction aims to recognize the subjectivity of the Other and defends non-human beings as subjects, not objects. In her Marxist criticism of science fiction and the forms of alienated subjectivity, Sherryl Vint claims that

> to address the property status of animals as part of an effort to imagine and create a less alienated life, overcoming human alienation not only from productive activity but also from nature, by resisting its commodification and returning to a relation in which nature is part of the sensuous world of a full human life—a world which also allows for the full species-lives of non-humans. (131)

That notion, hugely inspired by Haraway's *When Species Meet* (2008), allows one to turn science fiction of the Anthropocene from the challenges of ecological and environmental origin to the questions of biodiversity. It problematizes the images of the human and non-human relations not only as postcolonial but as of the Anthropocene and the Chthulucene. These images are not of multiculturalism, but they rather represent the world where the aim is to think with the Other: "Storying cannot any longer be put into the box of human exceptionalism. Without deserting the grounding terrain of behavioral ecology and natural history, this writing achieves powerful attunement to storying in penguin multimodal semiotics" (Haraway, *Making Kin* 43).

TRUE AND FALSE: THE POLITICS OF LANGUAGE AND LANGUAGE-GAMES

China Miéville, an award-winning British author, raises the question of the role of language in political communication and the formation of non-hierarchical relations with other cultures. His works, which diffuse the borders of genres and thus avoid any attempt at definition, often pose unanswered questions to politicians, sociologists, and anthropologists. In *Embassytown* (2011) he stresses the question of true and false statements in the spirit of twentieth-century logicians. It allows him to tie the question of the mutual dependence of language and culture with political discourse. Despite the fact that the narrative unravels in the interiors of the distant future, it is evident that Miéville is interested not as much in the question of a hypothetical conflict with another civilization as in the study of culture and language politics, which has already been carried out on Earth in respect of different ethnicities and cultures. The attempt to shift the anthropocentric paradigm, therefore, leads to a better understanding of the state of things here and now, and makes it possible to assess the already existing models of interaction with other cultures through the language impact.

The novel is set in the far future, when the humankind has not only mastered space technologies but also hardly remembers the planet on which it all began. The planet Earth is mentioned only once, as something located on the periphery of the universe and can hardly be considered the capital of the vast interplanetary empire. Even though humanity (the humanoid species in the *Embassytown* are referred to as the Terre) has encountered many different cultures and languages, it continues to regard itself as the dominant species, in comparison to which all others are exotic (*exot*) races.

Arieka, the planet where the main events of the novel take place, however, has a peculiar status. Here, humans have faced a culture that has never been seen before. The Hosts of the planet, therefore, are considered the natives. The Terre have only a small embassy town here, built to establish diplomatic contacts. That is why the city incubates the Ambassadors:

> The Ambassadors were created and brought up to be one, with unified minds. They had the same genes but much more: it was the minds those carefully nurtured genes made that the Hosts could hear. If you raised them right, taught them to think of themselves right, wired them with links, then they could speak Language, with close enough to one sentience that the Ariekei could understand it. (Miéville 66)

The uniqueness of the Ariekei lies in their language. Its difference is more ontological than formal. The Ariekei (the Hosts) are not able to grasp the meaning of the message being transmitted (using a speech statement) if the source of this statement does not possess consciousness. The peculiarity of the Ariekei Language lies not only in the fact that it requires the simultaneous pronunciation of various elements of a sentence, but also in the fact that phonetics itself means nothing in it. Even when articulated with maximum accuracy, the speech produced by a piece of technology and not by intelligent being is perceived by the Hosts as nothing more than a noise: "when they speak they do hear the soul in each voice. That's how the meaning lives there" (63); "Every time they talk to us, they taste our minds, and we're alien" (195–196). The Ariekei therefore understand the otherness of human minds, probably due to the dual nature of the Ambassadors. The question whether the Hosts consider the Ambassadors as one creature with two bodies or two different creatures is not resolved.

Thus, if an Ambassador's brain is not fully synchronized, there is a problem: "But if the two halves of an Ambassador aren't . . . quite enmeshed enough? Not two random voices: close enough to speak Language and for them to get it. But wrong? Broken?" (Miéville 196); "It's like a hallucination, a there-not-there" (196). Being under the influence of such speech, the Ariekei fall into stagnation, become addicted to the language, in a literal sense, like drug addicts: "The Hosts heard it and some of them got swoony and some of them wanted it again and again. [...] Oratees are addicts. Strung out on an Ambassador's Language" (196).

Another feature of the Language (capitalized L) is the fact that it does not allow lying. Everything that is said in the Language is a fact of reality. The Language does not allow metaphors, just some semblance of similes. Furthermore, the Hosts sometimes use people to express a new idea, to introduce a new fact of the Language. The Terre become figures of speech: similes, examples, analogies, and so on. For instance, Avice, who narrates the story, is a simile, whose full form sounds as follows: "there was a human girl who in pain ate what was given her in an old room built for eating in which eating had not happened for a time" (Miéville 28). Such comparisons are used by the Ariekei all the time, although their translation into human (the Terre) is not very clear. The uniqueness of Language is that "each word of Language, sound isomorphic with some Real: not a thought, not really, only self-expressed worldness, speaking itself through the Ariekei" (365).

The project of such a language, which would allow only true statements, was proposed in the first quarter of the twentieth century by Ludwig Wittgenstein in his famous *Tractatus Logico-Philosophicus*. Resting his ideas on the works of Frege and Russell, Wittgenstein posed the question whether it is possible and, if so, how it is possible, to create a language that, on a grammatical level, allows only ontologically true statements. The conclusion he reached was formulated in the final seventh thesis of *Tractatus*: "What we cannot speak about we must pass over in silence" (151). The language then becomes isomorphic with the world. As a well-known scholar of the philosophical heritage of the Austrian philosopher, Jaakko Hintikka comments on the ideal language of the *Tractatus*, arguing that such a language can be primarily labeled as phenomenological:

> The ideal language envisaged in the Tractatus is ideal precisely in that it captures faithfully what is given to me. The simple objects postulated there are therefore the objects of my immediate experience, that is to say, phenomenological objects. The world according to the early Wittgenstein is the world of phenomenological objects. (Hintikka 56)

Hintikka aimed to bring the philosophy of the *Tractatus* closer to the phenomenological philosophy of Husserl. Therefore, it is no coincidence that Wittgenstein's subsequent interest leads to the problem of verifying the existence of the consciousness of the Other, to which a significant part of his later *Philosophical Investigations* is devoted.

We are thus dealing with the language of pure phenomenology. The presence of such a language, which does not allow lies and transmits the world (and reality) as it appears to us, has some significant consequences. Due to the specificity of human cognition and the architecture of the human mind, human language is mostly based on the logic of comparison, that is, it is based on analogy (or metaphor) that makes it possible to compare objects with different ontological properties (the ability that Gilles Fauconnier and Mark Turner call "blending"). Thus, the language that is unable to make false statements turns out to be not only the language of total honesty but also the language in which fiction, as a result of sincere involvement in the world around us, is impossible. Without being able to talk about something that does not exist in reality, we are unable to create fictional narratives. Everything that was once said in it is an unambiguous fact of reality that cannot be questioned.

The Ariekei Language can also be classified as anti-language. In that case the Ariekei themselves are classified as "anti-humans, in a technical, non-evaluative sense of the word" (Głaz 337). On the basis of the ideas proposed in *Embassytown*, Adam Głaz claims that "the feeling of human superiority over non-humans is nearly palpable: humanness is about being able to think, which in turn is about being able to speak, rather than—as is the case with the Ariekei—being 'spoken by' Language *à la* Heidegger" (336). This notion seems to be legitimate from the postcolonial perspective as far as the transition from Language to language has an evident emancipatory effect. However, the situation featured in the novel appears to be more complex if addressed from the point of view of the Anthropocene or the Chthulucene.

We are dealing with a more complex political system, which includes the question of language. The Ariekei Language has a kind of protective mechanism that partly eliminates the possibility of manipulating the sincerity and naivety of its speakers. Not everyone can master the Language, but only those who have been specially raised to speak it (the Ambassadors). In this sense, the Ambassadors become not as much a subject of the political game as a mechanism, a translator, which carries out the connection between the two sides of the negotiation process. However, since it is possible to raise the Ambassador only on the planet itself, the influence of the Dominion on the policy pursued on Arieka is limited. Since the Ariekei cannot speak any other language but the Language, it is humans who are in need of representation. It turns upside-down the traditional postcolonial situation when the Other needs to be represented (cf. epigraph from Marx in Said's *Orientalism*: "They cannot represent themselves; they must be represented"). Although the Ambassadors are the embodiment of colonial power, they cannot govern the planet of Arieka. With that said, Miéville regards the lack of figurative potential of the Language as a weakness.

Had it not been for the unique Language, the Dominion would have turned Arieka into a port city long ago. Located on the very edge of the known universe, it is of great strategic importance. Thus, in the novel we are dealing with three main political forces: the Hosts, the Ambassadors mediating between the Hosts and human civilization, and the Controller from the Dominion, who oversees the order and acts as an actual subject of the political will of the human race.

The Ambassadors, on the one hand, are interested in maintaining their specific status. They seek to "freeze" the Language, not to let it develop, so as not to lose their power because they are well aware of the instrumental nature of their position. When humanity introduces the Ariekei to the concept of lies, the Ariekei begin to organize a festival of lies, trying to learn to lie. The festival itself becomes part of a political game expressed through language. In *Philosophical Investigations*, Wittgenstein writes, "Lying is a language-game that needs to be learned like any other one" (249). As the Ariekei Language is the language of pure phenomenology, it does not allow the existence of another language. It is not possible to teach human languages to the Hosts, only to learn their Language. At the same time, learning to lie will lead to a change in the status of the Language as the language of a phenomenological description of the world. The Ambassadors understand that the festival of lies is not a game of language fun, but a political game with specific political consequences. As soon as the Hosts begin to make their first progress, there is a murder with the apparent political motivation.

The Dominion, on the contrary, seeks to get rid of the Ambassadors in order to strengthen its authority and gain the opportunity to play a full political game (which requires raising the Ambassadors outside Embassytown, but since it is impossible to do so, the real power belongs to the Ambassadors, not to the Dominion). Human civilization seeks to get rid of its status as "being represented." By gaining power over Language, the Terre would secure their Dominion status, turning Arieka into a full-fledged colony. The Terre are not as interested in teaching the Ariekei to lie as in consolidating their status of Otherness through the language. By gaining control of the language, humans gain a powerful tool of political power and control over all the processes taking place on Arieka. Miéville, with his strong anti-imperialistic political views and sympathy for the Marxist ideology, lacks it for the imperial ambitions of the Terre. At the same time, he is not satisfied with the initial situation, which implies that the Ambassadors are an intermediary in the distribution of political interests. He therefore puts another political force into effect, represented by Avice.

A complicated situation emerges in which the Hosts themselves are excluded from the game and deprived of their right to vote. On the one hand, if the Ariekei learn to lie, they will lose their unique status and their true identity. They will become more human and will be included in the existing system as another exotic race which can be managed and used for human purposes. On the other hand, Miéville points out the limitations of the Ariekei Language, as it does not give the true freedom of thought.

The climax of the novel is the moment when the Terre send their own Ambassador to Arieka, the first one not raised on the planet. The effect of the new Ambassador's speech is astonishing. It is perceived by the Ariekei as both the speech of a rational being and a set of semantically meaningless sounds. It intoxicates, drugs their minds. Its influence cannot be called purely acoustic. First, the Hosts are influenced by the sound of the speech itself, because the consciousness of the two halves of the new Ambassador is not fully synchronized, and the confusion, which produces inability to determine whether a reasonable being is behind this stream of sounds, produces a narcotic, hallucinogenic effect. On the other hand, this speech is not wholly devoid of semantic content, because it soon becomes clear that the Hosts no longer want to hear the same phrase, repeated many times; they need more and more new statements, even if these represent a banal weather forecast or are semantically meaningless.

The situation in which the Hosts found themselves depending on the language of the new Ambassador is compared to the myth of the lotophagi. The lotus-affected Lotus-eaters were blissful drug addicts. The Ariekei, initially hard-working and disciplined, gradually become addicted to the new Ambassador's language, abandoning their factories and farmlands. The reference to the Greek myth allows Miéville to hint at the real historical events when Western civilization used this or that narcotic substance for its political purposes (a policy of the British Empire on selling opium in China, alcohol to Indians of North America, etc.). The language itself becomes the drug of the Ariekei. Getting rid of the drug influence of the new Ambassador's language is only possible through learning to lie. The language game based on it becomes an integral part of the political struggle for independence. When the language contains only true statements and there is no idea of a lie, it is impossible to distinguish between the truth and fiction because everything that is in the language is also in reality. In order to learn to distinguish between the truth and lies, one must learn to lie. This is the only way to find freedom.

As a result of prolonged political games, the civil war, and the fight against their addiction to the speech of the Ambassador with a split mind, the Ariekei are finally able to get free. They learn to lie, which inevitably changes their Language. On the one hand, this change leads to the loss of their true identity, to the displacement of the established picture of the world. Their status as unique, unlike any other culture, is lost. On the other hand, this change proves to be a necessary sacrifice to include the Ariekei into the real political process. Otherwise, the Ariekei would remain a colony on the periphery of human civilization, an important strategic point where the locals are deprived of the status of a political force, a cheap workforce that supplies colonial goods to the Dominion.

Aware of the cultural conditioning of ethics and the commitment to morality (and, in this sense, not recognizing the possibilities of ethical neutrality that Habermas writes about, although generally sharing the position of including the Other through the recognition of his rights and freedoms), Miéville proposes a compromise solution. Avice teaches the Ariekei not only lies but also metaphorical thinking that underlies human language and culture. A metaphor is "lie that truths" (Miéville 395). By acquiring the possibility of metaphorical speech, the Ariekei not only acquire the language of political freedom and independence but also reach the same level as human beings, acquiring the common ground of the two cultures.

CONCLUSION

In *Embassytown*, China Miéville is modeling political relations between the colony and the Dominion. Language, which determines not only the attitudes of its speakers but also the culture itself, is the main instrument of political influence. Language in such a system turns out to be a tool that determines the legal and political possibilities of its speakers, and the struggle to change the properties of the language becomes a struggle for liberation from the dominant political discourse. The expansion of political opportunities for language becomes a guarantee of cultural and political equality and diversity.

The monologue of Spanish Dancer, an Ariekei who is the first learner of the art of lie and metaphorical speech, is illustrative: "Before the humans came we didn't speak. We've been like countless things, we've been like all things, we've been like animals over Embassytown [. . .] we were mute" (Miéville 394). On the one hand, the comparison with animals is intended to show the changed status of the Hosts, the acquisition of political subjectivity. However, the emphasized role of human beings in changing the language (and the very need for this change) indicates the inability of Miéville to avoid anthropocentrism: the Language becomes a language, one among many.

The comparison with animals seems to be crucial in the context of the Anthropocene politics of non-human Others: "the underpeople equally and simultaneously represent animal lives alienated and exploited by a speciesist human culture" (Vint 121). Yet, the Ariekei unearth subjectivity and can no longer be treated as objects without the political will; they become more like humans and thus their Otherness turns into Sameness. However, the Chthulucene, as Donna Haraway states, does not need inclusion, which leads to autopoiesis, but needs sympoiesis, or "making-with," which is "a word proper to complex, dynamic, responsive, situated, historical systems. It is a word for worlding-with, in company" (Haraway, *Making Kin* 58). What is necessary is not the shift from the Other to the Same, but the hybridization of the Other and the Self—the vortex which is "neither One nor Other, that is who we all are and always have been" (98). That is the way "to practice the arts of living and dying well in multispecies symbiosis, sympoiesis, and symanimagenesis on a damaged planet, must be made without guarantees or the expectation of harmony with those who are not oneself—and not safely other, either" (98). That calls for not the One, the Whole, the Same, but rather conflicting constellation of the Same and the Other, languages and cultures which are creole, hybrid, and unstable.

In this case, the SF of the Chthulucene is the SF of the images of the symbiosis between human and non-human Other, of a transparent border between culture and nature, humans and aliens, humans and robots, animals, bacteria, cells, and the whole complexity of the world around. There is the need for creole and pidgin languages, rather than One.

Miéville bypasses a crucial ethical issue in the context of the Anthropocene/ the Chthulucene. The politics of language and cultural practices as presented in *Embassytown* reflects the ideas of class struggle and the postcolonial perspective. The Anthropocene demands "noncolonizing arts, sciences and politics" (Haraway *Making Kin* 57) as well as what Isabelle Stengers calls "cosmopolitics":

> Including human people, critters are in each other's presence, or better, inside each other's tubes, folds, and crevices, insides and outsides, and not quite either. The decisions and transformations so urgent in our times for learning again, or for the first time, how to become less deadly, more response-able, more attuned, more capable of surprise. (Haraway, *Making Kin* 98)

Sherryl Vint extends the idea: "the state of alive-with allows species-being to flourish for all species, human and non-human" (129). Miéville asymptotically approaches that image of creole and pidgin languages of the Anthropocene:

> The New Ariekei were astounded to learn that Terre have more than one language. I uploaded French. "I, *je*. I am, *je suis*," I said. Spanish Dancer was delighted. It said to me, "Je voudrais venir avec vous / I would like to come with you."
>
> That's not its only innovation. They don't speak Anglo-Ubiq here, but Anglo-Ariekei. (402–403)

But that is only a glimpse. The pledge of the Anthropocene. Miéville outlines the new politics, which Kathryn Yussof and Donna Haraway call for, but the general idea of the novel is rather postcolonial.

As a follower of Marxist views, Miéville is primarily interested in the issues of social stratification, which are associated with the possession or non-possession of tools of a political struggle, inclusion in or exclusion from the political discourse itself. In this sense, he cannot get rid of the anthropocentric paradigm, which has much more severe consequences. The struggle for the autonomy of different forms of culture is the struggle against the consequences of anthropocentrism. The world of the Ariekei has changed for good or for bad: "It would be foolish to pretend we know what'll happen. We'll have to see how Embassytown gets shaped" (Miéville 405). The fact is that the transformation of Arieka's culture stems from human impact. It is clear that Miéville searches for a way to deal with the Anthropocene, but the search is not enough.

WORKS CITED

Bhabha, Homi K. *The Location of Culture*. Routledge, 1994.
Beaumont, Matthew. "The Anamorphic Estrangements of Science Fiction." In *Red Planets: Marxism and Science Fiction*, edited by Mark Bould and China Miéville. Wesleyan UP, 2009, pp. 29–46.
Bignall, S., et al. "Three Ecosophies for the Anthropocene: Environmental Governance, Continental Posthumanism and Indigenous Expressivism." *Deleuze Studies*, vol. 10, no. 4, 2016, pp. 455–478.
Bould, Mark. "Introduction: Rough Guide to a Lonely Planet, from Nemo to Neo." In *Red Planets: Marxism and Science Fiction*, edited by Mark Bould and China Miéville. Wesleyan UP, 2009, pp. 1–26.
Clapperton, Guy. "The Internet is Helping Save Forgotten Languages." *Medium*, 25 September 2018. www.medium.com/s/story/the-internet-is-helping-save-forgotten-languages-dcc308509feb. Accessed 15 September 2020.
Davidson, Rjurik. "Writing Against Reality." *Overland*, vol. 188, 2007. www.overland.org.au/previous-issues/issue-188/feature-rjurik-davidson. Accessed 20 September 2020.
Donald, Merlin. *Origins of the Modern Mind: Three Stages in the Evolution of Culture and Cognition*. Harvard UP, 1993.
Evans, Rebecca. "Nomenclature, Narrative, and Novum: 'The Anthropocene' and/as Science Fiction." *Science Fiction Studies*, vol. 45, no. 3, 2018, pp. 484–499.
Fauconnier, Gilles, and Mark Turner. *The Way We Think: Conceptual Blending and the Mind's Hidden Complexities*. Basic Books, 2002.
Gibbs, Raymond W. Jr. "The Fight over Metaphor in Thought and Language." In *Figurative Language and Thought*. Oxford UP, 1998.
Głaz, Adam. "Reversals and Paradoxes: China Miéville's Anti-Language." *Extrapolation*, vol. 56, no. 3, 2015, pp. 335–352.
Glikson, Andrew Yoram. *The Plutocene: Blueprints for a Post-Anthropocene Greenhouse Earth*. Springer, 2017.

Habermas, Jürgen. *The Inclusion of the Other: Studies in Political Theorie*. MIT Press, 1999.

Hamilton, Clive, et al., eds. *The Anthropocene and the Global Environmental Crisis: Rethinking Modernity in a New Epoch*. Routledge, 2015.

Haraway, Donna. "The Promises of Monsters: A Regenerative Politics for Inappropriate/d Others." In *The Haraway Reader*, edited by Donna Haraway. Routledge, 2004, pp. 63–124.

———. "SF: Science Fiction, Speculative Fabulation, String Figures, So Far." *Ada: A Journal of Gender, New Media, and Technology*, vol. 3, 2013. doi:10.7264/N3KH0K81.

———. "Staying with the Trouble: Anthropocene, Capitalocene, Chthulucene." In *Anthropocene or Capitalocene? Nature, History, and the Crisis of Capitalism*, edited by Jason W. Moore. PM Press, 2016, pp. 34–76.

———. *Staying with the Trouble: Making Kin in Chthulucene*. Duke UP, 2016.

Hartley, Daniel. "Anthropocene, Capitalocene, and the Problem of Culture." In *Anthropocene or Capitalocene? Nature, History, and the Crisis of Capitalism*, edited by Jason W. Moore. PM Press, 2016, pp. 154–165.

Hintikka, Jaakko. *Ludwig Wittgenstein: Half-Truths and One-and-a-Half-Truths*. Springer Netherlands, 1996.

Hoagland, Ericka, and Reema Sarwal. "Introduction: Imperialism, the Third World, and Postcolonial Science Fiction." In *Science Fiction, Imperialism and the Third World: Essays on Postcolonial Literature and Film*, edited by Erica Hoagland and Reema Sarwal. McFarland, 2010, pp. 5–19.

Husserl, Edmund. *Cartesian Meditations: An Introduction to Phenomenology*. Translated by Dorion Cairns. Dordrecht: Springer Netherlands, 1960.

Kuehmichel, S. "Thriving in the Gap Visual and Linguistic Meaning Unmaking in the City & the City." *Extrapolation*, vol. 55, no. 3, 2014, pp. 349–367.

Lakoff, George, and Mark Johnson. *Metaphors We Live By*. U of Chicago P, 1980.

Latour, Bruno. *We Have Never Been Modern*. Translated by Catherine Porter. Harvard UP, 1993.

———. "Anthropology at the Time of the Anthropocene: A Personal View of What Is to Be Studied." In *The Anthropology of Sustainability: Beyond Development and Progress*, edited by Marc Brightman and Jerome Lewis. Palgrave Macmillan, 2017, pp. 35–49.

Le Guin, Ursula K. "American SF and the Other." In *The Language of the Night: Essays on Fantasy and Science Fiction*, edited and with introductions by Susan Wood and Ursula K. Le Guin. HarperPerennial, 1993, pp. 93–96.

Lévinas, Emmanuel. *Entre Nous: On Thinking-of-the-Other*. Translated by Michael B. Smith and Barbara Harshav. Columbia UP, 1998.

Levinas, Emmanuel. *Otherwise than Being, or beyond Essence*. Translated by Alphonso Lingis. Duquesne UP, 2006.

Miéville, China. *Embassytown*. Pan Books, 2012.

Milner, Andrew, et al. "Ice, Fire and Flood: Science Fiction and the Anthropocene." *Thesis Eleven*, vol. 131, no. 1, 2015, pp. 12–27.

Mithen, Steven, ed. *Creativity in Human Evolution and Prehistory*. Routledge, 2005.

Moore, Bryan L. "'Evidences of Decadent Humanity': Antianthropocentrism in Early Science Fiction." *Nature and Culture*, vol. 9, no. 1, 2014, pp. 45–65.

Neuwirth, Manuela. "'Absolute Alterity'? The Alien Animal, the Human Alien, and the Limits of Posthumanism in Star Trek." *European Journal of American Studies*, vol. 11–13, 2018. doi:10.4000/ejas.12464.

Nikoleris, Alexandra, et al. "The 'Anthropocene' in Popular Culture: Narrating Human Agency, Force, and Our Place on Earth." In *Anthropocene Encounters: New Directions in Green Political Thinking*, edited by Eva Lövbrand and Frank Biermann. Cambridge UP, 2019, pp. 67–84.

Pak, Chris. "Terraforming and Geoengineering in Luna: New Moon, 2312, and Aurora." *Science Fiction Studies*, vol. 45, no. 3, 2018, pp. 500–514.

Palmer, Alan. *Fictional Minds.* U of Nebraska P, 2004.

Quine, Willard. *From a Logical Point of View: 9 Logico-Philosophical Essays.* Harper & Row Publishers, 1961.

Satgar, Vishwas. "The Anthropocene and Imperial Ecocide: Prospects for Just Transitions." In *The Climate Crisis: South African and Global Democratic Eco-Socialist Alternatives*, edited by Vishwas Satgar. Wits UP, 2018, pp. 47–68.

Sawyer, Andy. "Foreword." In *Science Fiction, Imperialism and the Third World: Essays on Postcolonial Literature and Film*, edited by Ericka Hoagland and Reema Sarwal. McFarland, 2010, pp. 1–3.

Schlosser, Lourdes Arizpe. *Culture, International Transactions and the Anthropocene.* Springer Berlin Heidelberg, 2019.

Schwägerl, Christian. *The Anthropocene: The Human Era and How It Shapes Our Planet.* Foreword by Paul J. Crutzen. Synergetic Press, 2014.

Steffen, Will, et al. "The Anthropocene: Conceptual and Historical Perspectives." *Philosophical Transactions: Mathematical, Physical and Engineering Sciences*, vol. 369, no. 1938, 2011, pp. 842–867. doi:10.1098/rsta.2010.0327.

Thacker, Eugene. *In the Dust of This Planet.* Zero Books, 2011.

Treanor, Brian. *Aspects of Alternity: Levinas, Marcel, and the Contemporary Debate.* Fordham UP, 2006.

Trigg, Dylan. *Thing: A Phenomenology of Horror.* Zero Books, 2014.

Turner, Mark, ed. *The Artful Mind: Cognitive Science and the Riddle of Human Creativity.* Oxford UP, 2006.

Turner, Mark. *The Origin of Ideas: Blending, Creativity, and the Human Spark.* Oxford UP, 2014.

Tygstrup, Frederik. "The Politics of Symbolic Forms." In *Cultural Ways of Worldmaking: Media and Narratives*, edited by Vera Nünning et al. De Gruyter, 2010, pp. 87–100.

Vint, Sherryl. "Species and Species-Being: Alienated Subjectivity and the Commodification of Animals." In *Red Planets: Marxism and Science Fiction*, edited by Mark Bould and China Miéville. Wesleyan UP, 2009, pp. 118–136.

Waldenfels, Bernhardt. "Experience of the Alien in Husserl's Phenomenology." Translated by Anthony J. Steinbock. In *Edmund Husserl: Critical Assessments of Leading Philosophers*, vol. 4, edited by Rudolf Bernet et al. Routledge, 2005, pp. 345–358.

Wittgenstein, Ludwig. *Tractatus Logico-Philosophicus: the German Text of Ludwig Wittgenstein's Logisch-Philosophische Abhandlung with a New Translation by D.F. Pears & R.F. McGuinness; and with the Introduction by Bertrand Russell.* Translated by David F. Pears and R. F. McGuinness. Routledge & Kegan Paul, 1961.

———. *Philosophical Investigations.* Basil Blackwell, 1986.

Yusoff, Kathryn. "Biopolitical Economies and the Political Aesthetics of Climate Change." *Theory Culture & Society,* vol. 27, no. 2–3, 2010, pp. 73–99.

———. "Politics of the Anthropocene: Formation of the Commons as a Geologic Process." *Antipode,* vol. 50, no. 1, 2018, pp. 255–276.

Chapter 11

Mythological Aspect of Immigration in Fantasy

Case Study of Mercy Thompson *and* Alpha and Omega *Series by Patricia Briggs*

Dariya Khokhel

Contemporary fantasy is a mobile domain that covers a growing set of genres and subgenres with a wide variety of themes in its striving not to follow "simple imitation" (Attebery 208). Urban fantasy is one of the major genres that explore the purely Anthropocene space—that of the city, which is home for most of the "global geophysical force" that humans and societies have become in the era (Steffen et al., "The Anthropocene: Are Humans. . ." 614). The city is so ingrained in the image of today's geological age that the term "Urban Anthropocene" has been coined, combining "the global trend towards urbanization and the term 'Anthropocene'" (Hillel and de Oliveira). I argue that urban fantasy is a suitable medium for exploring the image of migration, as many of its core characters can be viewed as displaced people—either internally, as they have chosen to move to the cities from rural locations, or as immigrants. The city is "understood as both symbol and manifestation of the problems of modernity," indicative of the Anthropocene, especially when it comes to alienation and accompanying issues, which "might be characterized as identity troubles" (Young 141).

Many fantasy universes represent migration as a fact of life. Some works focus on this aspect, as it involves a lot of background information and establishes specific models of communication.[1] Michael Watts argues that there is more to migration then latching it to an appropriate spatial metaphor (125); hence different facets of it should be dwelt on. A number of fantasy texts highlight, or mention in passing, how certain national fantastic creatures appear in new surroundings, which often leads to encounters of preternatural beings from various cultures that would not have crossed paths but for migration.

The comprehensive body of research devoted to immigration literature allows insight into a number of approaches. Homi Bhabha offers the term "inbetweenness," explained as "estranging sense of the relocation of the home and the world" (6). Diane Krumrey indicates that in contemporary immigrant literature "multiethnic" works are being accepted as a more general approach, but the emergent trend is toward "celebration of the fragmentation" (252). G. H. Muller points out that "immigrants depicted in contemporary American fiction espouse unique mythologies of self and of their community that enrich and expand the social order" (234). Thus, there is a defined research trend that views immigrant literature not solely as the embodiment of "melting" into a unified homogenous nation but as texts that retain unique cultural identities in the new world. This transfer of traditions and their development can be viewed through the structuring prism of Raymond Williams's theory of culture, which consists of the dominant, the residual, and the emergent, and is seen as "the dynamic interrelations, at every point in the process, of historically varied and variable elements" (353). The usefulness of this approach for discussing fantasy has been demonstrated by Brian Attebery in his *Stories about Stories* (2014). According to Williams, "[t]he residual, by definition, has been effectively formed in the past, but it is still active in the cultural process, not only and often not at all as an element of the past, but as an effective element of the present" (353). Thus, many fantastic elements, derived from national mythologies, fall under this category. They cannot be viewed as dominant in the light of social and cultural changes, but they still exist within the dominant culture. The emergent is viewed as "new meanings and values, new practices, new relationships and kinds of relationship [that] are continually being created" (Williams 354). Brian Attebery argues that in fantasy "[t]he residual might turn out to be the emergent, or at least another face of the emergent" (42). He views both of these cultural components as "an oppositional or merely an alternative form of culture" (42), and states that "the hegemony of the dominant culture is challenged from two directions: from the past and its not-yet-vanished ways of living and seeing and from the future, the cultural alternative that will eventually take over" (42). This approach accommodates the cyclic nature of myth and opens the discussion on the use of national mythologies in authorial myth construction. Such constructs are especially complex when multiple national mythologies are involved. The cross-cultural interconnection in this case will involve the dialogue of multiple layers of residual mythological content in a new situation of "inbetweenness" (Krumrey 248) that forms "the new face of the emergent" in the universe.

The books comprising Patricia Briggs's *Mercy Thompson* series "don't receive much academic attention" (Cowles). The series has been primarily discussed in terms of the representation of sexual trauma in contemporary fantasy (Davis). However, Briggs's novels also provide ample material for research into the representation of migration in the fantasy universe, described in two overlapping series (*Mercy Thompson* and *Alpha and Omega*). Trauma and enrichment caused by immigration in Briggs's universe have not yet become the subject of analysis. The two series reveal different aspects of migration, such as the reasons for it, its timeline, the adjustments to the new medium all the parties had to make to coexist in close proximity and constant contact, especially in the urban environment. The issues comprising the comprehensive exploration of the theme of preternatural beings' migration from Europe to the New World are crucial both in terms of world-building and plot development. The newcomers and the indigenous creatures struggle to adjust to the combination of their residual mythological elements into the emergent fragmented whole, that is the Other in the universe.

The concept of "cultural appropriation" in the sense of a writer's approach to mythologies in order to include "characters from races they [the authors] themselves are not members of" (Young 158–159), and in a broader sense of "other" national heritages needs to be acknowledged in the context of Briggs's works. In the "Author's Comments" to *River Marked*, a Mercy Thompson novel, Patricia Briggs explains that her upbringing and previous job with the Museum of the Rockies helped her be "very aware of the exploitation of the Native American peoples and their cultures" (Briggs, *River Marked*). In order to introduce the different migrant and indigenous mythological characters, she undertook authorial research: "Then I decided to do [with the Native American stories] exactly what I've done with Russian, UK, German and Norwegian (among others) myths, traditions and histories. I mined the treasure trove of stories, treated them with due respect, but used them in ways they were never meant to be used" (Briggs, *River Marked*). The notion of cultural appropriation is widely debated and is viewed in terms of historical trauma, prejudice, stereotypes, ownership, moral values, globalization, and financial gain. Various interpretations show that it can have a "corrosive effect" on the misinterpreted cultures (Ziff and Rao 9), condone the tendency "to adapt and assimilate the cultural forms and practices of a dominant group," or form new emergent cultures, "linked to a residual culture" (7). Helen Young writes that "[t]aking signs—even multiple signs— from a culture and recombining them in ways that suit the needs of the story or imagined world but do not reflect their significance in the culture from which they derive is one kind of appropriation" (160). She adds that it most frequently occurs when "a culture is designated as Other" (160) and used to alienate the component of the fantastic universe. It can be argued that this is what happens with the cultural signs appropriated from national mythologies in Briggs's universe, as, for example, her "walker" is connected by Virginia Mclaurin with the nightwalker mythology rather than with Coyote tales (Mclaurin 87–88). The important aspect in the discussion of appropriation is the author's identity and the underlying attachment to the cultural signs native to them. Patricia Briggs's works constitute a challenge here, as she takes and interconnects signs from a wide range of cultures without implied disrespect or marked designation as "the Other". All these fantastic signs, irrespective of their origins, collectively comprise the fantastic component of this immersive fantasy, the Various within the Other. As Young states, "a new significance will be produced by the new context" (161). It can be argued that cultural appropriation as relocation and recombination of signs with insufficient cultural context is a structural strategy of Briggs's fantasy universe. The aforementioned approach, on the one hand, deprives the original mythology of the systemic context and can lead to misinterpretation of cultural signs; on the other, it is instrumental in creating the fragmented urban environment, rife with alienation and cultural misunderstandings.

This universe includes Native American deities, shifters, and spirits, an assortment of fae from different parts of Europe, werewolves, vampires, witches, and other magic users. These magic users (witches, druids, sorcerers) are basically humans with special powers, so there is little focus on their migration as part of the supernatural population of Briggs's universe, though they are also important to the city setting. Moreover, a number of characters appeared due to the new alliances, such as Native American werewolves, mixed-race Native American shifters, half-fae. The migration of preternatural beings and magic users into the United States can be viewed as a process taking place for three major reasons—escape, expansion, and exile. These three categories can be applied to discuss the migration of whole classes of magical beings and their individual representatives. The description of migration of the three main types of magical beings, that is, fae, vampires, and werewolves, varies in essence and purpose and is grounded in the nature of these magical beings. This chapter focuses on covering the movement and adaptation of such creatures.

In the novel *Moon Called*, in which the universe is introduced, the issue of migration is first voiced: "I knew that vampires, like the fae, and werewolves and their kindred were all Old World preternatural creatures. They'd come over for the same reasons most humans did: to gain wealth, power, or land, and to escape persecution" (ch. 11). The migration of these beings is compared and connected with human migration, which lends it the authentic "recognizable" aspect that is crucial to the construction of an effective fantasy universe, fortifying the coherence of the authorial myth. The combination of fantastic and historically and socially distinct features in a single image helps create a believable universe, one that is structurally and metaphorically sound, and strange enough to be intriguing and *other*, but familiar enough to be comfortable for perception.

The following passage offers the explanation of the preternatural beings' migration from Europe to the New World in the series universe:

> So vampires came to the New World, victims of religious persecution like the Quakers and the Puritans—only different. Werewolves and their moon—called kindred came to find new territory to hunt. The fae came to escape the cold iron of the Industrial Revolution, which followed them anyway. Together these immigrants destroyed most of the preternatural creatures who had lived in the Americas, until at last, even the bare stories of their existence were mostly gone. (Briggs, *Moon Called* ch. 11)

The information is provided in the third-person partially omniscient narrative of Mercy Thompson. The character is described as having a degree in History and a keen interest in it, which is meant to give the information credibility. The statement also sets the precedent for the consistent use of the terms "cold iron" and "moon called" throughout the series. Such consistency should be viewed as an integral part of developing a coherent fantasy universe throughout the series, as their uniqueness on the one hand and repetitive nature on the other help maintain the coherence of the narrative which contains multiple fantasy components. The images not only provide readers with a sense of familiarity due to consistent use, but also serve to distinguish Briggs's texts from other narratives that deal with similar themes.

Vampires "bear the past into the new world"; like the old-money families, they "re-establish old aristocratic norms and combine them with American culture to create an environment of decadence that is hostile to newcomers" (McGaughey 33). Hence, there is a marked similarity between the reclusive and hermetic establishment of the vampire society and the social separation that marked the life of privileged classes in the New World. In such a way, a parallel, which is also rooted in the traditional European representation of vampire migration going back to Bram Stoker's *Dracula*, is drawn in the texts.

Briggs's vampires are described as distinctively inhuman: "Her imitation of a human was very close, but not quite close enough to be real-and that small difference was giving me the creeps" (Briggs, *Moon Called* ch. 10). Their ability to emulate human behavior allows them to remain the only species hidden from people throughout the series. Vampires are also very deeply entrenched in European traditions. Their long existence and long-held grudges are presented as the reason for their move to the New World. In fact, most old vampires were exiled from the Old World, for example,

Marsilia, who was cast away by "The Master of Milan—or he was last we heard" (ch. 11). The indicated remark becomes relevant when the timeframe is revealed: "'When was that?' 'Two hundred years, more or less. He exiled Signora Marsilia here with those who owed her life or vassalage'" (ch. 11). The vampire community is depicted as closed-off and highly traditional—for example, their duels for power are still to elimination, unlike in the werewolf community, where this is a less likely outcome under the rules of the unified US werewolf community, which strives to integrate into the new world.

The vampire society is restricted in their integration into the larger social structures due to the inability to participate in their activities during daytime. They are only active at night, which, on the one hand, precludes them from most jobs and gatherings, and on the other hand, makes their lifestyle suitable to the urban environment rather than the rural one, as they thrive on vibrant nightlife of the cities. Furthermore, in contemporary cities they have associated themselves with organized crime: "In the Columbia Basin [...] every business the vampires considered under their jurisdiction (meaning anyone touched by the supernatural who was too powerless to stand against them) paid them protection money. And yes, just like the mob, the vampires only protect you from themselves" (ch. 8). Such a position suits the hermetic society of vampires in practical terms—it is a night activity that utilizes their inherent abilities to obtain maximum finance and fits their need for secrecy.

"Herd mentality" is considered inherent to any social being to a certain degree, due to its connection to the "us-them" principle of world division, and because of its strong prevalence in the structure of organized crime, it is sometimes also called "mob mentality" (Bond). In the descriptions of the vampire society there is a lexical interconnection with the terms used in defining this psychological phenomenon: the people, whom the vampire habitually feeds on and supports for this purpose, are called "flock" or "menagerie" as a group and "sheep" individually or generically. These terms are widely used metaphors that liken humans to animals (Krause and Ruxton). On the other end of the spectrum, there are multiple terms connected with the social structure of the nobility in the descriptions of Briggs's vampire community: vassalage, vassal, Signora, Master, menagerie (in the historical meaning of "management of a household," though the modern meaning of a "place where animals are kept and trained especially for exhibition" ("Menagerie") adds to the image of the inferiority of the non-vampire members of the society). Certain juxtaposition in approaches to the vampire society as a migrated unit is thus created: they appear connected to the unique lifestyle of the Old World nobility with the appropriate trappings and traditions, though they also constitute a system of secret organized crime groups in the supernatural world that ask for tributes from supernatural businesses in their teritory. It can be argued that both patterns have a lot in common: the need to follow the strong leader, ingrained prejudice against non-members, the "us-them" principle, the secrecy, and the exclusivity. Another aspect that turns this juxtaposition into a complex whole is the fact that Briggs's vampires see non-vampires as inferior and as a potential source to use unless they are in the enemy category: people are food, while weaker supernatural beings constitute the source of income. Their lifestyle feeds off the problems of the urban setting, primarily alienation, transience, and fragmentation. As a united force, vampires use the disenfranchised, the poorly adapted, and the lonely for their own purposes, thus highlighting the said problems of urban life.

What is more, the vampire society is described as hostile toward the indigenous preternatural beings: "Walkers are not popular among the vampires. I'd gathered that when the vampires first came to this part of the New World, the walkers here had made themselves enough of a pest that the vampires had killed most of them off" (Briggs, *Blood Bound* ch. 2). This hostility was primarily caused by the fact that, because of the inherent difference in their magic, which comes from a variety of sources in the universe (and the discrepancy stems from the diverse mythological traditions that come into contact in this instance), walkers were not affected by the vampires' powers: "Many of our powers do not work well on you. Most of our magic is useless" (ch. 8). Moreover, some walkers can see the ghosts that surround any vampire's lair and even interact with them: "Walkers also speak to ghosts" (ch. 8). Hence, the two species of preternatural beings are natural enemies, who met because of immigration, and the indigenous creatures suffered and were virtually eliminated by the newcomers. Virginia Mclaurin writes that there are certain stereotypes associated with Native characters, namely that "supernatural happenings seem to involve their identity as Native people" (88), and she mentions Mercy Thompson as one of the examples. Here the stereotype is not only used to draw attention to the adverse effects of immigration on Native American communities but also to provide a supernatural explanation for oppression. Despite the fact that indigenous characters are the heroes, the series arguably condones their historical trauma by means of this explanation.

Unlike the largely unwilling and selective migration of the vampires, the fae have basically moved the bulk of their population from Europe to the New World because of the growing urbanization and industrialization in Europe. As they are described to have moved from various parts of Europe, their society is extremely culturally diverse in itself, since it draws from a range of traditions. The inclusion of such a scope of characters as Baba Yaga, Gwyn ap Lugh, the Dark Smith of Drontheim, Nimue, the Lady of the Lake, and others, shows that even a single community of fantastic beings is not homogenous. These characters from different mythologies are also incorporated into Briggs's universe by means of cultural appropriation from a variety of European cultures, with the subsequent creation of new ties between them, resultant from their coexistence in the New World. The issue of appropriation is less commonly discussed if it involves the signs of dominant culture, but if "the white-dominated wider culture" (Ziff and Rao 32) of the United States is viewed as a complex heritage of a range of different European cultures, the issue of appropriation is also valid in this discussion. Both series incorporate the fae from numerous European mythologies and even include some folklore characters that are not normally associated with this class of fantastic beings (Baba Yaga of Slavic tales, for instance, originates from a deity connected to death and nature, and often serves as an initiation pythoness (Meletinsky 83); though she is not generally connected with fairy mythology, the essence of her nature is captured correctly in Briggs's novels). Moreover, the fae are different from each other in terms of the source of their power. In the past, the most powerful were those fae whose magic was connected with nature, but now in the urban setting they are actually on the brink of extinction. The destruction of their habitat and source of magic—the wilderness of various kinds—leads to the shift of power to the fae with affinity for metal after the Industrial Revolution:

> He was a forest lord whose greatest magic was to command beasts. When the last of the giants—who were beasts controlled by his magic—died, it left him a forest lord with no great power, and he resented it as Ariana's power grew. When the fae lost their ability to imprint their magic on things—like your walking staff, Mercy—she could still manage it. (Briggs, *Silver Borne* ch. 12)

This allusion to the Industrial Revolution as the trigger for the changes in the fae community and their consecutive relocation to the New World is closely connected to the ecological and cultural changes brought on in the Anthropocene. The extinction of the nature-bound fae, following the disruption of the ecological habitat they have occupied, drives home the idea of "the reality of anthropogenic climate change" (Steffen et al., "The Anthropocene: Conceptual" 860). It is a logical consequence of city growth and the gradual taming of the wilderness by humans. Such preternatural beings have no place in the urban environment that has become dominant in the Anthropocene.

These nature fae are later described in the book as enslaved by other fae and victimized to siphon off their residual creative magic:

> It was the creature that lay behind the fairy queen's throne that caught my attention. It lay huge and still, like a great redwood cut down by the woodsman's axe. It had bark and evergreen needles—but it also had four eyes as

big as dinner plates that glowed like ruby glass lanterns. It was bound with iron chains that glittered with magic. I didn't know what a forest lord looked like, but a giant tree with eyes seemed like a strong possibility. (Briggs, *Silver Borne* ch. 14)

This passage presents the most ancient of the powerful fae from the Old World, the forest lords. The indicated creatures suffered most due to the advance of the cold iron, but their connection with their natural habitat was also very strong, so they had issues with migration (not to mention the fact how logistically difficult their physical removal to the New World must have been). However, technology spread also into their new surroundings, so their powers slowly dwindled. Briggs's description is ripe with ecological imagery of nature's decline in the Anthropocene. If the protector of the forest is in such a miserable subservient state, the territory it protects is inferred to fare no better. Another part of the scene indicative of the victimization of nature in the Anthropocene is expressed through the embodied victimization of the forest lord at the hands of a black witch: "She gathered up her chains and moved to the farthest extent, which left her just able to reach the forest lord. She plunged the knife into the tree-like creature, and it bellowed, shook, and bled amber fluid onto the knife. The floor moved under my feet and the ceiling roots contracted and wiggled" (Briggs, *Silver Borne* ch. 14). It is important to note that witches are the only beings with preternatural power, who are human in nature; hence, it is a human being who draws power from victimization of nature's avatar.

It should be noted that the fae's adaptation process to the human world included the shift of power from the ones imbibing it from the wilderness to those who could safely migrate since they are disconnected from it. These creatures found it easier to settle in the urban environment and hide in plain sight among humans. As the human-made technologies develop, the fae leaders known as "the Gray Lords" (the name itself denotes the color between black and white and symbolizes moral ambiguity, which is often highlighted in fairy mythology) have found it more expedient to reveal their existence and make some weaker fae show who they are. This revelation leads to a dual reaction from the human population: they accept fae as a social minority, but out of fear they also form special reservations for them: "The wave of violence prompted the creation of four large reservations for fae. Zee told me that there were fae in the government who saw the reservations as damage control and used fair means and foul to convince the rest of Congress" (Briggs, *Moon Called* ch. 1). The community of fairy immigrants becomes a victim of violence caused by the fear of the "alien," thus reflecting the issues which immigrants face when settling into a new society and connected with the problem of "alienation" crucial in urban fantasy (Young 141).

The concept of "fae reservations" in itself is a merging of the residual cultural concept of Native American reservation with its emergent revival as fae territories. The use of the concept of reservation also allows to put the transferred Old World fae into the setting generally associated with Native Americans. The fae are subject to the laws and community-building programs that are poorly supervised by the authorities. The situation is hardly improved by the half-measures: "If a fae agreed to live on a reservation, he was given a small house and a monthly stipend. Their children (like Zee's son Tad) were given scholarships to good universities where they might become useful members of society . . . if they could find jobs" (Briggs, *Moon Called* ch. 1).

The described "damage control" attitude was a temporary measure. The fae could not defend themselves from this violence, as it was deemed counterproductive by the Gray Lords: "They couldn't defend themselves for fear of the Gray Lords. Whatever the humans did to them, the Gray Lords would do worse" (ch. 1). However, the reservations had an unexpected effect. The high concentration of fae meant the concentration of a substantial amount of power in one place. For all intents and purposes, these territories became populated and self-governed by the fae. The series thus presents a conflict between human authorities and the fae population on the grounds of discrimination. For instance, one trial acquitted a human serial murderer of preternatural beings despite overwhelming evidence: "They played up the strangeness of the fae and the werewolves and used it to scare the jury into acquittal" (Briggs, *Fair Game* ch. 13). The living victim of his crimes is a half-fae girl *lacking* any preternatural power, who was brutalized and her future in the human society was ruined. When the court ruled to let the perpetrator free, her fae father, a Gray Lord, announced the decision to remove the fae from the jurisdiction of human courts on the grounds of their injustice and prejudice: "But you all see us as monsters—so frightened of the dark that you cannot see truly your own monsters among you. Very well. You have made it clear that we and our children are not citizens of this country, that we are separate" (ch. 13). Indicative of the "us-them" alienation, this solution led to new tensions in the universe—both between humans and preternatural beings, and among various groups of preternatural beings of different origins. The dominant fragmentation is one of the central problems connected with urban life in the Anthropocene era, and it is the source of multiple conflicts throughout the series. In this particular case, discrimination stems from difference, and it is directed from the dominant majority (the human society) toward the Other.

The reappearance of the fae realm in the New World after its disappearance from its original location reinforces the importance of immigration not only as a cultural exchange but also in terms of cultural development of Briggs's universe. The fae realm is called Underhill, referring to the common component of multiple tales stating that the fae live under the hill, not in some more specific location, like Avalon (Keightly) or the Country of the Young (Yeats). Moreover, the realm is described as a transcendent place, which is now open to the New World fae: "'There is power in that kind of concentration.' He was careful not to say that the reservation had reopened a path or two to Underhill" (Briggs, *Silver Borne* ch. 13).

In her analysis of Caryl Phillips's *A New World Order*, Rebecca Walkowitz discusses "the different ways of arranging geography and of arranging the ways that people move through geography today" (540), mentioning cheap air travel, global news broadcasts, and tourism industry. This "arranging" is further complicated in Briggs's novels, as means of global connection are complemented with the travel to the reopened Underhill, the traditional fairy realm, lost to the fae in the early stages of their relocation away from the cold iron. This residual-turned-emergent dimension affects the power balance in the world of fantastic beings, leading to further fragmentation. Descriptions of magical beings in their new surroundings and allusions to their natural state or real appearance illustrate the author's interpretation of multiple national mythologies in a cross-cultural aspect. They also highlight the process of authorial myth creation.

The shift of supernatural power is crucial. Underhill disappeared in the Old World due to the decline of nature fae and reappeared in the New World, where the power in fae community shifted to those well-adapted to the urban setting. The residual image of ancient natural power is turned emergent with the shift of the driving force. It is not the few extremely powerful fae that managed to open the link with their place of power, but a big number of weaker ones varying in origin and power; this image is reminiscent of the notion of the "global geophysical force" (Steffen et al., "The Anthropocene: Are Humans" 614) of the Anthropocene era that is responsible for the sustainability of their environment, which in this case does not rely on "Earth's life support system" (618), but on the fae's unique magic in the urban environment. The urban fae also find it easier to produce powerful children with humans, in contrast to the ancient fae who rarely have children and their offsprings with humans are usually fully human.

The discussion of fae hybrids also adds to the issue of physical and magical merging in Briggs's novels. There are many characters that are of combined fae and human heritage—some of them inherited the power of the fae, while others did not. Examples of half-fae with inherited power include Tom, the son of Zee, the Dark Smyth of Dartheim, who inherited his father's talent in wielding metal, and Benedict Heuter, descendant of the "horned lord" (Briggs, *Fair Game* ch. 12). Tom is described as a well-adapted, kind, and thoughtful person with immense power; though he tries to hide it in order to live in the human society, he understands his power and is able to wield it at will. In contrast, Benedict Heuter was brought up cut off from his fae heritage, as his father was killed in his deer form in a road accident. He was brought up by a sociopathic uncle and taught to fear his power, repress it, and only use it to hurt other supernatural beings. Despite the significant power he possesses, the horned lord's descendant exercises poor control over it and is ultimately killed. This indicates the importance of cross-cultural upbringing and understanding of both sides of one's heritage.

In contrast, the daughter of a Gray Lord, Lizzie Beauclaire, is described as lacking any fae power, but having inherited from her father's side the desire to dance as a fae: "The only thing she gets from me is my mother's love of dance—and she has to train hours every day to do what my mother did effortlessly" (Briggs, *Fair Game* ch. 6). This incongruousness of ability and desire is a psychological issue all half-blood fae share, but understanding their dual nature and socialization helps them adapt to living among humans. The indicated conflict of desire and ability is a common theme in immigration narratives, and its treatment in Briggs's universe adds a fantastic layer to this theme.[2] The characters with mixed descent embody the question asked by Homi Bhabha: "How do strategies of representation or empowerment come to be formulated in communities where the exchange of values, meanings, and priorities may not always be collaborative and dialogical?" (6). In the universe of the series the lack of dialogue is described as an utter failure on multiple levels—magical, social, and personal. The half-fae children are part of both the fae and human societies, and if they possess magical abilities, they are part of the new power base.

Age is another layer to the complex picture of Briggs's preternatural species of various mythological origins as they have varying lifespans. Primordial indigenous deities have little power in this New World and are just a residual power. In contrast, the ancient werewolf duo of Bran and his firstborn son Samuel, who are over 1.5 millennia old, belong to the dominant culture of Briggs's universe and are reshaping the werewolf community into a hierarchical organization that favors civilizing influences over instincts. There are also ancient fae and vampires, who remain largely unchanged, and as such they can be seen as providing the element of stability in the universe. Many characters are described as having lived in both the Old and the New Worlds, and they hint at the difference in how their societies worked in the old territory. Highlighting the emerging tendencies, they also share primeval knowledge and traditions to ensure continuity. The discrepancy in the adaptation of the older beings to the new circumstances is indicative of the Anthropocene as a long and complex epoch that provides time for a gradual integration into the urban community in various roles.

The werewolves are the only supernatural beings described as having migrated by choice in substantial quantity. Their community is the one that the main characters of both series belong to. Hence, their integration into the New World is thoroughly detailed. The werewolves moved to the New World to spread their population. Like vampires and fae, they did not break ties with their past and traditions but did not shy from the integration into the new society either. Their perception of the New World as the land of opportunity is offered in the description of Boston through the eyes of one werewolf: "It wasn't just older; it felt older—and somehow still fresh and brash and still moving on. New World-ish, maybe. Built by people unsatisfied with their lives who crossed an ocean, risking and giving their lives for a new start, right here" (Briggs, *Fair Game* ch. 4). Such attitude allowed the werewolf community to, on the one hand, integrate with the American society and achieve political and financial success, and preserve their inherent magical and social features on the other.

The werewolf society is described as a unit with complex leadership issues, which stem from the pack structure convention: "For a werewolf, survival depends upon the pack—and a pack is a complex social and military hierarchy that depends upon each member knowing exactly what his place is" (Briggs, *Blood Bound* ch. 7). The pack members are obedient to the alpha through a magical contract, forged by ingesting his flesh, and in return, the alpha is bound to protect them. There is a magical and emotional unity to the pack:

> He took me to another silver garland and had me tell him whom it belonged to. After the third, I could find the strands myself without his guidance. The fourth was Paul's. He was running with Mary Jo—and just as anxious to find me. He still didn't like Warren, though. I could see that his garland and Mary Jo's were intertwined and connected to all the other garlands, too. One by one we walked by the rocks that were the wolves in the pack. (Briggs, *Silver Borne* ch. 15)

This passage presents the magical bonds existing between members of the pack: werewolves are separate entities, but they are magically connected to each other with durable but splittable bonds that they form by choice. The alpha is the strongest werewolf of the pack, who upholds the magical contract of the pack and ensures its unity: "All but buried in the pack magic was a very, very black rock" (ch. 15). A pack is a necessity for the werewolves due to their nature and social inclinations: "Werewolves don't do well on their own. They need someone, pack or family, or they begin to get odd" (Briggs, *Blood Bound* ch. 3). It results in a structured, adaptable, and inclusive society.

Moreover, these features help werewolves integrate into the urban environment. They are intrinsically team players, good at following orders. In the Anthropocene, when social integration within any given community is necessary for successful coexistence, this ability of the werewolves serves to strengthen their position. They are described as having varying careers: police, firefighters, medics, think tank executives, teachers, financial dealers, and so on, and these help them form close ties both inside and outside their community. Thus, they adapt well to the urban environment and are able to meet the restrictions which the Anthropocene era has placed on the wilderness, as exemplified by their transformation of urban warehouses into hunting grounds to allow werewolves to run on the night of the full moon without having to leave the city: "He's turned the whole thing into a maze—tunnels, lots of half stories and walls that can be moved to change it up" (Briggs, *Hunting Gound* ch. 5). Hence, werewolves have been able to adapt man-made areas to replace the natural space devoid of people—this substitution is a mechanism of survival in the face of the Anthropocene.

Both series provide numerous explanations of what a werewolf is and descriptions of how it shifts between two forms, but the most comprehensive and insightful explanations of the nature of a werewolf are offered through the voices of creatures that are either indigenous shifters or of mixed origin. This is due to the fact that the lead characters in both series are of mixed Old and New World heritage. The comparative description of werewolf nature is an example of cross-cultural dialogue in the text. The Native American Wolf deity describes the werewolf he encounters as follows:

> "Werewolf." Wolf frowned. "I had thought it an abomination when I heard it first. Wolf trapped in the same skin as a human—always in opposition with each other. And in some ways it is abominable. But look at you. You are beautiful."
> [. . .]
> "How is that different from our walkers?" asked Coyote in an interested tone. "They carry both spirits, too." "No," said Wolf absently, still lost in his examination of Adam. "In our descendants, there is only one spirit that expresses itself as either human or animal. This is different. The wolf is mine, and the man not at all. And yet it works." (Briggs, *River Marked* ch. 11)

This passage provides insight into the nature of the two main characters of the *Mercy Thompson* series—Adam, a werewolf, and Mercy, a coyote shifter. They exemplify the different approaches to the double nature of preternatural beings with two distinctive physical forms—human and animal. The descriptions of their change of shape reveal the difference between the spiritual organization of such beings in Native American and European mythologies. Native shifters have one spirit that is free to express itself in two forms—human and animal—and the transition is easy, fast, painless, and will-driven. European werewolves have two conjoined spirits: a wolf spirit and a human one, which are partially opposed and partially co-dependent; hence their transitions involve a struggle and bring pain. Also due to their partially split nature, werewolves are affected by outside forces to a greater extent and can go crazy if the split becomes complete. The Wolf deity forces Adam to keep his wolf shape for a while, making it apparent that the immigrant creatures, despite the described differences, are still similar enough to indigenous ones to fall under the control of a Native American avatar.

Thus, Briggs is able to offer this insight into the nature of a werewolf by applying another mythological system to the traditional European perception of a werewolf. The nature of a shifter is contrasted with a werewolf, and through this cross-cultural comparison both are defined more clearly. This juxtaposition results from the inclusion of various mythologies into a single universe but also reveals the insufficient context for the cultural signs that are combined. In this case, Briggs's appropriation lacks accuracy and does not reflect the complex differences in the way Native American cultures approach shifters, transformer gods, and nature spirits.

The Native American beings depicted in the series include shifters (also called walkers), spirits, and deities. Interestingly, the nature of these beings is described primarily from the point of view of the hybrid characters—Mercy Thompson, the child of Coyote deity and a white woman, and Charles, the son of Salish daughter of a shaman and a witch-born Welsh werewolf. In itself, this fact proves the essential role immigration plays in the series' universe and indicates the movement of cultural signs into a different medium. In both cases, the characters combine signs of indigenous and contemporary American Midwest and ancient Welsh cultures, and thus create a new cultural context. Such an approach is an instance of cultural appropriation from multiple sources that is employed to create a new, ambiguous, and fragmented environment; it rends the original ties between signs in their native cultures. On the one hand, there is no sufficient context for Welsh witch mythology and the legends about Sir Marrok, and, on the other, no sufficient background for the Coyote tales and Salish spirit lore.

The character of Mercy Thompson exemplifies the new category of preternatural beings of a mixed Old and New World origin. Mercy possesses the dominant magical characteristics of a walker, such as the ability to shapeshift into her coyote form and to see and put to rest ghosts, but she grew up with her Caucasian mother and then Bran's werewolf pack; hence, she is a product of two worlds. The protagonist's understanding of her adoptive werewolf family is deeper and her knowledge of their traditions more comprehensive than her attachment to her indigenous heritage. This shows the tendency to imbibe the dominant culture for easy assimilation into the powerful community. Mercy starts exploring the roots of her power in the fourth book of the series, when she meets indigenous deities for the first time, and they help her in understanding the basics of her nature. This investigation of one's origins in order to understand the complexity and richness of one's identity potentially promotes diversity, and the interest in one's roots is an emergent trend in the series. The indigenous deities possess the ability to exist in multiple planes—for example, "He [Coyote] walks in both places" (Briggs, *River Marked* ch. 11)—and the transitory nature of their power affects the powers of their descendants and facilitates their internal integrity as opposed to the werewolves' dual existence.

In contrast, the protagonist of the *Alpha and Omega* series, Charles Cornick, is brought up in two cultural surroundings. The first one is his mother's Salish tribe, where her shaman relative taught him the Native approach to magic and helped him develop his inherent gift. The second environment is his Welsh father's werewolf pack, where he was taught pack hierarchy and traditions. On the one hand, Charles looks fully indigenous, and his style reflects his upbringing and nature. Later, his appearance is noted to have a strong family resemblance to his Welsh brother's: "With that smile she could see past the superficial differences to the underlying similarities, a matter of bone and movement rather than feature-by-feature likeness" (Briggs, *Cry Wolf* ch. 3). The very phrase "underlying similarities" is indicative of their likeness not only in appearance but also in their magic power inherited from their common father and their upbringing.

Charles's magical power is a combination of werewolf powers, his father's witch blood, and his shaman ancestry. The fact that he is able to easily transform into his wolf form with little physical discomfort and could do so since birth is comparable more to Mercy's walker transformation than to the process experienced by werewolves. Charles and his wolf are two distinct entities that interact and are cognizant of each other: "In situations where I am better able, he allows me full control—and I extend him the same courtesy" (Briggs, *Hunting Ground* ch. 3). This is contrasted with how other werewolves deal with their dual nature: "To function, most werewolves have to make their wolf obedient if not completely subservient. After a while, the wolf spirit is reduced to a part of the man's spirit. An unthinking, violent part full of instincts and desires but no true thoughts" (ch. 3). They are not one being with two forms as indigenous shifters are; they contain and tame the wolf with their humanity. Traditionally, a werewolf, whose wolf side is unchecked by humanity, goes feral and follows the violent instincts of the wild animal. Charles is truly a being between the two traditions, with both spirits distinct yet united: "One soul, one man, two spirits. We are one, Brother Wolf and I. Inseparable. If he died, so would I" (ch. 3). He can willingly cede control to either spirit and change shape to fit the situation as both wolf and human sides of his nature are complete and cognizant. He is described as a uniquely powerful being, unhampered by his werewolf traits which make integration into the human society more difficult. He represents the emergent new type of creatures that, due to combining the most practical traits from both sides of their heritage, can function more easily in the Anthropocene. He embodies the most seamless merging of two mythological traditions in Briggs's series, presumably because he is described as having been brought up in both cultural environments and inherited magical properties from both sides. The importance of collaboration on fostering enduring values in children born to diverse heritage is repeatedly highlighted within both series. These characters are a direct result of migration and they embody both the unification of residual myths and their further fragmentation; they constitute new emergent power in Briggs's universe, and, through their unique experience, they enrich it.

In Briggs's series migration is heavily relied on to naturally include beings of various mythologies in a single comprehensive universe. Their encounters and interactions fall into the domain of cross-cultural relations; they are then united into a single multifaceted universe that, due to the significantly varied nature and powers of the characters, is subject to fragmentation and incongruence. The interactions and limitations of these different beings also condition their place in the author's magical universe.

The aforementioned diverse treatments of problems related to migration in Briggs's universe enrich and diversify the series' mythological foundation, allow for the coexistence of creatures from different national traditions, and reflect the condition of the globalized world. Briggs's preternatural creatures actively interact with each other; while the human society comes into the equation as a reactive force, it is presented as a homogenous structure in the dichotomy of fantastic (us) vs. human (them) that implicitly uncovers the creatures' alienation in the urban environment, which they struggle to overcome. Due to the series' unrestrictive world-building, new preternatural creatures are easily and seamlessly integrated into the fold at any given point of the plot. Such a strategy enriches the diversity of cultural background, provides an opportunity for plot development, and increases the capacity of the novels to include multiple social discourses. However, in some cases the introduction of these diverse cultural signs into the fictional environment lacks sufficient context.

Integration of the preternatural species in the New World is expressed on various levels, including the structuring of their inner society and interaction with others. The process of transition and adaptation of various preternatural beings is the embodiment of continuity of various traditions through transference and change in the society with rich immigration traditions. The diversity of problems connected with the settlement and interaction of various preternatural immigrants—social, environmental, political, identity, and community issues— correspond to the problems described in urban fantasy, notably alienation, fragmentation, and adaptation. Also, due to their connection to various mythological traditions, the characters of Briggs's novels reflect a number of temporal layers that coexist in the series' fantasy universe and embody the residual, dominant, and emergent features of the complex culture which exists and develops in its own fictional version of the Anthropocene.

Various communities are shown to have adapted in different ways after migration. Vampires thrive in the New World but are deeply estranged and hidden. Their society is the least changed one. The fae society has undergone deep transformation, due to the alteration of their circumstances brought on by the "cold iron" and the power shift. Similar to the dominant Anthropocene image of collective power and responsibility, the weaker fae have gained importance as a massive population unit, though a number of ancient fae have discovered hope due to the opening of the Underhill. Werewolves form the society most open to interaction and cross-cultural dialogue, and hence build extensive relations with other creatures. Moreover, the two well-adapted communities form personal relationships and breed with humans, while vampires interact with human outcasts or people who strive to join the vampire society. Both vampire and werewolf communities have a strict internal organization, but while in the vampire society the hierarchy is rigid and set in tradition, for werewolves it is dynamic and dependent on the personalities and relations of the members. This discrepancy explains the higher adaptability of werewolves in the urban setting.

The image of the Anthropocene does not only include that of a geological age, but also its social dimension. All the described preternatural societies can be viewed as "the Unseen" which is defined by Stefan Ekman as a combination of means that "produce a strong focus on that which in some sense or other is not seen" (463); "the Unseen" is important in emphasizing the juxtaposition or a certain interrelation of the notions of "fantastic," "urbanity," and "modernity" (463). In Briggs's series, the concept of "the social Other" covers a number of topics that are generally related to the central issue of alienation and acceptance, and it is differently embodied in the particular preternatural communities. The vampires distance themselves from the human society in a way similar to social stratification. In the wolf community, this concept is highlighted by showing the packs' gradual attempts to ensure freedom, safety, and a measure of equality within the pack structure to modernize it, for instance, in the strategies of placing an unmated female in the pack. The fae community's version of "the social Other" is based on the correlation of various degrees of separation they experience throughout the novels: from hiding from sight to being constrained in reservations. All these variations are united by two factors: they are residual-turning-emergent and their way to approach the Anthropocene is based on their supernatural power.

Briggs's series also explores the development of their preternatural societies. The emergent fantastic beings with various supernatural and/or human origin, the gradual unveiling of these creatures to the humans, and their integration into the global community lead to extensive changes in the universe. Another tendency is the connection of emergent and residual trends, such as the reopening of the fae realm of Underhill in the New World, and the interaction of Native American deities with the species of non-autochthonous preternatural beings. This allows Briggs to emphasize the continuity of various national mythologies, as well as their concatenation in the globalized fantasy universe of both series.

In Briggs's immersive fantasy, all fantastic beings constitute the element of Otherness of the fictional universe. The key conflicts in the series are driven by the consequences of migration and resultant alienation, fragmentation, misunderstandings, and adaptation in the Anthropocene world, which is dominated by humans and influenced by technological progress. Briggs is able to explore these topics by introducing various fantastic beings; cultural appropriation as migration of cultural signs into new media is used to both highlight these urban problems and unite the Various within the Other, as opposed to the human society. According to the series' premises, the changes wrought by the Industrial Revolution deeply altered the foundations of living conditions and led to the transformation of the concept of power. The most powerful communities and individuals are the most adapted ones, the ones most open to change and cultural enrichment.

NOTES

1. The novel *The Golem and the Djinni* (2013) by Helene Wecker explores the process of immigration and its immediate effects on the fantastic beings outside their natural habitat. *The Edge* series (2009–2012) by Ilona Andrews explores the life of the characters, locked in the universe that is on the boundary between human and fantastic worlds, who struggle to find their place in either as they are illegal aliens in both. In contrast to such novels, focusing their world-building on the diachronic reflection of migration, multiple novels accept immigration of fantastic beings as a ready fact. On the very end of this scale is the bare mention of the fact of immigration, as exemplified by Halyna Pahutiak's *Urizka Gothic* (2009), where the opyrs who aim to move to the New World are assured that they already have "their kind" over there.

2. Elizabeth Clifford and Maya Kalyanpur in their research on young adult fiction with immigrant protagonists explore a number of different literary representations of the three stages of the process of migration: the decision to migrate, the journey of immigration, and the adjustment upon immigration (15). They discuss the problem of desire and ability of the protagonists to fit into the new communities and participate fully in their life.

WORKS CITED

Attebery, Brian. *Stories About Stories: Fantasy and the Remaking of Myth*. Oxford UP, 2014.

Bhabha, Homi K. *The Location of Culture*. Routledge, 1994.

Bond, Michael. *The Power of Others: Peer Pressure, Groupthink, and How the People around Us Shape Everything We Do*. Oneworld, 2015.

Briggs, Patricia. *Blood Bound*, Kindle ed. New York, NY: Ace Books, 2007.

———. *Cry Wolf*, Kindle ed. New York, NY: Ace Books, 2008.

———. *Fair Game*, Kindle ed. New York, NY: Ace Books, 2013.

———. *Hunting Ground*, Kindle ed. New York, NY: Ace Books, 2009.

———. *Moon Called*, Kindle ed. New York, NY: Ace Books, 2006.

———. *River Marked*, Kindle ed. New York, NY: Ace Books, 2011.

———. *Silver Borne*, Kindle ed. New York, NY: Ace Books, 2010.

Cowles, Gregory. "Inside the List." *The New York Times*, 21 March 2014. www.nytimes.com/2014/03/30/books/review/inside-the-list.html. Accessed 26 September 2020.

Clifford, Elizabeth Joyce, and Maya Kalyanpur. "Immigrant Narratives: Power, Difference, and Representation in Young-Adult Novels with Immigrant Protagonists." *International Journal of Multicultural Education*, vol. 13, no. 1, 2011. doi:10.18251/ijme.v13i1.358.

Davis, Suanna. "Representations of Rape in Speculative Fiction. From the Survivor's Perspective." *Femspec*, vol. 13, no. 2, 2013, pp. 9–23.

Ekman, Stefan. "Urban Fantasy: a Literature of the Unseen." *Journal of the Fantastic in the Arts*, vol. 27, 2016, pp. 452–469.

Hillel, Oliver, and Jose Antonio Puppim de Oliveira. "The UN in the Urban Anthropocene." *United Nations University*, 14 August 2014. unu.edu/publications/articles/the-un-in-the-urban-anthropocene.html. Accessed 10 May 2020.

Keightly, Thomas. *The Fairy Mythology*. G. Bell & Sons, 1870. Project Gutenberg. www.gutenberg.org/files/41006/41006-h/41006-h.htm. Accessed 20 April 2020.

Krause, Jens, and Graeme D. Ruxton. *Living in Groups*. Oxford UP, 2002.

Krumrey, Diane. "Displacing the Nation: Contemporary Literature by and about Immigrants." *Caliban*, vol. 19, 2006, pp. 243–252. doi:10.4000/caliban.2486.

Mclaurin, Virginia. *Stereotypes of Contemporary Native American Indian Characters in Recent Popular Media*. MA Thesis, University of Massachusetts Amherst, 2014.

McGaughey, Clara. "Immigration, Glorification, and Forgetting in The Great Gatsby." *Verso: An Undergraduate Journal of Literary Criticism*, 2016, pp. 28–35.

Мелетинский, Елизар и пр. *Мифологический словарь*. [Meletinsky, Eleazar, et al. *Mifologicheskiy Slovar*. Mythological Dictionary]. Sovetskaya entciklopedia, 1991.

"Menagerie." *Merriam-Webster.com Dictionary*, Merriam-Webster. www.merriam-webster.com/dictionary/menagerie. Accessed 10 September 2020.

Muller, Gilbert H. *New Strangers in Paradise: The Immigrant Experience and Contemporary American Fiction*. U P of Kentucky, 1999.

Steffen, Will, et al. "The Anthropocene: Conceptual and Historical Perspectives." *Philosophical Transactions: Mathematical, Physical and Engineering Sciences*, vol. 369, 2011, pp. 842–867. doi:10.1098/rsta.2010.0327.

———. "The Anthropocene: Are Humans Now Overwhelming the Great Forces of Nature." *AMBIO: A Journal of the Human Environment*, vol. 36, no. 8, 2007, pp. 614–621. doi:10.1579/0044-7447(2007)36[614:taahno]2.0.co;2.

Walkowitz, Rebecca L. *Immigrant Fictions: Contemporary Literature in an Age of Globalization*. U of Wisconsin P, 2006.

Watts, Michael J. "Space for Everything (A Commentary)." *Cultural Anthropology*, vol. 7, no. 1, 1992, pp. 115–129. doi:10.1525/can.1992.7.1.02a00080.

Williams, Raymond. "Dominant, Residual, and Emergent." 1979. In *Cultural Theory: An Anthology*, edited by Imre Szeman and Timothy Kaposy. Wiley-Blackwell, 2011, pp. 353–356.

Yeats, W. B. *Fairy and Folk Tales of the Irish Peasantry*. Edited and Selected by W. B. Yeats. Walter Scott, 1903.

Young, Helen Victoria. *Race and Popular Fantasy Literature: Habits of Whiteness*. Routledge, 2018.

Ziff, Bruce H., and Pratima V. Rao. *Borrowed Power: Essays on Cultural Appropriation*. Rutgers UP, 1997.

Chapter 12

The Development of Realist Speculative Narratives to Represent and Confront the Anthropocene

Dwight Tanner

In the face of the ever-growing consequences of climate change, we require new strategies and modes of thinking to better grapple with not only the catastrophic effects of humans on the planet but also the role of literature to help narrate and consider the consequences of anthropocentric thinking. As the editors of *Manifesto for Living in the Anthropocene* (2015) claim, meaningfully addressing humanity's destructive tendencies requires the dismantling of various "traditional separations" that divide societal conceptions of, among other things, "nature and culture" and "economy and ecology," arguing that fealty to these constructed binaries both obscures and furthers humanity's destructive behaviors (Gibson et al., i). Reflective of this deconstructive process, I read Barbara Kingsolver's *Flight Behavior* (2012) and Ian McEwan's *Solar* (2010) as climate change novels that demonstrate the artistic development of specific—if not entirely new—modes of literary representation that seek to dismantle these perceived divides, partly in response to the exceptional challenges of depicting the fantastic nature of quotidian life in the Anthropocene.[1]

I first illustrate how McEwan and Kingsolver collapse and conflate traditionally separated literary modes of realism and speculative or fantastic literature, resulting in a mode of representation that I refer to as speculative realism. To be clear: these realist speculative narratives do not necessarily represent a radically new literary form entirely unique to Anthropocene fiction. On the contrary, literature has many examples, particularly from early modernists, of narratives that explicitly elide the spheres of the everyday and the exceptional.[2] However, as the effects of climate change become increasingly present in our day-to-day existences—and can also be linked to our quotidian choices—I argue that strategies that reveal the conflation of the fantastic and mundane are particularly vital and efficacious, especially given the desire to ignore the fantastic warnings of climate change by reconstituting these constructed binaries.

I use the term *speculative realism* to describe literary strategies for depicting literary elements of the fantastic and realism synchronously almost as a requirement of exploring life in the Anthropocene. Tzvetan Todorov's theories of the fantastic are particularly generative for understanding how and why we must think differently about the ways that fantastic events function in realist Anthropocene fiction. In *Introduction à la littérature fantastique* (1970), Todorov defines the *fantastic* as an event that occurs in the rational world that appears to be supernatural. In Todorov's formulation, if the strange event can be understood logically—as perhaps a dream or madness—then it is categorized as the uncanny or *das unheimlich*. If the supernatural event is determined to have actually occurred, what Todorov calls the marvelous, then a shift in rational understanding or the laws of reality must occur. The truly fantastic, according to Todorov, only exists in the hesitation or inability—by either characters or reader—to decide between the two.

However, in the Anthropocene, particularly in the twenty-first century, unnatural and fantastic events occur with greater frequency and severity, such as an increase in extreme weather situations. These occurrences are neither uncanny nor require a shift in the laws of reality because they are scientifically proven as inevitable given humanity's effects on the planet—but these facts do not make climate change any less incredible. Nor can we adequately confront humanity's effects on the planet if the unnatural is rendered familiar and normal. The logical but also unnatural destructive events of climate change are thus poorly rendered in this rubric since there can also be no hesitation between the uncanny or marvelous. While Todorov's fantastic necessitates engagement, the effects of climate change are often either effectively ignored without any shift required or passively acknowledged with the hope that an elusive solution to the problem will somehow be found. In other words, the fantastic effects of the Anthropocene result in a passive acceptance or denial that falls far outside the bounds of most definitions and expectations of how humanity might respond to these types of fantastic events. This process also is not legible within the bounds of magical realism, wherein events that may seem fantastic to the reader occur naturalistically—and are accepted as completely normal and unremarkable—within the story world. Speculative realism, on the other hand, depicts and explores the repercussions of how the fantastic occurs in day-to-day life while humanity finds new ways to keep ignoring them, most often by reconstituting other human-centric literary and cultural binaries.

In the opening passages of *Flight Behavior*, Kingsolver complicates these long-standing divisions as the protagonist, Dellarobia, an unfulfilled rural wife and mother, stifled by the monotony of her day-to-day existence, follows in the footsteps of fantastic storybook characters, taking a transformative journey into the woods behind her home. Dellarobia had once been a promising student with high hopes for her future career. Having married her high school boyfriend after getting pregnant, she now spends her days taking care of her two young children, taciturn husband, and messy home. Intending to meet and have an affair with a younger man, even Dellarobia admits that she is "manufactur[ing] a fantasy" (6) in order to escape the tedium of her mundane life, indicating how she views the quotidian and the fantastic as mutually exclusive. While both the quotidian and fantastic components (a bored housewife and a transformative journey into the woods, respectively) can be read as clichéd literary tropes, their coalescence in the opening pages is the first of many ways that Kingsolver's novel introduces the complicated and overlooked connections between the everyday and the spectacular. Other codependent elements of realism and fantasy are established formally—and in the specific context of climate change—in the narrative juxtaposition of Dellarobia's thoughts about the ordinariness of her life against the unsettling and even chimerical descriptions of the novel's otherwise realist setting.

While the third-person limited narration mostly highlights how Dellarobia is subsumed by anxieties about her mundane personal life and failing marriage, other narrative details—such as the descriptions of scenery—pointedly focus elsewhere: on the fantastic signs of a mounting ecological crisis. If Dellarobia's personal life is aching with realist humdrum, Kingsolver describes the land around her in strikingly dystopian terms. These fantastical descriptions of the foreboding landscape begin with the complete desolation of the neighbor's orchard, which is decaying and dying from too much rain (3). Tellingly, Dellarobia consistently repurposes these phenomenal sights as solipsistic pathos rather than something to be meaningfully considered or confronted. For example, as she gets higher in the mountains, she comes across a fallen tree: "the corpse of [a] fallen monster. The tree was intact, not cut or broken by wind. What a waste. After maybe centuries of survival it had simply let go of the ground" due to oversaturated soil (5). The narration invites readers to frame the scene as macabrely exceptional, describing the tree as a corpse and a monster. Dellarobia acknowledges that the tree represents something wrong, noting how she keeps reading about how this kind of thing "was happening all over the county," but she also strangely casts the agency on the tree for "simply let[ting] go of the ground" (5), refusing to see the global and fantastic nature of what the tree both represents and portends. Dellarobia further avoids perceiving the tree as both a causality and a sign of climate change by positioning what she sees in personal terms, noting that the tree, "like herself [. . .] seemed to have come loose from its station in life" (5). While Dellarobia clearly believes she wants a fantastic escape, the narration also reveals the ways that she pointedly privileges and refocuses on the spheres of the human, the personal, and the unexceptional, allowing her to further ignore the fantastic and ever-growing ramification of humanity's effects on the planet that surround her.

Similarly, the title of Ian McEwan's *Solar* most literally connotes the promise of solar energy that the book's protagonist, Michael Beard, fantastically believes—in a self-aggrandizing fashion—that he can harness in order to "save the world." But the title also invokes notions of the spherical, which is mirrored in McEwan's depictions of the overlooked but interconnected spheres of the fantastic, quotidian, global, and personal that the novel's characters—and perhaps readers—prefer to think of as unrelated or as existing on separate planes. However, McEwan, in his attempt to represent the failures of humanity to meaningfully consider and confront the effects of climate change, instead repeatedly highlights the actual coalescence or unification of these domains, partly by demonstrating how Beard's disastrous failures to save the world are inextricable from and often caused by his small-scale private squabbles and shortcomings.

Invoking James Phelan's notion of "extra artistic" events, which he defines as evolving sociocultural conditions that force "artists to develop new resources designed to better address the changing extra-artistic realm" (4), I argue that narratively representing the strange realities of human-made climate change through speculative realism both exposes and disassembles the traditional divisions that conceive of the quotidian and the fantastic, the global and the personal, and the human and non-human—as entirely separate spheres. I posit that the precarity and interconnectedness of climate change and other human-made issues have created unique literary challenges that problematize, among other things, artists' abilities to rely solely on realism or solely on speculative fiction to represent life in the Anthropocene. I ask, could analyzing literature's productive struggle to represent the ever-growing effects of climate change by bridging these bifurcations better equip us to approach the unique challenges of understanding and confronting the Anthropocene?[3] Inherent in this argument is the claim that these divisions are constructions—and in many ways, literary fabrications—that severely limit humanity's ability to confront and take responsibility for the Anthropocene, even as the consequences grow increasingly impossible to ignore.

CHALLENGES OF DEPICTING CLIMATE CHANGE

Many popular novels that explore and depict the cataclysmic ramifications of the Anthropocene, such as Margaret Atwood's *MaddAddam* trilogy, are, understandably, often categorized as Speculative or Science Fiction (SF), in no small part due to their portrayals of the fantastic, destructive consequences of human-centric thinking. The benefits of depicting climate change through SF are relatively obvious given SF's ability to engage with alternative conjectures, imaginative futures, and spectacular possibilities. There are, however, potential issues with a speculative approach, namely the fantastic, futuristic narratives that feel removed from reality can distract readers, essentially creating a type of erasure, from the fact that the real-life causes and repercussions of climate change, are, particularly in the twenty-first century, not necessarily speculative, futuristic, or—at least in their increased regularity—exceptional. While the fantastic global effects of climate change may *seem* like the stuff of fantasy and science fiction, living with these consequences is fast becoming a quotidian reality.

Amitav Ghosh helpfully explores this issue in *The Great Derangement* (2016), positing that literary fiction has struggled to adequately represent climate change—arguing that these failings are linked to long-established formal literary divides between fantastic and realist literature. He makes a compelling "history of the novel" argument, detailing how the novel shifted from depictions of "exceptional moments" and events (as in the narrative of *Robinson Crusoe*) to concentrate instead on more quotidian human actions and plots (as in the novels of Jane Austen), which Ghosh links to an Enlightenment rejection of exceptionalism. Tellingly, Enlightenment thinking also furthered a growing distinction between the human and nature, with an even further entrenched type of supremacy granted to the human figure. Granted, Ghosh's argument may be overly simplistic—and I think it is crucial to be clear that spectacular literature regularly utilizes naturalist conventions and that most realist literature engages in imaginative speculation.[4] Ghosh nevertheless demonstrates the challenges of depicting the ordinary nature of fantastic human-caused destruction in the Anthropocene, partly due to constraints of what is and is not plausible in conceits of realism.[5]

Much of the issue comes from the way we popularly conceive of cataclysm or apocalypse as far removed from reality and as definitively exceptional. In this regard, studies of apocalypse by Elizabeth Rosen and James Berger unpack how society far too often considers apocalypse only with a capital A and only end-of-the-world destruction on a global scale as apocalyptic—and thus we continually await cataclysm as opposed to recognizing and learning from the mounting destructions around us.[6] As anthropologist Matthew J. Wolf-Meyer reminds us, "the apocalypse is never singular" (1), but instead occurs slowly over time in fits and starts, a formulation inherent in Gordon Fraser's notion of the "long apocalypse," which he discusses in the context of Indigenous histories to describe the ways that destruction is generally slow and steady—and often willfully unseen by those it does not negatively affect.[7] In this regard, the speculative realism employed by Kingsolver and

McEwan depicts life in the Anthropocene while problematizing and conflating the traditional separations between fantasy and realism in order to render the mundane fantastic and the fantastic mundane.

Speculative Fiction is a valuable tool in this process, although its efficacy can be blunted if and when we think of it as the antithesis of realism. Most often positioned in contrast to realism or naturalism, SF is described as "substitut[ing] realism's what-was or what-is with other tenses: what-wasn't, what-isn't, what-might-be, what-could-have-been-if" (Carroll and McClanahan 658)—a formulation that appears, as indeed some particularly imaginative SF entries do, to make stark distinctions between realism and narratives of the exceptional. But even beyond the fact that these distinctions have always been fraught, the realities of living in the Anthropocene have further created scenarios where the "what-might-be" has become increasingly difficult to distinguish from the "what is." While we busy ourselves prognosticating the devastating effects of ever-rising temperatures and sea levels, the ocean continues to overtake coastlines across the globe, not to mention the stark reality of systematic droughts and floods. We also tend to move on quickly, or outright ignore, the destruction that is not happening in our immediate domain, refusing to see how choices we make individually can create repercussions outside our localized realm—or how the ripples of faraway destruction can suddenly appear in our own backyard. By overly categorizing literature that represents or explores climate change as engaging only with the "what might be," we run the risk of ignoring the ways that destructive, fantastic events have, unfortunately, become and will continue to become the "what is" most often associated with literary realism.

As evidenced by recent literary controversies, such as Margaret Atwood's and Ian McEwan's insistence that they write serious, realistic literature and not science fiction,[8] these traditional separations—and the corresponding condescension toward SF, and genre fiction in general—still retain power and influence in literary circles. But demarcating these categories has always been precarious and literature has long conflated the mundane and spectacular; the issue is that we still so often, even unwittingly, pretend that these categories are wholly distinct in literature. Disclosing the inconsistencies and illogics of our imposed bifurcations, Carl Joseph Swanson cites novels such as Michael Chabon's *Gentleman of the Road* (2007) and Colson Whitehead's *The Intuitionist* (1999) to demonstrate that "the commonplace opposition between literary and genre fiction certainly is no longer accurate" (380). But at the same time, in regard to Whitehead's zombie novel, *Zone One* (2011), Swanson cites reviews and the book's marketing by the literary establishment as demonstrating preemptive "anxiety over the pulp zombie's presence in a highbrow novel" (380), indicating how the ways that we popularly conceive of realism and the fantastic remain deeply oppositional despite the prevalence of novels being written and published that complicate or outright refute this constructed separation.

Many contemporary texts that represent climate change can and do function within the realm of the exceptional while actively avoiding the standard tropes, and fantastic settings, most often associated with SF. To a certain extent, this breakdown is inevitable in any contemporary text that attempts to depict life in the vastly interconnected, globalist twenty-first century. But many authors appear to take on this bifurcation more purposefully, partly to demonstrate society's desire to falsely equate destructive consequences of humanity with the futuristic and spectacular. Take, for example, the speculative realism in Thomas Perrotta's apocalyptic novel *The Leftovers* (2011), wherein a rapture-like event occurs and 2 percent of the world's population disappears. The "Sudden Departure" is clearly a fantastic event, and one that results in deep emotional trauma and loss but ultimately barely affects society's day-to-day operations. Perrotta's novel highlights the sometimes-quotidian nature of apocalyptic events, and challenges readers to consider how we process and deal with cataclysm when it does not affect us the way we thought it would (i.e., there is no visual proof or destruction of society). *The Leftovers* challenges bifurcations of realism and speculative fiction, while also countering humanity's penchant for viewing cataclysm as being futuristic and removed from our day-to-day realities. Perrotta makes this point doubly clear by repeatedly invoking actual, contemporary events—such as the horrors of 9/11—effectively reconfirming the notion that large-scale destructive events are not some far-distanced, seemingly remote possibility, but are instead firmly part of our lived reality.

FLIGHT BEHAVIOR

Barbara Kingsolver's *Flight Behavior* is particularly emblematic of realist literature that depicts contemporary life during the Anthropocene by eschewing and unsettling the traditionally constructed separations between the quotidian and the fantastic and the personal and the global. Literary critics such as Adam Trexler have understandably categorized *Flight Behavior* as "contemporary realism" (229) since Kingsolver's writing and much of the plot largely depict the mundane day-to-day life of Dellarobia, the poor, home-bound wife of a cattle rancher in rural Tennessee.[9] However, partly to depict the reality of climate change in the twenty-first century, Kingsolver also introduces fantastic and speculative events in the novel, such as the final pages that jarringly pivot to depicting an apocalyptic, large-scale global flooding event that may represent the end of humanity as we know it.[10] But, as I will demonstrate, Kingsolver overtly and covertly introduces fantastic elements into the realist story long before the shocking conclusion. To read the book solely as realism or solely as fantastic speculation misses Kingsolver's strategy of consistently engaging both registers and disrupting readers' ability and desire to keep viewing them as distinct.

While Dellarobia may, particularly in the first half of the novel, overlook the fantastic in her day-to-day life, the book's narration repeatedly highlights the liminality and porousness of what we consider fantastic and what we relegate to the quotidian. The book begins in media res as Dellarobia takes her clandestine flight into the woods, detailing her longing for an exciting and even dangerous escape from her mundane life. On the one hand, this potential affair can be read as a monumental rupture in the otherwise monotonous existence of Dellarobia. But, at the same time, could there be a more clichéd escape in literature than a meaningless affair? Even Dellarobia freely admits the banal nature of her supposedly fantastic escape as she repeatedly casts the situation in the context of repetitive narratives, claiming "This day had played in her head like a movie on round-the-clock reruns" (6) and that she feels like she is acting out "a script" (8). These admissions highlight the situational and equivocal nature of these categorizations, revealing how even the supposedly exceptional can be rendered trite and mundane. By grounding these moments in Dellarobia's quotidian concerns, Kingsolver disrupts our ability to read almost any particular scene or situation as either quotidian realism or fantastic.

At the beginning of the novel, the biggest threat to Dellarobia's existence centers around the family's mounting debt and the potential foreclosure of the family farm. On the one hand, this potential loss seems exceptional, but the book repeatedly reminds us that this is not an entirely unremarkable occurrence since the novel appears to be set around the economic crisis of 2008 and almost all neighboring farms are in default. While I do not disagree with Trexler's reading that "Dellarobia's preoccupation with quotidian life makes climatic disaster hard to absorb" (227), it risks overlooking how Dellarobia's quotidian concerns are *also* expressly linked to climate disaster. Indeed, the failures of the family's farm—along with the neighboring farms—can be read in the context of both climate change and the growing prevalence of corporate agro-farming, which both bankrupts smaller farms and leads to greater and even more untenable carbon emissions. While the family worries about their livelihood, they overlook how its potential loss is both unexceptional in the context of the Anthropocene and inherent to the fantastic causes and effects of climate change.

The book most overtly introduces elements of the speculative and fantastic when Dellarobia stumbles across something so unexpected that neither she, partly because she has left her reading glasses at home, nor the book's narration can even describe. As best as Dellarobia can tell, the forest seems to be alive or moving with flashes of bright orange color covering the trees. The narration notes that "The view out across the valley was puzzling and unreal, like a sci-fi movie," quite literally grounding the moment in conceptions of science fiction and narrative (13). To Dellarobia's eyes, the entire valley and forest appear to be on fire, a sight that she directly compares to both the burning bush of Moses and the apocalyptic destruction described by Ezekiel in the Bible (14), firmly establishing the fantastic nature of this plot point and highlighting how extraordinary events are often calibrated and understood through other improbable or miraculous narratives. Readers quickly learn that while the "burning valley" is not a Biblical miracle, it is nothing less unexpected or unbelievable: millions of monarch butterflies roosting in the trees. On the one hand, the presence of these butterflies can be read in light of the so-called butterfly effect, which, particularly in the context of the Anthropocene, accurately reflects the way that small-scale events or choices can ripple out in unexpected ways. But Kingsolver goes beyond using the butterflies as just a metaphor and instead provides concrete examples of how the butterflies function on both a mundane and fantastic scale that collides with Kingsolver's fictional world and real-life climate change destructions.

Indeed, we soon learn many tragic and portending facts about these butterflies. For centuries, they have come together to migrate south for the winter, nesting and breeding in a mountainside forest in Michoacán, Mexico. However, the entire mountain and forest were recently wiped out entirely after an unprecedented rainfall (linked to human-made climate change) triggered a massive, apocalyptic mudslide (linked to deforestation on the mountainside). Not incidentally, the mudslide also destroyed a village and resulted in the death and displacement of hundreds of poor mountain residents, powerfully illustrating how the early consequences of climate change tend to fall mostly on the shoulders of the least powerful.[11] Searching online to learn about this atrocity, Dellarobia is horrified to discover not only that the arrival of the butterflies is linked to a harrowing tragedy but also that she had somehow been unaware that such a cataclysmic disaster had even occurred. Readers may be similarly flummoxed to discover in an Author's Note at the end of the novel that Kingsolver based this occurrence on real-life mudslides that happened in and around Michoacán in 2010, which killed dozens of people and destroyed the homes of many more.[12] Overtly speculative, Kingsolver links the fantastic arrival of the butterflies in the novel to an equally fantastic real-life tragedy that has, in the context of the Anthropocene, been rendered so common to be forgotten or overlooked. Dellarobia's unawareness of this tragedy also hints at the reality of how we so often only learn about climate change disasters when they occur in our own backyard—to us or others that we identify with—and certainly not when they happen in other countries.

But the book also challenges our ability to think of the global as separate from our personal, small-scale realities. Dellarobia first learns about Michoacán from one of her son's schoolmates, who came to Tennessee with her family as migrant laborers after the rain and mudslide destroyed their town—further indicating the many ways that the aftereffects of a faraway disaster, even when we remain ignorant of it, can still show up on our doorstep, in much the same way that climate science indicates that behaviors and practices in one location can have negative effects globally. Within Kingsolver's speculative storyworld, the arrival of the butterflies can also be linked to fantastic climate-based events beyond the mudslide in Michoacán, since strange weather patterns across the globe have confused the butterflies so that they have now stopped to winter in Tennessee, where they will inevitably die once the temperatures drop below freezing.[13]

By inventing the arrival of the butterflies in Tennessee to speculate on the "what if" global effects of the real-life mudslides in Michoacán—and demonstrating how what happened in Michoacán was the result of actions and attitudes that happened well outside the physical sphere of Michoacán—Kingsolver affirms the mundane interconnectedness of the seemingly unconnected, or the things we refuse to see as linked. Even beyond just a revelatory symbol that something is wrong with the world's climate, the inevitable mass death of the butterflies, which play a vital role in pollinating agricultural crops, will surely trigger other cataclysmic consequences. These passages can thus be read in the context of Rob Nixon's crucial challenge to explore how we might "imaginatively and strategically render visible vast force fields of interconnectedness against the attenuating effects of temporal and geographical distance?" (38) Nixon's call is vital as a means of better developing strategies for assessing and confronting many of the unique challenges of the Anthropocene that coexist in the global and personal realm. An occurrence that is viewed by the townspeople as a miraculous sign of God's love is exposed to instead be inextricably linked to a variety of cross-continental—and real-life—climate events, but is also a powerful sign of global climate chaos *and* of future destructions.

Even as Dellarobia berates the others for their inability to understand the butterflies as a sign of climate change, the book repeatedly shows her falling again into the same habits of human-centric thinking. For example, Dellarobia worries that the involvement of others "made the butterflies belong to her less" (205). She also refers to the butterflies as "a gift. To herself in particular" (101). When scientists begin to arrive and explain the ecological catastrophe that the butterflies portend, Dellarobia becomes petulant, casting the event through a self-centered lens of possession: "These butterflies had been hers. She found them [. . .] in her name they were becoming beloved and important. They seemed to matter, like nothing she'd ever possessed" (149), demonstrating the human tendency, even in the face of awareness or incontrovertible evidence, to optimistically view the world and the non-human through a privileged, human-centric lens of ownership and control. Dellarobia cannot reconcile the connections between the quotidian and fantastic, so she either ignores the fantastic by rendering it simply mundane or pretending that it makes her quotidian life somehow exceptional.

Kingsolver thus uses something truly fantastic—a horde of butterflies that for centuries have migrated to Mexico but have instead arrived *en masse* in Tennessee—to interrupt the quotidian naturalism of the story with elements of the fantastic that are also steeped in realism and that foreshadow future disasters. To affect this, Kingsolver always ensures that the book's fantastic and speculative elements remain grounded in naturalism and the unfortunately probable—outside of Dellarobia's impoverished, parallel reconciliations. Consider the butterflies, a species that individually we regard as beautiful but also mundane. However, in this specific situation the butterflies have created a fantastic sight of wonder and beauty—but one that actually reflects and portends global catastrophes that is, just like the sight, difficult to understand through just the lenses of the everyday or the exceptional, indicating the dizzying ways that elements of the novel can be read as fantastic and mundane and back again multiple times.

SOLAR

In many ways, Ian McEwan's *Solar* is, on the surface, even more naturalistic than *Flight Behavior*. Focusing on the protagonist Michael Beard's philandering, gluttonous habits, and petty fights with everyone, much of the plot relates the private downfall of the middle-aged, misogynistic Beard as he lies, cheats, and steals in both his personal and professional lives. Much like Dellarobia's clichéd attempts at an affair, even the exceptional breadth of Beard's many liaisons (at the beginning of the book he is caught cheating on his fifth soon-to-be ex-wife) is rendered repetitive and mundane. But the novel also explores grander themes of the Anthropocene, largely through the has-been-physicist Beard's fantastically self-proclaimed—and self-aggrandizing—goal to "save the world" from climate change. Indeed, Beard's involvement with climate change issues places him in seemingly fantastic situations, such as an excursion to the Arctic and the implementation of advanced solar technology in the desert. Beard claims to have invented the tech, but he actually stole the ideas from his protégé following the young man's accidental death: a seemingly exceptional event that is also tied to, and bogged down by, Beard's personal squabbles.

As many critics have complained, these exceptional plot themes are ignored or abandoned in favor of constant digressions into the highly unlikeable Beard's poor quotidian life choices about food, his declining health, and his sadness over the loss of his sexual virility and sense of masculinity. In *The New York Times*, Michiko Kakutani criticizes how "McEwan repetitiously harps on Beard's gluttonous habits and growing waistline, his sexual promiscuity and his opportunistic efforts to cash in on global warming," ultimately calling the book a "lesser effort" by McEwan (Kakutani). Rather than read the novel's fixation on Beard's personal failures as a narrative flaw, I read *Solar* as demonstrating that Beard's hubris, poor life choices, and privileged sense of dominion and control reciprocally affect both his private life and the aspects of his life that engage with the exceptional and fantastic.

McEwan introduces his comingling of the quotidian and the fantastic—and humanity's desire to view them as separate—as early as the book's epigraph, which quotes John Updike's *Rabbit is Rich* (1981): "It gives him great pleasure, makes Rabbit feel rich, to contemplate the world's wasting, to know the earth is mortal too." Updike's novels feel particularly relevant as the four-book series tracked the routine—albeit privileged—existence of Harry "Rabbit" Angstrom from his twenties until death. But this particular passage from Updike also introduces the fantastic nature of "the world's wasting," and, more germane to my argument, presents a binary wherein the exceptionality of "the world's wasting" can be enjoyed with "great pleasure" by a privileged human only because both are conceived of as separate and distinct events and realms—and ones without actual consequences for the human subject.

To overlook *Solar*'s comingling of the speculative fantastic and the mundane is to, like Beard, overlook the vital ways that Beard's personal squabbles in the novel directly affect his pursuits in the realm of the exceptional (i.e., saving the world). *Solar* sometimes demonstrates these connections in overt ways, such as an early plot line about the climate-based Center where Beard is the nominal head.[14] Noting that the Center needs "a single eye-catching project" in order to receive media attention and funding, Beard devotes all of the Center's time, money, and resources to the development of a wind turbine, which soon reveals itself to be a useless project that will never actually work. Aware of the quixotic nature of the wind turbine, Beard nevertheless continues dedicating the Center's limited resources to the project, simply because "it had been Beard's idea, and reversing it would be a personal disaster" (32). The use of the term "personal" is striking, demonstrating how Beard's personal life is privileged over and negatively affects his larger aims to address global climate change. But the passage also indicates the extent to which Beard's private concerns dictate and affect his more global responses. Beard's personal problems are not merely a microcosm of his public disasters but are directly linked to his more exceptional failures. If this was not clear enough, as Beard notes the colossal waste the wind turbine project represents, the narration acknowledges how Beard allowed this project to happen in the first place: "Because Patrice [his current wife] was starting her affair [. . .] and he was not able to think of anything else" (34). Clearly, Beard's domestic dramas have a direct effect on the exceptional aspects of his life—all of which remains obscured to Beard by further focusing on his quotidian issues.

At the end of the novel Beard's self-centered plans to save the world are ultimately thwarted—and any meaningful attempt to combat climate change is abandoned—not due to any exceptional plot machinations, but by his own day-to-day, poor life choices and hubris. The novel ends not with a bang but with a whimper—not the end of the world but the end of Michael Beard's world. In a perhaps too convenient conclusion in a diner, Beard learns about the implosion of his career and the loss of the new solar panels due to issues stemming from: the last of his many divorces, a rivalry with another man, the unexpected arrival of his current partner, and yet another woman he is having an affair with, and hints that his doctor's repeated warnings of his unhealthy eating habits may have finally caught up to him. What is clear from the cacophony of his personal failings and the failure of his quest to save the world is that none of them are mutually exclusive. Instead, all are connected in a collapsing of the personal/quotidian with global/exceptional consequences. The problem is not solely Beard's failings, but rather his inability to understand how his day-to-day, all-too-human failings intersect with and affect his larger goals to save the planet.

Solar's engagement with speculation and realism is also evident in the book's setting. Published in 2010, the action of the novel takes place between 2000 and 2009, mostly in London. While it is certainly not odd for a novel to be set in the years leading up to its publication, this shift in time is outside the norm in much literary fiction that engages with the apocalyptic nature of the Anthropocene era. Other more speculative books that explore these themes, such as Cormac McCarthy's *The Road* (2006) or Claire Vaye Watkins's *Gold Fame Citrus* (2015),[15] tend to be set in the not-too-distant future after destructive events—functioning as an impending warning sign for readers about what might be. *Solar*, on the other hand, is set in the immediate past leading up to mounting climate change destruction that Beard supposedly works to prevent, effectively positioning the novel as a lament or elegy for what in reality might have been. This sense of speculative mourning litters the pages of the novel, including repeated reminders of the Bush vs. Gore saga that was playing out in the United States at the end of 2000, which Beard ironically thinks of as a distraction with an outcome that could not possibly matter. However, the temporal and physical setting of the novel bypasses any distancing effect that often occurs in futuristic worlds by focusing on the exceptional (saving the world) but in a story world that is nonetheless grounded in realism and an identifiable recent past.

Many critics have attempted to make sense of *Solar*'s conflation of realism, the quotidian, and the fantastic by reading the book as allegory, positing that McEwan downsizes and transposes "the apocalyptic scenario [. . .] into the private life of the protagonist" (Zemanek 58). In this allegorical reading, Beard's personal failures are a microcosm for society's destruction of the earth. The danger of this type of reading is that it reifies post-Enlightenment separations of the domestic and the global and replicates Beard's own unawareness; Beard's private life can only be read as symbolic for global disaster if the two spheres are also viewed as separate and distinct entities. In Orwell's allegorical *Animal Farm* (1945), the actions of farm animals can only represent the Russian Revolution of 1917 and the Stalinist era because they are entirely separate and distinct from those events. To read *Solar* as allegory erases the pointed ways wherein Beard's everyday private failings intersect with and result in his abject failures to enact meaningful change. Ironically, an allegorical reading essentially recreates the bifurcations that Beard prefers and that, I argue, the book actively collapses.

Perhaps the primary benefit of reading both *Solar* and *Flight Behavior* as speculative realism is that it also exposes how characters remain in thrall to this false bifurcation between the quotidian and the global—and how we perhaps refuse to see these connections by deploying another post-Enlightenment binary that separates and privileges the human over the non-human. As Myra J. Seaman argues, "[t]he human long presumed by traditional [. . .] humanism is a subject (generally assumed male) who is at the center of his world (that is, *the* world)" (246). In this conception, personal human influence extends beyond the personal sphere to the point of being seemingly inseparable from the actual global sphere. What is striking is that this collapse is not in service of acknowledging the symbiotic nature of the personal and the global, but instead privileges the human figure in order to justify dominion over the non-human. Even in their attempts to counter humanist hierarchical thinking, Posthumanists have largely failed to rectify this hierarchy. As Matthew Taylor has argued, many veins of Posthumanism, especially those that focus on human–nature hybridity, collapse the human–non-human binary while also further empowering the hybrid human in the process. Accordingly, "'persons' now *become* the 'world'" while "the nonhuman world serves our all-too-human agenda" (Taylor 7; original emphasis). These novels collapse the quotidian/exceptional binary through speculative realism but in the process also reveal the human-centric narratives we create and tell in order to re-privilege the human and further ignore the ways humanity's day-to-day choices fantastically affect the planet. For example, just as Beard seems to reach his lowest levels of doubt and despair following the fallout of his fifth failed marriage, he receives "an invitation to the Arctic" for an expedition that is little more than a PR stunt (52). By moving Beard to the exceptional setting of the Arctic, readers perhaps expect Beard to himself become exceptional—as the heroes of fantastic literature regularly do. But the novel thwarts this at every turn—instead showing how Beard's all-too-human, day-to-day pettiness and ineptitude still function in the fantastic setting of the Arctic.

Pointedly, Beard's incompetence is established using a mix of the quotidian and the fantastic. But the book also demonstrates both the small-scare and fantastic consequences of his unwillingness to recognize these connections. First, Beard arrives at the hotel late, cannot sleep, misses breakfast, and his fellow Arctic travelers leave for basecamp without him. In an extended, comical passage, McEwan details Beard's bumbling inability—complete with pratfalls—to dress himself in the required gear for travel in the approaching snowstorm. Just when things cannot get worse: "Hot and tired, an unpleasant combination, [Beard] stood suddenly in exasperation, turned, and collided with a beam or a column, he couldn't see," cracking his goggles and rendering him further sightless (62). While this may be the most literal occurrence, many other moments in the book detail how Beard is regularly hit in the face by things that he should have seen coming, but he has been blinded by his fixation on the personal.

And this imperceptiveness continues to reverberate in both ubiquitous and fantastic ways. For example, McEwan goes to great lengths to further humble and even emasculate Beard in the face of nature—calling to mind Myra Seaman's conception of the Enlightenment human as both male and in control of the natural world. Traveling across the Arctic on a snowmobile in a blizzard with cracked goggles, Beard is increasingly unable to see the landscape and drive his snowmobile, further highlighting the exceptional consequences of his mundane ineptitude. When things cannot get any worse, Beard must, despite his guide's dire warning, stop to urinate. In the process, however, Beard freezes his penis to the zipper of his snowsuit. After quickly pouring alcohol on it, he rips it free, but when climbing back onto the snowmobile Beard hears a sudden crack—which is tellingly compared to "a glacier calving"—and feels a sudden burning pain in his groin. Moments later, he feels something heavy drop down the leg of his pants. Beard, and by extension, the reader, briefly believe his compromised genitals have literally fallen off. Once he arrives at the basecamp, Beard discovers that what fell down the leg of his pants was just a tube of lip salve from his pocket. While his groin is definitely injured, the physical trauma is secondary to his wounded pride. Beard's seemingly literal emasculation represents a potentially fantastic moment, but one that reveals itself to be anything but—and is instead just another human misunderstanding and base failing brought on by Beard's inability to interact with the remarkable.

Rather than learn from these humbling experiences, Beard compensates for his feelings of inadequacy by engaging in the personal narrative creation of other binaries to reestablish his dominance over nature. This process is not dissimilar to the way Dellarobia, despite her growing awareness, continues to cast the butterflies in human-centric terms and narratives. Beard similarly ameliorates his wounded pride by using other classic tropes of narrative—specifically classic stories that pit humans vs. nature—to reposition and reconstruct himself as the dominant, privileged man. After a few days of sulking alone in his cabin, Beard joins a brief exploration of the surrounding area. After the group sees a polar bear over a mile away ambling toward them, the wary guide declares that they should return to basecamp. But as everyone else leaves, Beard is unable to start his snowmobile. Thinking he is alone, Beard is horrified to feel something large pushing into him, which he assumes is the polar bear attacking. Instead, it is his exasperated guide, who effortlessly starts the snowmobile; Beard had been incorrectly pressing the headlight switch, not the starter. Faced with yet another example of his continued ineptitude in the face of nature, Beard fashions a heavily revised narrative that reflects his preferred interpretation of himself as adventurous and brave rather than banal and ineffectual: "In the account he would give for the rest of his life, *the one that became his true memory*, a polar bear with open jaws was twenty meters distant and running at him when his snowmobile started forward" (82; emphasis mine). This is not merely an anecdote that Beard tells but one that he comes to believe. Perhaps more importantly, the story that Beard tells is specifically constructed to allow him to once again feel a profound sense of control and superiority over nature—leaving his quotidian failures behind to imagine himself as exceptional. The polar bear passage essentially depicts a reconstruction of precisely what the novel deconstructs: humanity's desire to position themselves as existing only within narratives of the exceptional or the everyday in order to avoid acknowledging the connections and fantastic effects of quotidian acts.

In another moment, Beard watches the Arctic dusk and feels, both literally and figuratively, on top of the world. But the book makes clear that it is an entirely socially constructed, human-centric narrative. Beard is actually hundreds of miles south of the North Pole, which he knows. Beard further acknowledges that: "it was an accident of cartography that placed the South Pole under the North" (83). As cartographer J. B. Harley argues, map making has always had "hidden agendas" that "work in society as a form of power knowledge" (275–276).[16] What is so powerful about this moment is that Beard ignores what he knows: he is not actually at the North Pole and the North Pole as top of the world is a false, constructed cosmography. Nevertheless, Beard uses this constructed positionality at the "top of the world" to reconfirm his own privileged human hierarchy: "[Beard] could not dispel the impression that he was near the top of the world and that everybody else, [his ex-wife] included, was below him" (83). In many ways, these passages echo Sara Ahmed's conception of straight lines and paths in *Queer Phenomenology* (2006) and the way that our ideologies are affected by how we are oriented in the world on a truly literal level. Perhaps even more telling is the way that Beard uses this narrative to orient himself over the entire planet, and specifically his soon-to-be ex-wife, granting himself power and dominion over both the quotidian and the exceptional components of his life, while still positioning them as separate spheres. If we read *Solar* as realist speculative literature that highlights and criticizes the false divides between the quotidian and the exceptional and the human and the non-human, Beard functions not as an allegorical concept of extraordinary destruction, as many critics prefer to read him, but as a painfully typical human who refuses to see the reality of quotidian and fantastic connections and uses human-centric narratives as a form of denial, absolution, and justification.

In conclusion, I cannot help but wonder if literature—and especially literary divisions that perceive and further a false separation between the fantastic and the day-to-day—has in some ways furthered these limiting bifurcations and human-centric ideologies and has thus reified the type of hierarchical thinking and denial that led to the Anthropocene. While I do not believe these novels provide easy answers or present alternative futures, they do, however, provide a valuable roadmap for understanding the power, allure, and danger of these traditional, false divisions. Additionally, speculative realism further uncovers how these divides can be easily manifested through both social and literary narratives. As Jason Moore argues, it is these human-centric ideologies and dualisms that "are fundamental to the thinking that has brought the biosphere to its present transition toward a less habitable world" (2), and these kinds of narratives, which also reposition the human as superior, are "unlikely to help us solve it" (1). *Solar* and *Flight Behavior* are just two examples of contemporary realist speculative fiction that responds to the unique challenges of representing both humanity's large and small effects on the planet by revealing and criticizing the false divides between both the humans and nature and our quotidian and exceptional acts and stories.[17] By failing to adequately account for this literary strategy, we run the risk of not only misreading these novels but also of continuing to reify these dangerous and consequential human ideologies, erasures, and practices.

The human-centric behavior that is exposed through speculative realism may even inform debates about the term Anthropocene: a hotly debated distinction due, in no small part, to the human-centric nature of calling an era the Anthropocene.[18] As Eileen Crist argues, "naming an epoch after ourselves" should make us question "What this discourse excludes from our range of vision: the possibility of challenging human rule" (14–15). Speculative realism powerfully demonstrates the allure of human-centric thinking—and unpacks certain limitations of attempting to confront and combat the effects of anthropocentric thinking when we keep falling back into—and at times running toward—human-centric and privileging solutions. As Rob Nixon demonstrates, anthropocentric thinking also furthers our reliance upon intra-human division and hierarchies, wherein the poor, racially othered, and otherwise disenfranchised are forced to shoulder the burden as part of the "solution" for privileged peoples and nations. In the end, I am not entirely sure we can look to books such as *Flight Behavior* and *Solar* as providing innovative solutions—and I am also not sure that fiction can or should be that proscriptive. But, at the very least, these texts demonstrate the frailty and futility of so many of the ways we keep approaching these issues with the very binaries and hierarchies that led to what we call the Anthropocene—and thus challenge readers to then imagine something else.

NOTES

1. Elizabeth A. Povinelli in *Geontologies* (2016) defines the Anthropocene as "a geologically defined moment when the forces of human existence began to overwhelm all other biological, geological, and meteorological forms and forces" (9). In this conception, the human essentially functions as a malignancy on the planet. Despite the debate among geologists regarding when to date the beginning of the Anthropocene, ranging from the origin of farming to the Industrial Revolution to the Atomic Bomb, it is telling that most possibilities occur after the rise of post-Enlightenment thinking that constructed a stark division between, among other things, humanity and nature, the natural and social sciences, and the individual and society.

2. As Jonathan Arac reminds us, Faulkner was a master at doing this in the context of ecological crisis, subtly alluding to the repercussions of the deforestation of the American South outside "the centre of his work" (139).

3. As I will discuss at the end of this chapter, there is much debate about using the term the Anthropocene to describe this era. For more on these debates (and alternative name suggestions), see the essays in editor Jason W. Moore's *Anthropocene or Capitalocene?* (2016), Elizabeth A. Povinellis' *Geontologies* (2016), and Donna J. Haraway's *Staying with the Trouble* (2016).

4. Among many other examples, consider just about any entry into the genres of historical fiction, alternative histories, or magical realism. Lisa Yaszek has also defined afrofuturism as "literature predicated upon both realist and speculative literature" (41). There are, indeed, many literary forms, genres, or movements that have problematized the separation between realism and speculation to various ends. I, however, focus on the specific development and use of these strategies to represent climate change and the Anthropocene.

5. Ghosh perhaps best illustrates this point with a personal story of walking to a meeting in Delhi and having his normal, peaceful day interrupted by the appearance

of a tornado, which causes some destruction but no loss of life. The tornado quickly disappears and Ghosh dusts himself off and continues to his meeting. Ghosh argues that incorporating such a story into one of his novels would result in criticisms of improbability. But he is quick to point out that the increasingly extreme "weather events of this time," which are becoming both more common and normalized, "have a very high degree of improbability" (26). Ghosh's tornado anecdote indicates how narrative conceptions about naturalism and probability inhibit our ability to represent the growing quotidian nature of the advancing effects of climate change through stories.

6. See Elizabeth Rosen's *Apocalyptic Transformation: Apocalypse and the Postmodern Imagination* (2008) and James Berger's *After the End: Representations of Post-Apocalypse* (1999).

7. Another literary example of the long, slow apocalypse can be found in Octavia Butler's *Parable of the Sower* (1993).

8. To be fair, after the controversy surrounding Atwood's comments about science fiction in 2003, she has actually used the term to describe her novel *The Handmaid's Tale*. For more on Atwood and McEwan's comments, see Sarah Ditum's 2019 article "'It drives writers mad': why are authors still sniffy about sci-fi?" For more on the consequences of literary bifurcations between science fiction and literature, see also Ursula K. Le Guin's "Science Fiction and Mrs. Brown" (1976).

9. In *Anthropocene Fictions* (2015), Adam Trexler helpfully explores the varied forms of the development of the climate change novel in a variety of different genres and literary styles, largely in an attempt to "contribute to a bidirectional exchange of ideas between literary and science studies" (23). I am not attempting anything as exhaustive, nor am I claiming that there is only one way to textually depict life during the Anthropocene. I also do not wish to present speculative realism as a new, wholly distinct formal mode—but instead use it to challenge readers and critics to consider the porousness of realist and fantastic depictions, especially as they relate to representing life in the Anthropocene.

10. Similarly acknowledging the melding of the fantastic and realism, but referring to this process as depicting "a fictional event in a rather realistic way," Rajadivya and Palanivel categorize *Flight Behavior* as a "tentative imaginary tale" (368).

11. See Sebastian Bathiany, et al., "Climate Models Predict Increasing Temperature Variability in Poor Countries" (2018).

12. For a discussion of how the butterfly population has been affected, see José López-García, et al., "On the Landslide Event in 2010 in the Monarch Butterfly Biosphere Reserve, Angangueo, Michoacán, Mexico" (2012).

13. The scientists in the novel also postulate that the unseasonably warm and wet weather in Tennessee has tricked the butterflies into thinking that Tennessee is a good place to spend the winter.

14. A position Beard only holds due to his ability to help the center receive funding due to the prestige of the Nobel Prize that Beard won, perhaps undeservedly, decades earlier.

15. For a discussion of climate change in McCarthy's *The Road*, see Adeline Johns-Putra's "'My Job Is to Take Care of You': Climate Change, Humanity, and Cormac McCarthy's *The Road*" (2016).

16. For more on cartography as a social construction, see Jeremy W. Crampton's "Maps as Social Constructions: Power, Communication and Visualization" (2001).

17. Other texts that engage in this type of exploration, in various ways, include Ruth Ozeki's *A Tale for the Time Being* (2013) and Annie Proulx's *Barkskins* (2016).

18. The original intent of the name was to call out the reality of the ways that humanity has negatively affected the environment. But if issues such as climate change are the result of anthropocentric thinking, might we not be replicating that kind of thinking with such an anthropocentric name?

WORKS CITED

Ahmed, Sara. *Queer Phenomenology: Orientations, Objects, Others*. Duke UP, 2006.

Arac, Jonathan. "*The Overstory*: Taking the Measure of a Major New American Novel." *The Critical Quarterly*, vol. 61, no. 4, 2019, pp. 137–144.

Bathiany, Sebastian, et al. "Climate Models Predict Increasing Temperature Variability in Poor Countries." *Science Advances*, vol. 4, no. 5, May 2018, p. 5809.

Berger, James. *After the End: Representations of Post-Apocalypse*. U of Minnesota P, 1999.

Carroll, Hamilton, and Annie McClanahan. "Fictions of Speculation: Introduction." *Journal of American Studies*, vol. 49, 2015, pp. 655–661.

Crampton, Jeremy W. "Maps as Social Constructions: Power, Communication and Visualization." *Progress in Human Geography*, vol. 25, no. 2, 2001, pp. 235–252.

Crist, Eileen. "On the Poverty of Our Nomenclature." In *Anthropocene or Capitalocene? Nature, History, and the Crisis of Capitalism*, edited by Jason W. Moore. PM Press, 2016, pp. 14–33.

Fraser, Gordon. "Troubling the Cold War Logic of Annihilation: Apocalyptic Temporalities in Sherman Alexie's *The Lone Ranger and Tonto Fistfight in Heaven*." *PMLA*, vol. 130, no. 3, 2015, pp. 599–614.

Ghosh, Amitav. *The Great Derangement: Climate Change and the Unthinkable*. The U of Chicago P, 2016.

Gibson, Katherine, et al., eds. *Manifesto for Living in the Anthropocene*. Punctum Books, 2015.

Harley, J. B. "Deconstructing the Map." In *Classics in Cartography: Reflections on Influential Articles from Cartographica*, edited by Martin Dodge. Wiley-Blackwell, 2011.

Haraway, Donna J. *Staying with the Trouble: Making Kin in the Chthulucene*. Duke University Press, 2016.

Johns-Putra, Adeline. "'My Job Is to Take Care of You': Climate Change, Humanity, and Cormac McCarthy's *The Road*." *Modern Fiction Studies*, vol. 62, no. 3, Fall 2016, pp. 519–540.

Kakutani, Michiko. "The Planet Be Damned. It's All About Me. Review of *Solar*, by Ian McEwan." *The New York Times*, 30 March 2010: p. C1.

Kingsolver, Barbara. *Flight Behavior*. Harper Collins, 2012.

López-García, José, et al. "On the Landslide Event in 2010 in the Monarch Butterfly Biosphere Reserve, Angangueo, Michoacán, Mexico." *Landslides*, vol. 9, no. 2, 2012, pp. 263–273.

McEwan, Ian. *Solar*. Anchor Books, 2011.

Moore, Jason W. "Introduction." In *Anthropocene or Capitalocene? Nature, History, and the Crisis of Capitalism*, edited by Jason W. Moore. PM Press, 2016, pp. 1–14.

Nixon, Rob. *Slow Violence and the Environmentalism of the Poor*. Harvard UP, 2011.

Perrotta, Tom. *The Leftovers*. St. Martin's Griffin, 2011.

Phelan, James. *Reading the American Novel, 1920–2010*. Wiley-Blackwell, 2013.

Povinelli, Elizabeth A. *Geontologies: A Requiem to Late Liberalism*. Duke UP, 2016.

Rajadivya, G., and R. Palanivel. "The Angle of Ecocritics: The Study of Environment and the Narrative Situation in *Flight Behavior*." *Language in India*, vol. 18, no. 11, 2018, pp. 367–373.

Rosen, Elizabeth K. *Apocalyptic Transformation: Apocalypse and the Postmodern Imagination*. Lexington Books, 2008.

Seaman, Myra J. "Becoming More (than) Human: Affective Posthumanism, Past and Future." *Journal of Narrative Theory*, vol. 37, no. 2, Summer 2007, pp. 246–275.

Swanson, Carl Joseph. "'The Only Metaphor Left': Colson Whitehead's *Zone One* and the Zombie Narrative Form." *Genre*, vol. 47, no. 3, 2014, pp. 379–405.

Taylor, Matthew A. *Universes Without Us: Posthuman Cosmologies in American Literature*. U of Minnesota P, 2013.

Todorov, Tzvetan. *The Fantastic: A Structural Approach to a Literary Genre*. Translated by Richard Howard. P of Case Western Reserve U, 1973.

Trexler, Adam. *Anthropocene Fictions: The Novel in a Time of Climate Change*. U of Virginia P, 2015.

Wolf-Meyer, Matthew J. *Theory for the World to Come: Speculative Fiction and Apocalyptic Anthropology*. U of Minnesota P, 2019.

Yaszek, Lisa. "Afrofuturism, Science Fiction, and the History of the Future." *Socialism and Democracy*, vol. 20, no. 3, 2006, pp. 41–60.

Zemanek, Evi. "A Dirty Hero's Fight for Clean Energy: Satire, Allegory, and Risk Narrative in Ian McEwan's *Solar*." *Ecozon@: European Journal of Literature, Culture and Environment*, vol. 3, no. 1, 2012, pp. 51–60.

Index

adaptation, 21n8, 96, 183, 216, 221, 224, 229, 231; film, 83n2, 84n5, 152n1; parody, 5

agency: collective and individual, 185–86; geological, 177, 181; human, 83n2, 178, 186, 194; human-geologic, 179; lithic, 185–86; nonhuman, 55, 58, 69, 77–82, 83n2, 187–88; systems and processes, 46. *See also* human, as a geological agent; human, and nonhuman

Age of Ecocentrism, 89, 97, 99–100

Ahmed, Sara, 251

Alaimo, Stacy, 47, 51, 57, 69

Aldiss, Brian, 115

alienation, 194, 200–201, 213, 216, 219, 221, 222, 229–31

Almeida, Mara and Diogo, Rui, 140

Alter, Alexandra, 186

Anthropocene: and catastrophic disease, 114–17; as challenge/demand, 5–6, 11, 48, 59, 67, 137, 192, 197, 201, 244, 251–52; concept of, 2, 4, 5, 6, 45, 47, 67, 105, 135, 158, 161, 179–80, 236; consequences of, 1, 4, 27, 46, 56, 58, 121, 126, 182, 187, 188, 230, 243; criticism, 192, 193, 194–95, 196; and ecocriticism, nature, 68, 75, 76, 77, 78, 89, 96, 99, 220, 221, 223, 239, 247; end of, 132, 157, 158; and fantasy, 178, 184–86; and heroism. *See* speculative fiction, heroism in; and hope, 4, 21n8, 41, 58, 62, 137; origins of, 2, 6, 177–90, 21n6, 57, 88, 252n1; post-Anthropocene, 137, 152; and quest, 62; responsibility for, 5–6, 8–11, 117, 251; Seeds of a Good Anthropocene, 21n8; and speculative fiction, 12–13, 15, 28, 51, 60, 162, 166, 172, 178, 192, 208, 235–38, 240, 252n4, 253n9; and storytelling, narration, 2, 6, 7, 11, 53, 146, 178–79, 184; term, 10, 88, 252n3; as a tool of perception, 20n2, 20n4, 200; urban, 213, 220; and wilderness, 87–102; and young adult (juvenile) literature, 45–66, 136–37

anthropocentrism, 13, 47, 54, 88, 149–50, 196, 207, 209

apocalypse, 117, 124, 125, 127, 132, 133n2, 145, 150, 177, 189, 239; apocalyptic disease genre, 106; in Christian tradition, 122, 145; the role of, 13–16; in Russian Speculative fiction, 158, 165, 172; zombie apocalypse, 124; in Zoroastrianism, 122. *See also* post-apocalyptic fiction

Applebaum, Noga, 136, 141

Arac, Jonathan, 252n2

Index

Arias-Maldonado, Manuel, 5, 10, 11, 13, 20n2, 21n7
Asafu-Adjaye, John (et al.), 21n8
Ascott, Roy, 99
Attebery, Brian, 17, 30, 43n14, 49, 61, 213, 214
Atwood, Margaret, 115, 238, 240, 253n8
Austen, Jane, 239

Baccolini, Raffaela, 28
Bacigalupi, Paolo, 4–5
Baker, Deirdre F., 54
Bakhtin, Mikhail, 110
Banerjee, Anindita, 159, 163
Barash, David P., 141
Barker, Chris, 77
Barnosky, Anthony D., 179
Barron, T. A., 75–76, 84n8
Barry, Peter, 68
Barthes, Roland, 191
Bathiany, Sebastian, 253n11
Beck, Ulrich, 4
Bednarek, Agnieszka, 170
Berger, James, 125, 126, 239
Berlatsky, Noah, 183
Bernardo, Susan M. and Murphy, Graham J., 29, 34, 40, 42n8, 43n10, 43n13
Bevan, David, 105
Bhabha, Homi K., 199–200, 214, 224
biosphere, 27, 42, 115, 123, 251
Bloch, Maurice, 76
Boccaccio, Giovanni, 108–10
Bond, Michael, 218
Bonneuil, Christophe, 10
Booker, M. Keith, 123
Bostrom, Nick, 87, 89, 97–98, 138, 148
Braidotti, Rosi, 88, 98, 140, 150
Brawley, Chris, 68, 69, 73
Breyer, Melissa, 84n7
Briggs, Patricia, 213–33
Broderick, Mick, 125
Brooks, Max, 109
Buell, Frederick, 45

Buell, Lawrence, 14, 46, 47, 69
Bugajska, Anna, 135, 136, 138, 147, 148, 151, 152n1, 153n7
Bulgarin, Faddey, 159
Burke, Brianna, 90
Burke, Edward, 95
Butler, Octavia, 253n7
the butterfly effect, 4, 243
Buttsworth, Sarah, 91
Bynum, Caroline Walker, 57

Calavarro, Mike, 136
Campbell, Joseph, 49, 142, 144
Camus, Albert, 115
Capitalocene, 10, 88, 193
Caracciolo, Marco, 35, 39–40, 43n16
Carey, M. R., 121–34
Carretero, Nacho, 141, 151
Carroll, Hamilton, and Annie McClanahan, 240
Carroll, Jane Suzanne, 54
Carroll, Lewis, 52
Carson, Rachel, 84n4, 88
Cassirer, Ernst, 195
Cavaliere, Guilia, 141
Chabon, Michael, 240
Chakrabarty, Dipesh, 10, 45–47, 54, 57, 59, 178, 181–84, 186
Chan, Sarah, 141
Chernus, Ira, 124
Chief, Karletta, (et al.), 10, 11
Christian, Christianity, 18, 47, 122, 137, 141, 144, 145, 147, 150–52, 153n6, 158. *See also* Myth, Christian
Christopher, John, 112, 116
Chthonic, 163, 169–72
Chthulucene, 10, 19, 180, 192, 193, 201, 204, 207, 208
Clare, Cassandra, 49–50
Clark, Timothy, 4, 6, 7, 11, 12, 20n1, 20n4, 21n5
Clarke, Bruce, 143
Clarke, Bruce and Rossini, Manuela, 135
Clifford, Elizabeth Joyce and Kalyanpur, Maya, 231n2

Clifford, James, 46
climate change, 1, 7–10, 27, 45, 48, 53, 60, 93, 121, 126, 136, 137, 139–40, 151, 178, 180, 182–83, 187, 195, 196, 220, 235–38, 254n18; challenges of depicting, 238–47, 253n5, 253n9, 253n15; Climate Change Denial Disorder, 14; climate crisis, 19, 47, 52, 58, 68, 69, 70, 83, 183
Cohen, Jeffrey Jerome, 185
Colebrook, Claire, 47, 59, 60
Colfer, Eoin, 136
Collins, Suzanne, 14
colonial/colonialist/colonialism, 9, 19, 21n6, 90, 92, 93, 99, 113, 177, 180–84, 186, 188, 189, 193, 196–99, 204, 207
Coltelli, Laura, 6
Commager Jr., H. S., 107
commodification, 184, 188, 201
Comos, Gina and Rosenthal, Caroline, 7, 9, 11
consciousness, 35, 39, 72, 79, 81, 100n2, 193, 202, 203, 206
consumption, 5, 9, 182, 184
Cooper, Susan, 49
Cowles, Gregory, 215
Crampton, Jeremy W., 254n16
Crist, Eileen, 251
Cronin, Justin, 109
Crutzen, Paul J., 2, 45, 88, 105, 135, 158, 179
cultural: appropriation/appropriate, 73, 93, 144, 198, 215–16, 220, 227, 231; context, 18, 50, 216, 227
Curtis, Claire P., 14–15
Cyranoski, David, 141, 151

dance, 27, 33, 36, 38, 41, 224
Dashner, James, 14
Davis, Heather and Todd, Zoe, 11, 13
Davis, Heather and Turpin, Etienne, 10, 14
Davis, Suanna, 215

De Cristofaro, Diletta, and Daniel Cordle, 45
deep time, 9, 157, 177, 179, 181–86
Defoe, Daniel, 108, 115, 118n1
dehumanizing/dehumanization, 139, 162, 184
de la Cadena, Marisol, 179, 187
Derrida, Jacques, 199
Dick, Philip K., 5, 77, 115
disaster: cataclysmic, 178, 243; climate, 183, 242; ecological. *See* ecological, disaster; environmental, 20, 159, 188–89; as fantasy, 123; global, 161, 248; human-induced, 122, 136, 157; movies, 123; natural, 1, 106, 121, 146, 159–60; nuclear, 159, 168
diseases, 98, 105; catastrophic, disastrous, 105–19; man-made, 108; in speculative fiction, 112–17; supernatural, 109. *See also* Anthropocene, and catastrophic disease; apocalypse, apocalyptic disease genre
Ditum, Sarah, 253n8
Divov, Oleg, and Max Rublev, 164, 165
Drozdov, Nikolay (et al.), 158
Dvorsky, Georg, 152n3
dystopia/dystopian, 2, 3, 12, 14, 21, 29, 42n2, 47, 48, 87, 89, 94, 125, 137, 140, 145, 147, 151, 152, 237; young adult, 148

ecocriticism, 17, 67–86, 87, 88
ecological: catastrophe, 244; crisis, 9, 71, 136, 237, 252n2; destruction, 180; disaster, 146, 183
Ekman, Stefan, 48, 55, 230
Eliade, Mircea, 142
Elliott, Robert C., 140, 141
Ellis, Erle C., 20, 158
Elroy, James Mc and Emma Katherine Mc Elroy, 92
embodiment, 7, 33, 36–40
environmental humanities, 179–80, 186
environmental justice, 186

Epic of Gilgamesh, 98
Eurocene, 10

fantasy: cyclical patterns in, 49–50; and ecocriticism, nature, 55, 67–86; of human survival, 122–23, 132; as lenses, a vehicle for understanding, 177–78, 179, 184–85, 188, 196; and migration, 213–33; and myth, 67–86; mythic, 132; noir, 191; quest, 45–65, 247; and realism, 13, 237, 239, 240; urban, 191, 213, 221, 229; young adult, 45–65. *See also* realism/realistic, YA fantastic realism; science fiction, science fantasy; speculative fiction
Farzin, Sina, 47
Fass Leavy, Barbara, 112, 115
Fauconnier, Gilles, and Mark Turner, 198, 204
Faulkner, William, 252n2
Ferrando, Francesca, 98
Filenko, E., 161
Fishman, Leonid, 171
Flanagan, Victoria, 136
Flieger, Verlyn, 73, 79, 83n2
Ford, Thomas H., 10
forest ecology, 71–76
Foucault, Michel, 70, 195, 199
fragmentation, 214, 219, 222, 223, 229, 231
Fraser, Gordon, 239
Frege, Gottlob, 203
Fuller, Steve, 138
futurity, 197

Galina, Mariya, 162–63, 171
Gardiner, Michael, 110
Garrard, Greg, 67, 84, 88–90, 94, 95, 97
Gaydamaka, Natalya, 161
geology, 178, 179–80, 185, 186; and history, 180, 181
Gevers, Nick, 42n6
Ghosh, Amitav, 239, 252n5
Gibson, Katherine, 235

Gifford, Robert, 15
Gilyarovsky, Vladimir, 163
Głaz, Adam, 191–92, 204
globalization, 9, 46, 162, 163, 182, 215
Glotfelty, Cheryll, 68
Glukhovsky, Dmitry, 157–74
Goga, Nina, 47
Goldschmidt, Eugeniy, 162
Gonik, Vladimir, 164, 165, 169, 171
Goodbody, Axel, 47, 53
Gramsci, Antonio, 195
Grechko, Matvey, 163, 164
Green, Amy M, 127
Greer, John Michael, 7, 20n3
Grigorovskaya, Anastasiya, 171
Grusin, Richard A., 7, 158
Guanio-Uluru, Lykke, 90, 93, 97, 99

Habermas, Jürgen, 199, 207
Hamilton, Clive (et al.), 16, 196
Haraway, Donna J., 10, 88, 89, 98, 150, 180, 182, 192, 195, 200, 201, 207, 208, 252n3
Harley, J. B., 250
harmony, 27, 30, 33, 34, 36, 41, 42, 72, 76, 208
Harrison, Jennifer, 136, 137, 149
Harrison, Robert Pogue, 70
Hartley, Daniel, 192
Harvey, Michael, 14, 46, 57
Hauskeller, Michael, 135, 142, 146–48, 152n1, 153n7
Hayles, N. Katherine, 88
Heise, Ursula K., 9, 45, 46, 55, 59, 96
Heller, Jason, 15
Heller, Peter, 112
hero, heroes, heroine, 50, 53–55, 87, 90, 93, 97, 100, 136, 146, 219, 249
Hillel, Oliver, 213
Hintikka, Jaakko, 203
Hoagland, Ericka, 197, 200
Hoffstadt, Christian, 122
Hogan, Patrick Colm, 39
holocene, 67, 158, 180
Hornborg, Alf, 180, 182

Hovanec, Carol, 72
Hughes, Lesley, 145–46
human: enhancement, 98, 135–56; as a geological agent, 6, 59, 178, 181, 186; and nonhuman, 62, 69, 149, 179, 196, 248; and unhuman, 192, 193
Hume, Kathryn, 20
Hunt, Peter, 54
Husserl, Edmund, 197–98, 203
hybrids/hybridity/hybridization, 18, 128–32, 133n5, 136–47, 149, 151–52, 199, 200, 208, 223, 227, 248
hyperobject(s), 4, 7, 21n5

indigenous, 9–11, 19, 71, 72, 84n8, 90, 92, 93, 184, 187, 192, 193, 197, 200, 215, 219, 224, 226–28, 239
Itäranta, Emmi, 1–4, 15
Ivanova, Elena, 159
Izpisúa Belmonte, Juan Carlos, 151

Jackson, Peter, 83n2, 84n5
James, P. D., 114
Jameson, Fredric, 125, 148
Jaques, Zoe, 48, 55, 58, 136
Jeffers, Susan, 74
Jemisin, N. K., 19, 177–90
Jensen, Kristian, 90, 93
Johns-Putra, Adeline, 47, 53, 253n15
Jonas, Hans, 136, 138
juvenile literature. *See* young adult literature

Kakutani, Michiko, 246
Kareiva, Peter, 21n8
Kass, Leon, 136, 138
Kaveney, Roz, 89
Keightly, Thomas, 223
Kermode, Frank, 124
Kern, Robert, 68
Kerridge, Richard, 68
King, Stephen, 109
Kingsolver, Barbara, 235–37, 239, 241–45

Kocher, Paul H., 73
Kolbert, Elizabeth, 88
Konijnendijk, Cecil C., 70
Koplin, Julian, and Dominic Wilkinson, 141
Koplin, Julian J., and Julian Savulescu, 141
Kowalska, Hanna, 172n1
Krause, Jens, and Graeme D. Ruxton, 218
Kriegman, Sam, 145
Krumrey, Diane, 214
Kuprin, Alexandr, 159–60

Lacan, Jacques, 199
language-game, 201–7
Larson, Nina, 10
Lasik, Marta Magdalena, 167
Łaszkiewicz, Weronika, 153n6
Latour, Bruno, 10, 194
Leggatt, Judith and Kristin Burnett, 90, 91
Le Guin, Ursula K., 13, 16, 17, 27–44, 47, 71–72, 76, 84n4, 84n8, 195–96, 253n8
Lehmann, Lisa S., 140
Lévinas, Emmanuel, 194, 198, 199
Levitas, Ruth, 153n5
Lewis, C. S., 75, 77, 80–81, 84n8
Lewis, Simon L. and Maslin, Mark A., 4, 6, 7, 20n2, 21n6
Liao, Matthew S., 140, 151
Lima, Manuel, 84
Lindow, Sandra J., 29, 31, 33, 36, 38, 42nn2–3, 42n7, 42n9, 43n12, 43n15
Livingstone, Niall, 116
London, Jack, 106, 113, 114, 116
Longrigg, James, 118n2
López-García, José, 253n12
Lowenthal, David, 67
Lu, Marie, 136
Lucretius Carus, Titus, 106–8, 118n2
Luczak, Ewa Barbara, 113, 114
Lyotard, Jean-François, 9

MacArthur, Sian, 116
MacFarlane, Roger, 126
Maitland, Sara, 58
Malm, Andreas, 180, 182
Manlove, Colin N., 69
Markley, Robert, 47
Marland, Pippa, 69, 84n4
Marshall, Kate, 50, 57
Martin, George R. R., 14
Massey, Doreen B., 46, 52, 53, 59–62
Matheson, Richard, 109
McCallum, Robyn, 49, 53
McCammon, Robert, 106, 108, 116, 117
McCarthy, Cormac, 114, 133n3, 136, 247, 253n15
McCausland, Elly, 50
McClanahan, Annie, 240
McCulloch, Fiona, 51
McEwan, Ian, 235, 238, 240, 246–51
McGaughey, Clara, 217
Mclaurin, Virginia, 216, 219
Meletinsky, Eleazar, 220
Mercer, Calvin, and Tracy J. Trothen, 141, 153n7
Merle, Robert, 112
Metro 2033, 157–74
Meyer, Stephenie, 50, 87, 89–93, 98
Miéville, China, 191–12
migration, 213–19, 221, 229–31, 231nn1–2
mimesis, 28, 29, 31, 33, 41; in fantastic literature, 30; through language, 34–35
Mirzoeff Nicholas, 10
Misseri, Lucas E., 141, 148, 153n9
Mitchell, David, 8
Mitchell-Boyask, Robin, 118n2
monomyth, 49
Moore, Jason W., 9, 196, 251
More, Max, 148
More, Max, and Natasha Vita-More, 99, 153n8, 153n10
More, Thomas, 141
Morton, Timothy, 16, 46, 56, 150
Moscow, 157, 162–72

Moylan, Thomas, 140
Muller, Gilbert H., 214
Mustazza, Leonard, 116
mythical time, 49–51, 61
mythic landscapes, 54–55
myth/mythology, 12, 17–19, 37, 43n14, 59, 90, 93, 105, 110, 124, 140, 148, 151–52, 162, 169, 214–16, 219, 220, 223, 226, 227, 229, 231; ancient, 49; Christian, 137, 141, 144–6; of a global identity, 10; Greek, 116, 128–29, 206; of human enhancement, 140–47; of Icarus, 142, 146; as means of understanding the world, 128; Moscow Metro, 163–65; popular, 146; of Saviour, 167; of the underworld, 169; urban, 164; and utopia, 137, 141, 144–46; of the wilderness, 17, 87
mythopoeisis, 17, 61

Naess, Arne, 88
Nakauchi, Hiromitsu, 151
natural history, 201; and human history, 46–47, 58, 182
Niewiadomski, Andrzej, 171
Nijakowski, Lech M., 157, 171
Nikolajeva, Maria, 38, 41
Nikoleris, Alexandra, 196
Nixon, Rob, 182–83, 252
Nodelman, Perry, 52
Nuzum, K. A., 50
Nyrnes, Aslaug, 94

Occidentalocene, 10
Odoyevski, Vladimir, 159
Olesha, Yuri, 160
Oliveira, de, Jose Antonio Puppim, 213
optimism/optimistic, 7, 11, 21n8, 117, 141, 160, 171, 245
Orwell, George, 248
the Other/otherness, 19, 57, 110, 137, 150, 166, 191–12, 215–16, 231
Ovchinnikov, Oleg, 165–66

Ozeki, Ruth, 254n17
Oziewicz, Marek, 42n4, 61

Paffenroth, Kim, 124
Pak, Chris, 196
Paolini, Christopher, 75, 81, 84n8
Park, Bum Jim, 72
part and the whole, 27, 33, 35, 37–38
Patterson, James, 135–56
Pearce, David, 148
Perrotta, Thomas, 241
Persson, Ingmar, 140
Phelan, James, 238
Pilsch, Andrew, 148
plague. See diseases
Plantationocene, 10
Plumwood, Val, 9
poetry, 34, 41, 74
post-apocalyptic age, 182
post-apocalyptic fiction, 18, 114–15, 132, 157, 159, 161
postcolonialism/postcolonial, 99, 178, 181, 182, 192, 199–201, 204, 208; postcolonial fiction, 193, 197
posthumanism/posthuman, 77, 88, 93, 97–98, 129, 132, 133n5, 135–56, 248
Povinelli, Elizabeth A., 252n1
Prashkevich, Gennadiy, 160
Pratchett, Terry, 12
Pronin, Igor, 165
Proulx, Annie, 254n17
Pushkin, Alexei, 110, 111, 114

quest. See fantasy, quest
Quine, Willard, 199
quotidian, 19–20, 235, 237–53

Rafnsøe, Sverre, 157–58
Rancière, Jacques, 195
realism/realistic, 12–13, 21n8, 48, 235–55, 106, 113; socialist realism, 160; speculative realism, 20, 235–55; YA fantastic realism, 51
relational space, 46–48, 52–62
Rice, Anne, 98

Rival, Laura, 76
Robinson, Stanley Kim, 136, 184
Rochelle, Warren G., 33
Roden, David, 140, 152n4, 153n8
Rodnykh, Alexandr, 163
Romanov, Alexandr, 163
Rosen, Elizabeth, 106, 117, 253n6
Roth, Veronica, 14
Rousseau, Jean-Jacques, 94
Rowling, J. K., 49, 50, 55, 82
Rubincam, Catherine, 118n1
Rublev, Maksim, 164, 165
Russell, Bertrand, 203
Russian literature, 158, 161, 168; post-Soviet, 159, 162, 168, 171; Soviet speculative fiction, 168

Said, Edward, 199
Sandberg, Andrew, 149, 153n10
Sartre, Jean Paul (Sartrean), 106
Sarwal, Reema, 197, 200
Schell, Jonathan, 123
Schimelpfenig, Mary Jo., 32
Schmeink, Lars, 146, 152n1
Scholes, Robert, 15
Schrey, Dominik, 122
Schwägerl, Christian, 158, 194
science fiction, 5, 12, 57, 93, 98, 122, 127, 136, 191, 193–201, 238–40, 243, 253n8; dystopian, 89; elements of, 178–79; Russian, 160, 163, 180, 184, 188; science fantasy, 188, 195
Seaman, Myra J., 248, 249
Sedgwick, Marcus, 136
Segal, Charles, 118n2
Senior, W. A., 49
Serres, Michel, 4, 10
Shaviro, Steven, 124
Shaw, Ali, 17, 76–78, 83
Shelley, Mary, 106, 122
Sheshnyov, Alexandr, 158
Simmons, Dan, 109
Sinisalo, Johanna, 12
Sixth Extinction, 2
Skult, Petter, 125

Sloterdijk, Peter, 10
Sontag, Susan, 123
Sorel, George, 153n5
speculative fiction: and defamiliarization, 13, 196; and ecology, 158–59; heroism in, 87; as means of accepting responsibility, 15–16; as means of altering perception, 12, 20, 145, 178; as means of understanding the real world, 69; possibilities of representation, 81, 238, 240; and reality, 99; Russian, 157–74. *See also* diseases, in speculative fiction; post-apocalyptic fiction; Russian literature, Soviet speculative fiction
Stapleton, Patricia, and Andrew Byers, 148
Starobinets, Anna, 162, 165, 169
Steffen, Will, 4
Steffen, Will, (et al.), 3, 67, 196, 213, 220, 223
Steger, Manfred B., 9
Stengers, Isabelle, 208
Stiefvater, Maggie, 45–65
Stoermer, Eugene F., 2, 45, 105
Stripling, Mahala Y., 141
Strugatsky, Arkadiy and Boris, 160–61, 167
subway, 158, 162–63
Swanson, Carl Joseph, 240
sympoiesis, 192, 200, 207, 208
Syvitski, James, 71, 78
Szynkiewicz, Sławoj, 144

Tarasevich, Grigoriy (et al.), 161
Tarr, Anita and White, Donna, 136
Tatar, Maria, 164
Taylor, Matthew, 248
Technocene, 10
Thacker, Eugene, 194, 196
Thucydides, 106–8, 118n1
Todd, Zoe, 11
Todorov, Tzevetan, 236

Tolkien, J. R. R., 12, 17, 48, 55, 69, 73–75, 79–81, 83, 83n2, 84n6, 84n8
Traill, Nancy, 102
transhumanism, 17, 89, 97–100, 135–56
Treanor, Brian, 198
trees, 42, 55, 57, 58, 60, 67–86, 94–97, 243
Trexler, Adam, 47–48, 56, 58, 88, 93, 100n1, 241, 242, 253n9
Trischler, Helmut, 105
Truccone Borgogno, Santiago, 135
Tuan, Yi-Fu, 165, 169, 170
Turner, Mark, 198
Tygstrup, Frederik, 195

Uexküll, Jacob von, 89
underground, 157–74
universe, 33, 88, 131, 161, 202, 204, 213, 214; fictional universe, 126, 167, 196, 215–17, 219, 220, 222, 224, 227, 229–31, 231n1; *Metro Universe*, 157; shared universe, 157
Updike, John, 246
utopia/utopian/utopianism, 14, 18, 27, 38, 125, 135–56, 157

vampire, 50, 87–102, 109, 132n2, 135, 146, 216–19, 225, 230
van Dooren, Thom and Rose, Deborah, 179, 187
Varley, John, 125
Vint, Sherryl, 201, 207, 208

Waldenfels, Bernhardt, 198
Walkowitz, Rebecca L., 223
Waller, Alison, 48, 61
Waters, Colin N., 179, 180
Watkins, Claire Vaye, 241
Watson, Ian, 72
Watts, Michael J., 213
Weik von Mossner, Alexa, 178, 184, 185
Wells, Dan, 136, 139

werewolf, 149, 218, 225–28, 230
Westerfield, Scott, 87, 93–97, 99
Whedon, Joss, 49
Whitehead, Colson, 240
Wiater, Paweł, 157, 166, 167, 171
wilderness, 57, 69, 70, 79, 87–102, 125, 161, 220, 221, 226
Williams, Justin, 46, 56, 59
Williams, Raymond, 214
Wilson, Edward O., 88
Wilson, John, 110–11
Wittgenstein, Ludwig, 198, 203, 205
Wohlleben, Peter, 70, 83n3
Wolf-Meyer, Matthew J., 239
Woodford, Riley, 91
Woodruff, Charles Edward, 114

Yaszek, Lisa, 252n4
Yeats, William Butler, 223
Yefremov, Ivan, 160, 161

Young, Helen Victoria, 213, 215, 216, 221
young adult literature, 47, 148, 231n2; young adult readers, 14. *See also* Anthropocene, and young adult literature; fantasy, young adult
Yusoff, Kathryn, 182, 195, 197
Yusoff, Kathryn, and Jennifer Gabrys, 185, 189

Zalasiewicz, Jan, 158
Zamyatin, Evgeniy, 161
Zapf, Hubert, 11
Zemanek, Evi, 248
Ziff, Bruce H., and Pratima V. Rao, 215, 220
Zipes, Jack, 91
zombie, 109, 110, 121–34, 153n9, 240
Zylinska, Joanna, 6–7
Zywert, Aleksandra, 167

About the Authors

Sylwia Borowska-Szerszun, Ph.D., is an assistant professor at the Faculty of Philology (University of Białystok), where she teaches courses in English literature. She is the author of *Enter the Carnival: Carnivalesque Semiotics in Early Tudor Moral Interludes* (2016) as well as the coeditor of *The Fantastic and Realism* (2019) and *Polish Science Fiction and Fantasy Literature: Anglo-American Influences* (a special issue of *Crossroads. A Journal of English Studies*, 2017). She has also authored a number of articles and anthology chapters. Her research focuses on various aspects of fantasy literature, cultural memory, and medievalism in popular culture.

Anna Bugajska, Ph.D., is the head of the Institute of the Modern Languages and the Language and Culture Studies Department of the Jesuit University Ignatianum in Kraków. She is also the collaborator of the Department of General and Applied Ethics at the same university and a member of the Utopian Studies Society—Europe. Bugajska is the author of *Engineering Youth: The Evantropian Project in Young Adult Dystopias* (2019), and has written articles on young adult literature, dystopias, and posthumanities.

Britta Colligs is a lecturer and Ph.D. student in the English Literature Department at the University of Trier, Germany, since 2016. Her doctoral research investigates the representation and significance of fictional forests within fantasy and speculative contemporary fiction with an ecocritical approach. She has published an article on "The Loss of Ancient Forests: An Ecocritical Reading of T. A. Barron's *The Ancient One*" (2020). She is furthermore examining forms of empowerment in literature, especially female and character empowerment in George R. R. Martin's *A Song of Ice and Fire*, which she discussed in the radio interview "Why Is 'Game of Thrones' So Successful?" (SWR2 Forum, 2019).

Tereza Dědinová is an assistant professor at the Faculty of Arts (Masaryk University, Czech Republic), where she teaches theory and history of fantastic literature and creative writing for academic purposes. She holds a Ph.D. in Czech literature. She is the author of research articles, of a monograph *Po divné krajině. Charakteristika a vnitřní členění fantastické literatury*, 2015 (*Through a Strange Landscape. Characteristics and Inner Structuring of Fantastic Literature*) and the editor of *Na rozhraní světů: fantastická literatura v mezioborovém zkoumání*, 2016 (*At the Edge of the Worlds: Fantastic Literature in Interdisciplinary Exploration*). In her research, she focuses on a theory of fantastic literature from the perspective of cognitive sciences and ecocriticism.

Lykke Guanio-Uluru is professor of Literature at Western Norway University of Applied Sciences, Norway. Her research focus is on literature and ethics, with an emphasis on ecocriticism, climate fiction, fantasy, game studies, and reading research. She is the author of *Ethics and Form in Fantasy Literature: Tolkien, Rowling and Meyer* (2015) and coeditor of the anthology *Ecocritical Perspectives on Children's Texts and Cultures: Nordic Dialogues* (2018), both published by Palgrave Macmillan UK. She is also the author of numerous research articles and anthology chapters.

Jiří Jelínek, Ph.D. is an associate professor at the Hradec Králové University, Czech Republic. His scholarly interests consist of constructed languages, poetry, and language and style in general. He has been teaching courses on constructed languages, post-apocalyptic fiction, and Tolkien's writings, but also on lexicology and stylistics. Among other studies, he has published chapters in the monographs *Hlasy míst* (on poetry and places, 2016) and a study on Jiří Gruša's dystopian prose *Mimner* in the periodical *Česká literatura* (Czech literature, 2016).

Dariya Khokhel, Ph.D. in Comparative Literature, is a teaching assistant at Ivan Ohienko Kamianets-Podilsky National University, Ukraine. She holds two bachelor's degrees (in Education (English and German Languages and World Literature) and History) and a master's from this establishment. Her research interests include the poetics of fantasy texts, this genre's functioning in contemporary British, American, and Ukrainian literatures, and teaching contemporary fantasy texts to English majors. She is also a translator and has published translations of fantasy fiction.

Aleksandr Kolesnikov is an associate professor at the Department of World Literature of the Institute of Philology and Journalism of the Lobachevsky

University (Nizhniy Novgorod, Russia). His research interests lay in the areas of narrative studies, science fiction, and fantasy and myth studies with focus on contemporary English fiction of North America and Great Britain. Aleksandr Kolesnikov defended his Ph.D. dissertation ("Myth and Mythopoeia in English Literature of the Second Half of the 20th Century") in 2018. He has published several essays in Russian periodical academic journals and the chapter in the collective monograph "Searching the Borders of Fantasy: On the Way to Methodology" (Wroclaw, 2017).

Weronika Łaszkiewicz, Ph.D., is an assistant professor at the Faculty of Philology (University of Białystok), where she teaches courses in American literature. Her research interests focus on British and American popular literature and culture, particularly on the various aspects of fantasy fiction. She has published a number of articles and coedited *Visuality and Vision in American Literature* (2014), *Dwelling in Days Foregone: Nostalgia in American Literature and Culture (2016)*, and *Tekstowe światy fantastyki* (2017). She is the author of *Fantasy Literature and Christianity* (2018) and *Exploring Fantasy Literature: Selected Topics* (2019).

Maria Quigley is a Ph.D. candidate in International Cultural Studies at NUI Galway. Her research explores the representation of the child in post-apocalyptic fiction, focusing on the aspect of gender. She holds a B.A. in English Literature and Linguistics from University College Dublin, and an M.A. in International Contemporary Literatures and Media from NUI Galway. Her research interests include contemporary science fiction, horror, and gender and queer studies.

Joanna Krystyna Radosz is a Ph.D. student of Russian literary studies at Adam Mickiewicz University in Poznań, Poland. She studied at Nicolaus Copernicus University and Adam Mickiewicz University. She is currently working on a thesis on manifestations of the Russian national character in the post-Soviet speculative fiction. In the last five years she has attended over thirty conferences in Poland, Czech Republic, Russia, and Latvia. Her fields of interest include contemporary Russian literature and cultural aspect of sports and sociocultural background of politics in Russia.

Keygan Sands, a graduate of the Creative Writing and Environment MFA program at Iowa State University, explores the confluence between science, non-human environments, and society. Her writings appear in *Cold Mountain Review*, *Cleaver Magazine*, and the climate fiction anthology *Nothing Is As It Was* edited by Amanda Saint. She was a 2019 Summer Writer in Residence at the Iowa Lakeside Laboratory. She has also presented literary research at the Fantasy and Myth in the Anthropocene International Conference, creates visual art, and teaches others about the non-human world as a naturalist. Find out more at keygansands.com.

Carrie Spencer is a third-year Ph.D. candidate in Children's Literature at the University of Cambridge. This research takes an ethics of care approach to portrayals of mad mother characters and adolescent protagonists in Young Adult literature. Her chapter, "The New Alpha and the Ethics of Care," in the MTV series *Teen Wolf in Healthcare in Children's Literature* edited by Naomi Lesley, Abbye Meyer, and Sarah Hardstaff is forthcoming.

Dwight Tanner teaches courses on speculative fiction and world literatures at Winston-Salem State University. He holds a Ph.D. in English and Comparative Literature from the University of North Carolina at Chapel Hill. His teaching and research also focus on ethnic US literatures, critical race theory, climate fiction, and performance studies. Dwight's work has been published in *South Atlantic Review* and the *Journal of Asian American Studies*. His current research project considers the role of marginalized identities and futurity in apocalyptic narratives.

www.ingramcontent.com/pod-product-compliance
Lightning Source LLC
Chambersburg PA
CBHW050900300426
44111CB00010B/1320